5 Years *of* 4th Genre

5 Years *of* 4th Genre

Martha A. Bates, editor

Michigan State University Press • *East Lansing*

♾ The paper used in this publication meets the minimum requirements of ANSI/NISO Z39.48-1992 (R 1997) (Permanence of Paper).

Michigan State University Press
East Lansing, Michigan 48823-5245

Printed and bound in the United States of America.

12 11 10 09 08 07 06 1 2 3 4 5 6 7 8 9 10

LIBRARY OF CONGRESS CATALOGING-IN-PUBLICATION DATA
5 years of 4th genre / Martha A. Bates, editor.
p. cm.
ISBN 0-87013-776-X (pbk. : alk. paper)
1. American prose literature—20th century. 2. American prose literature—21st century. 3. American essays—20th century. 4. American essays—21st century. 5. Autobiography. I. Title: Five years of Fourth genre. II. Bates, Martha A., 1947–
PS659.A154 2006
818'.540808—dc22
2005032968

Cover design by Sharp Des!gns, Inc.
Book design by Michael Brooks

green press INITIATIVE Michigan State University Press is a member of the Green Press Initiative and is committed to developing and encouraging ecologically responsible publishing practices. For more information about the Green Press Initiative and the use of recycled paper in book publishing, please visit *www.greenpressinitiative.org.*

Visit Michigan State University Press on the World Wide Web at *www.msupress.msu.edu*

Contents

Preface

Looking over nearly eight years of publishing innovative essays, we see contemporary practitioners of the "fourth genre" forging new routes into subjects that have long defined some of the highest literary aspirations of essayists writing in the past century.

Contemporary literary nonfiction carries on a legacy of the American essay that values introspection and iconoclasm while probing subjects, far from congenial or genteel, that comprise our common, lived humanity. The essays gathered here in this retrospective volume carry on the tradition of the American essay Joyce Carol Oates has described as "springing from intense personal experience . . . linked to larger issues." Even those writers who stretch the conventional boundaries of essay technique are only exercising the independence and inquisitiveness that Emerson, the sage of American prose, had in mind when he challenged future generations of freethinking writers to "insist on yourself; never imitate."

Among the many reasons for the current resurgence of creative nonfiction is the moral populism of the form. Its skillful practitioners remind us that seemingly ordinary, even ephemeral things—like a train whistle, a mantle photograph, some misplaced keys, a snow fall, the smells of a mother's cooking—often hold the key to unlocking extraordinary insight into family, culture, personal history, place and time. Many—if not all—of the writers featured in the pages of this anthology find sharable insight in these unique particulars of their experience, the universe in a grain of sand.

The Uruguayan writer and iconoclast Eduardo Galeano, interviewed in our Fall 2001 issue, spoke of what it means as a writer to be "a voice of voices." "Deep down" Galeano said, "we all contain many people even though we don't know it."

Because it liberates these common voices, the contemporary personal essay is the most democratic among nonfiction subgenres. It is doubtful that writers can forge as close a connection to readers through more expository forms such as the feature story, polemic, commentary, or reportage. The moral populism hard at work in the contemporary personal essay continuously reminds us that every life worth living well is one well worth writing about.

In a *Fourth Genre* roundtable on the art of the personal essay (Fall 2001) Steven Harvey summed up a basic claim that guides much of our editorial work and consequently much of the work in this volume. "Writing becomes art," Harvey said, "the moment that we care as much about the way it says what it says as we do about what it says." Many of the writers featured here explore that "way." What is particularly useful about their experiments is how they treat technical concepts—imagery, structure, voice, juxtaposition, dialogue, narrative line, closure, etc.—as open invitations to aspiring writers "to take risks on the page," as Scott Russell Sanders put it in a *Fourth Genre* interview, "to venture out from familiar territory into the blank places on those maps" (Spring 1999).

It is in that willingness to "venture out" that the essays reprinted here engage a variety of subject matters. Some writers strike cheerful poses, wearing their subjects loosely. Others, knowing they are headed into painful territory, are wary, cautious, severe.

We also believe that a literary form ought to live, as Diane Ackerman said of the natural world, "as variously as possible." Some of our writers, for example, probe the human infatuation for things nonhuman, for the flora and fauna that make our world whole and complete. Their essays often remind us of the dual nature of insight: a simultaneous perception of the inner, sometimes hidden nature of a subject or a thing that poses as the subject of an essay and a discernment of the writer's own consciousness and moral complexity. We are left wondering whether the literary nonfiction essay has a special capacity, perhaps even a *calling*, to merge these inner and outer worlds.

One of our own teachers, mentors, and special friends—James Laughlin, the late founder and publisher of *New Directions*—once reminded us that "literature, a whole culture in fact, goes dead when there is no experiment, no reaching out, no counter-attack on accepted values." It should come as no surprise then to see writers experimenting in the following pages. Still, we realize that you cannot get so precious over counter-attacking accepted literary values that you dismiss what traditional and established essayists

(Montaigne, Emerson, E. B. White, and personal favorites like Jane Addams and Susan Sontag) have to teach us about how to make an essay. While Laughlin was actively publishing radical new poets like Charles Olson and writers like Gertrude Stein who would eventually form the modernist literary movement, he always reminded us that he was busy reading the Troubadours and ancient Chinese poets so he could have some plumb line as a publisher of poetry that broke from traditional forms. That's why *5 Years of 4th Genre* includes essays that are conventionally drawn (although hardly conventional) and solidly grounded narratives.

The work we publish in *Fourth Genre* is sometimes graceful and dignified, sometimes flip and playful, sometimes factual, sometimes truth-seeking. The best of these essays reside somewhere in the gray spaces. The contemporary essay looks to us more tentative and complex, still evolving, and, as such, hard to pin down and explain. We tend to view the fourth genre as exploring the ground between truth and imagination rather than as defying or assaulting the traditional boundaries of factuality. One thing we know for certain: there's an entire landscape between hard gravel and soft marshes, and there are many, many good writers occupying that ground, using new techniques, redeploying traditional ones, making discoveries, and revisiting old places. The vast array of writers and subjects represented here, therefore, are perfectly at home in what has long been considered the freest of literary forms.

David Cooper

Introduction

The personal essay has been a viable form since Montaigne's early efforts in the fifteenth century. And the memoir's legacy dates even further back, to St. Augustine's *Confessions.* Yet it is only during the last five or ten years that the genre now widely known as creative nonfiction began to gain widespread recognition as a literary form.

We have published more than 350 personal essays and memoirs since *Fourth Genre*'s inaugural issue appeared in 1999. As a result, the journal has been at the forefront of a vital, evolving conversation about creative nonfiction's place in the literary spectrum.

Partly to document *Fourth Genre*'s evolution, and partly to chart the rapid and remarkable growth of contemporary literary nonfiction, we have decided to now offer a representative sampling from the journal's first ten issues.

Fourth Genre's subtitle, *Explorations in Nonfiction*, epitomizes our belief that creative nonfiction's roots as a literary form are more closely connected to the spirit of Montaigne's work than to matters of subject, reportage, and scholarly research. Consequently, many of the pieces that editor Martha Bates has chosen for *Five Years of "Fourth Genre"* are exploratory, intimate, and personal. As such, they reflect the autobiographical and "literary" impulses (discovery, exploration, reflection) that characterize the kind of writing we call the "fourth genre."

Reflecting another aspect of what we mean by the term fourth genre, the authors represented here are writing not simply to confess or tell their personal stories. Rather, they use their personal experiences as a way of connecting themselves (and readers) to larger human subjects, issues, and ideas. As essayist/critic Marianna Torgovnich reminds us, "All writing about self and culture is personal in that writers and critics find some of their richest material in experience." "Often," she adds, "our search for personal meaning is precisely what generates our passion and curiosity for the subjects we research and write about."

Memoirist Mary Clearman Blew writes that "the boundaries of creative nonfiction will always be as fluid as water." Since *Fourth Genre*'s inception, we have made it a point to highlight the work of writers who, in their search for meaning and understanding, are not afraid to push at boundaries. Therefore, as you read through these twenty-five selections, you will find that a good many writers have borrowed techniques and strategies freely from other literary genres as well as from other writers. Some pieces, for example, combine narrative with fictional and poetic techniques, while others weave self-portraiture and reflection with reportage and critical analysis.

And because the genre encompasses such a broad range of sensibilities, forms, and approaches, *Five Years of "Fourth Genre"* includes writers who are exploring the roots of their identities, others who are chronicling personal discoveries and changes, and still others who are examining personal conflicts and interrogating their thoughts and opinions. All are, in one way or another, attempting to connect themselves to a larger human legacy.

The writers whose works appear in this volume share a common desire to speak in an intimate, singular voice as active participants in their own experience. This impulse often overlaps with the writer's need to mediate that experience by serving as a witness/correspondent—thus creating a synergy that is unique to this literary form.

Another of the genre's identifying characteristics is its hybrid nature. Patricia Hampl, one of our finest literary memoirists, has described creative nonfiction as a "mongrel" form. Several writers in this anthology utilize plot, character development, dialogue, and dramatic scenes in some of the same ways that fiction writers and playwrights do. And a number of pieces reveal a heightened sense of language and a use of rhythm, image, and metaphor that for centuries have been the hallmarks of lyric poetry.

In keeping with its hybrid qualities, another of creative nonfiction's hallmarks is its flexibility of form. Annie Dillard says, "The essay can do everything a poem can do, and everything a short story can do—everything but fake it. It can also do everything a diary, a journal, a critical article, an editorial, a feature, a report can do."

Dillard is suggesting that the genre offers writers license to explore some of the more whimsical twists and turns of their imaginations and psyches.

In their quest for value and order, then, many of the writers in *Five Years of "Fourth Genre"* are experimenting with a variety of structures—ranging from chronological narratives and flashbacks to non-linear, disjunctive, and associative devices such as montages, mosaics, and collages—several of which mirror the fragmentation and confusions of our inner—and outer—worlds.

As you can see from the table of contents, we have tried to illustrate both the genre's expanding range and the variety of voices it embraces. We have also chosen a representative mix of distinguished and emerging writers who differ widely in their approaches and techniques. Some, for example, blend reportage and straightforward narrative with dramatic scenes and dialogue, while others explore their subjects and ideas in more lyrical, discursive ways. And readers will find that the temperaments and dispositions of the authors vary considerably. A particular piece, for example, might by turns be lyrical, analytical, meditative, expository, self-interrogative, reflective, and/or whimsical.

Still, despite the differences in sensibility, each piece is marked by the discernible authority of the author's presence. As essayist Scott Russell Sanders writes, "the essay is distinguished from the short story, not by the presence or absence of literary devices, not by the tone or theme or subject, but by the writer's stance toward the material."

Where, for example, does this narrator stand in relation to the subject or situation he or she is investigating? In other words, who is this person—or persona—taking them on this journey? A number of *Five Years of "Fourth Genre"* selections demonstrate a variety of ways in which writers establish their personal presence. Some writers are self-interrogative, others reveal more pensive personas, and some deliberately maintain an emotional and psychological distance from their subjects.

And yet, whatever their narrative stance(s) are, we are always aware of the authors' presences, partly because they allow us to be privy to their inner struggles—their thoughts, ruminations, and feelings—as they wrestle with what Marianna Torgovnich describes as "some strongly felt experience, deeply held conviction, long term interest, or problem that has irritated the mind."

As the body of work in this anthology demonstrates, the artfully crafted personal essay/memoir is uniquely suited for our times. We say this because today the need to pay attention to the singular, idiosyncratic human voice is perhaps more urgent than ever before. As essayist/editor W. Scott Olson asserts, "As the world becomes more problematic, it is in the little excursions and small observations that we can discover ourselves, that we can make an honest connection with others, that we can remind ourselves of what it means to belong to one another." This is precisely the intent and spirit that characterizes all of the writing in this anthology. We hope you'll be surprised, enlightened, and enriched by the journey.

MICHAEL STEINBERG

Reading History to My Mother

Robin Hemley

"Your silence will not protect you."
Audre Lourde

"Everything's mixed up in those boxes, the past and the present," my mother tells me. "Those movers made a mess of everything." I'm visiting her at the Leopold late on a Monday night after reading to my kids and being read to by my eldest, Olivia, who at six is rightfully proud of her newfound reading ability. My mother and I have been readers for many years, but in some ways, she finds it more difficult than does Olivia. At eighty-two, my mother's eyesight has deteriorated. Glaucoma. Severe optic nerve damage to her left eye. Macular degeneration. Tomorrow, I'm taking her to the doctor for a second laser operation to "relieve the pressure." We have been told by the doctor that the surgery won't actually improve her eyesight, but, with luck, will stop it from deteriorating any more. After that there's another operation she'll probably undergo, eighty miles south in Seattle. Another operation that won't actually make her see any better.

"I always had such good eyesight," she tells me. And then, "I wish there was something that could improve my eyesight." And then, "When are we going to go shopping for that new computer?"

"Well, let's make sure you can see the screen first," I say, which sounds cruel, but she has complained to me tonight that she wasn't able to see any of the words on her screen, though I think this has less to do with her eyesight than the glasses she's wearing. Unnaturally thick and foggy. My mother looks foggy, too, almost drunk, disheveled in her dirty sweater, though she doesn't drink. It's probably the medicine she's been taking for her many conditions.

My mother owns at least half a dozen glasses, and I know I should have sorted through them all by now (we tried once) but so many things have gone wrong in the last five months since my mother moved to Bellingham that sorting through her glasses is a side issue. I get up from the couch in the cramped living room of her apartment, step over the coffee table—careful not to tip over the cup of peppermint tea I'm drinking out of a beer stein, careful not to bump into my mother—and cross to the bedroom crammed with wardrobe boxes and too much furniture, though much less than what she's used to. On her dresser there are parts of various eyeglasses: maimed glasses, the corpses of eyeglasses, a dark orphaned lens here, a frame there, an empty case, and one case with a pair that's whole. This is the one I grab and take out to my mother who is waiting patiently, always patient these days, or perhaps so unnerved and exhausted that it passes for patience. She takes the case from me and takes off the old glasses, places them beside her beer mug of licorice tea, and puts on the new pair.

She rubs an eye, says, "This seems to be helping. Maybe these are my reading glasses." I should know, of course. I should have had them color-coded by now, but I haven't yet.

She bends down to the photo from the newsletter on the coffee table, and says, "Yes, that's William Carlos Williams."

A little earlier she told me about the photo. "It's in one of those boxes," she told me. "I saw it the other day. I thought I'd told you about it before," but she hadn't, this photo of her with William Carlos Williams, Theodore Roethke, and other famous writers. So I spent fifteen minutes rifling through her boxes of bills and old papers mixed up on the kitchen counter (a Cascade Gas Company bill, final payment requested for service at the apartment she moved into in December, when we still thought she could live on her own; a letter from the superintendent of public schools of New York City, dated 1959, addressed to my grandmother, a teacher at the time, telling her how many sick days she was allowed), looking for the photo, until she explained that it was actually part of a newsletter from the artists' colony, Yaddo, in Saratoga Springs, New York. Armed with that crucial bit of information, I found it.

The photo is captioned "Class picture, 1950."

"Can you pick me out?" she says.

Not many of these people are smiling. Eugenie Gershoy, seated next to Jessamyn West, has a little smirk, and Mitsu Yashima, seated next to Flossie Williams, smiles broadly, and also Cid Corman in the back row, whom I met in 1975, when I was a high school exchange student in Japan. My mother visited me in Osaka and we traveled by train to Kyoto, to Cid Corman's ice-cream parlor where I ate a hamburger, had an ice-cream cone and listened to a poetry reading while my mother and Cid reminisced.

From left, top: Willson Osborne, Theodore Roethke, Robel Paris, Harvey Shapiro, Elaine Gottlieb, Beryl Levy, Cid Corman, Simmons Persons, Gladys Farnel, Hans Sahl, Clifford Wright, Richard Eberhart. From left, bottom: Ben Weber, Nicholas Callas, Jessamyn West, Eugenie Gershoy, William Carlos Williams, Flossie Williams, Mitsu Yashima, Charles Schucker, Elizabeth Ames, John Dillon Husband. Photograph was taken in July 1950, at West House on the Yaddo grounds in Saratoga Springs, New York, and is used courtesy of The Corporation of Yaddo.

"Don't I look prim?" my mother says, and she does. Or maybe it's something else. Scared? Intimidated? Shocked? My mother was 34 then. This was a year or so before she met my father. My sister, Nola, was three, and my mother was an up-and-coming young writer, one novel published in 1947. John Crowe Ransom liked her work, publishing several of her stories in the *Kenyon Review*. I wasn't born until 1958.

She stands up straight, hands behind her back, a scarf tied loosely around her neck, draping down over a breast, a flower pinned to the scarf. Theodore Roethke stands, huge, imposing, dour. In an accompanying article Harvey Shapiro tells of how publicly Roethke liked to display his wounds, how he told Shapiro of his hurt that John Crowe Ransom had rejected "My Papa's Waltz," though Roethke was famous by then and the poem had been widely anthologized. What remained, still, was Roethke's pain, perhaps the pain of rejection meshed with the pain of the poem's subject matter—abuse at the hands of his drunken father. Shapiro also tells of Roethke's claim that he'd bummed his way to Yaddo after escaping in drag from a mental institution on the west coast earlier that summer. "He liked to romanticize his mental illness," Shapiro writes. Perhaps, but something honest still comes across in that picture, the despair clear for anyone to view head-on.

In the front row, William Carlos Williams sits cross-legged, dignified.

"He dreamed of my legs," my mother tells me.

"William Carlos Williams dreamed of your legs?" I ask.

"At breakfast one day he said he'd had a dream about my legs. 'That girl has nice legs,' he said."

We have to keep going back over histories, our own and the histories of others, constantly revising. There's no single truth . . . except that, perhaps. History is not always recorded and not always written by the victor. History is not always written. We carry our secret histories behind our words, in another room, in the eyeglass case on the dresser in the bedroom. Maybe someone comes along and finds the right pair. Maybe we have too many, unsorted.

⌐ ⌐ ⌐

My mother's former landlord, Loyce, wants to know the history of the "L." I was gone for the past week in Hawaii, and that's the only reason I haven't called before now. Loyce has left messages on my answering machine twice, ostensibly to see about getting my mother's deposit back to us; minus a charge for mowing, the ad for renting the apartment again, a reasonable charge for her time, and of course, for painting over the "L." She'd also like the keys back from us. But the "L" is the real reason she's called. My mother wrote an "L" on the wall of the apartment in indelible magic marker before she left. "I'm dying to know the story," Loyce says. "I know there's a good story behind it."

Loyce appreciates a good story, and this is one of the things I appreciate about Loyce, that and her compassion. She moved to Bellingham several years ago to take care of her ailing mother, and now lives in her mother's old house on top of a hill with a view of the bay and the San Juan Islands. So she understands our situation. She knows that my mother can't live alone anymore, that all of us were taken by surprise by her condition when she moved here five months ago. Until then, my mother had been living on her own in South Bend, Indiana, where she taught writing until ten years ago. She'd been living on her own since I moved out at the age of sixteen to go to boarding school, and had been taking care of herself since 1966 when my father died. But in the last several months things have fallen apart. Our first inkling was the mover, a man in his sixties who worked with his son. He took me aside on the first day and told me that in his thirty years of moving he'd never seen an apartment as messy as my mother's. When he and his son went to my mom's apartment in South Bend, they almost turned around. "You don't have to do this if you don't want," the mover told his son.

No, the first inkling was my brother's call from L.A., where my mother was visiting a few days prior to her big move. The van had loaded in South Bend and she'd flown off to L.A. to visit him and his family. The night before her flight from L.A. to Seattle he called me near midnight and said, "Mom's hallucinating."

I asked him what he meant, what she was seeing, and he told me that she was seeing all these people who didn't exist and making strange remarks. "When I picked her up at the airport, she said there was a group of Asians having a baby. She said they were a troupe of actors and they were doing a skit."

Still, the next day, he put her on the plane to me, and I picked her up and brought her to her new home. Since then, we have gone to three different doctors and my mother has had brain scans and blood tests and sonograms of her carotid arteries and been placed on a small dose of an anti-psychotic drug. One doctor says her cerebral cortex has shrunk and she's had a series of tiny strokes to individual arteries in her brain.

At three A.M. one morning, the police call me up and tell me that my mother thinks someone is trying to break into her apartment.

"Is there anyone living with her?" the policeman asks.

"No."

"She says a handicapped woman lives with her. You might want to see a doctor about this."

I take her to doctors and try to convince my mother that she needs to live where she can be safe, but she refuses to even consider it. "I should have stayed in New York," she tells me. "I never should have left." And then, "I should never have come here. Why can't you be on my side?" And then, "I'll move down to L.A. Your brother is much nicer than you are."

I spend a few nights at her apartment, and she tells me about the Middle Eastern couple who have taken over her bedroom and the children who are there, and the landlord comes over and puts a lock on the door from the kitchen to the garage, though we know no one was trying to break in. And homeless people are living on her back porch. And she keeps startling people in the garage who are removing her belongings.

But finally.

After my cousin David flies up from L.A. After visiting a dozen managed care facilities, after my brother says he thinks it's the medicine that's doing this and I talk to the doctors and the doctors talk to each other and they talk to my mother and she says, "The doctor says I'm fine," and I say "No, he doesn't," and she hangs up, turns off her hearing aid.

And coincidentally, a friend of my mother's in South Bend wins second place in a poetry competition run by the literary journal I edit. The poems were all anonymous, and I had nothing to do with the judging, but my mother's friend has won second prize for a poem about her delusional mother, called "My Mother and Dan Rather." I call her up to tell her the good news of her award, but she assumes, of course, I'm calling to talk about my mother. So that's what we do for half an hour. She tells me she's distanced herself over the last year from my mother because she seemed too much like her own mother, and she tells me that several of my mother's friends wondered if they should call me and let me know what was going on.

I almost forget to tell her about her prize.

No, the first inkling was two years ago. My wife, Beverly, wondered aloud about my mother's memory, her hold on reality. I told Beverly my mother had always been kind of scattered, messy, unfocused.

And finally. After I come into her apartment one day and feel the heat. I go to the stove and turn off the glowing burners. My mother has a blister on her hand the size of a walnut. Beverly tells me that it's insane for my mother to live alone, that somehow we have to force her to move. "What if she sets the apartment on fire? She might not only kill herself, but the people next door."

"I know," I tell her. "I'm trying," but I also know that short of a court order, short of being declared her legal guardian, I can't force her.

And finally. I convince my mother to come with me to the Leopold, an historic hotel in downtown Bellingham that has been converted into apartments for seniors, one wing assisted living, the other independent. We have lunch there one day. My mother likes the food.

And finally, she agrees to spend a couple of weeks there in a guest room.

Famous people stayed at the Leopold, I tell my mother. Rutherford B. Hayes. Jenny Lind, the Swedish Nightingale. This doesn't impress her, of course. She has known more famous people than can fit on a plaque. But she has a nice view of the bay, somewhat blocked by the Georgia Pacific Paper Mill. And she likes the food but the apartment is only two cramped rooms, and across the street at the Greek restaurant, people party until two each night and climb trees and conduct military rituals. And the Iraqi Army rolled through the streets one night. And a truck dumped two bodies, a man and a woman dressed in formal evening attire.

"They sometimes flood the parking lot," she tells me, "and use it as a waterway."

Or, "Look at that," pointing, reaching for nothing.

She keeps returning to the apartment, driven by the woman I've hired to clean it. My mother wants to drive again, and I tell her no, she can't possibly, and I read articles and watch programs that tell me not to reverse roles, not to become the parent, and I wonder how that's possible to avoid. One day, I walk into her apartment and find signs she's posted all around on the bed, in the guest room, on the kitchen counter. "Keep off." "Stay out." "Go away." I ask her about these signs and she tells me they're just a joke. She's become wary of me. I tell her she's safe, ask her why she feels so threatened. She tells me, "I've never felt safe in my life."

During this period, my mother writes her "L" on the wall of the kitchen.

And the weeks at the Leopold have turned to months, and now most of her belongings are stuffed into a heated mini-storage unit. More of her belongings are stuffed into the basement of The Leopold.

Finally.

⌐ ⌐ ⌐

I almost don't want to tell Loyce the story of the "L" when she calls. I'd like to keep her in suspense, because sometimes that's stronger than the truth. She probably thinks it's about her, that the "L" stands for Loyce, but it doesn't. It stands for Leopold. One day my mother was at the apartment, after we finally convinced her she had to move, and I gave her a magic marker and asked her to mark the boxes she'd like taken to the Leopold. Apparently, she thought she was marking a box, but she was really marking the wall. This is what she really wanted. That was not lost on me. She loved that apartment. She wanted her independence, but this was just too much for me to move.

Loyce and I say goodbye after I assure her I'll return the keys and she assures me she'll return most of the deposit. It's already eight-thirty and I told my mother I'd be over around eight, but I had to read to my kids first. I haven't see them in a week. I've just returned from Hawaii.

⌐ ⌐ ⌐

In Hawaii, where I've been researching a new book, I probably had more fun than I should have. Not the kind of fun with life-bending consequences, but fun nonetheless, hanging out with a former student, eating out every night, smoking cigars, drinking. For ten dollars a day more, I was told at the airport, I could rent a convertible—a Ford Mustang, or a Caddie, and I'm not ready for that, so I take the Mustang. Stupid. The wife of the friend I'm staying with laughed when she saw it in her driveway. "Oh," she tells me. "I thought maybe Robbie was having a mid-life crisis." No, it's me probably, even though I hate to admit it. I refuse to believe such a thing could happen to me at this pre-ordained age, a month from forty, that I could be saddled with such a cliché crisis, such mediocre regrets.

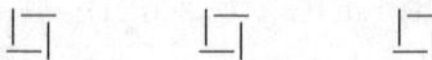

Olivia wants to read to *me* tonight, all seven stories from an Arnold Lobel book. "They're short," she assures me. We compromise on three, her three favorites. One of these she read last week to her class while I was in Hawaii. Beverly, who sometimes works in Olivia's class as a volunteer, has already told me that the class was enthralled by Olivia. "She acted so confident. She took her time and showed them the pictures."

The one she read to her class, "The Journey," is about a mouse who wants to visit his mother, and in a sequence of transactions, acquires a car, roller skates, boots, sneakers and finally a new set of feet. When he reaches his mother she hugs him, kisses him and says, "Hello, my son, you are looking fine—and what nice new feet you have!" Olivia's whole class broke out in hysterical laughter, she assured me.

I've brought my mother a box of chocolate-covered macadamia nuts. She looks at it, bewildered. "Oh, I thought it was a book," she says.

I make tea for us, but she only has a few tea mugs and they're dirty, so we have to use beer steins. "I've ended up with such an odd assortment of things," she tells me, and she blames this on the movers.

A week before my trip to Hawaii, I visited her and she showed me a notebook in which she'd kept a journal during the mid-seventies. My mother has kept journals from the time she was sixteen, a series of secret histories written in any notebook she can find. But now, she cannot read these histories, and she asks me to read this one to her.

"I might use it in a story," she tells me. "It's about Moe and Helen." Moe is Moe Howard, of the Three Stooges. He was a cousin of ours by marriage, and whenever she visited California, she'd stop by to see them. Moe, who had such a violent on-screen persona: Think of him saying, "Wise guy, eh?" Poking the eyes Larry, Curly, Shemp, or one of the later pseudo-Stooges, Curly Joe and Joe Besser. I met him once, a frail old man with white hair, too quiet to seem like Moe. Off-screen, he was a gentle family man, kind and grateful to his fans, never refusing to sign an autograph. What my mother wants me to read to her is an account of the last time she saw Moe and his wife Helen, when they were both dying.

Seeing Moe and Helen was touching—a beautiful hill of purple flowers outside that Moe said was all theirs—a beautifully furnished, expensively comfortable house through which they glide, ghost-like. They don't kiss me because of the possibility of germs. Helen is in a loose purple nylon dressing gown. She has been recuperating from a breast operation and says in a slightly quaking voice that she will be going to the doctor soon and will probably have cobalt.

Moe is red-faced and very thin. His thinness, wispiness, makes him look elfin—because he used to be heavier, he seemed bigger. His hair is white. He smiles proudly, talking about his appearances at colleges and his memoirs which comprise many books. Talk about the film I am supposed to have made with him. He reminds me that I acted in it (at the age of about 19) 8mm, I think, with his children. But it is packed somewhere with thousands of feet of other film.

As I'm reading this to my mother I feel odd, wondering if she notices the similarities between this passage and her own present life—the things packed away, the memories, the frailty—but I say nothing about this, though it moves me. Instead, I ask her about this film she was in, and she tells me it was an impromptu home movie in which Moe was cast as the villain, of course, and she was the protector of his children. She has never seen it but it exists somewhere. Moe's daughter, Joan, once showed me the huge roll of home movies in her attic. Towards the end of his life, Moe took every home movie he made and spliced them all together onto one monstrous cumbersome roll that no one could ever possibly watch in its entirety. Somewhere on this roll exists a movie with my mother, age nineteen, circa 1935.

Silently, I flip through other pages in my mother's journal, as she sits near me, lost in her memories, needing no journal really.

I am not in fantasy land. I am painfully living out my loneliness and nostalgia. I dream of my son every night and wish he were here. Those who have died are intolerably absent and I feel that all the love I need and want will not come because I had my chance and lost it, and what man will be responsible for or will react to my aging, my passion, my intolerable loneliness . . . ?

I am with her now, but not. We see each other through veils. We have battled for this moment, and neither sees the other as we would like.

William Carlos Williams dreamed of my mother's legs, as did other men that summer of 1950 at Yaddo.

As we bend over the class photo, circa 1950, she tells me the official history of that summer, how special it was for her, how it was so exciting to be around such vital intellects, such talented writers. "It was really something, going down to breakfast and having conversations with all these people. The talent was never quite the same after that."

I tell her I'd love to have a copy of this picture. "You could write to Yaddo," she says. "They use it for publicity." She tells me I could write to one of the writers pictured with her. "It's the least he could do," she says, with what seems like bitterness, and I let this remark wash over me because I think I know what's behind it.

Once, a number of years ago, Beverly and my mother and I were on a drive, and I was telling her about a friend of mine who'd done his dissertation on the poetry of one of the poets pictured in the photo. From the back seat my mother blurted, "You know, he raped me."

Beverly and I looked at one another. We didn't say anything. We didn't know what to say. The remark was so sudden, so unexpected, we hardly knew how to react. We were silent, all three of us. Neither Beverly nor I mentioned this to each other later.

My mother starts talking about him now, though I haven't asked. She says, "One time, he invited me to a private party, and innocent that I was, I went there." In memory, she's lucid. Only the present is slippery, tricky, untrustworthy.

"There were all these men there. They were all leches. Ted Roethke kept lunging for me, just making grabs. He really had problems," and she laughs. She mentions the name of the poet who was her friend, whom she trusted. He was younger than her, than all these other famous men. "I thought he'd protect me." She laughs again. This time, there's no mistaking the bitterness.

I think about asking her. What term to use? "He assaulted you?"

"Yes," she says.

"Did it happen at Yaddo?" I ask.

She nods.

"Did you ever confront him?"

"No," she says. "I don't want to talk about it."

But then she says, "There wasn't much I could do. In those days, there wasn't much to do. I just pretended it didn't happen. For a little while, he became my boyfriend."

I don't know what to say. I probably shouldn't say anything. I sigh. "He should have been locked up. How could he be your boyfriend after that?"

"He was drunk when it happened," and I want to say that's no excuse, but I keep my mouth shut and let her talk. "I left the party early and he followed me back to my room. I tried to lock the door, but the lock was broken.

"I turned things around. I had to. I was confused. In my mind, he became my protector from the other men there."

I study the picture again. My mother's expression and the expressions of the men. I wonder when this photo was taken, before or after the assault my mother describes. The photo has taken on the quality of a group mug shot to me. I think they look like jerks, most of them—except for Cid Corman, whom my mother says is a wonderful person, and maybe some others, too, maybe William Carlos Williams, who dreamed of my mother's legs and "had an eye for the ladies" as my mother says. Maybe even dour Theodore Roethke, though he lunged at her as though she was something being wheeled by on a dessert tray.

"They weren't famous for their personalities," she tells me.

I think about these people in the photo, how unfair it seems to me that someone can go on to have a career, hide behind his smirk, have dissertations written about him, how the actions of some people seem to have no visible consequences. I think of my mother's secret histories, her journals, her blurted comments, her assertion that she has never felt safe.

I flip the newsletter over to the section titled "Recent Works Produced by Yaddo Fellows," and see that the latest works reported are from 1987. For an absurd moment, I believe that none of the Fellows at Yaddo have been productive for over ten years, and this makes me happy, but then I realize the newsletter itself is ten years old.

My mother has taken to carrying a picture of me, Ideal Robin, I call it, skinny, sitting languorously, smiling beside a life-size cardboard cut-out of Rudolph Valentino. The son she longed for in her journal perhaps hardly exists anymore—I was away at boarding school that year, my choice, not hers, and I never returned.

I have come to visit her now. I've knocked lightly. I've used my key. She can barely see me when I walk into her apartment. I've told her I've returned from Hawaii, that she can expect me around eight, but I'm late and as I push open the door she's looking at me almost suspiciously, because really her eyesight is that bad, and until I speak she has no idea who's entering. The Iraqi army? A stranger who wants her belongings? A poet she thinks is her "protector" but means her harm? I half expect to see signs, "Keep Off," "Stay Out," "Go Away." I have brought a box of chocolate-covered macadamia nuts. I am wearing new feet, but she doesn't notice. Tomorrow she will have surgery on her eyes that will not improve anything, but keep things from getting worse. How much worse could things get for this woman who loves words, but can neither see nor write them anymore? Does her history go on inside her, on some gigantic roll of spliced-together home movies? Tell me the story of the "L." Tell me the story of the wall of your apartment. Tell me the story of those talented writers who publicly display their wounds and the writers who secretly wound others. Tell me which is worse. She kisses me lightly and I give her her gift. And she says, once, only once, though I keep hearing it, the disappointment, and strangely, even fear, "Oh, I thought it was a book." ■

My Father Always Said

Mimi Schwartz

For years I heard the same line: "In Rindheim, you didn't do such things!" It was repeated whenever the American world of his daughters took my father by surprise. Sometimes it came out softly, in amusement, as when I was a Pilgrim turkey in the P.S. 3 Thanksgiving play. But usually, it was a red-faced, high-blood-pressure shout—especially when my sister, Ruth, became "pinned" to Mel from Brooklyn or I wanted to go with friends whose families he didn't know.

"But they're Jewish," I'd say, since much of our side of Forest Hills was. The eight lanes of Queens Boulevard divided the Jews, Irish, and Italians pushing out of Brooklyn, the Bronx, and Manhattan from the old guard WASPs of Forest Hills Gardens. No Jews or Catholics over there—except for a few blocks near the Forest Hills Tennis Stadium where, from fifth grade on, we kids all went to watch what is now the U.S. Tennis Open, our end-of-summer ritual before school.

"You're not going," my father would announce before all such rituals.

"But everybody's going."

It was the wrong argument to make to a man who fled Hitler's Germany because of everybody. But I couldn't know that because he rarely talked about *that* Germany, only about his idyllic Rindheim where everybody (as opposed to the everybody I knew) did everything right. If my friends didn't have an aunt, grandmother, or great grandfather originally from Rindheim or vicinity, they were suspect. They could be anybody, which is exactly why I liked them—not like the Weil kids whose mother was "a born Tannhauser," as if that were a plus.

"I don't care about everybody!" my father would shout (that was his second favorite line); but it was a losing battle for him. My sister smoked at fifteen, I wore lipstick at twelve, we had friends with families who were third-generation Brooklyn and Rumania, and we didn't give a hoot that "In Rindheim, you didn't do such things!"

The irony of those words were inchoate—even to him, I realize now—until we went back to his village to visit the family graves. It was eight years after the war, I was thirteen, and he wanted to show me, the first American in the family, where his family had lived for generations, trading cattle. He wanted me to understand that "Forest Hills, Queens is not the world" (his third favorite line). A hard task to tackle, but my father was tough, a survivor who had led his whole clan out of Nazi Germany and into Queens, New York. He was ready for an American, newly turned teenage me.

"So Mimi-a-la, this is Rindheim!" my father boomed as the forest opened upon a cluster of fifty or so red-peaked houses set into the hillside of a tiny, green valley. We had driven for hours through what looked like Hansel and Gretel country, filled with foreboding evergreens that leaned over the narrow, winding roads of Schwarzwald. Even the name, Schwarzwald, which meant Black Forest, gave me the creeps after being weaned on Nazi movies at the Midway Theater; but I was optimistic. Life did look prettier than in Queens.

We drove up a rutted main street and stopped before a crumbling stone house with cow dung in the yard. "This was *our* house!" my father announced, as I watched horse flies attacking the dung, not just in *our* yard but in every yard on Eelinger Weg. And there were cows and chickens walking in front of our rented car. What a bust! My mother at least came from a place with sidewalks (we had driven by her old house in Stuttgart, sixty kilometers north, before coming here), but my father, I decided at once, was a hick. All his country hero adventures about herding cows with a book hidden in one pocket and his mother's raspberry linzer torte in the other were discounted by two cows chewing away in stalls where I expected a car to be.

A stooped, old man with thick jowls and a feathered leather cap came out of the house with a big smile and a vigorous handshake for my dad who, looking squeezed in his pin-striped suit, nodded now and then and looked polite, but did not smile back.

"Sind Sie nicht ein Loewengart, vielleicht Julius oder Artur?" The man kept jabbering and my mother translated. He was Herr Schmidt, the blacksmith, and had bought the family house in 1935 from Uncle Julius, the last of the Loewengarts to leave Rindheim. The man was reminding my father about how he and his brothers, Sol and Julius, liked to play in his shop with all his tools. "Eine nette Familie, sehr nette," he kept saying.

I understood nothing because I had learned no German in our house in Queens. When my father reached Ellis Island, he announced that our family would not speak the language of those who drove them out of Germany.

Which was fine with me. It was embarrassing enough in those days to have parents who, for all my coaching, couldn't stop saying 'fader' and 'moder' to my friends.

The man beckoned us towards the house, but my father shook his head, "Nein, Danke!" and backed us quickly away. I wanted to go in and see his old room; but it would be forty years until I followed Frau Hummel, the blacksmith's daughter, up the narrow, dark stairs to a loft with two windows like cannon holes and searched the heavy low beams for his initials—A. L.—carved in the worn, smooth wood.

"And here's *my* downtown! No Penn Drug to hang around here!" my Dad said cheerfully, as we drove past four buildings leaning together like town drunks. "And here's where Grunwald had his kosher butcher shop and Zundorfer, his dry goods. And here's the Gasthaus Kaiser! It had all the Purim and Shuvuott balls with green branches and ferns and pink flowers like marbles in the candlelight. . . ." I could picture Mr. Grundwald—he sold sausages in Queens—but I couldn't picture my big-bellied, bald-headed Dad dancing, a kid like me.

We turned into an alley and stopped next to a grey stone building with stone columns in the doorway and what looked like insets of railroad ties decorating the four corners. I wouldn't have noticed it tucked among the houses.

"Here's where we spent *every* Shabbat," my father said, getting us out of the car to look at the old synagogue. He pointed to a Hebrew inscription carved onto a stone plaque above the doorway: "How great is God's house and the doorway to Heaven," he translated haltingly in his rusty Hebrew. Right below the stone plaque was a wooden beam with another inscription, this one in German. It said the same thing, my father said, but it was new. He'd never seen it before.

I found out later that the German inscription had been added the year before we came. That's when the Jewish synagogue was converted into the Protestant Evangelical Church to accommodate an influx of East Germans who had fled the advancing Russians troops late in World War II. They had resettled into the empty Jewish houses, which had been one-third of this tiny village of Catholics and Jews. Keeping the same words over the doorway was meant as a tribute of respect: that this building was still God's house. But the Rindheim Jews who had fled to America and Israel were never grateful. Their beautiful synagogue was no more; that's what counted.

"Well, at least it didn't become a gymnasium or a horse stable, like in other villages," one villager told me huffily in 1993 when I returned to

Rindheim on my own. Two other villagers nodded vigorously, but a lively woman, who said she used to live next door to my great uncle, said, "Na Ja, I wouldn't be so happy if our Catholic church became a mosque—and believe me, we have plenty of Turks here . . ."

". . . They are our new Jews," someone interjected.

". . . Na Ja," the lively woman shrugged and continued, "and I wouldn't feel good just because the Moslems said our church was still God's house."

I had passed "the Moslems," four men squatting around a table and sipping Turkish coffee in a terraced yard below the synagogue. They had come, the lively woman's husband said, in the 1960s as guest workers from Turkey and Afghanistan and now made up twenty percent of the village. Quite a few lived in the old Gasthaus Kaiser, where my father used to dance at Purim Festivals and where my Aunt Hilda and family once lived above the restaurant. This village is more like Forest Hills than you thought, Dad, I told myself, wishing he were around to discuss these ironies of migration. (The Forest Hills Gardens of my childhood is now owned by wealthy Asians and our block on 110th Street is now filled with Iranians.)

My father loosened his tie and wiped beads of sweat from his forehead with a checkered handkerchief. "And if you weren't in your synagogue by sundown on Friday, and not a minute later, *and* all day on Saturday, you were fined, a disgrace to your family. Three stars had to shine in the evening sky before anyone could go home."

I thought of his fury whenever I wanted to go bowling on Saturday at Foxy's Alley where all the boys hung out. Not that my father went to synagogue in Queens. The most religious he got, as far as I could see, was to play his record of Jan Pierce singing Kol Nidre on Yom Kippur. And he fasted—which I tried once or twice but got hungry when my mother ate a bagel. She never fasted.

The sun was high, the car seat sticky on my thighs, so I happily sat in the shade of four tall, arched windows which someone had been fixing. But my mother was heading for the car, saying she didn't like standing in the open where everyone could see us. In fact, she would have skipped Germany altogether and stayed in Belgium with my sister who had married a Belgian Jew instead of Mel from Brooklyn.

"Aren't we going in?" I asked when my father started to follow my mother. He was usually the leader on everything, the man who, as soon as Hitler was elected, convinced his brothers, sister, cousins, and parents-in-law, forty people in all, to leave Germany as soon as possible; the man who figured out schemes for smuggling money taped to toilets on night trains to

Switzerland—it took two years—so that they'd have enough cash for America to let them in. (Jews without a bank account or sponsor had no country who would take them from Hitler's Germany.)

"No reason to go in. The building is just a shell. Everything was gutted by fire during Kristallnacht."

"What's that?"

I imagined some Jewish festival with candles out of control. In 1953 there was no *Schindler's List* or Holocaust Museum, so I never heard about the Nazis burning all the synagogues in Germany on one night of a country-wide pogrom in 1938. All I knew was that good Americans, who looked like Jimmy Stewart and Gregory Peck, fought mean-looking men in black uniforms who clicked their heels a lot and shouted, "Heil Hitler." And we won.

"Kristallnacht was when the Jews finally realized they had to leave—and fast—even from Rindheim where it wasn't so bad. People felt safe—until the synagogue was torched, everything in flames."

He stopped talking. "Go on!" I urged, but he held back, tentative. Not at all like him.

"My cousin Fritz . . . he's dead now, he lived over there, said that he smelled smoke and raced over—he was part of the Fire Brigade, many Jews were—and began shouting, 'Why don't we do something?' Men he knew all his life were standing around, silent. 'Against orders!' a Nazi brownshirt said, 'except if Christian houses start to burn," and pointed his rifle at Fritz. So everything inside was lost—the Torah, the Ark. . . ."

I thought about the old blacksmith who lived in our house. Was he there? Was he one of those firemen? Why was he so friendly if he hated the Jews?

"But these people weren't from Rindheim," my father said quickly. "They were thugs from outside brought in trucks by the Nazis to do their dirty work."

My father, already in America by then, had heard this from Rindheim Jews like Fritz who left as soon after Kristallnacht as they could get exit visas. "The Rindheimers would not do such a thing!" he'd been assured by many who resettled in America.

My father opened the car door. "In fact many Christians helped the Jews fix the store and house windows also smashed that night. But for that they got in trouble. Everyone who helped was sent to the Front as cannon fodder."

"What's that?" I asked.

"It's what you feed to guns so they'll shoot."

I imagined a young man being stuffed into a cannon aimed at American guns, his mother in the red doorway of the house we just passed, getting a telegram, crying like in the movies. But I wasn't going to feel sorry, not when they let the synagogue burn.

Later I would hear this term, cannon fodder, used again and again by Rindheim Jews—and always with the same "broken window" story. It was as if they had decided collectively on this tale and how it illustrated that their Christian neighbors meant well. "It wasn't their fault. They were afraid, too," they'd say with more sympathy than anger. But, like my parents, those who returned to Rindheim to visit the family graves did so quickly, never wanting to chat out in the open or re-enter old rooms of memory.

I was hungry, but my father stopped again, this time in front of a shabby building with three tiers of windows. This was his school, he said, and it looked like mine, but P.S. 3 had a paved playground and good swings. This just had dirt.

"We Jews had the first floor and one teacher, Herr Spatz, who taught everybody everything. The Christians had the other two floors."

"How come?" I asked, for I'd never heard not dividing kids by age.

My father looked surprised. "That's how it was done. We learned Torah and they didn't. They went to school on Saturdays and we didn't. But to high school, we went together, six kilometers to Horb, those who went."

"And did you talk to each other—and play games?" I thought of Tommy Molloy in the schoolyard, saying that I killed Christ, but then he asked me to play stickball on his team, and I said okay.

"Of course. We all got along. Rindheim was not so big."

I wouldn't argue about that! The schoolyard was deserted, and looking for movement in a meadow on the far hill, I saw a giant white cross ringed by forest that kept its distance, like dark green bodyguards. It was also new, my father said. It wasn't even there when he came home for an occasional Shabbat, after moving to Frankfurt in 1921 to work and marry.

"Remember how we had to park the car two kilometers away and walk to my father's?" He nudged my mother. "No Jew dared to drive here on Shabbat! Am I right?"

"Absolutely not. You'd be run out of town!" My mother laughed for the first time all day and turned to tell me about how she, a big city girl from Stuttgart, first came to this village for her cousin Max's wedding. She wore a red, lace dress. Very shocking! Her shoulders eased with nostalgia, wisps of black hair loosened from her chignon, and I leaned forward, close to her neck that always smelled of almond soap, to hear more about my parents having fun.

My father made a sharp left turn up a dirt road that zigzagged up a hill and stopped in front of a low run-down farmhouse with half a roof. We needed a key for the Jewish cemetery and it was hanging on the peg "where it has always been," my father said. The Brenner family were the gravediggers; they'd been burying the Rindheim Jews for generations. A quarter of a mile farther, a giant stone portal emerged from nowhere—the kind that led to castles—and the fat key opened the heavy gate that led us deep into woods.

I still remember the sunlight on that day, how it streamed on the gravestones, a thousand of them tipped but all standing in an enchanted forest light. It was a place to whisper and walk on tiptoe, even if you were an American thirteen. I remember the softness of the ground, a carpet of moss and leaves, and the stillness, as if the trees were holding their breath until we found everyone: my grandmother, Anna, born Tannhauser (1872-1915) and my grandfather, Rubin (1866-1925), both marked by sleek, dark marble gravestones that looked new despite the underbrush. And Rubin's father, Raphael (1821-1889) and his father, Rubin Feit (1787-1861), their pale sandstone gravestones carved with elaborate vines and scrolls eroded by time.

I tried to imagine faces: a grandfather who enforced strict rules about work, manners, and Torah; a grandmother who, in the faded photo over my parents' bed, laughed with my father's twinkle when life pleased him. She had died when my father was not much older than I was, of infection, not Hitler, my father said. So had his dad, who refused to go to the hospital two hours away.

But all I could picture were the grandparents I knew: the Omi and Opa who lived three blocks away in Queens and "babysat," against my loudest objections that I was too old for that. This grandfather walked my dog so I didn't have to and wove yards of intricately patterned shawls and slipcovers on his loom in our attic. This grandmother made delicious, heart-shaped butter cookies and told stories of how they escaped in a little boat from Denmark to Sweden, and then to a chicken farm on Long Island where she, a city woman from Stuttgart, sang to her hens every morning—until my grandfather's heart attack made them move three blocks from us.

"Do you want to put down stones?" my father asked, placing small ones on his father's grave, his lips moving as in prayer, and then on his mother's grave—and on the others. He had found the stones under the wet leaves, and my mother, wobbling in high heels, was searching for more, enough for both of us.

"What for?" I asked, not wanting to take what she was offering. I would find my own.

"It's how you pay tribute to the dead," my father said looking strangely gaunt despite his bulk. "The dead souls need the weight of remembrance, and then they rise up to God more easily . . . If we lived nearby, there'd be many stones," he said softly to his father's grave.

In later years, there would be more stones, as more Rindheim Jews came to visit the graves of their ancestors, but eight years after the war there were no others. I placed a smooth, speckled white with mica on Anna's grave and rougher, grey ones on the men's. My father nodded. Some connection had been made, he knew, the one he had run from and returned to, the one I resisted even as I lay stones.

There were Loewengarts all over the place, mixed in with Pressburgers and Froehlichs and Grunwalds and Landauers, the same names again and again for they all married each other—or someone Jewish from a nearby village. There were four or five with Jews. My father said he had been daring to marry a woman from so far away—sixty kilometers! But when my mother found a gravestone that might be her second cousin on her mother's side, I thought: not *so* daring!

We were next to a wire fence in the far end of the cemetery where the weeds were high. My mother had disappeared, so it was just my father and I among rows of tiny graves no higher than my kneecaps, their writing almost rubbed off.

We were among the children's graves, my father said, slipping on wet leaves, but catching himself as I reached for his hand. I wanted him standing, especially with my mother gone. Above me, I heard the warble of a single bird and shivered. My father pointed out a headstone carved like a tree trunk but with its limbs cut off. It meant the person died young, in the prime of life, he said, and I thought of my sister Hannah who died soon after they arrived in America—before I was born. I didn't know the details then—how their doctor, also a German refugee, didn't know about the antibiotics new on the market—only that the sweet face with green eyes who hung over my parents' bed was buried in New Jersey somewhere.

I was glad to move back among the larger stones, worn and substantial like adults. I saw one dated 1703. You could tell the older stones, my father said, because all the writing—what little was left—was in Hebrew. The newer gravestones were mostly in German because by 1900, Jews no longer had to pay extra taxes as Jews, so they had started to feel very German, as if they really belonged.

"Do all the Rindheim Jews now live in New York?" I was thinking about how many came to our house in Queens and pinched my cheeks over the years.

"Many, yes," he lectured, "but some moved to Palestine as a group. Others went to Chicago, Paris, even Buenos Aires . . ." We were now before a headstone carved with a broken flower, its stem snapped in two. He touched it. "And some stayed," he said quietly. "There were many, especially old people, who were like my Tante Rosa and thought no one would bother her. 'I'll be fine' she kept saying. Later . . . we tried to send her money, but then . . ." His voice trailed off.

"Is she buried here?"

He shook his head. "She was deported." I asked no more, for I knew what deported meant, had seen the pictures of Auschwitz in *Life* magazine. I'd always been relieved that my Dad was smart and had gotten the whole family out in time—except for this Tante Rosa. I imagined a handful of old people getting into a wagon, but no one I knew, so it didn't seem so bad.

The sun rays had faded, the forest turned grey and dank, and we were near the entrance again, standing before a large, monument in black stone, erected "to honor the victims of the persecution of the Jews—1933-1945." No individual names were listed, so I kept imagining a handful of old people and walked over to a memorial that had a face: Joseph Zundorfer, his features carved in bronze above his name. He had been a Jewish fighter pilot in World War I with many medals. "Shot down!" my father said, placing a stone on the grave, and I pictured a hero like Gregory Peck.

Eighty-seven Jews, not a handful, were deported from my father's village during 1941 and 1942, I found out forty years later. They died in the concentration camps of Lublin, Riga, Theresienstadt; but with no names engraved in stone and no faces to admire, they remained anonymous to me that day. What registered to an American teenager who lost no one she really knew was the sunlight on my family's graves, and how a thousand Jews, related to me, were buried, safe and secure for centuries in these high woods.

"In Rindheim, we didn't do such things!" suddenly carried more weight, giving me a history and legitimacy that would have made me not mind, as much, if my father had kept saying that line. But he didn't. When we came home, he took up golf and played every weekend with American friends who never heard of Rindheim. Their world of congeniality became ours and I was to enter its promise. "Smile, smile! You are a lucky girl to be here!"

is what I remember after that as his favorite line. His magical village of memory had disappeared among the graves that were not there and the weightless souls with no stones of remembrance. ▀

The Stranger at the Window

Rebecca McClanahan

"Here's your first assignment," says the hospice coordinator, "if you want to take it. White male, seventy-four years old." My father's age, I'm thinking. "I see by your records that you're okay with Alzheimer's. Some volunteers won't touch it."

"My mother nursed her father for years."

"His wife says his hands are busy all the time—a scratcher and a grabber. And his language is gone."

"I'm fine with that."

"She's exhausted. She can really use the help."

"I'll be there tomorrow."

"She says he's a sweet man, not a mean bone in his body."

* * *

The woman who answers the door is trim, about seventy, with a full sensuous mouth painted coral. Her thick dark hair is coifed in a '60s bouffant. She smiles and leads me to the den where a man with silver hair is propped against a sofa back, a flowered sheet tucked neatly beneath him. "We've been married fifty-two years," she says. "Can you believe it? Where did the time go?" Her husband is dressed in steam-pressed peach-and-white striped pajamas over a clean white T-shirt. "Do you think he might be cold?" she asks. Together we maneuver her husband's stiff limbs into a velour robe. He smiles up at me, his blue eyes squinting mischievously.

"He's over the angry stage," she says. "And the wandering. He used to get lost. He'd just wander out the door." Apparently his wandering is now confined to his mind—and his hands. Every arm of the chairs and sofa is shredded. "I tried an Alzheimer's apron. Do you know what that is?" I tell her yes, I've seen them in nursing homes—aprons stitched with buttons, shoelaces, snaps to keep the patients' hands busy.

"But he kept pulling off the fringe balls, putting them in his mouth." He yanks free the sheet that's been tucked over the sofa, then pulls at the belt of his robe, as if to say *where is the end of this thing*, seeming not to understand that it is attached to him. She takes his hands, smoothes them, clucks soothingly, "There, there." She reaches behind the couch and brings out a bright yellow box of Legos. "He likes the red ones," she says.

⌶ ⌶ ⌶

Volunteering is only in part a way to repay that which has been given. It is also a cry to be needed, to be used. Volunteers often say that they get back more than they give, and I used to consider this a false sentiment, equivalent to the modest pooh-poohing that follows a compliment. Now I know they are right. We do what we do because *we* need to. Something in the act of volunteering confers on even the most selfish individual a mantle of generosity and caring. The middle-aged man sitting beside me at the first hospice volunteer session needs badly to tell us how badly he is needed. He frowns, crosses his arms over his chest. "People say, how can you do this? I mean, how can you *not* do it, how can you *not* help someone? What kind of world would that be?"

It's an eclectic group gathered around the table—black, white, young, old, male, female. Most have been caregivers to family members or friends and wish to repay the hospice community for the help they received. The burly, bearded computer salesman, who more closely resembles a lumberjack, has buried a mother; the elderly gentlemen with an eastern European accent, a wife; the blond middle-aged woman, a brother to AIDS. Others have different agendas. The energetic nurse wants something useful to do on her day off. The dark-haired, dark-eyed girl wearing all black is a graduate student in architecture, studying how to make buildings that encourage the best kind of dying.

What I end up telling the group is how, for many years, I watched my mother care for her father. Alzheimer's is a slow and excruciating descent to the grave, and at times my mother appeared to suffer more from his disease than he did. Exhausted and confused, at times despairing, she carried on with little outside help.

I don't tell the group my fears—that I'm made of weaker stuff than my mother, that when the time comes, I won't have what it takes to care for my dying parents, siblings, or husband. I don't relate my own experience with my sister, who contracted a severe bacterial infection while giving birth to her second child. Although it's been nearly ten years, it still hurts to talk about that time, to think of how close she was to death. Had I known at the time how close, I might not have been able to manage—taking care of her newborn son and young daughter while trying to administer, every four hours for four weeks, the infusions of antibiotics that dripped from the IV tube into the catheter the surgeon had installed directly into my sister's heart.

Each infusion lasted an hour. My sister would sleep but I couldn't; I'd watch the syringe for air bubbles, the tubing for crimps, the wound for swelling or reddening. Then it was time to disconnect the tubing, disinfect the area, wash my hands, change another diaper, wash my hands again, prepare another bottle of formula, another meal, wash another load of clothes, watch the clock for the next infusion time. I was too tired to cry, too frazzled to do anything but the tasks set directly before me. Well-meaning friends and neighbors dropped by, but their presence was more troubling than helpful. They didn't seem to know what to do. One morning while taking the babies for a stroller ride around the block, I began to weep, crying aloud to the air—I can't do this anymore, I need help, someone has to help me. The streets and yards were empty. I rolled the stroller to the neighborhood church and began to bang on the door. When no one answered I went next door to the parsonage. I knocked, but no one answered. Exhausted, I collapsed on the steps and wept until no more tears came. Then I stood up, tucked the blanket around the babies, who had miraculously fallen asleep, and wheeled the stroller back to the little brick house where my sister waited. Turning the corner into her driveway, I made a pact with the universe. Save my sister, get me out of this mess, and I'll repay the debt.

I don't tell the group that it's taken me nearly ten years to make good on my promise. I also don't express my other fear—that my vocation, the daily emphasis on words and ideas, has estranged me from the physical world, lifted me further and further away from the body's lessons. A therapist once accused me of loving my stepson only in the abstract, suggesting that the reason I chose not to bear children is because I live primarily outside my body. Maybe working with dying patients, especially Alzheimer's patients, will provide a guide not only for the years of caretaking ahead, but also for the world *beneath* language, a universe of feeling, gesture, touch, sensation that I seem unable to fully enter. Gardening, cooking, dancing, sex pull me briefly into this world, but I sense there is a deeper frontier to explore, what the poet Rilke calls "a place where, from each to each/there is something that might be language, without speech."

"I'm late," BJ says. (BJ is the name I'll use here; as a hospice volunteer, I have signed a form promising not to reveal the names of patients and their family members.) "I need to go. Are you sure you'll be all right?" She shows me the food tray, the telephone, emergency numbers. "He isn't much trouble. There's not a mean bone in his body." She says she's unhappy with the young woman who comes to bathe C. Apparently the bather has been hurrying him through his bath, talking sternly to him. "I don't want someone treating him like that," she says. "He can't help the way he is."

As soon as she leaves, I wish she hadn't. It's the way I always felt as a teenager when the parents left for the evening and I was left alone with their children. Suddenly the house seemed bigger. Responsibility loomed. What if something went wrong—the baby choked on a cracker, a stranger came to the door? C reaches for a red Lego, pats it, rubs it, then tries to fold it into the hem of his robe, looking up at me with a smirk, as if he's getting away with something. His face is open, trusting, delicately lined in those places where emotion marks us; if he ever hurt anyone, it does not show. I once heard an aging actress say that we get the faces we deserve. If so, C must have done something right.

He smiles, licks the instruction book. I snap three pieces together. He takes them apart. He lifts up his pajama bottoms to reveal broomstick legs, brown socks pulled up to his knees. I take his fingers and gently disentangle them from the fabric. Then I smooth the pajama bottoms down to cover his knees, which are knobby and chapped. What trust, to leave your husband in the hands of a stranger. In exchange for a little peace, a few hours away, you relinquish control over the one you love.

The glass-fronted cabinet beside the sofa is filled with figurines of elderly people, their faces suggesting serenity and intent concentration as they bend over their work. One woman is quilting; another embroiders; the others shell peas, shuck corn, churn butter. Purpose defines their eyes. A bald man in blue overalls, one leg tossed over the other, is whittling. At his feet a wooden horse and small toys validate the end of his labor. I recently read a news article about the death of "the mitten lady," who, for forty-four years, knitted mittens and hats for poor children. She always kept yarn on her needles; as soon as one pair was finished, she started another. According to her daughter, the woman believed that God would not take her if she was in the middle of a work in progress. A few days before her mother's death, the daughter noticed that the needles were empty.

C's hands are busy picking imaginary lint from the carpet and stuffing it into the Lego box. His pajama bottoms are slack, and he folds, pleats, repleats them, then gestures with his hands like an umpire—two fingers, three. He lifts his head to stare out the window: "The man at the hotel, he saw it. Five, ten, fifteen, twenty twenty twenty." Outside, a neighbor's white undergarments flap on the line.

卐 卐 卐

Although *hospice* is linked etymologically with *hospital,* its emphasis is not on cure, but on care. At the hospice unit of the local hospital, miracle is redefined. Time and people move slowly—no CPR, resuscitation, or other heroic measures. Hope may be the thing with feathers, but you won't be flying out on its wings. You are in the hospice unit to die, or to return home to die. A hospice patient, by definition, has been diagnosed with a terminal illness and is expected to live less than six months. Seventy-five percent of our city's hospice patients have cancer; fifteen percent, AIDS; the remaining ten percent suffer from other diseases. C is one of only three hospice patients whose primary diagnosis is Alzheimer's.

According to the hospice nurse, if you are one of the miracles, one who defies the odds and is discharged, you may find to your surprise that you mourn your release, that you miss the attention, the intimate world of care you had grown accustomed to. The nurse, who is leading our third volunteer session, has been present at the death of hundreds of patients. "Death is a lot less scary than we imagine," she says. Her gaze shifts to the window behind my chair. "The angel often appears in the window in the corner. The moment of death can be filled with joy and light."

I want to believe this, but I'm cynical, having recently heard my aunt's account of the death of my paternal grandfather thirty years ago. It had been an excruciating year, her father living on canned oxygen and pain, her mother worn down to raw nerves. Near the end, because my grandparents were no longer "good for each other," Ruth began sleeping on a cot in the dining room and administering a shot of morphine to her father every four hours and then, because he called out in pain, every three hours, then two, and finally—because he begged her—every hour. Early one morning, while my grandmother was stirring oatmeal in the kitchen, he cried out. Both women ran to the room in time to witness his last minutes: no heavenly light, no angel in this window. My grandfather was sitting up in bed, his arms spread wide, eyes wild with terror. "Mom!" he cried. A cry of anguish, my aunt recalls. Then black blood began pouring, spewing from his nose and mouth. Ruth caught what she could in the bedpan, but it kept on coming, the remaining seconds of his life emptying, his body's fluids spraying against the bedroom wall.

It's a rainy May afternoon, one month since my first visit. I come every Wednesday and Saturday and stay three or four hours. Eight visits so far, although it feels like more. Working with hospice patients, you quickly cut to the chase, no time for formalities. BJ has left for another dental appointment and C, dressed in new beige print pajamas, seems happy to see me. His eyes are bright as he reaches for the sleeve of my sweater. I touch his head, tell him how handsome he looks in the new pajamas.

"We need to make a punk for the king and queen," he says. I nod, reaching for the Legos. C grabs the edge of the sheet and the hem of his robe, pressing them tightly together. "Five ten fifteen twenty twenty twenty," he says, peering out the window. "We can go out and catch it from here." His hands are shaking, his mouth drawn in tightly—a sign, as BJ has explained, that he needs a nap. I move to the sofa and sit beside him, propping a pillow beneath his head. His forehead is creased, mouth tense, his blue eyes narrowed in worry. This must be one of his lucid moments, the kind my mother's father occasionally had. Last week BJ told me that a few nights ago as she sat on the couch beside C, he suddenly called out, "Hold me!" It frightened her that *he* sounded frightened. She held him, his head in her lap, stroking his hair until he fell asleep.

Sitting beside C, I massage his forehead, smoothing out furrows. His mouth begins to work, his lips moving silently, quickly. "There, there," I say, borrowing BJ's rhythms. Maybe a lullaby would soothe him, or some song from the past. My grandfather always liked old songs, especially hymns. Near the end, only music brought him back to himself. I'd sit at the piano and play "Annie Laurie" or "The Church in the Wildwood" and my grandfather would join in. His voice, though it had thinned over the years, was still strong, and the words seemed to come from some well deep within. I lean close to C's face and begin to sing "Amazing Grace." His eyes fly open, his hands claw the air. "What's that?" he says. "What's that?" He begins to cry, as if in pain. "What's that?"

When BJ returns, she is holding her jaw and grimacing. The dentist has made a plate to keep her from grinding her teeth during the night. "From stress," she says. C is sipping invisible drinks, licking his fingers, pulling at the sheet and blanket. "He wasn't always like this," she says. "When he retired, he was supervisor of the composing room. Before that, he was a typesetter."

That makes sense, of course, things are falling into place—the endless counting, C's busy hands. His working life was spent stacking letter beside letter, building words, assembling, reassembling typefaces, counting out sizes. I wonder what he'd think of my new poems, the ones I've been struggling with these past months. "About a fifteen," he says to the folded end of the sheet. "Fifteen fifteen fifteen fifteen."

BJ sits beside him and takes his hands in hers, then leans her head on his shoulder. He stares straight ahead through the large window that faces the back yard. BJ's eyes are closed, and her head jerks slightly as if in sleep. If some stranger were to pass by the window just now and look inside, he'd see an elderly couple snuggled close on the sofa, the man sitting tall and straight, handsome in his silver hair and sea-blue eyes, the woman resting against him. It's the way I sit with my husband every night while we watch the evening news. We have it down to a science now, no words necessary. I move close, he reaches in his shirt pocket to remove his reading glasses, then lifts his arm to pull me into the cave between his shoulder and his ear. Usually I don't even watch the screen; the news is just an excuse. I close my eyes and take in my husband's smells, his end-of-day tiredness, the pulse beating softly in his throat.

Suddenly BJ rouses, blinks her eyes. "My goodness," she says, almost guiltily. "Did I fall asleep?"

"You needed it," I say. C is still wide awake, his hands performing some task in the air. She places a pillow on her lap and repositions his body, pressing his head onto the pillow. She begins to stroke his face, and for a moment it's just the two of them in the room. She caresses his cheekbones, forehead, the hollows around his eyes. "If you touch his face, like this," she says, "it calms him." Although I discovered this technique weeks ago, I don't tell her this. It's the kind of thing only a wife should know.

⌐ ⌐ ⌐

"*Hospice,*" the social worker is explaining to the group, "is derived from *hospis*, which means both *stranger* and *host*; in Latin *hospis* also means *enemy*. As a volunteer, you may be called upon to be that stranger. You're asking to be part of the most tender time of a patient's life. In exchange, you must expect to be used. However," she continues, "it is your right and your responsibility to set your own boundaries. Some volunteers refuse to work with AIDS patients; others can't bear the sight of a dying child. Some volunteers welcome the chance to work with a patient of a different race or religion or socioeconomic level; others are terrified to venture into certain neighborhoods. A back rub, a massage, is a godsend to most patients, but if it makes you uncomfortable, don't do it. If you don't want to feed a patient or diaper him, tell us. If you can't bear the sight of blood, or if the smell of feces makes you gag, let us know. These are not judgments, simply facts. Know your boundaries and stick with them."

At the coffee break the bearded computer salesman presses me into conversation, seemingly desperate to recount his last few months with his mother. "I fed her, I diapered her, I held her head when she threw up," he says, rubbing his hand across his bristly beard. "But I couldn't bear to bathe her. Something about it just didn't feel right." He seems to need some sort of absolution.

"I understand," I say. For my mother, diapering her father was the most difficult part. It wasn't the smell or even the mess, she told me. After all, she'd diapered six babies of her own and a dozen grandchildren. It was more the thought of it, the shame she was afraid he must have felt. "Daughters aren't supposed to diaper their parents, that's not the way the world should be." I haven't yet diapered C, but I've watched BJ do it, and I think I'm ready now. It's harder than it looks, she says. He's heavier than a baby.

After the coffee break, a nurse introduces us to the tools of our new trade: rubber gloves, sponge swabs for moistening the patient's mouth, face mask and nose cannula, plastic urinal, "fracture" bedpan, large-size disposable diapers. We handle each item and are shown how to use it. The demonstration concludes with a Foley catheter of the "in-dwelling" kind. The nurse points to each part of the catheter and names it. She's given the spiel so many times, her instructions seem to have evolved into a rhyming quatrain:

This is the catheter
This is the tube
Don't worry about the pigtail
It inflates the balloon

After everyone has handled the catheter, we practice making an "occupied" bed. This is war, after all—the patient is under siege. The nurse reminds us of universal precautions: Wear gloves. Wash your hands often and well. Don't touch blood or any secretion that might contain blood. The most important thing to remember, she says, is that *everyone* is potentially contagious. Not C, I'm thinking. There's nothing I can catch from him. Last week the coordinator asked if I'd consider working with an AIDS patient when my time with C is over. We have a lot of requests, she said. Think about it.

I told her that certainly I'd consider it. But right now there's C, I said.

"Of course," she said. "But we need to look ahead. It won't be long now. You need to start preparing yourself."

⌊⌉ ⌊⌉ ⌊⌉

A balmy day in late July, C smiling up at me in his blue pajamas with the green trim. Blue is his color; it shows off his eyes, his silver hair. I've brought my radio headset, tuned to a classical station that plays only instrumentals—no vocals, no hymns. When I place the headset on his head, it slides down over his eyes. I readjust it. His eyes fly open in surprise that quickly turns to delight. Every few minutes I press my ear to his, checking to see if the music has become too loud, or grating, or has modulated to a minor key.

BJ is kneeling on the carpet, picking breakfast crumbs from C's socks. "Do you think he looks tired?" she asks. BJ has a habit of asking questions she already knows the answer to. Most are trivial, though perhaps comforting in their triviality, serving as reminders that life, banal and daily, keeps happening. Last week a neighbor brought zucchini from his garden. "Do you like zucchini?" BJ asked me, with the same intensity with which she now says, "People say he doesn't understand anything, but I think he does. Do you think he does?"

The hospice nurse who visits once a week has explained that hearing is the last sense to go, that we need to be careful what we say in C's presence. The most important thing, she advises, is to keep listening. And to listen not only to his words, but to what his body is saying. The body knows when it's time to die, she says. Nearing the four-month mark, C is still alert, energetic, and able to eat the food delivered each noon by Meals on Wheels. His body is giving few signals that it's ready to leave this world, unless his spurts of language hold some code I've yet to crack. Most are voiced as interjections—suddenly here, then gone, little flags thrown up then dropped. Between them is the gesture. "We don't see any, do we?" (peering at the carpet) "Got any money? Is everybody ready to go?" (brushing the carpet) "Finally found one" (scratching his sock) "Might not see anything" (picking at the waistband of his diaper) "They'll be racking up any time now"(gazing out the window) "It's all for sale" (throwing a piece of imaginary lint into the air).

While I'm feeding C his lunch—a compartmentalized tray of roast beef, whipped potatoes, and green beans—the nurse arrives. BJ is quite fond of M, even though, according to BJ, she "dresses funny." Today M is wearing a long shapeless tie-dye dress and brown gladiator sandals. Her toes are brown and stubby, her right ankle wrapped in an elastic bandage. "Skiing," she says when she notices me staring. Her laugh is deep, her manner with C easy and affectionate, and he responds in kind. Watching them together, I feel a twinge that could almost be jealousy. "Here," she says, taking the spoon from my hand and turning her attention to C. "So, how're you doing today?" she asks, straightening his collar with her free hand. "You're looking handsome as always."

C smiles broadly, winks, opens his mouth for the potatoes. Her practiced hands maneuver the spoon effortlessly. "That pudding looks mighty good," she says. I study her gestures, pleased to see that she, too, screws up her mouth the way I do when I feed him—the sympathetic reflex of a mother feeding a baby. She spoons in another serving of potatoes, turning to answer my questions, which I've been saving for weeks. She tells me that his father died from Alzheimer's, and that apparently C was already failing even before the quadruple bypass several years ago. "Six weeks after the operation he had an aortic aneurysm, and he's never been the same since. But he just keeps going. Don't you?" she says warmly, her eyes again on C.

"His wife's afraid they might drop him from hospice care," I say.

"It's possible. The waiting list is long, and he's not showing too many signs yet. Are you, Good-Looking?" she says, lifting the roast beef to his open mouth.

⊑ ⊑ ⊑

BJ's bathroom, like every room in her house, is meticulous and neatly organized. On the counter is a plastic container holding at least twenty lipsticks. "My sister-in-law asks me why I keep all those lipsticks. Why not? I like to keep myself up." Beside the container is an aqua box of dusting powder—Estee Lauder Youth Dew, the same kind I use. I sprinkle it on after my bath each night, right before I climb into bed. "Mm, you smell good," my husband always says. When he's away on business, I don't use the powder; it seems wasteful. BJ feels differently, I guess. Whenever I hug her—we've taken to hugging each other whenever we part—she smells sweet, as if she's just emerged from a scented bath. Although C has long ago forgotten who she is, she still dresses nicely every day and applies her make-up with care. "I still like to look nice for him," she says.

When BJ answered the door today, her first words were, "I'm not put together yet." Now she pats her hair. "I wear a wig, did you know that?" I answer that I wasn't sure, that I thought maybe she just had very thick hair.

She laughs. It's strange, I think, to be vain enough to wear a wig, yet not vain enough to keep it a secret. Or maybe I'm becoming family now, part of C's inner circle, his genogram. According to the social worker, every patient has a support web that includes not only family members, friends, and support staff, but also a patient's hobbies, religion, and work. If you're a hospice patient, there's even a support group that cares for your pets during your illness and places them in adoptive homes after you die. Although, as the social worker has pointed out, quite often a surviving spouse who never even liked the pet his dying spouse doted on, finally finds he cannot give up the pet, and ends up keeping it. I'm wondering how far my genogram would extend. I have a husband, a stepson, two parents, five siblings, eight nephews, six nieces, several aunts and uncles, a few close friends, and a cat—a larger and more tangled web than C's.

He's breathing deeply, eyes closed, mouth open, but his hands have already awakened and begun their work. Soon he will yawn, move a foot, open one eye then the other. Sometimes I mimic his actions, having recently discovered that the best way to be *with* C is to try, as much as possible, to *be* C. So I sit where he sits, look out the window and try to see the world as he sees it, stripped of linguistic and logical context. It's not a bad view, but it requires new eyes. One day last week, after I'd brushed his teeth and given him a capful of Listerine to swish, I held the dishpan to his mouth. "Spit!" I said. He pressed his lips tightly together. "Come on," I said, "time to spit!" His lips tightened even more, he was not *about* to spit. He kept staring at the square red dishpan, his eyes narrowing in frustration, hands clenching a Lego cube. I looked down at the dishpan, trying to see what he was seeing. He opened his hand, stared first at the red Lego cube and then at the dishpan. Of course! The dishpan was the same color, the same shape, as the Lego. Quickly I swished imaginary Listerine, brought the dishpan to my mouth, and pretended to spit. His eyes widened and cleared, as if a veil had lifted, and when I moved the dishpan to his mouth, he spit.

Now his shoulders are rigid, drawn up tight, signaling that he is cold. His body, unlike his mind, seems to remember what has been lost. I reach for the velour robe and begin my maneuvers. When I first started working with C, I kept trying to force his body into position—cramming the knee down, yanking the arm. I've since discovered that it works better to move close, then dance him into position. ("He was a good dancer," BJ says. "Women told me he was good at leading. I wasn't a good follower. Are you?") I lay my arm beside his, making one arm out of our two. Together we move into the sleeve. Once his arm is inside, I slip mine out, slide it away. He claps his hands, looks squarely into my eyes. He asks if I've found my barn yet, and I say yes.

⌴ ⌴ ⌴

It takes a village to raise him from the sofa—BJ, a neighbor, C's granddaughter, and me. As he rises I realize this is the first time I've seen C vertical—or as vertical as C can get, bent over as he is, a storm-damaged tree. We're a conga line, two in front of him, two behind, moving in unison down the steps toward the car which will take him to the clinic. It's nearly ninety degrees outside, and C's granddaughter is adamant that he doesn't need the robe. Impossible for a seventeen-year-old, bronzed and finely-muscled, to imagine being seventy-five. I doubt that she can even imagine being my age—not that she's noticed my age, or anything else about me. Each time we meet, she looks right past me, directly into her future: graduation, boyfriends, prom pictures, after-school jobs, spending money, savings account. I was the same way at seventeen, looking past older people as if they did not exist. Once I nearly ran over Great Aunt Bessie as I was hurrying to answer the door—some boy come to call. The granddaughter's dismissal shouldn't surprise me. Who am I to her? Some middle-aged woman, hired help. Or worse. A volunteer. Some stranger with time on her hands.

⌴ ⌴ ⌴

Today for the first time in five months the sofa is bare, emptied of the sheets and of C. After a five-day stay in the hospice unit—his lungs had filled, his breathing stopped—he is now settled into a hospital bed squeezed into the corner of their bedroom, beneath a sunny window. An oxygen tank has been rolled in, and the nurse has fitted him with a nose cannula, which he keeps putting into his mouth. His stork legs, pulled tightly to his chest, are working hard to pull free the sheet and afghan. BJ comes in, a fresh tear on her cheek. "Do you think he's changed much?" she asks.

"Yes," I say, and my eyes begin to fill. He does not seem to remember me. I touch his head, stroke his hands, massage his legs in an attempt to release them from their clench. For such a bone-thin man, he is amazingly strong, a *death grip* (what else?) on sheet, blanket, diaper, my sleeve, as we struggle to lift him (together, on the count of three) and remove the soiled diaper. I have diapered him many times in the past few months, but when BJ is here I step aside and let her take charge. I dip a fresh washcloth into the pan of warm water and hand it to her, then lean down to lift his knees so she can get to him. She wipes his thighs and genitals, rubs cream into his skin, and shakes powder onto the clean diaper. "At first it was hard to do," she is saying. "But after a while you get used to it. I hope he doesn't understand this part. Do you think he does?"

I shake my head no, though I'm not so sure. Usually when I'm diapering him, he looks straight into my eyes the way a baby does—innocent, trusting. But sometimes he averts his eyes, turns his head to face the window.

BJ tells me she's afraid to be alone with him at night, in case *it* happens here. I tell her not to worry, that if *something* happens—she's not yet ready to name it, and I'm trying to follow her lead—she should call the hospice number immediately. The something which will happen will probably be a heart attack, according to the doctor, although it's possible that C's lungs will fill again.

"I need to start making arrangements," she says. By *arrangements* she means the minister, organist, soloist, pallbearers, honorary pallbearers. The funeral home has already contacted her. She tells me she doesn't want an open casket, doesn't want to see him "that way."

I offer to help her with lists, phone calls, and correspondence, secretly hoping I won't be here when the undertaker comes for his preliminary visit. He may remember me from last month's training session; I was the one who said *undertaker* and asked too many questions. He wore a navy blue three-piece suit with a brass nameplate on his lapel, his skin an unfortunate pallor—unfortunate in that it reinforced the typical undertaker stereotype, one which he attempted, right off, to dispel. "Those of us in the profession prefer to be called *funeral directors*," he said. I prefer undertaker. It's straightforward, free of expectation or deceit: an undertaker takes us under. And wherein lies the shame of being called *mortician*? Its genogram is deep-rooted in Latin, German, and French, webbing wide and deep to claim kin to some of our most respectable words: mortal, mortgage, amortization, moratorium, remorse, mortar (as in 'ground down'). But this man wanted no part of the ground. "I like to think of myself as one who lifts the load," he said.

Then, just as I was thinking how easy it would be to dislike him, he began relating his first experience with death. For a moment his face broke its stiff, smooth exterior and revealed the little boy he must have been. He told of making trips to his dying grandmother's house, sitting beside her bed, being present at the funeral and the burial, both of which he described as calm and soul-stretching events. I was just warming up to his story when he suddenly segued into a history of the funeral business, skimming over the

Egyptians and skirting the Civil War—when embalming was first used in the United States so that soldiers could be brought home for burial, an event related somehow to William Harvey and the discovery of blood circulation. Lincoln, we were told, was embalmed so that his body could be displayed, but grave robbers kept exhuming it, so finally his body was placed under twenty feet of concrete. Nowadays, the undertaker told us, embalming cannot occur without written permission of the family; otherwise, it's considered mutilation. I made a note of that fact, followed by several large question marks.

He moved on to a discussion of ethnic and cultural differences regarding funeral practices (shiva, visitations, wakes, the cooling board, the dining room table). Even within cultures, every situation is unique, he said, relating a recent case in which a woman's cremains were divided into four equal parts and sprinkled on each of her four husbands' graves. He gave us practical tips: If you're present when the technicians come to "collect" the body, it's best to encourage family members to move to another room, because sometimes the body has to be stood up or otherwise repositioned in order to get it onto the stretcher, and this can be disconcerting to the family. Toe tags are usually either blue or black; if technicians see a red one, they will know to use universal precautions. And yes, we always use black zippered bags.

Then he distributed a list of expenses, ranging from full standard service to direct donation of a body to a medical school. Apparently there are payment plans for every situation. The funeral home accepts credit cards; survivors can even receive frequent flyer miles. He reminded us that the local paper charges for obituaries that are longer than seven lines, and that head shots can be as small as a thumbnail.

* * *

A dark-haired teenage boy opens the door. BJ has left early today for a hair cut—"The hair under the wig," she told me over the phone. "But my grandson will be there to let you in." The boy is about fourteen—tall, polite, and plainly uncomfortable, his eyes darting side to side. C's lunch sits on the folding tray. According to BJ, the grandson refuses to touch C or feed him, and is terrified that C will die in his presence. I ask the boy if he remembers much about his grandfather before his mind began to change—that would have been about seven years ago. "Not much," he says, shrugging.

I try to make small talk, but his eyes are focused on the television, one of those talk shows where the studio audience is prompted for applause and laughter. When I was his age, the closest I'd been to death was my paternal grandfather's sickroom, where he began a slow climb toward the violent end Aunt Ruth would witness years later. For three consecutive summers, when our family drove to Illinois, I voiced what I thought would be my final good-bye to my grandfather. His answer was always the same, a wet racking cough accompanied by the silent passing of a twenty-dollar bill from his hand to mine, a bill so crisp and seamless it might have been ironed. I remember feeling guilty for taking it—at the time, it seemed like a lot of money—but I never had any trouble spending it.

卐 卐 卐

C has passed the six-month mark, yet he seems barely changed, having regained much of the strength and pluck he lost during his hospital stay. A month ago, when it appeared that death was imminent, each visit felt precious, sweetened with impending loss. Tasks took on a tender, slow-motion quality. Now suddenly it's back to business, the jobs piling one upon the other, our hands busy, hearts dulled, BJ moving like some exhausted wind-up toy: diapering, re-diapering, wiping, disinfecting, changing sheets, washing pillowcases, suctioning mucus, checking oxygen levels. I retrieve the nose cannula from C's mouth, where he's been sucking it like a straw. His eyes are bright, and when I bring the glass to his mouth, he grabs it, spilling cranberry juice onto the clean sheet. I have to pry his hand loose, finger by finger.

The rest of the day is filled with visitors, webs of C's genogram. The new bather, a young black woman with skin like toasted almonds. The delivery man from Meals on Wheels, followed by the new nurse (M, the funny dresser, has been reassigned). BJ stops in for a moment between errands, just in time to greet the retired couple paying a visit on behalf of the Baptist church where C and BJ are members. The woman is stylishly dressed, her make-up applied artfully, and while I feed C, she keeps cooing at him as if he were an infant, applauding each bite. I hope this is not one of his lucid moments. It's demeaning, *mortifying*. For God's sake, I'm thinking, just let the man die in peace.

卐 卐 卐

It's a cool October day, sweater weather. BJ is in the bedroom trying to diaper C, a job that now requires four hands. Each time we touch him, he winces and cries out, against some pain we cannot locate. In the past few weeks, his flesh has pulled away from what little muscle remains. His skin is thin, slack, rubbed raw at contact points, despite the ointments and creams

BJ applies several times a day. The hollows behind his ears are chafed from the oxygen tube; when I try to adjust it, he whimpers. Is this pain or suffering? There's a difference, according to the hospice chaplain.

Earlier today, I passed along this fact to my parents, who are visiting from Indiana. Ever since my father's heart attack and valve-replacement surgery, he's been compulsive about keeping track of his children, so twice a year they make the journey, 1,400 miles round trip. After breakfast we were sitting in the living room, each holding a cup of coffee. My father takes his black; my mother, with a touch of cream. I like mine milky, light. We were talking about hospice and I mentioned the distinction the chaplain had made. Pain is just something the body gets through. Suffering, on the other hand, is pain with *meaning*—that is, suffering is the *meaning* we attribute to pain. Which hurts more, I wondered aloud. To be attacked from within and without, the body dumb against the meaningless assault, or to be granted, in addition to the pain, the *meaning* for the assault? Does knowing the meaning of our pain make it hurt any less?

My father set his coffee cup down, threaded his long fingers together as if preparing for prayer, then spoke quietly. "We say pain, anguish, sorrow. They're just words. What does it matter? Only the person inside of it knows what it means to him." A holy silence filled the room. I thought of my grandmothers and Aunt Bessie, each of whom had died alone, in stray moments between visitors. I looked across the room at my father, then at my mother, and I knew in the silence between our words that when the time comes, no matter how hard I try to get inside their suffering, I will be refused entry.

卐 卐 卐

Throughout the training sessions, we have practiced moving from seeing ourselves as "the living" toward imagining ourselves as "the dying." This is in keeping with the philosophy of Elisabeth Kübler-Ross, who wrote, "We have to take a good hard look at our own attitude toward death and dying before we can sit quietly and without anxiety next to a terminally ill patient." *Next to* is an essential concept in hospice care, as is *compassion*, which means, literally, *to suffer with*. So we've answered questionnaires regarding our personal fears and hopes regarding death. We've practiced *disclosure* as we gather in small groups to tell our childhood death stories. The elderly man with the European accent, whose mother died when he was six, recalled walking behind the horse-drawn wagon carrying her coffin to the cemetery, where he was admonished by his uncles to be a man and not show his tears.

We've even played a game called "Fancying Your Own Death," in which we plan our last earthly scene, every detail, down to the lighting and music. Mine is a mob scene consisting of all the people who might even *remotely* love me encircling my bed, which has been wheeled into a sunlit gazebo where champagne is flowing, waiters are serving caviar and barbecued ribs, and a black gospel quartet is singing "Walk Him Up the Stairs." This is probably not the way it will happen. If family tradition continues, I'll either go out in blood-spewing agony like my grandfather or die alone in a hospital—in brief moments between family vigils—like my grandmothers and great aunt.

Today as I enter the hospice training room, I see that someone has placed stones at each volunteer's place. Mine is darker and smaller than the stones on either side. I pick it up, turn it over in my hand, rub its sharp edges. The bereavement counselor speaks from the front of the room. "By now I'm sure you've all noticed the rock in front of you. If you haven't already, go ahead and pick it up, feel it, study it." The others comply. "Now, trade stones with your neighbor." The woman beside me holds out a large smooth river stone. I don't want to trade, I want the one I have, but I hand it over and take the river stone from the woman's hand.

"Every death is different," the counselor says. "It's hard to imagine someone else's, how it feels to them." The man with the European accent, the one who lost his wife last year, is sitting across the table, his eyes moist, as if he's just finished crying, or is about to. Sunlight through the narrow window halos his bald head and the delicate hairs lining his ears. He picks up a small pale nugget and begins to caress it.

⌷ ⌷ ⌷

Today I help out in the kitchen, peeling potatoes, preparing the pork chops for dinner. BJ, though exhausted, refuses to relinquish her housewifely duties. I reach for the pepper, sprinkle it on the pork chops. BJ collects salt and pepper shakers and all kinds of matched sets. Beside the kitchen table, in a bin labeled *Taters & Onyuns,* two cloth potatoes with painted cartoon faces are bedded down in a burlap sack. The shelf near the bay window is a veritable aviary: a hen nesting beside a rooster with cliché-red wattles and a brisk fan of tail; the identical heads of two white ducks; a pair of ceramic pheasants, the male's colors more showy than the female's, his topknot tall as he leans toward her; a couple of bronze cranes, one bending low, the other pointing heavenward.

As we work, conversation turns to marriage vows. No, she says, she doesn't feel it's been a burden. Yes, she'd do it all again. She asks when I expect my husband home—he's been out of town for several weeks—and if I'm planning a dinner celebration for his return. "The years go fast," she says. "Enjoy them while you can." Last week the volunteer coordinator opened our session with a startling announcement: the computer salesman had died over the weekend. Around the table, there was an audible, collective gasp. None of the training activities, not even the fancying of our own deaths, had prepared us for one of the living being swept away so suddenly. Apparently he had gone out to dinner, eaten a steak, and—due to complications from diabetes—died shortly thereafter of kidney failure. He had only recently moved to our town and had not yet made any friends, so he died in the hospital among strangers. After he died, the authorities located a sister who lived in the eastern part of the state. She supplied a photograph (was his face the size of a thumbnail? I wondered) and seven lines of obituary copy. He probably didn't even have time to fancy his death, I thought. No songs were sung, no lover held his hand, no mountaintop was visible from his bed.

If I'd known in advance, I would have treated him differently, lingered a while at the coffee pot, listened more intently to his stories about his mother. He'd seemed so desperate to talk about her last days. Maybe he'd had a premonition, seen the angel in the window. If *my* death were imminent, or the death of one I loved, I'd like to know in advance so I could set things straight. Once I dreamed I gave birth to a baby who had a message stamped across her forehead like those warnings on dairy products or prescription bottles: *Use before 6-1-94.* If children were born with expiration dates, would we love them more or less?

And what if we were issued at birth an itemized list of each future pleasure, and beside it the number of times that pleasure would be granted. When Kübler-Ross asked dying patients what they would change if they could live their lives over, hundreds of them answered, "I would eat more chocolate." Maybe I've already eaten my last piece of pineapple upside-down cake, and I don't even know it. My mother's father, like C, died slowly, each pleasure subtracted, one by one, in preparation for a naked end. Others, like the computer salesman, are taken whole, at once—in one quick boil of the brain, a head-on collision, a diabetic seizure during a steak dinner. Already so much is gone I can't retrieve. How much more is left? Filling the teapot, 7,062 times. Hearing the waves, 692. Playing cards with my father. Making dinner for my husband. One night, years (or days?) from now, I will call out for my mother, as from a childhood nightmare, expecting to see her in the doorway, the light from the hallway filtering through her gown. I cannot imagine the universe without my mother. I need to start imagining.

卐 卐 卐

Two weeks before Christmas, I help BJ unpack the silver tea service, wipe down the good china with a tea towel. There will be a Christmas dinner—her daughter and son-in-law, the grandchildren, and a friend of the family whose wife died earlier this year. "The adults will eat at the good table," she says. "The children can eat in the kitchen." The plates are English bone china painted with delicate roses. "When I chose it, the pattern was eleven dollars per place setting. Do you think it was too extravagant, to pay so much? But I've enjoyed it, I've used it." She wipes the gravy boat with the tea towel. "That was fifty-two years ago. Just think what it would be worth today."

Our diapering days are over; the nurse has installed a catheter of the indwelling kind. And C no longer makes his own saliva. We swab his mouth with sponge-tipped sticks dipped in Saliva Substitute, feed him liquids through a syringe. Today as I enter the bedroom, I see that the doctor has fitted C with moon boots, devices made of white foam and designed to wrap his feet in a cushion of air so as to prevent chafing. Lying in bed—with my radio earphones wrapped around his head, oxygen tubes in his nose, moon boots strapped to his feet—he resembles a sci-fi astronaut poised for landing, or a deep-sea diver about to make the plunge. His lips move silently. Lately he hasn't spoken, except with his eyes, which seem fathomless. What is it like where he is? What is he thinking, what universe moves inside him? I think of the "deep light" that scientists' cameras have recently discovered at the bottom of the sea, light too faint to be perceived by human eyes.

When his breathing changes, signaling sleep, I curl up on the double bed BJ and C shared for fifty-two years. Exhausted, I fall instantly into a dream: I've grown a giant fleshy ear, just below my left rib. I hold it gingerly with a gloved hand, trying to shield it from damage. What enters through the huge ear is a symphony of strange and beautiful sounds—underwater gurgles, muffled heartbeats, oriental music in a five-tone scale played at a slow and mournful speed.

When I wake the room is too quiet. I switch on the television, letting the room fill with voices, pictures, mouths opening and closing on words. It's a holiday special, a made-for-TV movie about a teacher who works with a retarded teenager named Jack. The first half of the movie focuses on her attempts, over several months' time, to teach Jack how to write his name. In the climactic scene, he takes the pencil from her hand, the music swells, and by the time he's added the last stick to the bottom of "K", he's weeping, his teacher is weeping, I am weeping. Is this what I've been reduced to, a woman weeping over daytime TV? Now Martha Stewart is showing me how to light a candle when I cut an onion, to keep my eyes from tearing.

When BJ's car pulls into the driveway, I turn off the TV and hurry to the kitchen for a tissue. She enters carrying grocery bags, her cheeks flushed from the cold, her dark eyes luminous with what looks like joy. She puts the bags on the counter and wraps her arms around me. I begin to cry, what am I doing, *I* should be comforting *her*. "You know," she says, her voice calm and steady. "When they put him in the ambulance to bring him home, I climbed in beside him, and when they closed the door, something came over me. It felt like peace, the kind they tell you about. Do you think it could be peace?" In a Buddhist parable, Gotami's child died, leaving her inconsolable. Buddha told Gotami that he would make medicine for the child, to bring him back to life, if she would gather mustard seed from a house where death had not visited. She went from door to door, searching, and when she could find no such house, understanding was granted her. She threw her child's corpse upon the pyre.

卐 卐 卐

"In my father's house," the Baptist minister begins, "are many mansions." How did it happen, how did he slip away so quickly? In the midst of the Christmas rush, I failed to call BJ for a few days. On Saturday, and again on Sunday, there was no answer when I rang the house. When the volunteer coordinator called, I knew what she was going to say.

The minister reminds us that God has already gone ahead to prepare a place for C. I try picturing C in a mansion, but the image won't come. I keep seeing a brick ranch house, a narrow bed beneath a window. Soon C's mansion will be renovated. The bed will be rolled out, the bedroom cleared of oxygen tank, medicine tray, sipping cup, feeding syringe, talcum, disinfectant, the stash of rubber gloves, the afghan, the bright box of Legos.

When the minister suggests that C may be teeing off right now, on the green beside the apostle John, there's a ripple of laughter down the pews. I hadn't known he was a golfer. I wonder how much else I don't know. The pallbearers and honorary pallbearers are seated together, twelve aging men. I survey the backs of their heads: nine gray, three balding. We stand and sing all four verses of "When We All Get to Heaven," a typical major-key Baptist hymn in 4/4 time, its predictable harmony allowing for the boom of basses and the chance for ambitious sopranos to soar. The minister says a few words about C, about his love for his wife, his family, his friends, reminding us that, finally, what really mattered was his love for his Lord. You're wrong, I want to say. It wasn't God who slept with C all those years, who sat across the breakfast table and in the car seat beside him, who ironed his pajamas and sheets, bathed him, diapered him, suctioned him, fed him through a syringe. "We are promised," the minister continues, "a new body. Our corrupted, corruptible flesh will be no more. We will put on incorruptibility." I imagine C putting on his incorruptibility, slipping into it like a pair of clean pajamas.

The pallbearers remain seated through the benediction. No one lifts the casket, bears the pall. Accompanied by two black-suited undertakers, it rolls soundlessly down the aisle on wheels engineered for smooth exits. As the casket approaches my pew, I try to conjure up C's spirit, clothed in light. What comes is the memory of his body, corruptible and corrupted—his busy hands, the thin smile edging on mischief, that perpetual smirk, as if he was pulling one over on me, getting away with something (the sipping straw, the Lego block, the food right out of my hand). Getting away with more than I'd ever expected. He glides past my pew, the casket draped with an American flag which lies perfectly flat and undisturbed. I half expect it to rustle, to see C's hands rise up, give an umpire signal, flick away the words the minister is speaking, so much imaginary lint. Earlier this morning, as I'd sat at my desk trying to write, the blank page seemed to stretch on and on, its surface pale and vulnerable as skin. Outside, the silhouettes of winter trees were smeared, indistinct, their sharp edges softened by fog. Close to the window—so close I could almost touch them—two gray doves tipped precariously across the granite stepping stones. The leaves of the holly, still damp from the night's rain, appeared varnished, and the knot of a squirrel's nest provided the only heft to the bare white birch. ■

King of the Cats

Kathryn Watterson

My cat Blake spent most of his life in a cage before he met my big brother John.

At the time, I was a teenager, and John was in college at Arizona State, where he had a job milking scorpions in Stankey's Poisonous Animals Lab. John sat behind a glass table, put his arms through portholes, and, wearing thick rubber gloves, used tweezers wired to a voltage regulator to pick up scorpions by the last joint in their tails. The current running through the handles of the tweezers caused the scorpion's tail to contract—and to shoot its venom into a capillary tube. John would go through a whole tray of scorpions—about twenty to thirty of them—to fill one glass capillary with scorpion venom.

From the time we'd moved to Arizona, I'd known that little scorpions, the translucent ones you could hardly see, were the most dangerous. Their poison could kill you. Even if you were an adult, you were dead if you couldn't quickly get to a hospital that had scorpion antivenom. The big scorpions could kill young children, but usually bigger kids, like my eight-year-old sister Alice, or someone like me, who weighed 110 pounds at the time, would only get very very sick from their sting.

In Stankey's Animal Lab, John milked the big scorpions as well as the small ones to make antitoxin. And around the room, about fifteen cats in cages watched what he did. These cats—Blake was one of them—were test cats. Each of them was given a series of scorpion venom injections, and when a cat had developed antibodies to the venom and was fully immunized, John and the other scientists took the cat out of its cage, injected it with Sodium Nembutal, shaved its breast area, swabbed it with alcohol, and then, with a big horse needle, punctured its chest and withdrew about 80 cc's of blood directly from its heart. My brother told me that this horrible "cardiac puncture" was the only way to withdraw such a large amount of blood from such a small animal. Sometimes a cat lived through this procedure; sometimes it didn't.

After the scientists got the blood, they set it aside for a few days to let the blood serum separate naturally. Then they partitioned the serum, which was scorpion antivenom/antitoxin, put it in a vacuum chamber, freeze-dried it, and sent it all over the world.

None of this stuff seemed yucky to John or anyone else in our family but me. From the time he'd been small, John had been exercising his scientific muscles. While I was naming worms and speculating whether they could smell with their little pink noses, John—who mostly was in his basement laboratory tanning rabbit hides and mixing disgusting potions—advised me that if I cut the worms in half, they'd regenerate. He hunted and dissected frogs to understand their anatomy, while I stayed outside in my favorite tree, listening to birdcalls and making up stories about me and my husband Tarzan swinging on vines through the jungle.

One day when John came home from work, he told us about a huge old tomcat. "This old guy—I call him Blake—has been a test cat for years," John said. "This cat has gone through eight series of immunizations. That means he's lived through *eight* cardiac punctures. He's so big that they take 120 cc's of blood from him each time, rather than the normal 80. For some reason, his tailbone has been broken in a number of places, and he's totally emaciated. Basically, he's a wreck." John, who talked even in those days like the scientist he would become, said that he had just done a cardiac puncture on Blake—the last one he'd ever do. He said he hated doing it and had apologized to Blake ahead of time. "I doubt that he can recover from it," he said, "but before I injected the Sodium Nembutal, I told him, 'I'm sorry to hurt you, kiddo, but if you survive this one, I promise I'll put you out to pasture.'"

Four days later, John brought Blake home in a cardboard box. This cat was big, but he looked more like a prehistoric relic than a living, breathing animal. His heavy-boned skeleton looked as if it had dried cat skin stapled to it. That cat skin, punctuated with patches of flea-bitten bits of gray fur, looked like old worn leather left too long in the sun. The spot of chest hair over his sternum was all shaved off and stubby and other large patches of fur had been shaved as well, showing red traces where needles had left their tracks. His head was all skull and bones, no fur, and the enormous sunken eyes that looked out from that hellish cranium were as terrified as they were terrifying. He edged himself into the corner of the box, looking up frantically and scratching his way backwards.

Our other cats—Charlie, Penelope, and Huey Schroeder—hissed and ran away when John set Blake's box down on the ground, close to the house, in our back yard. Wag, our mellow old dog who sometimes in a frenzy chased and ate desert frogs that made her sick and crazy, lay by the rose bushes and watched, her brown tail flapping against the ground in its own form of welcome. Blake backed further into the corner of the box, cowering and breathing so hard it sounded as if he would choke to death on his own inhalations. John turned the box on its side, so Blake would be able to walk right out the opening on to the ground. But Blake didn't move. He stayed in his corner, trembling and shaking and hacking into the air. He lay there all that day and all the night. In the morning, he still hadn't moved from his spot.

Day after day, Blake wouldn't come out. I tried to understand why. He probably had no memory of ever stepping outside a cage, I figured, so how could he know what to do? I thought he might never leave. He might spend the rest of his life in that box. We carried him food and set it inside his "cage." Then we set it a short distance from the edge, hoping he would venture out to eat when we weren't there. For several days, we substituted new cat food for the old—but it remained untouched.

The pain in Blake's eyes was so morose, so deep, so terrible, that you knew the suffering he'd experienced was beyond imagination. It reminded me of pictures I had seen of concentration camp survivors—all skull and eyes and heartbreak. Just to look at him made me feel like crying, but I thought, I won't touch him until he gets used to me. I thought, his hideous-looking skin must hurt him, so I won't pet him.

Sometime during the second week, Blake began to creep parts of himself out of the box. He put his nose out and then pulled it back inside. Later, we saw a paw. Then two paws. When he finally came all the way out, his legs shook, but he walked out, stretched, and went back in. Every day, he explored more territory before returning to his box. I squatted nearby, trying to get him used to me. The first time I tried to touch him, I did it carefully, barely passing my hand down his bumpy backbone. Bits of hair stuck up on his bony, broken vertebrae. My sister Alice said, "Yuk. Gross! You'll probably get a fungus."

The first time Blake approached me, I was standing, talking to Alice. At first I had no idea what was happening. I just felt an odd sensation crawling up my leg, like a slow growing awareness of something dangerous. I held very still and looked down, imagining that I might see a tarantula or a rattlesnake—even a small man with a gun. Instead, I saw a revolting cat skeleton rubbing against me. The impulse to jerk my leg away was so strong that I had to take deep breaths to keep from moving. It was one thing to observe or pity this creature of death, but quite another thing to allow him to breathe and rub against me.

"Look what's happening," I whispered to Alice. "This is *so* sickening, but it's great. Don't move. Don't scare him." I held myself as still as a tall saguaro for as long as I could—trying to contain my runaway emotions. When I'd finally conquered my revulsion, I tried slowly squatting down to pet him, but he bolted. He was even more conflicted than I was about life; he *knew* people were out to hurt him, while I only feared it.

Eventually, although he was still tensed to bolt at any sudden movement, Blake began to let us pet him while he rubbed against us. As the days passed, and then the weeks, he began to eat his food when we walked away. He slowly began to gain weight—and his skeletal frame began to fill out. His bald spots filled in with gray peach-fuzz. After about four months, he began jumping into our laps. At first he would jump up, and then jump down. After he got used to that, he would lie in our laps purring.

And then the miraculous happened.

Six months after he had come to our house, Blake had turned into an extraordinarily beautiful, regal cat. He weighed nearly eighteen pounds and his thick gray coat was silken and luxurious, with a luminous sheen that cast a glow around him. If cats had a dynasty, he would have been king. My brother John looked at him one day and started singing, "King of the Road."

And that's who he was. Blake radiated a sense of peace, a kingly serenity. He padded around the yard with his head held high, as if surveying his kingdom. He lay on his back in the sun and batted at butterflies with his paws. He slithered along the ground and then leaped into the air, trying to catch birds that flew overhead, teasing him, as they dived for water. He ate with the slurping satisfaction of a creature who has known hunger all too well. And when Blake purred, which was any time he was touched, any time he was fed, any time he was petted, you could hear the hum and rumble of that purr long distances away. Blake purred with his whole heart—the heart that had been punctured eight times—and it made his entire body vibrate. If he sat in my lap and purred, my hand, resting on his head or back, vibrated as well. My legs were warmed. His large brown eyes—those eyes that had looked so haunted and hunted—reflected contentment and trust. He didn't jump when one of us moved toward him; he moved toward us. Blake, I know, thought he was in heaven.

And for me, he was a gift. Watching him mend his heart had melted mine. For me, his recovery was a healing, a sign of hope. If Blake could survive, if he could become so calm and content, maybe anything was possible.

Blake's story might have gone on that way forever. And, for more than two years, it did.

But then somehow, another of our menagerie, Penelope, the very ladylike longhaired cat who licked her paws with great fastidiousness after every meal, got ringworm. The ringworm spread to Huey, whom John had brought home from a filling station a few years earlier. (Initially we had called her Huey Schroeder, but when she gave birth to seven kittens, we changed her name to Huey Jane.) From Huey, the ringworm spread to Charlie, the successful bird hunter who almost always got his prey. And then, small circles of raw skin appeared on Blake.

The vet said we should have all the cats dipped. This is where things get hazy. I thought that my brother and my mom took the cats, one by one, to the Animal-Veterinarian Center. They recall it differently. My brother swears he never went—that it was me. My sister says she carried a cat in her lap for at least one of the trips. My mother doesn't remember anything about it. But I do know that somehow we took all the cats to get dipped in ringworm solution—and that the last cat we took in was Blake. What happened then—whether I pieced it together later or whether it happened in this exact form—I can't guarantee. But this is what happened to Blake, and I'm telling it the way I remember it.

Blake had no desire to go to the veterinarian's. He struggled to stay out of the car, he did not want to travel. Mom drove, and I held Blake wrapped in a towel against my chest. When we got there, I carried Blake into the vet's office, and he was anxious and quivering in his skin, burrowing against me like a baby in a bunting. In the reception room, he calmed down and got quiet again as I stroked him.

But when I stood up to carry Blake into the vet's office, he began quivering again. Inside that office, with its steel examining tables, bright lights and cages where sick animals recovered after surgery, his quivers turned to full body shaking.

Maybe the smell of the room reminded Blake of the odor of the lab. Maybe it was the sight of the vet's white lab jacket. But when the vet took him from my arms and started to carry him across the room to dip him into a tank of medicated solution to rid him of the ringworm, Blake went wild. His eyes looked frantic, and for a moment it seemed he was climbing the vet's arms as if they were branches of a tree. The vet wasn't putting Blake into a cage, but Blake didn't know that. He bucked and heaved.

"Stop!" I screamed. I would take Blake out of this office, away from here. He didn't have to get dipped, he didn't have to be so scared. Why hadn't I thought of this? I would take him home. But in the moment I was screaming and crying and rushing toward him, Blake grew still in the vet's arms. Very still. Too still.

The vet, a tall and pale blond, looked from Blake to me and back to Blake. I took Blake from his arms and held his heavy limp body against my chest. The vet, nodding at me to quiet my sobbing, felt for a pulse inside Blake's thigh.

He stood there for a while, and then he said, "I think he had a heart attack."

We buried Blake in the desert, knowing his bones would rejoin the earth where he had walked and played. I planned to paint his name on a gravestone, but never did. I got distracted by growing up, by learning how to dance, by shrieking with laughter and staying out late, by lying to my mother that I was at my girlfriend's when I was really with my boyfriend, by going to work as a nurse's aide where I took care of people whose bones stuck out in knobs through their skin, just like Blake's had at the beginning.

Not long ago my sister Alice and I went back to visit our old house in the Arizona desert. Other people live there now, but they said they didn't mind our stopping by. We walked around the house, past the cacti our mother had illegally dug up and replanted so many years before, past her rose bushes, which were still blooming after all this time, past the pine tree we'd planted one Christmas and that was now the tallest tree around. Alice and I stopped at the spot Blake used to hover and jump at birds, back when he was King. I looked at the place, imagining how smooth Blake's gravestone would look by now if I'd put it there after he died. I imagined Blake leaping into the air again, tasting freedom. ■

Toward Humility

Bret Lott

5

Once it's over, you write it all down in second person, so that it doesn't sound like you who's complaining. So it doesn't sound like a complaint.

Because you have been blessed.
You have been blessed.
You have been blessed.
And still you know nothing, and still it all sounds like a complaint.

4

You are on a Lear jet.

It's very nice: plush leather seats for which leg room isn't even a matter, the jet seating only six; burled wood cabinets holding beer and sodas; burled wood drawers hiding bags of chips, boxes of cookies, cans of nuts; copies of three of today's newspapers; a stereo system loaded with CDs.

Your younger son, age thirteen, is with you, invited along with the rest of your family by the publicist for the bookstore chain whose jet this is. When you and your wife and two sons pulled up to the private end of the airport in the town where you live, there on the tarmac had sat a Lear jet, out of which came first the publicist, a young and pretty woman in a beige business suit, followed by the pilots, who introduced themselves with just their first names—Hal and John—and shook hands with each member of your family.

"You're all welcome to come along," the publicist had said, and you'd seen she meant it. But it was an invitation made on the spot, nothing you had planned for. And since your older son, fifteen, has a basketball tournament, and your wife has to drive, it is left to your younger son to come along.

Your younger son, the one who has set his heart and mind and soul upon being a pilot. The one whose room is plastered with posters of jets. The one who has memorized his copy of Jane's Military Aircraft.

"I guess we can get you a toothbrush," you'd said to him, and here had come a smile you knew was the real thing, his eyebrows up, mouth open, deep breaths in and out, in his eyes a joyful disbelief at this good fortune. All in a smile.

Now here you are, above clouds. In a Lear jet, your son in the jump seat—leather, too—behind the cockpit, talking to Hal and John, handing them cans of Diet Coke, the publicist talking to you about who else has ridden in the corporate jet. Tom Wolfe, she tells you. Patricia Cornwell. Jimmy Carter. And a writer who was so arrogant she won't tell you his name.

This is nowhere you'd ever thought you might be. Sure, you may have hoped a book you wrote might someday become a bestseller, but it wasn't a serious hope. More like hoping to win the lottery. A pretty thought, but not a whole lot you could do about it, other than write the best you knew how.

But getting on a list wasn't why you wrote, and here, at 37,000 feet and doing 627 miles an hour over a landscape so far below you, you see, really, nothing, there is in you a kind of guilt, a sense somehow you are doing something you shouldn't be doing.

Riding in a Lear jet to go to a bookstore—four of them in two days—to sign copies of your book.

Your book: published eight years before, out of print for the last two. A book four books ago, one you'd thought dead and gone, the few copies left from the one-and-only hardcover print run available in remainder bins at book warehouses here and there around the country.

A book about your family, based on the life of your grandmother, who raised six children, all of whom were born in a log cabin your grandfather built, the last of those six a Down's Syndrome baby, a daughter born in 1943 and for whom little hope of living was held out by the doctors of the time. It is about your grandmother, and the love she has for that baby, her desire to see her live, and her own desire to fix things for her daughter as best she can, if even at the cost of her other children and, perhaps, her husband.

A book recently anointed by a celebrity talk show host. Not a celebrity, but an icon. Not an icon, but a Force. A person so powerful and influential that simply by announcing the name of your book a month ago, your book has been born again.

Bigger than you had ever imagined it might become. Bigger than you had ever allowed yourself even to dream. Even bigger than that. And bigger.

Guilt, because it seems you're some kind of impostor. Even though it is based on your family, you had to reread the novel for the first time since you last went through it, maybe nine years ago, when it was in galleys, you sick of it by that time to the point where, like all the other books you have published—there are eight in all—you don't read them again. But this one you had to reread so that you could know who these characters were, know the intricate details of their lives so that if someone on the television show were to have asked you a question of an obscure moment in the whole of it all, you would have seemed to them and to the nation—Who would be watching? How many people? As many as have bought the book? And more, of course—to be on close terms with the book, with its people, its social context and historical and spiritual significance.

You wrote it ten years ago.

And yesterday you were on this talk show host's program.

Tom Wolfe, you think. Jimmy Carter, and you realize you are dressed entirely wrong, in your dull green sweater and khaki pants, old leather shoes. Maybe you should have worn a sport coat. Maybe a tie. Definitely better shoes.

You can see the soles of your son's skateboard shoes, worn nearly through at the balls of his feet, him on his knees and as far into the cockpit as he can get. He's got on a pair of cargo shorts, the right rear pocket torn, and a green T-shirt. He'd been lucky enough to wear a polar fleece jacket to the airport this February morning in the sunny South.

This is all wrong.

The publicist continues on about who has ridden in the corporate jet, and you nod, wondering, How did I get here?

All you know is that you wrote this book, and received a phone call the first week in January, a call that came on a very bad day for you, a call that found you out a thousand miles from your home, where you were teaching others how they might learn to write. A job in addition to the daily teaching job you have so that you might make ends meet, and so that your wife wouldn't have to work as many hours as she has in the past.

The Force found you there, on a very bad day, and gave you unbelievable news. And now your book is on the lists.

You think about that day. About how very bad it was, how empty, and hollow, and how even the news that was the biggest news of your life was made small by what happened.

And now the plane begins its initial descent into the metropolis, and your son returns to the seat beside you, still with that incredulous smile, though you have been airborne nearly an hour. Hal and John happily announce you'll be landing in moments, the landscape below hurrying into view—trees, highways, cars, homes. Nothing different from the view out any airplane window you have looked before, but different all the way around.

Everything is different.

The jet settles effortlessly to the ground, taxies to the private end of an airport you've flown into before, the public terminal out your window but far, far away, and you see, there on the tarmac as the jet eases to a stop, a Mercedes limousine.

Yep. A Mercedes.

You look at your shoes, and at your son's. His cargo shorts. This sweater you have on.

"When we were here with Jimmy Carter, the lines were all the way out the store and halfway around the building," the publicist says. "This is going to be fun," she says, and smiles, stands, heads out the door past smiling, nodding Hal and John.

Then John asks, "What would you guys like for dinner?"

You and your son look at each other—he's still smiling, still smiling—and then you look to John, shrug, smile. "Subs?" you say, as if the request might be too much to manage.

"No problem," John says, and both he and Hal nod again.

Here is the store: brick, tall, a presence. A single store in a huge bookstore chain, every store complete with a coffee bar and bakery, a gift shop with coffee mugs and T-shirts and calendars.

And books.

You climb out the limousine before the chauffeur can get around to open your door, because you don't want to make him feel like you're the kind of person who will wait for a door to be opened. Then you and your son, the publicist in the lead, make your way for the front doors.

Inside is a huge poster in a stand, the poster two feet by four feet, advertising your being at this store for a signing. In the center of the poster is your picture, formidable and serious, it seems to you. Too serious. This isn't you, you think. That person staring pensively off the photographer's left shoulder is somebody posing as an author, you think.

There are a few people in the store, and you wonder if the line will form a little later on, once the signing gets underway, and you are ushered by a smiling store manager in a red apron to the signing area.

It's in the middle of the store, and is a table stacked with copies of the anointed book, and with reprints of the earlier three books, and of the four that have come out since the anointed one first appeared all those years ago. Your books, you see, are piled everywhere. Books, and books.

"Look at this!" the manager exclaims, and points like a game show hostess to a rack of paperback books beside you, the Bestseller rack. "You're the number one book," the manager says, and you see the rows of your book, beneath them a placard with #1 printed on it.

You look at your son to see if he's as impressed as you are beginning to be.

He smiles at you, nods at the books, his eyebrows up.

He's impressed.

You take your seat behind the table laden with your books, and see between the stacks that there is a kind of runway that extends out from the front of your table to the other end of the store, a long and empty runway paved with gray-blue carpet. Big, and wide, and empty.

"We'll get you some coffee and cookies, if that's all right," the publicist says to you, then, to your son, "Hot chocolate sound good?" and your son says, "Yes ma'am," and, "Thank you."

You are here. The signing has begun.

But there are no customers.

You wait, while the manager announces over the in-store speakers your presence, fresh from yesterday's appearance on national TV. This drives a couple of people to the runway, and they walk down the long corridor of gray-blue carpet toward you. It seems it takes a long time for them to make it to you, longer even than the flight up here from your hometown, and you smile at these people coming at you: a young man, tall and lanky; a woman your age with glasses and short brown hair.

They are smiling at you.

You know them. Students of yours from the program where you teach a thousand miles from home. They are students of yours, friends, writers. Both of them.

You stand, hug them both, introduce them to your son, to the manager back from the announcement, and to the publicist returning now with that coffee and hot chocolate, those cookies. Then the three of you remark upon the circumstance of your meeting here: they live in the same city, and have been waiting for your appearance at the store; how wonderful and strange that your book has been picked, what a blessing!; when Jimmy Carter came here, the line was out the door and halfway around the building.

You talk, sip at the coffee, don't touch the cookie. There are no other customers, and the manager promises they will come, they will come. He's had phone calls all day asking when you will get here, and if the lines will be too long to wait through.

You talk more, and more. Talk that dwindles to nothing but what is not being said: where are the customers?

Now, finally, fifteen minutes into a two-hour signing, you see an older woman rounding the end of the runway. She has bright orange hair piled high, and wears a tailored blue suit. She's pushing a stroller, and you imagine she is a grandmother out with her grandchild, the child's mother perhaps somewhere in the store right now, searching out children's books while Grandma takes care of the baby.

It's an expensive suit, you can tell as she moves closer, maybe thirty feet away now, and you see too the expensive leather bag she carries with her. The baby is still hidden under blankets, and you smile at the woman as she moves closer, closer, a customer heralding perhaps more customers, maybe even a line out the store and halfway around the building by the time this is all over.

Maybe.

Then here is the woman arriving at the other side of the table, and you see between the stacks she is even older than you believed. Heavy pancake make-up serves in a way that actually makes her wrinkles bigger, thicker; watery eyes are almost lost in heavy blue eye shadow; penciled-in eyebrows arch high on her forehead.

And you are smiling at this person, this customer, as she slowly bends to the stroller and says in the same moment, "Here's the famous writer, Sophie, the famous writer Mommy wants you to meet," and she lifts from inside the blankets, the woman cooing all the while and making kissing sounds now, a dog.

A rat dog, a pink bow in the thin brown fur between its pointy ears.

"Sophie," the woman says to the dog, "would you mind if Mommy lets the famous writer hold you?" and her arms stretch toward you between the stacks of your books, in her hands this dog with a pink ribbon, and without thinking you reach toward her, and now you are holding Sophie.

The dog whimpers, shivers, licks its lips too quickly, tiny eyes darting again and again away from you to Mommy.

You don't know what to say, only smile, nod, and let your own eyes dart to your students, these friends, who stand with their own smiles, eyes open perhaps a little too wide, and then you glance behind you to the publicist, whose chin is a little too high and whose mouth is open, and to the manager, who stands with her arms crossed against her red apron. She's looking at the gray-blue carpet.

And here is your son. He's standing at the end of this line of people, hands behind his back, watching. He's not smiling, his mouth a straight line, and your eyes meet a moment.

He's watching.

"Sophie would love it," the woman begins, and you turn to her. She's plucked a copy of the anointed book from one of the piles, has opened it to the title page. Those watery eyes are nearly lost in the wrinkles gathering for the force of her smile. "I know Sophie would absolutely love it," she continues, "if you were to sign this copy to her."

You swallow, still smiling. "For Sophie?" you say.

The woman nods, reaches toward you for the dog, and you hand it out to her while she says, "She'll love it. She'd be so very proud."

Here is your book, open and ready to be signed.

You look at your students. Their faces are no different, still smiling. They are looking at you.

You look at the publicist, and the manager. They are both looking at you, too.

And you look to your son. He has his hands at his sides now, his mouth still that thin, straight line. But his eyes have narrowed, looking at you, scrutinizing you in a way that speaks so that only you can hear, This is what happens when you're famous?

These are the exact words you hear from his eyes, narrowed, scrutinizing.

"She would be so very proud," the woman says, and you look to her again, Sophie up to her face now, and licking her cheek, that pancake make-up.

You pull from your shirt pocket your pen.

3

Everyone is here, your living room choked with friends, maybe fifty people in all, all there to watch the show. You and your wife have laid out platters of buffalo wings, fresh vegetables, jalapeño poppers, various cheeses and crackers and dip; there are bowls of chips, a vast array of soft drinks. Cups have been filled with store-bought ice, paper plates and napkins and utensils all spread out.

They are here for the celebration. You, on the Force's talk show, your book the feature.

Kids swirl around the house and out in the yard, their parents laughing and eating and asking what it was like to meet her, to be with her, to talk with her. Some of them tell you, too, that they have finally read your book, and tell you how wonderful your book was.

You've known most of these people for years, and there are moments that come to you while these friends tell you how wonderful your book was when you want to ask them, Why didn't you read it when it came out eight years ago? But you only smile, tell them all the same thing: thank you, thank you, thank you.

You tell them, too, that the Force was incredibly intelligent, disarming, genuine, better read than you yourself are. A genuine, genuine person.

This was what she was like when you met her, when you taped the show for three hours two weeks ago, you and her book club guests—four women, each of whom wrote a letter about the effect of your book on their lives that was convincing enough to get the producers of the show to fly them in, be these book club guests—and there were moments during that whole afternoon when, seated next to her and listening to one or another of the guests, you stole a look at her and told yourself, That's her. That's her. I'm sitting next to her. Moments that startled you with the reality of this all, moments that in the next moment you had to shut down for fear that thinking this way would render you wordless, strike you dumb with celebrity were the conversation to turn abruptly to you.

Then the show begins. Kids still swirl, and your wife has to pull two preschoolers from the computer in the sunroom off the living room, where they are banging two-fisted each on the keyboard, no one other than you and your wife seeming to notice this, everyone watching the television. There are no empty chairs left, no space on the sofa, the carpet in front of the TV spread with people sitting, paper plates in hand heaped with buffalo wings and jalapeño poppers and veggie sticks, and you have no choice but to stand in the back of the room, watching.

Here is what you were warned of: this episode of the book club show—your episode—happens to fall during sweeps month, when ratings are measured so as to figure how much to charge for advertising time, and since the viewership for the monthly show featuring the book and the author always plummets, the producers have decided to spend the first half of the hour with bloopers from past shows. "Forgettable moments," these fragments have been called by the promotional ads leading up to the air date.

This was what you were warned of, two weeks ago when you were through with the taping. Officials from the show told you all this, and you'd nodded, smiling, understanding. What else was there for you to do? Demand equal time with everyone else?

No. You'd nodded, smiled, understood.

Now the Force introduces video clip after video clip of, truly, forgettable moments from past episodes: two people argue over whether the toilet paper is more efficiently utilized if rolled over the top or out from beneath; a woman tells a Viagra joke; the Force marches down the street outside her studio in protest of uncomfortable panty hose.

Your guests look at you.

"I had nothing to do with this," you say, too loud. "It'll be on the last half of the show," you say, too loud again.

They are quiet for a while, then return to ladling dip onto plates, loading up wings and poppers, pouring soda, until, finally, you are introduced, and the book, and there you are for two minutes talking about your grandmother, and your aunt with Down's Syndrome, your voice clear and calm, and you are amazed at how clear and calm you are there on the television, when you had wanted nothing more than to jump from the sofa you were seated on in the studio and do jumping jacks to work off the fear and trembling inside you. Now comes a series of family photos, a montage of images with your voice over it all, calm and smooth, the images on the screen pictures your family has had for years.

Pictures of your grandmother, and of your aunt.

The people you wrote about, whose lives are now here for the world to see, and you realize in this moment that you had nothing to do with this. That these photos—of your grandmother, your aunt, and your grandfather and aunts and uncles and your father too, all these family photos that have existed for years—simply bear testament to the fact they were lives lived out of your hands, and all you had to do was to write them down, getting credit for all those lives led.

You think about that bad day in January. About how this all began, and how all this credit has come to you.

Yet you are still a little steamed about losing the first half of the show, when every other author you've seen featured on the show has gotten most of the program. You are a little steamed, too, about not having some place to sit here in your living room, and about those kids banging on the keyboard. You are a little steamed.

Then the discussion with you and the four women and the Force begins, and you see, along with everyone in your house, and everyone in the country, the world, a discussion that had lasted three hours squelched down to eight minutes, and six or so of those given to a woman who gave up her Down's Syndrome child at birth because of the "life sentence" she saw being handed her. You see in your living room choked with your friends this woman crying over her life, her decision, and see her somehow thank you for your book and the meaning it has given her life.

You knew this would be what was included on the air. You'd known it the moment her voice wavered and cracked that afternoon two weeks ago, there in the studio. You knew it then, and now here it is: this woman, crying over giving up her baby, and thanking you for it.

And you see yourself nod on the air, looking thoughtful.

She makes great TV, you think. This woman who missed the point of your book entirely.

2

You are answering the phones for a while, because of the terrible thing that has happened this bright, cold January day.

"We'll send you a brochure," you say to someone on the other end of the line, no one you know, and as she tells you her address you do not write it down, only sit with your back to the desk, looking out the window onto the late afternoon world outside: snow, sky.

A little after lunch, this day turned very bad, a turn that has led to you here, in the office of the program in which you teach a thousand miles from home, to answer the phone for the administrative director.

She is in the other room, too much in shards to answer the phone, to field the bonehead questions that still come to a program such as this one no matter what bad things happen and when. People still call to ask about the program, about costs and applications, about credits and teachers. About all things.

Earlier today, before you began answering the phone, before lunch, your agent called here, where you are teaching others to write because it seems you know something about writing, to tell you the novel you have just finished writing is awful.

You are here for two weeks, in workshops and seminars, lectures and readings, the students adults who know what is at stake. Though they have lives away from here, just as you have your own, you and they converge on this New England campus from all over the country, the world, twice a year to study the word and all it can mean. They come here to study writing, because they want to write, and some of them become friends to you and to the other writers teaching here, because it is this love of the word that unites you all.

Some of them become your friends.

Your agent said to you this morning, "What happened to this?" She said, "Where was your heart?"

Her call, you'd recognized with her words and tone, had not surprised you. You knew it was coming. You knew the book was dead and gone to hell in a hand basket, had known it for the last month as you'd tried to get to the end of the thing. You knew it had gone to hell in a hand basket even before you missed the deadline last week.

You knew.

The novel: a sequel to the last one you published, early last year. That one had done well, better than any of the others you've published this far. A novel you'd had a tough time trying to get published, seeing as how your books have never done that well. You're a literary author, and publishers know that means you don't sell many books. You're not a bestseller, they know. You write well enough, but you're just not a bestseller, a fact you reconciled yourself to many years ago.

But the first hardcover run of this latest book—a run in the low five figures—sold out in a few months, the publisher electing not to reprint. They'd sold as many as they'd believed they could sell, had also sold it to paperback with another publisher.

Everything was great, with selling out the print run. So great they asked ten months ago if you would write a sequel to it, and you agreed, though it wasn't anything you'd thought much about. Not until you saw how well the book was selling.

Now, here you were, ten months later, teaching people to write on a day cursed with the sad and empty curse of a startlingly blue winter sky. A day in which you have been informed of what you have known all along: this one didn't work.

You know nothing about writing.

But this is not the bad thing. It had seemed bad enough to you, walking across campus to lunch after the phone call, three hours long, from your agent, a phone call in which you both reconnoitered the train wreck before you, pieced out what was salvageable, shrugged over what was lost.

The day seemed bad enough then.

And then.

Then, after lunch, one of the students was found in his room, dead. Not one of the students, but one of your students.

Not one of your students, but a friend.

Some of them become your friends.

You were to have had dinner in town with him tonight, to talk about the novel he is writing, the novel you had been working on with him all last semester, when he was a student of yours and during which time he became a friend. A big, ambitious, strange and haunting novel.

A novel that will go unfinished now.

He was found in his dorm room, sitting at his desk, having gone to his room the night before, students have said, complaining of a headache.

He was found sitting at his desk, reading a copy of one of your books. A novel. A lesser known one, one it seemed no one really cared for.

Your friend was reading it.

He was found at 1:30 on this blue and cursed January afternoon. Now it is 4:00, between that time and this a somber and hushed chaos breaking out all over campus. Everyone here knows everyone here. No one has ever died here before. He was too young. He was your friend.

And now you are answering phones for the administrative director who is in the other room. You told her you wanted to answer the phone to give her time away from the bonehead questions, but you know you offered as a means to keep yourself from falling into shards of your own. You offered, so that you would have something to do, and not have to think of this very bad day, when the loss of your own book, you see, means nothing. A book means nothing.

You have lost a friend. A friend who is here, a thousand miles from home, too. A friend not much older than you, his death a complete and utter surprise. He lives with his mother, you know, where he takes care of her, an invalid, and where he is writing a big, ambitious, strange and haunting novel.

The phone rings. You are looking out the window at the afternoon sky growing dark, the blue gone to an ashen violet, and you turn to the phone, watch it a moment as though its ringing might change how it appears, like in cartoons when the phone jumps from its place and shivers.

It rings, and nothing happens, rings again, and you pick up the receiver, hold it to your ear knowing another bonehead question is on its way.

"May I speak to ______ _______?" a man says, all business, a solid voice that carries authority with it, and you think perhaps this is an official from the college, calling on business. Not a bonehead.

"Hold on," you say, and place the phone down, go to the room next door, where she is sitting, gathering herself.

"Can you take a call?" you ask, and try to smile. "It's for you," you say, and she nods, sniffs, tries at a smile herself. She stands, and you follow her back into her office, her domain, you only a brief tenant this afternoon of a very bad day.

She picks up the phone, says, "Hello?" and her eyes go immediately to you. "You were just talking to him," she says, and hands you the phone, trying to smile.

You take the receiver, bring it to your ear, say, "Yes?"

"I'm calling from Chicago," the businessman's voice says to you, "and my boss is working on a project she needs to talk to you about. I need to break her from a meeting. Can you hold?"

A meeting, you think. My boss. What is this about?

You say, "Sure," and now music comes on the line, and you glance up at the director, who is looking at you, wondering too, you can see, what this might be about. You don't live here. You're a thousand miles from home. Who knows you are here, and why?

You shrug at her in answer to her eyes, and then the music stops with a phone connection click, and a voice you think you may recognize says your name, then her own, then shouts, "We're going to have so much fun!"

Who is this? Is this who you think it is? Is this who she says she is?

Is this her?

"Is this a joke?" you shout. "Is this for real?" and your eyes quick jump to the director, who sits in a chair across from you, watching you in wonder.

This makes the woman calling—her—laugh, and she assures you this is no joke, this is for real, and that she has chosen a book you have written as her book of the month next month.

It's a book four books ago, a book out of print. A book about your grandmother, her Down's Syndrome daughter, your family.

This isn't happening. It hasn't happened. It will not happen.

But it has happened: you have been chosen. Your book has been anointed.

"This is secret," she says. "You can't tell anyone. We'll announce it in twelve days. But you can't tell anyone."

"Can I tell my wife?" you manage to get out, and she laughs, says you can, but that's all, and she talks a little more, and you talk, and you cannot believe that you are talking to her, you here a thousand miles from home and with a secret larger than any you have ever had lain upon you. Even bigger.

Yet all you can think to say to her is, A friend of mine died today. A friend of mine died. Can I tell you a friend of mine died?

But you do not say it. You merely talk with her, her, about things you won't be able to recall five minutes from now.

And then the phone call is over, and you hang up, look at the administrative director.

She knows who it was, you can tell. She knows, but asks, "Was it her?"

"It's a secret," you say, your words hushed for fear someone else in the office might hear. "You can't tell anyone," you say, and you are standing, and you hug her because she is the closest person to you and you have this secret inside you, and because she is the only other person on the planet to know.

You will call your wife next. You will call her and tell her of this moment, of this delivery. Of this news beyond any news you have ever gotten.

You let go the director, and see she is crying, and you are crying now, too. You are crying, and you are smiling, and you look back to the window, see the ashen violet gone to a purple so deep and so true that you know none of this is happening, none of it. This is what you finally understand is surreal, a word you have heard and used a thousand times. But now it has meaning.

A friend has died. The Force has called. The sky has gone from a cold and indifferent blue to this regal purple. A secret has been bestowed. A novel has been lost. Another gone unfinished.

This is surreal.

You go to the window, lean against the frame, your face close enough to the glass to make out the intricate filaments of ice crystals there.

You want to feel the cold on your cheek, want evidence this is real, all of this day is real. You want evidence.

You listen again to her voice on the phone, the words exchanged. You feel this cold.

A friend has died, and you did not record his passing with the Force.

And now you cry openly, watching the sky out there in its regal color, regal not for anything you have done. Only assigned that value by your eyes on this particular January day. That color has nothing to do with you, exists as it does as a kind of gift whether you are here to see it or not.

What does a book matter?

Still you cry, and do not know if it is out of sorrow or joy, and decide in the next moment it is out of both.

1

Your newest book is pretty much going to hell. In a hand basket.

Late afternoon, December, and you and your wife are in lawn chairs at the soccer field, watching your younger son play in one of the last games before Christmas.

Christmas. Your deadline for the next novel. The advance you were given, a sum the same as you were paid for your last book, even though it sold out its print run and sold to paperback as well, was spent months ago. Ancient history. Now here's Christmas coming hard at you, the novel going to hell.

Your son, a wing, is out on the field, your wife sitting beside you on your left, your older son a few feet farther to your left and in a lawn chair too, and talking to a schoolmate sitting on the grass beside him. Long shadows fall from across the field toward you, cast by the forest there. Other parents, schoolmates, brothers and sisters are spread across your side of the field, those shadows approaching you all. Maybe thirty or forty people altogether. It's a small school, new and with no field on campus, this one a municipal field at a city park. Lawn chairs is the best anyone can do.

And of course here with you, too, is your book pretty much going to hell, and this fact, its lack of momentum in your head and heart coupled with that looming deadline, might as well be a dead body propped in yet another lawn chair sitting next to you for all its palpable presence in your life. The world knows, it seems to you, that you are flailing.

You are cranky. That's what you would like to think it is. But it is more than that, and you know it, and your wife knows it, and your children do too. You are angry, resentful. You are in the last fifty pages, but the book is leaving you, not like sand through your fingers, but like ground glass swallowed down.

You believed you had something, going in to the writing of it nine months ago. You believed you were headed somewhere.

You thought you knew something: that you could write this book.

So, when you see your son lag behind on a run downfield, you yell at him, "Get on the ball! Run! Get in the game!"

It's too loud, you know, with the first word out of your mouth, and you turn to your wife, say, "Why doesn't he get into the game?" as though to lend your outburst credence. As though to find in her some kind of agreement that it's your son slacking off, when you know too well it's about a book you are writing going down like ground glass.

She looks at you out the corner of her eye, says nothing.

Your older son gets up from his lawn chair, and moves even farther away with his friend, and you look at him, too. He's got on sunglasses, a ball cap on backwards. He's embarrassed by you, you know.

You would have been, too, were you him.

But the book is dying. It is dying.

You yell, even louder, "Let's GO! Get in the GAME!" and feel your hands in fists on the arms of the lawn chair.

This time your younger son looks over his shoulder, though far downfield, and his eyes meet yours. Then, quickly, they dart away, to others on the sidelines, then to the ground, his back fully to you now, him running and running.

"He's always just hanging back like that," you say to your wife, quieter but, you only now realize, with your teeth clenched. "It's like he's always just watching what's going on." You know your words as you speak them are one more attempt to give your anger, your resentment a clear conscience: you're yelling because of your kid. Not because of you.

And now your wife stands, picks up her lawn chair, moves away, settles her chair a good fifty feet from you.

This is no signal to you of the embarrassment you are. It is nothing cryptic you are meant to decipher. It is her truth and yours both, big and dumb: you are a fool.

And it is because of a book. A stupid book. There are more important things, she is shouting to you in settling her lawn chair that far from you. There are more important things than a book.

You are here in your chair, alone with yourself. And the corpse of your book propped beside you.

You look off to the right, for no good reason but that it's away from those you have embarrassed, and those who know you for the fool you are.

And see there near the sideline, almost to the corner of the field, a blond kid, down on one knee on the sideline, his back to you. He's maybe ten yards away, the sun falling across the field to give his blond hair an extra shimmer to it, turning it almost white.

He's talking to himself, you hear, his voice quiet but there, just there. He's got on a black T-shirt, cargo shorts, skateboard shoes, and though his back is to you, you can see he has in one hand a plastic yellow baseball bat, in the other a plastic Day-Glo orange squirt gun.

He's holding them oddly, you can see, the bat by the thick end, where the ball makes contact, the handle up and perpendicular to the ground, like a flagstaff with no flag; the squirt gun he holds delicately, thumb and first finger at the bottom of the grip, as though it might be too hot.

He's still talking, and you can see the gun and bat moving a little, first the gun, his hand shaking it in sync, you hear, with his words, then the bat, the movement small, like the sound of his voice coming to you across the grass, and over the shouts of players at the far end of the field. Then the gun shakes again, and you see too by the movement of his head that he looks at the gun when he moves it and talks, and looks as well at the bat when he moves it and talks.

What is he doing?

Then he turns, rolls toward you from the knee he is on to sitting flat on the ground. He's facing you now, still holding the bat and gun in this odd way, and you see, now, now, he is a Down's Syndrome boy: almond eyes, thick neck, his mouth open.

He speaks again, looks at the bat, moving it with his words, and you only now realize he is speaking for the bat, that the bat itself is talking, this boy supplying the words, and then the gun answers the bat.

They are talking one to the other: a yellow bat, a Day-Glo squirt gun.

The boy is about your younger son's age, you see, and see too the shimmer of late afternoon sunlight in his hair the same as a few moments before, when his back was to you, and you hadn't known. You hadn't known.

You look at him. Still they talk one to the other, the words nothing you can make out, but there is something beautiful and profound in what you see. Something right and simple and true, and just past your understanding.

It's a kind of peace you see, and can't understand, this moment.

I wrote a book about that, you think. I wrote a book about a Down's Syndrome person, my aunt, and her mother. My grandmother, you think.

That was a good book, you think. That one was a gift, given to you without your even asking.

A gift, you think, and you wonder who this boy is with, who his own family is, who he is a gift to, and just as you wonder this you hear a rise in the crowd.

Parents and children in lawn chairs are growing louder now, clapping, hollering, though nothing as bombastic as what you knew you let out a few minutes before, and you turn to the sound, see your son's team moving and moving before the goal down there, the ball popped to the left and then right, and now you hear from the boy the word, "Go," then louder, "Go! GO!" and you look at him, see him turned to that end of the field now too, see the bat and gun held still, this boy back up on one knee and in profile to you. "GO JOHNNY!" he yells, and you know he has a brother out there.

The gun and bat talk to one another again, while the shadows from the far side of the field grow closer to you all, to everyone, and now you know you knew nothing in writing that book. It was a gift, this story of a mother and daughter, but has it made you a better father to your son? Has it made you a better husband to your wife?

The answer, of course, is no, because here you are, chewing out the world around you because a book is going down like ground glass swallowed.

This is when the boy happens to glance up from the dialog he creates and lives at once, to see you looking at him. Your eyes meet a moment, the talking toys now still, and you say, "Hi." You say it just to be nice to him. You say it because your eyes have met, and he has seen you watching him.

But you say it to try and save yourself.

He looks at you, looks at you, and even before he goes back to the dialogue at hand, his friends these toys, you know he won't say a thing.

You are a stranger.

You look beside you. There is no corpse of a book here, not anywhere around. Your wife is gone too, her to your left and away from you, your older son even farther away. And there is your younger son, out on the field and running away from you as best he can. Your son, a teammate to this boy's brother.

There is, you know, only you here with you, and though you wish it were possible, pray it might be possible, there is no way for you to stand and lift your lawn chair and walk fifty feet away from you.

Which is what you want to do. To be away from you, here.

Because you have been blessed.

You have been blessed.

You have been blessed.

0

You have everything to learn.

This will be what keeps you. What points you toward humility: knowing how very little you know, how very far you have to go. As far now, in the second person and once it's all over, as on an afternoon soccer field, shadows growing long.

I know nothing. I know I know nothing.

I have been blessed.

for Jim Ferry

Ours or the Other Place

Anna Monardo

New York is like a guy who doesn't like you as much as you like him. You know it's time to let this crush go. It's been too long with no phone calls, nothing. And still, you arrange your days and evenings so you'll be there for his call if it ever comes. The phone rings differently when it's him. It's a better ring.

One day, you admit to yourself that this romance lives nowhere but in your own head. You admit to the hard work of keeping it alive. You ask yourself, finally, Why am I doing this?

Because there was that one heightened bit of time when he made you feel like someone grander than yourself, some better version of yourself—freer, happier, funnier, smarter, more beautiful, wiser, more worldly, kinder, braver.

Only a passing glance can have this intensity, this jumped-up pulse. Afterward, you are addicted—not to him, but to the enhanced vision of yourself. It's like crack, a fast and solid addiction. You need this person so you can feel that way again. Nothing matters but to feel that way again. Your whole being is in need of this person. Your bones feel the need for him and the absence of him.

New York is like that.

* * *

It was 1977 and I was twenty-one years old. I thanked God when I arrived in New York. I had flown just one hour from Pittsburgh, but I was as grateful as an immigrant, as relieved as a refugee who has finally escaped. I don't mean to equate the enormity of exile with the comparative ease of my departure from suburbia, but I can't lie about this: landing in New York felt as lucky to me and as monumental as it must have felt for anyone who ever sailed into Ellis Island. In leaving my family's home, I was an anarchist.

Our women had never lived in this place I was going to. For my Italian grandmothers, my mother, my aunts, a life between the home of the father and the home of the husband had never existed.

But now it did exist. At last, I was in the right place.

The city was completely new to me but felt completely known. I can put it no other way but to say that I was happy in my skin. A few years later, working a book-publishing job, I glanced through the glass wall of an office and got a glimpse, two rooms down, of a man—tall and large, dark-haired, in a heavy overcoat. I did a double take. He was stunning in a roughed-up sort of way I had never known I was attracted to. But now I was. He startled me. Who is that? I'd never seen him before but I felt that premonition of familiarity, the beginning of loyalty. I just knew that this man and I would have some kind of business together. (Eventually, of course, we did. It was with him, one of my first close friends in the city, that I learned about the particular sexiness of talking late into the night, in the booth of a bar or at the tiny table of a coffee house, working your way toward the possibility of lovemaking. Then veering right past it, just so you can keep on talking. Here's the magic trick: If you keep talking past sex, the possibility of it stays there between you, around you, like the aroma of a meal that is almost ready to be served, but not quite. Our times together were delicious because we never did become lovers, which was of course what I'd had in mind the first time I saw him through the glass and my breath caught.) Flying into New York in September of '77 I looked through the double-paned window of the USAir jet, down into a misty Friday morning, and I felt that same astonishing tug.

I had just left my family and my college boyfriend, who, the day before, had sent me roses, and my mother, in a last-ditch plea to keep me home, had said, "But how can you leave? What about your roses?" I later learned that after I left, my mother cried in the kitchen to my boyfriend, and that this scene took place at just the same time I was looking from the plane down onto the apartment complexes of Queens, the willowy grasses along the shores that hug the runway at LaGuardia, and, enchanted by this harsh beauty, I was thinking, "I like this." And I was praying, Please God, let there be a place for me down there.

And there was.

In New York when I was twenty-one I felt sure I could not die. I'd been a cautious girl going to college in the Midwest, but I knew that wasn't my real life. I'd kept myself safe, not wanting to squander my luck there.

Now, rushing through Central Park after midnight, on work nights, in cabs driven by drivers who were sometimes stoned, some who spoke to me with the accents of the faraway places they had run from, speeding to the uptown bad neighborhood where my new boyfriend lived, I had a sense of mission. Destiny had meant for me to live these days. These nights.

And because these nights were about art as much as they were about love, there was in my canvas bag, along with my work clothes for the next day, some manuscript or other to show him. (*Him!* A few years older than I was and an experienced writer; for a young woman who wants to write, this is a dangerous combination in a first city boyfriend.)

When I was finally in the vestibule of his building, my heart galloped. With trembly hand ringing the buzzer for apartment 5F once, then again, caught for a moment in the tight space between the outer door that opened freely to the dark street and the locked inner door that led up to the dubious safety of this man's home, I felt the solitariness you feel in the confessional.

When you're alone like that, it's just you there, with your limited strength, with all your sins (like abandonment of loved ones, or greedy grabbing for too much in life), sins that will someday demand a price.

But not yet. There's the click, the door unlocked, then that rush of relief, almost as good as salvation. Spasm of adrenaline, just what's needed to be able to run up the five flights.

And I did run, fast enough to ignore the choking knowledge that most likely this man would one day break my heart.

But not yet. Tonight he's coming down the steps to meet me, all sweet words and smiling. Tonight we are happy. New York is still doling out only generous, good love. Hadn't the bountiful heavens given me everything I had just to risk it for this?

Risk. How we love our brave selves.

And just as gorgeous were the moments, middle of the night, when I'd leave 5F in a fit (Just who does he think he is?). I'd run down the flights of steps for one more last time, run the half-block past the dark garage, past the hoods' hangout, the soles of my boots crunching broken-bottle shards all the way to the avenue, where I raised my arm, defiant, to four angry lanes of traffic coming toward me while now and then a drunk approached from behind, but I'm saved by the yellow of a taxi, and I slam the door shut and ask the driver to take me home. Please.

In moments like these, New York City gives birth to us, as if the city were some savvy mother who knows that the best thing she can do is toughen us up.

That is Year One. The next year, Ed Koch becomes mayor. Even after moving into Gracie Mansion, he won't give up his downtown apartment. By now I've moved from West 72nd to West 82nd to West 102nd, so I don't blame Koch one bit for holding on. His place is rent-controlled and has a terrace. If I were him I'd sooner give up the mayor's mansion, which is basically a sublet with an extension clause, than give up that apartment in the Village. One year follows another, Koch is still mayor, my real-estate odyssey continues (to East 80th Street to West End Avenue to Brooklyn and back). Each spring, wherever I'm living, I clean my closet(s) out thoroughly, telling myself I will leave the city by September. And each September I clean again and tell myself, By spring I'll be gone—there've got to be easier places to live. One spring, during a subway strike, women begin carrying their good shoes in their briefcases and wearing sneakers to work. This practice continues after the strike, but I refuse to do it. I've been in New York $2^1/2$ years and am working now at a magazine, and every morning, wearing thick-heeled boots, I walk the long walk to the Helmsley Building and indulge in long noisy fantasies about becoming a rock star. I'll call myself Infanta and sing scathing hard-rock versions of Motown hits like "Get out of my life, why don't you, babe." By now my first city boyfriend is sleeping with a former friend of mine. By now the city is changing.

My first apartment had been a gigantic prewar, shared with roommates, across the street from the Dakota, dirt-cheap. In those early days, if I wanted to visit my friend who lived on 79th Street at night, I ran up Columbus because there were long dark stretches of the avenue where the storefronts were empty. Then real estate went up, disco went out, business picked up. Danger shifted to safety. Enter: The '80s. People walk in the evening from shop to shop. My favorite Italian restaurant on Columbus, a tiny place with pipes low and dusty on the ceiling, and sawdust on the floors, now has a glassed-in sidewalk café; a line has formed at the door. Mrs. Fields cookies bake on every other corner of the Upper West Side. One bright expansive afternoon, walking up Central Park West, I see skywriting over the park: *Happy Birthday, Yoko. Love, John and Sean.*

By Year Four, I am a graduate student in creative writing, walking everywhere (but rarely venturing below 96th Street, hardly ever below 72nd Street). Wandering up and down Broadway, to and from Columbia, I am constantly trying to figure out how to make a story of the series of events that led to the marriage of my first city boyfriend and my former friend. That night at the Mudd Club when he told me, "You have no *joie de vivre*"—is that the ending of the story or where it begins? What is the connection between what you live and what you write and what people want to read? What, exactly, is *story?*

Then one Friday afternoon the news on NPR is all about a recent Brinks truck robbery in which cops were killed. The suspects have just been identified as former members of the radical anti-establishment protest group the Weather Underground, men and women who have been living in the city under aliases for years, since they blew up a brownstone in the Village in March 1970 and got away. For ten years, they've been holding down jobs, taking care of their children, going about their business, the whole time pretending they were people different from who they really are. Just a few blocks north of where I live, there have been people waking every morning and stepping into a solid fiction. Meanwhile, I've been pacing the paths of Columbia's campus, worrying, wondering, practically memorizing the cobblestones, as if story could be revealed in the pattern of stones.

By now John Lennon has been killed. There is that cold cold winter when everyone begins wearing puffed-up coats stuffed with down feathers, and in the Korean delis loaves of bread and boxes of doughnuts are always being knocked off the shelves. People have to make lots of room for each other. The headlines are all about disease. You can no longer stand on line and socialize in front of the Thalia and the Regency because those theaters are closed. There is a period of eight months when, early in the morning several times a week, I go to a church on Amsterdam to light candles, but still my grandmother dies. And then there is a spectacular September Friday when my niece is born at Mt. Sinai Hospital, and every fall after that, whenever a certain quality of pink light washes over the pediments of brownstones or the facades of high-rises, I will think *Clare.* The Berlin Wall falls.

I start going downtown once in a while. At a party at Westbeth I meet a musician who visits me one afternoon and brings his bass viol because, he says, he wants to play music for me. When he does, all the apartments on my floor tremble and someone complains to the doorman. Another afternoon there's a different musician—subtler, a jazz guitarist. His side line is selling clothes to vintage dress shops, and one day he arrives at my apartment with two hockey-equipment bags full of never-worn shoes from the '40s, '50s, '60s. He bought the shoes from a man emptying inventory from an old store in Jersey, and I'm very lucky to have first pick at this stash. We spend a couple of hours talking while I try on shoes: open-toed pumps, slingbacks, tassel loafers, bowling shoes; he's brought more than forty pairs. Some are still in the original boxes. I like this musician. He's funny in a quiet way, and kind, and I buy four pairs of terrific shoes, hugely discounted. Thereafter, my friends refer to the musician as "your dealer."

One night the dealer and I walk out of a bar onto Christopher Street after listening to Mike Stern play guitar, and a street guy approaches us. "Spare some loose change?"

You can tell a lot about people by the way they handle panhandlers. My dealer is too savvy to dole out money, but he can't bear to leave anyone empty-handed. "What size shoes do you wear?" he asks, as he leads the guy over to his vintage Volvo, parked nearby, opens the trunk and begins looking through boxes of sneakers. When we find his size, the street man is very happy.

The clothes dealer and I don't become intimates, nor do we fall in love (though I think we'd both like to), but after that night, I will think of him and his sweet funny ways every time I walk through that intersection by the Christopher Street subway station, usually on my way farther west, to Elephant & Castle or to the Paris Commune, to eat omelets with a handsome vegetarian who likes to smoke. There's another smoker, someone I sit in Caffe Vivaldi with a lot, and we talk about how we're wasting our time—we really should be sitting in coffee shops in Rome. There's one evening when a seriously contemporary architect surprises me with a no-nonsense kiss outside of Time Cafe, but the whole night has been very hip, very downtown, and I don't have the right clothes for this particular nightlife. In my heart of hearts, I love the Old New York places (just as I love the old shoes), and a three-year relationship with a journalist begins with a first date at Sevilla, where we drink a lot of Sangria, and before we've even finished ordering I have a premonition: I see the two of us sitting in a café in the Mediterranean, the Caribbean, someplace hot. So three months later, in January, I'm not surprised when the journalist and I are spending a week in Puerto Rico, sitting on a sunny patio together eating paella again.

There's an enthusiastic long walk one spring Sunday with an old friend who takes me for a great hamburger on the lower deck of the Water Club. For a nice long time we just watch the water, then we watch Geraldine Ferraro and her friends arriving for her birthday party. He's a great listener, this guy, and we talk aimlessly all afternoon, but it will make me sad years later when I find out that that spring, my friend was working hard to get over a significant cocaine habit, which I wasn't sharp enough to guess, let alone give him a chance to talk about; I thought we were just eating hamburgers and getting some sun.

In my work life around this time I'm part of a neurotic group of friends playing out an assortment of half-baked romances at the Old Town Bar just up from Union Square. There are all kinds of Saturday nights—early ones, late ones, uptown, downtown, expensive ones that involve taxis, cheaper ones riding the subway or bus—but they all end the same way: at the H & H Bagels counter, where I get a sesame bagel for Sunday breakfast and one of whatever's just out of the oven, which I eat warm from the white bag while I walk the rest of the way home.

The dilapidated facade of an SRO hotel is what my bedroom window faces in one apartment I live in for a while. One night the old building across the street lights up in flames. No one dies in the fire, but that last-chance home for so many old or sick or poor people burns down to a charred haunting frame that looks like the ruins of Rome. Months later, when the building is restored, it is a high-priced condo. New stores and chains of stores have come to the neighborhood. Nightly, homeless people break into vans on Riverside Drive so they have somewhere to sleep. Years earlier, on my way to one of my first jobs, I used to see a homeless woman every morning pushing her junk-loaded shopping cart up Broadway, moving against the crowd headed for the subway, and she'd sing at the top of her lungs, "Hi ho, hi ho, it's off to work we go," and everyone around her smiled. I remember a bedraggled old man crossing Fifth Avenue, dodging noontime traffic while the horrified crowd on the corner of 79th Street watched him, and when he arrived safely at the corner, he gave us an elegant bow and said, "Time is money, time is money!"

There aren't so many jolly moments on the street anymore. One afternoon as I am walking the aisles of a new Food Emporium, a news broadcast comes on over the store's PA system and I hear George Bush's voice, and I think, I'm bored with all this.

So in 1993, after seventeen years in the city, when I get a call telling me about a job opening in the Pacific Northwest, I'm ready for it. I know this means it's time to leave, at least try something else for a while. I know I'm lucky to have the chance for this. What I don't know, have no way of knowing, is that within six months my life will be something I can't even imagine while I'm sitting on a subway or riding the cross-town bus. I will be living in a place where the skies are porcelain. The Inland Empire of Washington State, just east of the desert. The air will be dry and polite, not humid, not pushing up against me in any way that feels like unwanted seduction or malicious intent. It was the genius of glaciers that shaped this land into moonscapes of wheat fields called the Palouse, and just down the street from my apartment and as beautiful as ancient tragedy, there will be volcanic rock. The light will be an army of angels blessing me as they march through my large rooms. I will have many rooms, including a separate room to write in, and when I lie on my office floor, on the sun-warmed, honey-colored floorboards, look out the five windows, each one will be a canvas of perfect blue.

So what.

I still won't be able to let go of some jazzed-up version of my life. I'll still want to walk on streets that spark fire under my feet, send me walking faster. During my early days in the West, my first drive through the eternally rolling hills of the Palouse, I will cry. The land there is uninhabited and there is no horizon. Remember those childhood dreams of being in a crowd, safe with your mother holding tight to your wrist, until some force of the crowd breaks the lock of your mother's hand and suddenly you're worse than dead? You're lost, not able to get to anyone who would care who you are. How I will miss the hug of skyscrapers around me.

⧉ ⧉ ⧉

From a distance, New York is a trompe l'oeil, a trick. You don't remember the boring fear of taking the subway home to Brooklyn at night when you lived in Brooklyn, the bad smell on the street during summers on the Upper West Side. The howl of the insane so close it seems they're living in your apartment, or closer. The exhaustion, too, is boring after a while. Too many too-odd jobs. The sterile loneliness of days at the desk. The tedious heft of grocery bags. The dilemma of dirty laundry and kitchen trash and running out of shampoo. You forget that life in New York is lived like life anywhere, day by day.

A crush is a shattered attraction, made up of fragments. What got you was how the guy looked in the midst of a certain gesture, some one beautiful moment. There is the way the sky turns lilac at the foot of West 72nd Street at the end of the day. City sunset filtered through chemical sky, it just gets you, the way a cigarette voice late at night seems to be talking to some neglected part of your soul. The rarefied beauty that aberration brings.

Of course, this kind of beauty has so much to do with sex. Some cities are female, some are male. New York is the world's most provocative, sexual, bisexual, transsexual, extra-sexual monster creature, daily swallowing virgin offerings of every type. New York City will love you in any way you ever imagined yourself being loved.

New York will have you, but you can never have New York. It is always slipping away from you, always with a wandering eye, always threatening to love someone else better than it ever loved you.

Your friends tell you this love affair is not healthy. You know it yourself.

You have heard there is a kind of love that grows in absence. Some men will fall in love with you while they are away from you. The friends say, Go ahead. Try it. Leave town. Now he'll see, they say. Everything you ever said to him will resonate. He'll walk the streets, eyeing the crowds, hungry for a glimpse of you. On the serene raft of his therapist's couch he'll have that moment of clarity (provoked by the intelligent questions of the therapist, who realized from just the few details he told her that you are this man's one best chance for happiness in this life, and she'll use all her skills to help him see that). It's only a matter of time, your friends say. He will run into people who know you and they will tell him the name of the place you moved to. Your new phone number is listed. He will call.

Okay, so he doesn't call. But after a few seasons in this new place (after the pine straw jamming up your windshield in autumn, after the yellow blanket of pollen over everything in spring), you decide it's time to plan a visit back home. For the first time in years you are living by the calendar, like a child waiting for Christmas. Your days are lived simply to get to that date when you will leave for your trip to New York. You're getting closer, crossing off each day with a big red marker, moving deeper into the hot heart of summer. It really is dry here. Suddenly, the day before you are to leave, there are fires in the forests, the landscape is aflame. The fires get bigger. The radio news reports that the fires have jumped the river.

Something has happened. It's evening in the neighborhood, everyone is out, and you don't feel like going inside to pack your suitcase. You want to stay to watch the last bit of sunlight, which goes on and on. Suddenly you realize that your eyes will miss what they're seeing—the unfailing blueness of this endless Western sky. The green over green all around your white house. Your ears will miss the mysteriously sweet sound of these summer nights (big mystery—it's really just the absence of subways and sirens). You are happy and you realize that you have been for quite a while. Happy in the most unobtrusive way, a pleasure you weren't aware of because it just kept happening. It didn't end and come back and end and leave you needing more. You have never felt this way before. What is this?

It can't be love because there's no pain in it. Is this what they call contentment? Peace? Is this peace? The night before you are to leave, you lie in bed, eyes open, listening, wanting to touch every corner of this life. You are stunned by it. It is as upsetting as finding that you are in love with someone you weren't supposed to love. Someone else's husband, someone who speaks nothing but a foreign language, someone who is a Republican. You never expected it. The fire has jumped the river.

Two characters in a Chekhov story, a young man named Savka and an older man, are sitting in the forest when suddenly they hear "a hollow sound of timid footsteps in the dark, and from the spinney emerged the silhouette of a woman." The apprehensive woman approaching them is Agafya, the signalman's young wife. Agafya is also Savka's lover. Just before she appeared, the two men had been discussing bird migration, the older man asking Savka, "And what place do the birds like best? . . . Ours or the other one?"

Talking about the difficulty of maintaining allegiance to one love at the exclusion of other attractions, a psychiatrist once told you, "We all had a mother and a father, didn't we?" How different the atmosphere of the mother from that of the father. A friend called recently with this story: Her small son had asked her, "Is it okay if you love one of your parents more than the other one?" At that moment this woman knew herself to be the less-loved parent. She is the familiar terrain, with no sunrise or sunset. Home with the child day in and day out. She doesn't thrill the boy the way his father does, with his disappearances and appearances each day when he goes to work and comes back. The little boy was so upset he was crying when he asked, "Is it okay?"

There is that point at the beginning of every love affair when all you feel is sadness for the last love, no matter how long ago it ended. You know that feeling? And for a day or two you can't make love with your new lover because if you do you will cry and cry? After that spell of grief, you can admit, with joy, that this new love is happening. You can let go of the old life. You can let your allegiance shift.

By the time you begin to think this place you've come to may be your new home, it has already happened. When you get to that bend in the road your heart leaps a bit for the muscular shoulder of mountain that you know is just about to appear. There's that elbow of rolling river out your kitchen window every morning while you make your coffee. On your way home from work, at sunset, the hills are a net gathering gold light. You hardly recognize your days now that they are lived against this grandiose backdrop. Is this your life? Is this you? Maybe you really have been transformed.

With time, if your imagination becomes engaged, the landscape becomes more than beautiful, it gains power. It's a little like writing fiction, when you move to a new place. You have to take the details and juice them up a bit. Some stories are a circle. Some are a straight line into the future. Without a willingness to work your details, though, you won't be able to push your story into that all-important free fall, a sinking into unexpected depths.

⎿⏋ ⎿⏋ ⎿⏋

I was very much in love with a man once, and we had a game we played, mostly in bed, of making up stories together, different epics set in different times in history and on different continents—a dacha in pre-Revolution Russia, a port city in Brazil, Trieste during World War II. Each story involved lovers who met, underwent enormous turmoil, withstood heartbreaking separation and were miraculously reunited. The lovers' names were always our names. It was always us, coming together despite huge obstacles, living over and over again the incredible joy we had felt when we found each other.

We were so happy, except that after a while, sometimes we weren't. It took us a long time to decide whether to get married or separate. Now, looking back from several years' distance, I see the decision was made long before we decided. Our dis-engagement began when we stopped making up stories together. I remember one of the last times. We were sitting on a beach. There was a sailboat offshore. I tried to begin, "See that boat, there's a man out there . . . " but it was forced. We couldn't breathe life into the man or build the boat or navigate the sea he traveled over on his way to find his lover. The details took us nowhere. Our imaginations were no longer engaged with each other.

⎿⏋ ⎿⏋ ⎿⏋

Psychology tells us that the way we experience love as adults is largely determined by what happens in our childhood. There is, in the earliest years, days, hours, the danger of a faulty bond being set, a pattern established that we will, wittingly or unwittingly, pace out for the rest of our days. (Are there actually people who were received into the world in such a perfect way that love for them is painless, unambivalent? Have you ever met these people?)

Is it because I am the daughter of immigrants that I have, all my life, invested geography with the allure and the dangers and the voluptuous attractions of romantic love? That ineffable longing to get closer to some perfect happiness that almost but never quite was? That constant yearning to be someplace else, with some one perfect beloved? Call it what you want.

In my family, we called it Italy. Childhood, I know, was the beginning for me of the ground/figure conundrum of place and love.

But maybe geography, with its wordlessness and bulk, is a natural way to talk about love. So much happens in the body.

What if it's just lust?

And what if it is lust? Is it possible to call it love if you're not feeling lust, that glorious painful state of unsatisfied desire? Lust, with its compelling incompletion.

It's not that the West isn't sexy—it is—but the thing about it is that it happens in the eyes. Only in the eyes. Why is it that sometimes the vistas leave me feeling hollow? Inherent in the glorious escape of this place is the loneliness of this place, the complete absence of everything I knew before.

I want depth. I want what Leonardo da Vinci wanted—the sense of skin over muscle and bone. That's why he did autopsies. So he could draw the human form with a more knowing hand. He wanted his figures on the page to have blood and marrow and a pulse.

⊑ ⊑ ⊑

Let's say that by now it's your second year in the West. As you're getting ready for another of your pilgrimages back to New York, you're invited to stop in the Ozarks for a visit. A new man. He'd been passing through the Northwest when you met him in April. He hung around. For two months you were friends. In June, lovers. A few weeks later, when he had to go back home to Arkansas (Arkansas? You had to look it up on a map), he said, "Will we see each other again?"

"We'll do what we do." So, you have learned something out West. You've learned not to talk everything to death. You've learned to rely on the weather, the silences, the bulk of the body.

When you arrive in Arkansas with your small suitcase and a few books and a laptop computer, it's the season of the cicadas. There is nothing but the puffed-up humid heat and the insects' trilling, which is as constant as unanswerable questions, and familiar to you for some reason you haven't figured out yet. Once or twice you wonder, Am I in love with this man? Rather than try to answer the question you notice you have no desire to leave. You figure out that the cicadas' buzz reminds you of the constant hum of traffic in New York—irritating only if you stop and pay attention to it; otherwise, it provides a pulse for your days, an energy in the air every morning. You just have to get up and latch on.

The landscape in Northwestern Arkansas is lower than what you're used to. From here you see that Manhattan and the Rockies are similar in many ways. Both places are magnificent, pushing the outer limits of what they are. Both are among the most impressive examples of their type. In contrast, the Ozark Mountains are slow-rising slopes, comforting as warm bread. Nothing towers over you here. This terrain doesn't do that Alice-in-Wonderland number of aggrandizing you and dwarfing you at the same time. From the start you found it very easy to talk to this new man. Now he shows you his unadorned patio and his untended lawn (he hasn't lived here long; divorce, etc.) and says, "It's all yours. Do what you want."

"Anything I want?"

"Anything you do is fine."

That's in July.

August is a string of nights warm as a bath, and the low ride of his car, and jazz on the car radio, and the fast pictures your eyes snatch from the side of the road. Low stone houses and old stone walls. A flash of tile roof, clay pot. Broken cement column climbed over with ivy, the base of a fence buried in moss. Solid stone structures aged and vintaged and worn. Color muted within stone. These rushing-by scenes have the quality of fresco, and for that reason they are provocative to you, forcing your eyes off the road, as if you've caught a glimpse of someone you know.

Dance teachers talk to their students about the phenomenon of muscle memory. If you perform a movement enough times, your muscles will incorporate the movement and memorize it forever (hence the importance of doing the movement correctly from the start). The thing about these Arkansas nights is that as you drive through them they feel old the way Europe does. Italy, let's say. You are the daughter of immigrants, and your body remembers—and is loyal to—what it has known: the spiraling roads into the Calabrian hills you and your family visited when you were a baby, a little girl, a teenager. The dry stone of the fountain in the village in the summer. The clay-pipe roofs spread out before you when you opened the shutters over the windows in your grandmother's house, when the house was full of everyone, when everyone was together and your father was alive. The lost empire of your family. Stone. Hills. Clay. The scenes go by so quickly that while you are seeing, you are also remembering and hoping to see more. Wishing. The present is layered with the future and past, the living and dead. Under the skin of these summer nights, there is muscle and bone.

When the eye sees what the heart desires, the body immediately knows what to do. Lust, that gap, pocket of open air where flint makes spark and combusts.

In September you marry the man in Arkansas. You don't know exactly when this new loyalty began or how. You remember a moment of noticing his hands on the steering wheel and thinking, Beautiful hands. By now there are plants in the back of the house and the front of the house, voices inside and outside, the man, his young sons, the cat, you. A civilization. Empire restored. At night the backyard is filled up with stars.

卐 卐 卐

The problem with the empire restored is that it is entirely restored, with all its imperfections. Never as highly polished as you remember, always as faulty as it really was.

When you neglect the plants they die. The cat becomes burdensome and is given away. You keep the sons, of course. They are wonderful. But there is the constant complicated question of whether or not to bring another child into this mix. Sometimes the house shudders with arguments. Arguments that haunt you with familiarity. The heart remembers and repeats the words it has known. At other times the rooms are silent, thick, impassable.

It is impossible to know the rooms of marriage until you are actually living within them. The rooms of your marriage are full of the man's good looks and the delicious way his body moves around within the space. You're living with his jokes and his intelligence and the information stored in his head. You're living with his scents and his habits and books and the phone calls that come for him. You're living with his junk mail, his magazines. And you're living most profoundly with his problems. As he lives with yours. His temperament, confusions, frustrations. As he lives with yours. The walls that mark the place where your wisdom has reached its limit have been adjoined to the walls that mark where his wisdom ends. This is your new home—side by side, the two of you living in a hut, surrounded by the wilderness of your mutual ignorance about everything you haven't managed to figure out yet.

卐 卐 卐

Within the first six months of marriage, I had two miscarriages. After the second, I had to go to the hospital for a same-day surgical procedure. They told me to arrive at the outpatient station very early in the morning. It went smoothly, an assembly line. Check clothes into a locker, sign forms, lie down on the bed in the assigned cubicle. One doctor, another doctor, a couple of very nice nurses. Some were dressed in whites, some in surgical greens, several in brightly illustrated smocks that made them look like large children wearing pajamas. I wasn't allowed to eat or drink anything, but they gave me a shot of tranquilizer, and before long I was in a good mood again for the first time in weeks. My husband was relieved. Eventually they made me scoot over onto a stretcher and they wheeled me somewhere else.

There was another injection. Then grogginess. Time passed.

I remember an anesthesiologist leaning over me, his cap as tight as a bandage around his forehead, making him look like someone with a very bad headache. He turned my face toward him with a soft fatty hand. "Can you hear me?" he asked.

"Yes."

"Is your blood pressure usually low?"

"Yes."

"Good. For a minute there we were afraid you were dead."

Later, I felt the faraway pressure of a man's fingers on my thigh and I opened my eyes. "Do you feel that?" It was a different anesthesiologist. "Do you feel me pinching you?"

I felt the lightest indentation, vague as a dream memory, but there was something. It was so nondescript, though, and moved me so little. "No," I said, "I don't feel anything."

"Okay," the doctor told the nurse, "we're ready."

All day long, at every stage of these quickie surgeries, they check in with you. A capped or masked or unmasked or smiling or worried face suddenly hovers above the patient and asks, "Do you know what procedure you're having done today? Do you know your doctor's name?" These questions are asked at least a dozen times.

And in the same way, during the days following, I regularly asked myself, Do you know who you are? Do you feel anything? Do you know why you're here? I was living in a place I didn't know at all yet, it was February and seemed to me that the weather was strange—too mild for what was supposed to be going on in winter, unsettling, unnatural. The day after the day at the hospital, I walked down our country road. When I got to the narrow overpass that bridges the skinny creek, I stopped and kicked stones into the tiny bit of water below. I was crying, and in that spot—that overpass, that creek—that was where my imagination chose to bury the babies, my invisible babies. I had to rest them somewhere. In this huge wide world they, too, needed their place.

I remember that day. It was warm, but I was wearing my husband's big old sweater, just for the feel of arms around me. This detail strikes me now—the sweater instead of the man. Had I gone for a walk without telling him? Was he not home? What we didn't know then and wouldn't know for a long time was that my short walk down that road was the beginning of the distance between our life together and seven months lived apart.

He stayed in Arkansas. I went back to New York.

* * *

Being in New York when you're married but "single" is, in some ways, better than being in New York when you're utterly single. There's an edginess that's gone, but when you walk the streets you're relieved of the feeling that you're missing out on something that everyone else knows about. Now you know. You don't hate the streets for their refusal to offer up *him*. In short, you don't take the city's rebuffs so personally. You're just grateful for your old work contacts that make it possible for you to pay the rent. Mostly, you're glad that a few years ago when you left the city you held on to your apartment, and when you returned, your subletter was ready to move out.

You are now a ghost wandering around in your past life.

* * *

During those months back in New York, sitting with friends in Starbucks and Vietnamese restaurants and a Cuban-Chinese place on the Upper West Side, I told no one the full story. Maybe because I sensed the story was not finished yet, mostly because it's one we'd all heard too many times. There's a man, there's a woman. They recognize something in each other—an aura of sadness surrounded by a halo of hope. Middle-aged but ignorant as teenagers in the way they know nothing about each other but are convinced they've found that one someone who will know their wish before it is even wished, some god of a lover, fairy godmother, both god and mother, some perfection. They marry.

Always, the story goes the same way: Eventually, the tulle that swathes this marriage will unwrap, a Christo sculpture in reverse. And after the sheets of illusion are taken away, if the couple are lucky—and my husband and I were lucky—a bridge will be standing, a stretch of solid framework that fighting hasn't corroded completely and that a long separation hasn't flooded away.

"What happened?" we ask each other, surprised not by our separation—we were clearly headed there from the very first day—but shocked that we managed to find each other again. We retrace often. First we met, lust origamied into love, love into loss, and then it was Easter weekend and he came to visit me in New York. We were eating piroshki at Veselka on Second Avenue, and I remember those piroshki as the first joyful meal we had together after more than a year of mute grief. Earlier, we'd gone into a church and lit candles for the memory of our babies. Now he was saying, "If you're leaving—" He put down his fork. "If you're leaving, take me with you."

⌴ ⌴ ⌴

Looking over our journey and its wild terrain, we're awed, a bit reverent, the way we used to be when we watched those trains out West. They traveled along tracks cut way up into the hills. A string of freight cars so long they wrapped an entire mountaintop, so far away and slow that in the first moment our eyes believed those trains were moving landscape, big beautiful chunks of it being loosened and pulled along.

⌴ ⌴ ⌴

You and your husband are together again? You're leaving the city again? Now what are you going to do?

All I know is this, a feeling that happens when I am flying down into New York: before the active seduction begins, when I am as full of expectation and hope as I am wise to the inevitable disappointments, the jagged skyline of high-rises is as familiar to my eyes as the feel of my tongue along the edges of my teeth. Inevitable.

Loyalty is what we're talking about here. That locked-in Calabrian-brand of loyalty. When a person has in some way become yours, when you belong to a place, when you find work you love, questions of right or wrong are beside the point.

Three years I lived out West. People were always pointing to the clock in my car and saying, "That's wrong. You should fix it."

"It's not wrong. That's what time it is in New York." ∎

Why I Played the Blues

Richard Terrill

We were four white guys trying to play the blues in rural Wisconsin. We were patch-jeaned and unshaven at a time when the bar crowd was spackled in polyester and slapped with cologne, overdressed for nightclubs and lounges in towns too small to have them. Or the people shot pool in PBR-on-tap, plastic-cup saloons, shitheels listening to George Jones and Charlie Rich, *a big ten-four, partner*, before country wasn't cool. Trying to make a living at the blues, we split a hundred bucks a night four ways—a hundred minus gas money and a twelve pack of Walter's Beer for the ride home from the gig.

Walter's slogan was "The Beer That Is Beer," a nifty tautology that matched our youthful cynicism. Wallie's was brewed right in our town, and it had that American-lager clarity of purpose and bargain price that made sense in the days before microbrews. Like microbrews, Walter's was better than the national brands, better even than Leinenkugel's, which, since it was brewed in the next county, we considered an import.

In Bloomer, Wisconsin, we have set up in a bar dominated by foosball tables and pinball machines, our small stage in one corner. The jukebox blasts out country and western. During our first tune, the Foosballers, in work boots and newish cowboy hats, pack up one by one. The young women kibitzing by the bar and pretending not to notice the action at the tables, one by one, go with them. By the end of the first set only the bartenders are left in the joint.

"If you guys quit now," the owner tells us, "I'll pay you for half the night. Just forget the last three sets and we'll call it square."

"Do we have a choice?" Lee the drummer asks Will, the guitar player. Lee's voice has a throaty rasp, so that even serious things he says are funny. Will's voice is low and even pitched, perfect for irony.

"Not really," Will answers. We take the fifty bucks and begin to pack: the black speakers with the beer rings on top, the trap case and drum cases,

Will's amp, my axes, the bass player's stuff, the board, the garage-built monitors, the mikes and stands. It all goes into the trailer rented from Brackett Avenue Sinclair and into the hatchback of Lee's eleven-year-old baby blue '68 Ford Pinto. The trailer cost us twenty bucks for the weekend. The car will do only thirty-five in second gear uphill on the interstate. Ted the bass player and I have to hunch over to fit in its bench back seat. Ted is not very tall.

By the time the car is loaded, the same foosball players in the same boots are back at the same tables. Their girlfriends continue to pretend to ignore them, seated along the bar. Apparently the word spread down the street to the other saloon in town that the band was leaving. The four of us are standing in front of the empty stage.

"So let's get the hell outta Dodge," Lee says. "Score a six pack first?"

"Let's make it a twelve," Will says, handing Lee a five-dollar bill. "Get Walter's. Go down the street to the Bloomer Tap, though. I don't think we want to give this guy our business. Bring back the change."

And as quickly as that we were off, in our car so loaded that the exhaust pipe scraped. Loaded with equipment, but also loaded down with the burdens of being the Burner Blues Band. The first burden: it was 1979, and disco, having peaked by now on the coasts, had finally made it to the heartland; we didn't play that stuff. Problem number two: not every country bar sold Walter's Beer. I had gone to college with the Walter girls. Barb played first chair flute in the concert band and was stern and unapproachably beautiful. Her sister Margaret had dated my friend Gary, a trombone player. Brand loyalty counted and Walter's was our brand. Our third burden was that the uninhibited teen-age brother of the bass player was half right when he said about our music: "Nobody wants it. You should quit."

He was right that no one wanted the music. He was wrong that we should have quit playing it.

⌐ ⌐ ⌐

Out of grad school for nine months before joining the Burner Blues Band, I'd been working at a job more opposite to the spirit of the blues than any imaginable. No job was less like what they sang the songs about. I wasn't a drug dealer, an auto worker, a repo man, a factory geef, an unemployed anything. Rather, I worked as a teacher of speed reading.

No job was more unlike the blues, except for one thing: mine had been a traveling job. I worked for a small private company in New England, run by a rich tightwad who sent me around to small private colleges, blue blood schools. I was in residence at each for a month, then I'd move on to the next, sometimes hundreds or even a thousand miles away. Tight Pockets paid his teachers a flat fee out of which we had to cover all travel, food, and living arrangements. I was a ramblin' man, teaching the children of privilege to read faster—but for a price. I stuffed everything I needed into my 1975 Corolla sedan. It was good practice for later stuffing Lee's little Ford. In the Corolla I packed a portable cassette player (Walkmans were expensive in the late '70s; only my reading students had them), portable black-and-white TV, hot pot, electric typewriter, one decent sport coat, two ties, plus all the speed reading junk I needed: pacing machines with little plastic bars that were like treadmills for your eyes; scanning machines that only let you see parts of a sentence for a split second of time, like on some quiz show; other machines to enhance peripheral vision, which probably didn't work, but impressed the students; and reading samples graded and color coded for difficulty.

With this burden, I wandered. I had no home. I lived for two weeks once in a youth hostel, sparsely heated in November, my sleeping bag on a bare bunk. Nuclear submarines cruised the Thames River outside my uncurtained window (they pronounced it the way it looked in New London, Connecticut, as if it rhymed with James). I spent a month in the third floor of a tenement in Brockton, Mass., sharing the apartment with a young restaurant manager whom I saw exactly four times. He slept little, and always while I worked. His former roommate had walked out owing two months rent and he was glad to have me since I paid in advance. It was the year the Red Sox blew the pennant in September, the year Bucky Dent hit that pop fly that barely drifted into the first row of seats in that one-game play-off. I knew no one in Brockton nor cared to, the ghost of Rocky Marciano in the Italian streets and in the corner delis, the tired brown skyline. I watched the Sox on TV every evening alone, watched the collapse, when Dewey Evans tried to carry the team, and Yaz and the pitching let them down. I became a fan just in time for that latest Red Sox heartbreak.

In a closed up mining town in central Pennsylvania I lived four weeks in the spare room of a sixtyish woman who spent the whole day smoking Parliament cigarettes and baking a lot. I can still smell the yeast and hear the theme music from nightly *Gunsmoke* reruns, drifting up the stairs together to my room in this too-small frame house. "She's a grass widow," a local bartender told me, the town small enough for everyone to know everyone else's business. "That means her husband left her for a younger woman," he added when he figured I didn't know what he was talking about. I remember her hanging her underwear outside on the line to dry, pee stains for all to see, and if I paid her a few extra bucks she'd do my laundry and, microtipped cigarette dangling from her lip, hang my shorts out next to hers.

Sometimes I had friends within a half day's drive of where I was staying, and I could crash on their couches on the weekends, drink with someone familiar. Have a life for a couple of days. If I had no friends within a reasonable drive, my non-working existence—which is to say my existence since the job itself was almost too stupid to be true—consisted of whatever friend or contact I could make in four weeks at whatever little college I hitched my horse to. Thus during my tour of duty I met a few women younger than the grass widow. There was one freshman girl slender as a birch, with eyes of marble blue and olive skin, friends with the Kennedys, rich to my middle class, tennis player to my trout fisherman, and eighteen to my twenty-six. I went home with her to her parents' house on break once, and I'd never seen anyone in my life so relieved as her mother when I was on my way out the door. "I hope you find," she told me probably meaning to be nice, "whatever it is you're looking for."

There was a Vietnamese refugee, who'd strolled into my class one day dressed like the back cover of a good magazine. She spoke five languages and was the daughter of an ambassador from the former government. I was too inexperienced to think of her as a woman to make a life with, which she clearly was. We made love in her dorm room at the women's college one weekend when it seemed that everyone on campus was away. In the mornings she'd play a record of a Chopin nocturne arranged for classical guitar. Long light shone through the breath condensed on her east window. *"Prenez soin votre mains,"* she left me a love note after class—"take care of your hands." She thought them extraordinary, whereas up to that point in my life I'd just thought of them as smaller than average.

At one particularly exclusive college there was a graduating senior interested in everything, including me, my writing, my music, even the vagabond nature of my strange job. She was cheerful, intelligent, and challenging. And, unlike the tennis player or the refugee, she could read fast. Most would also say, if they were less than sensitive, that she was not beautiful. Again I was too stupid, this time not to know that that didn't matter, not to know that I should have made love with her, so apparent these years later. "Yes," she agreed, "sex makes things complicated," but it needn't have except for the youth of both of us, me the few years older that should have known the difference. I hope she's having a happy life.

I remember these women (not many women), these apartments and furnished rooms (many of them), even some of the bars in which I drank too much and talked too little, because of the loneliness of the job and the travel that went with it. And because I couldn't see a clear way out of either the job or the loneliness. They could lead nowhere. When I drove those interstate miles from New England back to my Midwest home, from colleges in Michigan to Connecticut to Pennsylvania, I propped that monaural cassette player (the cheapest model RadioShack made) on the passenger seat, and played the same three or four tapes over and over, the only ones I owned: Bob Dylan's *Blood on the Tracks*, two old Sarah Vaughn tapes I'd found on a discount rack in Harvard Square, and only one pure jazz tape, the name of which, strangely, I can't remember now. Later I dubbed Frank Sinatra's *A Swingin' Affair!* and *Songs for Swingin' Lovers!* off my vinyl collection at home. It helped add variety to my listening. But the Voice, in his melancholy mode, singing "Night and Day" or "I Thought About You," sometimes made me feel even lonelier. More even than did public radio.

Later still I added Keith Jarrett's *The Köln Concert*, which I dubbed off a record owned by a woman I'd met in grad school. Truth be told, I'd taken the job to be near her in New England, where I thought most of the speed reading work would be. She was the reason I was so stupid and romantic not to follow through with other more willing and just as fine women I'd met on the road. Truth be told again, most of my speed reading colleagues had also taken the job to be close to someone. Or to be away from someone.

I was overeducated and underexperienced. I was too controlling and lacking in spontaneity, despite my time improvising jazz in college and dashing off poems in dumpy apartments in grad school. But even not knowing it then, I had flowing in me that undercurrent of despair, that bad stream that nevertheless feels like it should be there. There was the obligatory series of women, no matter how truncated were the encounters, and the one unobtainable love. Even as a teacher of speed reading, with my pacers and flashers and colored folders, there was the landscape, that interstate mindless repetitive roadscape, the trucker hotels and greasy spoons, the strange bars. America was out the window always, trying its damned best to be the same place no matter where I slept or ate or cried. Not only that, I didn't have much money.

It's safe to say I had the blues.

⌐ ⌐ ⌐

My right ear still carries a buzz from Will Dowling's amplifier. He always set up to that side of me. I can conjure, effortlessly and in the right key, his high and grinding opening lick to "Hoy Hoy Hoy." "I dreamed of heaven and saw my baby tonight," he'd sing, then we'd play the unison line: *da do da DOO duh, da DOO da do duh.* His guitar notes have made an impression on the part of my brain in charge of sound, something like the path worn in a carpet. Or sometimes you might look directly into too bright light, then close your eyes and see the negative of what you saw floating upwards on the insides of your eyelids. That's the sound. It's an engraving, it's silk touched by acid fingertips.

Will introduced himself to the people in the crowd as "Coyote Will," perhaps his chance to construct an identity for himself the way we'd all like to. His chance to create a myth about a ramblin' blues man, coming into town, playing the gig, then leaving town again. Will Dowling was scholarly, particular, liberal, and involved. A reader and a thinker; "Coyote Will," though I knew him only on stage and not as well, was a guitar player. He was unlettered, undiscriminating, folksy and noncommittal. In Will Dowling's future was a doctorate in seventeenth-century literature and a professorship at a state university in a quiet town where he home-schooled his daughter, installed a recording studio in his basement, and developed an interest in literary theory; in Coyote Will's past was the unspoken, the unimaginable, whatever created in him that need to wince at the high notes on his solid body Gibson guitar, whatever made him smoke too much and eat too little. Maybe it was a mean daddy who whipped him, maybe leaving school to work in the fields or factories, maybe a jail term or unfaithful woman. Only Will knew what those imaginary eyes had seen.

Will Dowling's pointed features, hook nose, long face, deep lines running from eyes to mouth, did indeed suggest an animal, though maybe not a coyote. More a snake, but without the devilish connotations unfairly ascribed to that good beast. Maybe a very thin bird.

I'd known Will as a bookish grad student during my own unserious undergrad years, and as a rock-and-roll guitar player who'd gigged around our town. But, as a confirmed jazz musician myself, I'd never heard him or played with him. Will always wrote poems with images borrowed from classical mythology—"through Herakles' thighs strangled Nemean beast vanquished in vain," or "Phoenician script, worms in Iberian clay." Those of us on the campus literary magazine thought Will's work high toned and impersonal. Not only that, we never knew what he was talking about. We were busy writing poems with images borrowed not from myth, but from our lives—our fantasy lives, really: the thighs of some magically pliant woman or the script above the urinal in the men's john. When I told Will once, in a moment of directness, that his poems seemed distant to me, he said he thought his Odysseus and Herakles poem was the most personal one he'd ever written.

Four years later seemed like a lifetime, since we'd all grown. I was off the road from speed reading and hoping to stay home for a while and play music. It seemed backward to me—being a traveling teacher and stay-at-home musician—only because I was still young enough to expect experience to be logical.

A friend told me Will Dowling was putting together a blues band and wanted to talk to me. I'd been commuting two hours to Minneapolis (already too many miles given what I'd just been through!) to play in a nostalgia band that was just starting up: the music of the '60s, for weddings, parties, and reunions. There'd probably be a market for that, I was told, and when I wasn't playing sax on some tunes, they said they'd let me strum an acoustic guitar into a mike on a Beatles song, sing harmony on the Rascals, or shake something Latin on Santana. It sounded like fun.

But Will, like many youngish people who are intelligent and searching, who have had a few hard knocks and are basically unsure of themselves, had a gift of making other people believe what he believed. He was a man of plans and ways. He made dreams sound more like goals. What was far away was really near.

"I want to do this partly for fun, which means I want to have a lot of sax solos," I told Will first off. We were sitting in his living room on one of those days at the end of winter in Wisconsin when you'd just as soon have it over with—if not winter, then your life. I was trying to think of everything I could in answer to Will's persuading me to join his band.

"We're going to have a lot of sax solos," Will said. "I imagine you'd take a ride on every tune."

Still young enough to remember my jealousy of the "other" tenor sax player in the college big band, of the guitar players in rock bands who got all the solos and attention, I thought that sounded pretty good.

"I need to make something of a living doing this," I added. "I don't want to have to go back to this speed reading jive."

"I've been on the road most of the last two years," Will said. "I know club owners, I've got contacts, I think there's a market for this. It's good music. And we'll have good musicians. Like you."

". . . Yeah, to make a living, but I don't want to do just commercial material. I'd like to have a variety of tunes. Just the same old three chords gets pretty boring. Tunes like 'Chameleon,' 'Since I Fell for You' will work . . ."

"I've got a whole list of tunes, and those two are already on it. I think we should do some jazz tunes, and R&B, maybe even some standards thrown in, some ballads. Do you have any ideas?"

The guys in that novelty band certainly hadn't asked my opinion about the choice of material. "How about 'Here's That Rainy Day?'" I asked.

"Let's see, how does that one go . . ."

I sang a few bars and recited the chords for Will, who strummed them on his unplugged guitar. "Of course we could do it as an instrumental, but people like to have the words, and if we're going to make some money, I guess someone could sing it."

"I think *you* should sing it," Will said.

My thinking stopped in its tracks. I'd never sung in a band before, not more than a few back-up lines in high school rock-and-roll groups, lines that often consisted of one syllable words like "Shout!" or "Hey!"

That night, I called Minneapolis and told the show band I wouldn't be making it to any more rehearsals.

After three quick weeks of working on tunes with Will and a drummer, we had our first gig at a local college bar on the street in town that was filled with college bars. I think it was a Thursday night before spring break because the place was packed. We didn't really have enough tunes yet to play four hours, so we had to stretch out on the ones we had, which meant long solos for me. We even had to repeat a few tunes. There were just four of us, and one of them was filling in—Jeff, a bass player friend of Will and mine from college, who was making a small fortune running the local music store. We all thought that he'd gotten his start-up cash selling dope, but either way he knew his business. We hadn't been able to find anybody permanent on bass yet, just one mark of how unprepared we were for this gig. But all of our friends were in the bar in anticipation.

And, for whatever reason, so was the rest of the town. People standing at the bar, people crowding the tables, people stuffing in through the door, as if the bar were some overstuffed suitcase. And most of all, people on the dance floor. Gyrating and drunk, laughing and down, lovin' the blues. Coyote Will's angular face took on the expressions of his highest notes. Lee "Boogey Shoes" Doerner, was introduced as "from Naples, Florida" (where he'd lived once) and "formerly of the Drifters" (with whom he filled in one night. "They were real dolts," Lee always said); Lee spiked his fat 2B drumsticks on the set in such a way that the beat was tangible as night. Jeff the bass player played as loud as I remember him playing in college jazz band rehearsals. And I sang "Here's That Rainy Day" with a smoothness that surprised even me, not to mention my friends.

And they loved us—my friends and those college kids and those people who poured in from the other bars on the street. Ten minutes after last call the people were still going wild, screaming for a second encore. We played "Seventh Son" again. It might have been the third time. I couldn't hear the lyrics right, the way they bounced around the room and off the beer signs and bar mirror and off the butts and backs of the dancers who, seen up high from the stage, looked like nothing as much as a very large ant farm. I never could catch the first line, which went something like, "I can tell your future just by lookin' at your past." Maybe that's the way Will Dowling sang it, even though I'm sure that's not the way Willie Dixon wrote it. Maybe that's what we believed—that given our separate pasts, musical and otherwise, our collective future was just bound to be better.

And so we played "Seventh Son" one last time for the crowd, and cop cars were beginning to cruise the street as they always did this close to 1:00 A.M. "Bar's closed," the fat bartenders bellowed. But they still couldn't get the people out.

"I didn't think Will knew what he was talking about," Jeff leaned over and said to me. A drunken college girl was trying to untie my shoelaces. "If I didn't have the music store, I'd keep doing this for sure. You guys are going to make a fortune."

Most writing about the blues as a philosophy or state of mind makes me wince because it's usually contrived to help somebody make money. A kid who grew up in a middle-class suburb pretends to be down and out or working class. I don't mean the way Will Dowling pretended to be Coyote Will, since we never made much off that, and it was a labor of love, not money. I mean a calculated cultivating of an image of the blues, a marketing device. I'm wary of those deep-chested singers who do a rap behind the drummer's heavy back beat and guitar's wail, who start sentences with "The blues is like . . . " as if these modern blues players didn't own microwave ovens, didn't have back yards or library cards or retirement savings.

In its contemporary context, I've always thought the blues was less a feeling or a way of life than it was three chords that got along with each other well, and a style of playing as dependable as it was boring after too long a time. But the blues depends on energy, ironically (more than finesse or even "soul"), and energy is the component of playing music that I had the most in abundance. Even as I admired most the dexterity and complexity of players like John Coltrane and Bill Evans who seemed less blues-influenced than most, what I did best at that time in my musical life was wail, honk, and growl on the saxophone. What I'm saying is that I was equipped to play the blues better than your average teacher of speed reading.

Most human effort culminates in failure. I'm not sure I want to say that in front of my children, even though it's true. I'm not sure I want too often to hear myself say it, since the undeniability of the fact makes it hard for me to get out of bed in the morning. Suffice it to say that success is overrated, unreal as television commercials and high school sports teams. Success, finally, isn't all that necessary.

We learn to live within the confines that reality sets for us. Not just race, class, and gender stacking the deck. Also politics and charm shuffling and dealing; obsession, foolishness, and luck telling us whether to stay or fold. One friend of mine says it's like a trajectory, that we're all bound by circumstance to a certain arc, but how far we progress along it is more or less a matter of individual agency. But as certain as the fall is the fact that we are probably not going to be what we dreamed we would someday be. At twenty-six, I still didn't know that. Nobody in the Burner Blues Band did. Finding that out: *that's what the blues is. . .*

For years afterward, I thought that if only we'd had a fifth member in the band, say a keyboard player or rhythm guitar player to fill out the sound, and if he'd been someone who sang better than Will, the band would have made it. Will's singing had improved a lot, said a friend who'd heard Will's last band. I'm sure it was true, but not true enough. Unlike any coyote I could think of, Will struggled with the high notes. That didn't prevent him for reaching for them, though, and I think people could tell. That and the fact that we took tempi too slow. People didn't know how to dance to blues that desperate and intense. Our blues wasn't good-time fare.

I had my part in the failings of the band: playing whole tone scales over Cannonball Adderly's "Work Song." Trying to sing like Frank Sinatra on "Here's That Rainy Day" ("One for my Baby" perhaps, but "Rainy Day"? In a blues band?) Trying to play the flute when I had never had a lesson. Taking long solos over every tune. But who else to do so? The bass player was hanging on for dear life. It's always hard to find a bass player—in any town, any style of music. We picked a folk guitar player we liked and sent him home with a pile of records and a rented Fender. His self-effacing walking fifth to root was a mantra, a foundation more than a groove.

But the band was not bad, good enough for the bars and parties we played. We were just stuck in the wrong time, which happened to be the present, and never established an identity with most other people living then.

"BERnard? That's the name of your new band?" one particularly offensive young faculty at the local college asked Coyote Will. "Couldn't it at least be berNARD?'"

She had a point. "Burner" sounded more like the name of an old racehorse than the title of the classic blues tune from which Will had lifted it. Maybe a distant cousin of "Hayseed" or "Bag o' Bones." No one could say "Burner" without thinking of burned out. Or Bunsen. Or a stove.

But as with everything else with the band, Coyote Will had a vision and because he was the leader and we at least knew that *we* didn't know what we were doing, we didn't try to talk him out of it ahead of time. After our first gig though, I forced a compromise. Instead of just "Burner," How about "Burner Blues Band"? At least that would identify the kind of music that we played. Good enough, except that in the world of disco and country, would that truth in labeling be an advantage? Or would it only ensure that we wouldn't get a foot in the barroom door? We'd try the new name, we agreed. Maybe that would make the difference.

If I tried now, I think I could list, though not remember, almost every gig we played over the following six months. We played the aptly named Corner Bar in River Falls, the one place that loved us without reservation, though even there we had to play for the door, so we never once topped a hundred bucks take home, and that had to cover expenses. Still, the audience at the Corner Bar was a bunch of graying hippies who all seemed to know each other and for whom dancing was an act of abstract expressionism. I remember liking them so much that at closing time once I sat on the edge of the stage and played to rapt attention a chorus of "In the Wee Small Hours of the Morning" a cappella while the other guys schlepped the amps into the trailer. Then we got invited to a party.

Somebody took pictures of the gig in La Crosse, some bigger nightclub along the Mississippi downtown, I think called "the Loading Dock," with décor to match. Years later I realized it was so named because people were supposed to get loaded there—pretty subtle for my beloved Wisconsin. I still have copies of the pictures. There are lots of shots of the band wailing, close-ups of me wailing, of Will or the bass and drums wailing. Coyote Will in his pink long-sleeved T-shirt, form fitting, collarless, with the row of little buttons down the front. Me in Levi's and a striped, crepe shirt, unblues-like. The background looking black and cool as a warehouse, which is what the place had been. Then, at the end of the roll, like a punch line, a shot of the four of us on break with our girlfriends (I was hanging around with a married older woman then; all part of my blues image, I think now). We all had chins on hands, nursing a beer, looking six or eight different ways at empty tables.

I remember some bars only as "the hot place" or "the small place." In the latter, we set up in a small back room behind a small and friendly bar, on a highway somewhere. The place had a window cut into the wall between bar and kitchen from which underpriced burger baskets would magically appear. The room we played in was so tiny that no one could sit inside it to listen—too loud. Everybody—everybody in town, I think, young and old in the best Wisconsin country bar tradition—drank out of sight in the adjoining barroom. But they liked us.

There was the one where a highway crossed a river—a bar where they rented inner tubes for people to float away summer evenings. All I remember about that gig was how hot it was outside, and that there was sand all over the dance floor. Nobody was there because they were all floating down the river. Then there was the gig in Upper Michigan, a five-hour drive in wintry March, far away from everything. We got there to find a homemade poster, in colored construction paper and magic marker. "BURNER," the big letters said, then sitting in each corner at an angle, "Rock" "Disco" "Funk""Country." We played what we always played. I had a cold, and took antihistamines between sets, drank Coke instead of beer to keep going. We were so broke we drove an hour south to my parents' uninsulated cottage to save on a motel bill and make the trip pay. We kept the fireplace going late nights, froze by morning, spent most of our bread on beer (we couldn't get Walter's), and had to slosh through icy puddles in the gravel tire track driveway to get to the car and back. It was miserable.

And there were the gigs close enough to home that our regulars would come out to hear us. One English professor friend who'd just left his wife was trying to have an affair with a new colleague. A lot of us had tried to have an affair with her, and most never got anywhere. But these two were always the first on the dance floor and they looked great, he not knowing, I imagine, whether to be angry or relieved he was out on the town; she, I imagine, happy for more attention from someone she could keep safely at arms' length. Another prof friend had better luck always than his newly divorced colleague, and would leave toward the beginning of the third set, a step and a half behind some much younger beauty. He clenched his cigarette in an understated grin, conspicuous and loving it.

There was a lesbian friend who complained regularly about the woman-beating lyrics of one tune we covered, and the tastelessness of others that described women's anatomies. It was a mark of the times, I think, that we played those songs, and that our friend came out to hear us anyway.

Most of the songs were harmless enough, though. I can remember our first set, worked out in order. We started always with "What a Difference a Day Makes," by Esther Phillips, then Horace Silver's "Sister Sadie," followed I think by "Soul Man"—this before the Blues Brothers' version made the tune acceptable again. The problem was that no one in the audience had heard of the first two tunes, and the third they thought of as an "old" song, a novelty. Their confused silence after the first two tunes gave way to a knowing smile after the third: So it *is* a joke, I could hear them think.

There was our Wilson Pickett medley: "Midnight Hour" and "Mustang Sally," both sung by Lee the drummer in his pseudo black soul voice: "HUH. UGH. LOOKIE HERE" and the like. Even in 1979 I had to laugh—only because he did it so well. It wasn't politically incorrect, if the term had existed in those days. Raspy-voiced Lee really liked the music, and it made him smile.

But people who want to dance want to make love or have sex, and people wanting that, young people at least, don't want music to be funny. We did about a twenty-minute version of Herbie Hancock's "Chameleon"—this right as funk was dying. And what did they make of my wail on "Georgia on My Mind"? Of Will's strained vocal on "If Lovin' You Is Wrong (I Don't Wanna Be Right)"? In one of the sets we actually played the samba from the Brazilian movie *Black Orpheus*. In each of our venues we were the only band to have that tune on our list. Ever.

Somehow Will got us a job at the Alma Center High School prom, for which we were ill-suited, but it didn't matter since the kids were eager to get out of the dance and go drink and party and park with their dates. We made more money there than on any gig we had. I think the gig had been booked a year in advance for Will's old band, which played the kind of rock-and-roll that might hold a high school kid's attention a little ways past the grand march.

Alma Center was a farm town in some rolling hills a two-lane road away from the interstate. The couples danced close to "Since I Fell For You," as I played that crystalline and bluesy melody. How foreign to them, that sound, more even than the body of their partner! How small we all seemed, the little band, the little number of couples, in the big gym empty and dark, in the world that would grow bigger for all of us too soon. Everybody was enjoying the slow dance, and so I played another chorus, and Will sang one, and Will played one, and I played one. Everybody in the universe knows that song: some poor sap leaves his happy home for a temptress—and on "leaves" the melody whines up to that flatted third, that blues smile. And from there the grand generalization: Life brings misery and pain. Life is bad. And of course he still loves her anyway. Wherever she is. Everybody in the universe knows that song. Except those kids we were playing it for.

When we finished the grand march, everyone left, and we packed up a set early, our pockets stuffed with money from the student council. One of the chaperones, a social studies teacher, told us how much he dug the band.

Why are these four men standing along the shoulder of the interstate highway, hazard lights flashing on their stuffed, light blue, ten-year-old Pinto hatchback, and on the rented trailer from Brackett Avenue Sinclair, the young men pissing, after a twelve pack of Walter's beer for the ride home (beyond whatever they drank during the gig)? What's more, why, after driving for two hours and working for four, and doing so for twenty-five bucks a man, minus what they paid Sinclair for the trailer and Walter's for the beer, why are they smiling, why are they happy? Why are they happy not only as they're being remembered, but happy even in that moment?

After all, things are not so good and won't get better soon. One of them, the sax player, after those six months of spring and summer at home as a musician, will have to go back on the road teaching speed reading. That September he is off to Alma, Michigan; Norton, Mass.; and points beyond in the academic galaxy. After the deliberation of blues, he speeds up until he could speed up no more. Another of them, Lee "Boogie Shoes" Doerner, the drummer, after the band's gigs wither away to none, will round up all the Walter's empties in the house to take to Super America to buy cigarettes. He thinks he might go back to Texas and work in his father's plastics factory, and so he does. He never has to play the drums again. And so he never plays the drums again, or sings with his raspy voice in a smile. And Ted the bass player (his parents are both college professors), has already gotten his GED and he thinks if he gets steady work he can marry his girlfriend, and so he does and so he does. He will buy a car he can sit up straight in, go back to strumming acoustic guitar. The Burner Blues Band doesn't break up. It winds down. And when Will Dowling gets an offer to teach freshman English in Illinois, Coyote Will will have to go back from wherever he came.

But the four young men don't know this now, yet even not knowing, why do they smile and inhale the smoke and the stars, just as they did the stares of the uncomprehending farm kids, the red noise of the juke box on breaks, the dim lights of the small Wisconsin service stations, their own modest ambitions passing for a dream. Why don't they pack up their smiles with their cynicism in that crowded car?

So my point is that the beer was pretty good. Coyote Will pops the top on the first Walter's in the front seat of the Pinto on the way back from Tony or River Falls, Spread Eagle or Somerset. Lee is driving since it's his car and he knows how to coax it up hills. In the back seat Ted and I don't see much of the Wisconsin landscape going by out the little back windows in the dark. We're sitting back there as straight as we can so we don't get beer down our chins.

"No other taste like it," Coyote Will reflects as the interstate night grows warmer, almost curved with the road over which it hangs. And of course we agree. "The Beer That Is Beer," the enigmatic slogan proclaims on the bottle. We can read it by dome light.

And we were the blues that is blues. And that's why.

Red

Carol Guess

I am fifteen and I have no name, but I am learning how to get into a car without showing my underwear to the men surrounding me.

A woman is teaching me.

She has long nails, a short skirt, willowy heels.

"Girls," she says. There are ten of us in beauty school, ages thirteen to thirty-nine. "Girls, pretend you are surrounded by handsome men. One of them opens the car door for you. How do you enter?"

I begin by imagining the men in great detail. I give them faces and names because one of them might be my husband. When it's my turn, I totter in my spiky heels to the center of the circle. I sit in the passenger seat, my back to the driver, and swing my legs gracefully, torso twisting in sync.

"Now get out," she says.

And later: *remember to keep your knees shut tight, like a secret you can't tell.* Her nails are red. One of the men I imagine is real. He has a name and a face and a zippy red car. He is ten years older than me, and a bad driver.

After everyone has had her turn in and out of the car, we leave the parking garage and return to the classroom. One by one we strip to our underwear, step on the scale, and sink.

Think about numbers for the first time that week.

When I step on the scale, the women surround me. I feel their stares like heat on my shoulders and thighs. One writes the number in a folder; another tugs on her straps—powder blue. There is so much lace in the room. It makes me happy. At fifteen I like lace and complicated colors—mauve, violet, silver. I like frills and words such as "full-face" and "uplift." They assuage my fears that I do not fit in, fears I cannot name because I cannot point to anything different about me. I look like all the other fifteen-year-olds at my high school: thin, diffident, pastel. We are all anorexic and painfully, almost parodically, feminine. We look like drag queens, except for Jessica, a star on the swim team.

She looks like a linebacker.

I avoid her.

My locker is covered with pictures of ballerinas. At fifteen, for reasons I can't explain, I flip through dance magazines, culling pictures of muscular male stars, which I paste carefully over the bodies of Suzanne Farrell, Kyra Nichols, and Heather Watts. When I get to my favorite photo, of Heather Watts twisted into a pretzel, I can't bring myself to cover her with Peter Martins. Instead I leave her, a tiny woman with legs muscled into perfect figure eights, suspended like a question. I also pin up pictures of girls I dance with, their legs twisted into cautious letters. I would like a picture of the man with the red car, but he laughs when I say I want one for my locker.

When he calls, my mother summons me from the bedroom lair where I am sprawled on my bed eating rice cakes and drinking diet soda. She murmurs his name in a studied whisper, but her eyes betray her pleasure. Because I don't have makeup on, I feel self-conscious. I twirl my hair around my finger and shift from foot to foot.

He is a bad driver because I distract him.

At least, this is what he tells me. But when I say *sorry*, he puts his hand on my thigh and twists the steering wheel in an abrupt, deliberate jerk. He was my brother's babysitter last summer, while my parents were in Europe and I was at dance camp. My brother liked him, his roguishness, the thick shock of pale hair falling over his left eye. They played good games, my brother says—catch and half-court and Pac-Man—and ate McDonald's six nights out of nine. He was a good babysitter, my parents agree, and when he calls to ask if I want to go for a walk in Larrett Park one Saturday, I imagine we will play good games, too.

Thirty minutes before he arrives at the house, I am lounging in my bedroom, biting my nails and reading teen magazine articles on bulimia. I am thinking about throwing up, how it would feel, what my mouth would taste like after. In one story a girl eats half a cake and two pints of ice cream before she lets the food slide from her gut to her throat to her lips, then rejects it. I love the articles, love the descriptions before the girl vomits—the decadence of the orgy, the long lists of forbidden foods.

I am daydreaming about ice cream when my mother knocks. She looks startled to find that I am in my nightgown. Her whole face contracts into a clock. "He'll be here in half an hour," she says, folding her hands over and over. They look like water as she waves me into the bathroom, as she sits me on the toilet lid and begins to do my face.

When the man with the red car arrives, I am ready. I am wearing a short black skirt safety-pinned around my thinning middle, a long velour black sweater, and a gargantuan pink bow at the back of my head. My bracelets and earrings make a great deal of noise as we walk around the park. Once I burp. I am mortified. He pretends not to hear and when no one is looking, plucks a rare flower and tucks it behind my ear.

In beauty school I am learning about illusion—how to create the simulacrum of depth. When I make up my lips I use a pale, creamy base to destroy their actual shape, so that the face in the classroom mirror has no mouth. Then I outline a new set of lips with brick-red pencil and fill in the outline with movie-star red. For the finale, I smudge a dab of light pink in line with my nose, at the center of the bow-shape everyone in class is envious of.

Once I emerge with a spectacular Betty Boop smirk that Tara, our Tri Delta coed, singles out with the right index finger of her French manicure. "You look twenty-one," she says, her voice a mixture of envy and something else. I don't like the envy, but I like her gesture, which happens in slow motion. I even remember touch, soft soft at my skin, but perhaps I made that up, or make it up now—me, Carol, the storyteller.

The day of our walk in the park, our first time alone together, the man with the red car drops me off in time for dinner. I thank him and ask if he'd like to come inside and visit my brother.

He is, after all, the babysitter.

He cocks his head. His right eye is autumn-amber. "I didn't come for your brother," he says. And he reaches for my lips with his whole hand.

After our lessons, after we have created our faces for the week, we put cheesecloth bags over our heads before we tug our smocks off. The bags emerge stained with cheeks, eyes, lips, as the pink of our smocks is replaced by cool tans and crisp navys. We learn to fix snags in our hose with nail polish, spreading the sticky stuff over the runs carefully, without concern for the flesh beneath. We learn to fix anything that runs, sags, or bleeds with acrylic and cotton, bobby pins and saccharine.

Every week we weigh ourselves. Although I hate the scale's bold proclamations, hate the tears of the women who have come for this reason, I love the flowers we become when we strip down to our bras and panties. The older women wear sophisticated colors—greens, grays, violets that shimmer when they brush past me, biting their lips. We leave our jewelry on, but not our heels; they lie jumbled in a pile like obscure weaponry. Once, as I am tugging my skirt back over my hips, Tara leans toward me, still shirtless, and congratulates me on losing another pound. In the grace of her gesture I see only a shadow, the faint darkness of a line where her cream-colored push-up bra cups meet in a satin bow. My difference is there, in that moment; though I write it off as envy, as wanting to be like Tara, some part of my mind knows it is something else.

In the lunchroom at school, Jessica passes my table carrying a tray filled with food. My friends and I tug the foil tops off plain yogurt, exchange carrot sticks, sip diet soda through bendable straws. When Jessica returns for seconds before Nancy has even finished her symmetrical apple slices, Claire nudges me and I take care of it.

"*Hungry,*" I hiss. The other girls pick it up. *Hungry,* then *Greedy,* then, although Jessica is muscular, a swimmer, *Fatty.*

Fatty becomes *Lezzie.*

And I am safe.

In beauty school I am learning about perspective. One day my teacher, Glory Sue, hands me a bra with breasts already in it. They are flesh-colored, though not the color of my flesh, mottled pink and freckled, nor the color of Jasmine's, dark brown with red undertones, but the fragile jaundice-yellow of a sickly baby, whiny and urine-scented, longing for milk. The cloth around the breasts is red—red satin—and Glory Sue winks as she hands it over. When I fold it double, the cups make a hand puppet, red mouth without a voice. Years later, I find it wadded in the back of my dresser and tie it to a doorknob, knowing my cat will show no mercy, knowing that animals use things in useful ways.

He parks the red car where no one will see its color. He wanted hunter or pewter, something masculine, something stark. Instead there is this red, and me, spread open. I watch the stars through the window when I'm on my back. On my belly, there's nothing to see, so I close my eyes. Once, in the middle of a contortion, he bursts out laughing. When I sit up, frightened, he is holding the red bra.

When he drops me off, the house is dark. In the morning I eat breakfast with my brother, who calls me a slut until our mother shushes him.

At Christmas the man with the red car's parents give me a necklace—a tiny amber bead encased in gold. They hand me the package, then go into the living room and drink cocktails with my parents. When I show my mother the necklace, she holds it in her palm for a long while. There is something in her eyes; I can't name it. When she gives it back, the amber feels warm.

When the man with the red car comes to our door, my mother checks my makeup and my father hands me money. Every week, excluding holidays,

I earn ten dollars because I pocket the cash. It's meant to cover the usual fancies. But the man with the red car pays for everything, so I think of my time with him as free.

He comes. My parents welcome him. Often he sits inside for several minutes, joshing about stock options, baseball, films. He is serious and pseudo-intellectual, which suits his startling eyes and golden hair. He lives with his parents because he is struggling to open his own law business—at twenty-five, no less! *Wunderkind,* my parents joke when they think I can't hear them. They both kiss my forehead before I leave the house. They don't wait up, but they show their concern for our safety—his as well as mine—in the bend that signals *kiss.* Then my father opens the door and everyone watches as I leave the house first. Once, when I turn back, the man with the red car is standing between my parents, the longed-for son of their senior years.

He opens the car door for me. I totter in my spiky heels to the car's gaping red mouth. I sit in the passenger seat, my back to the driver, and swing my legs gracefully, torso twisting in sync.

"Now get out," he says later. We are parked in a deserted lot. The railway station shimmers, ghostly; I will remember its faint outlines better than his hands. I will remember the ghostly silhouettes of buildings, benches, tracks, and the whistle of the trains that pass by but don't stop. Years later, when I see steamed-up cars, I will wonder if the girl waited for her date to open her door and help her out, then into the backseat; if the seat belts left bruises; if the radio was on.

Sometimes he says my name.

At first I don't understand that the moment of naming precedes expulsion. I think that my name, shifting between his lips, is a gift, a moment of identification. But the name is a release, a rush of air that parallels the rush his body makes, all strength and density. No part of me admires it; there is nothing beautiful in it, though years later I will fall in love with a man and try to understand what he calls *pleasure.* But for now there is only the dark triangle his body makes, hovering, and his words, sounds really, letters chosen not for meaning but for motion.

Sometimes he says my name, but that name never reaches the world beyond his car. In school I take a nickname, while he calls me by my birth name. In school the kids call me *Kate* and the letters do not remind me of him.

I am safe. And thin. In beauty school we fix dinner at the end of every lesson—vegetables wilting like sylphs dying onstage. We eat carefully, admiring each other's manners, sticking to the assigned topics: movies, weather, domesticated animals, art.

And Him.

"The key to a successful date is to make him feel like a Great Man."

We learn to listen to men, to nod, to agree. We learn *yes yes yes* and *thank you please.*

Years later I take a self-defense class. The first thing the instructor asks us to do is scream. Around me women open their mouths and form the nameless syllables that signify fear. I open my mouth, too, widening the lips my grandmother bequeathed me, the bow-shaped lips that are the only thing linking me to her ghost, to the woman I believe would have understood me. I open my mouth and inhale, silent.

The instructor is gentle with me. But I leave the class crying because I cannot scream.

The man with the red car makes small talk with me, shies away from anything serious. Once I mention the word *abortion* and he frowns, so I know exactly how he feels. I am in tune with him, with his red car; I am empathetic and sympathetic both; I make him feel a Great Man. In turn, he tells me I am beautiful, desirable, a rare flower.

But in the mirror at school, I do not look beautiful. His stubbled cheeks leave scratches, as if someone has struck a match against my skin. I am thin, thinner, thinnest. My friends and I pretend not to notice as each of us picks at her lunch.

One day I am in the bathroom, redoing my lips—two colors only, I do not have time for my mouth to vanish and return—when Jessica bustles in. I pretend I'm not watching as she rummages for change.

When her search fails, when her palms come up empty from her pockets, she turns to me and asks for what she needs in a surprisingly soft, low voice.

I am startled. No one—not one of my friends—still bleeds. No one weighs enough. It is understood that to bleed is to be fat.

I put the cap on my lipstick. She is looking at me and when I turn away from her eyes in the mirror, I look at the floor. It will be years before I understand that the something else she sees in my eyes before I turn away, the gaze that takes in her solid body, her incautious gestures, her gentle muscularity, is desire.

Yes yes yes.

Thank you.

I do.

Sometimes he asks why I'm so quiet. Once, we watch a film in which the heroine whispers sexy things to her husband. After the film is over, he picks at his hamburger.

"Can't you be more like that?"

I try.

I try to speak, to say things that will light the dark hum of the red car. But years later, in college, four boys will surround me on a dark walkway, surround me and begin, inexplicably, to tickle, then kiss me. The kisses will feel sharp, like needle pricks. And I will stand, shouting distance from a clump of passersby, shouting distance from students clustered at the steps of the library, and my throat will dry and my body will harden and I will not be able to make the sounds that might save me.

In school I stop speaking. My teachers appreciate my polite, discreet presence. My teachers are men, and we do not read books by women. The women in the books we do read are quiet—victims, mothers, maids. My teachers tell me I am a good listener. They suggest I apply to Ivy League schools like other promising students, white, wealthy students, students who have attended private schools like mine, students like me.

Somehow I doubt the existence of others like me.

But I hide my sense of my difference. When my teachers comment admiringly on my poise, my sweetness, my dresses, I smile, knowing perfectly well by now what effect that has. I am a dancer. I know how to work an audience. At night, in the red car, I perform.

My real self, the girl between two names, is somewhere else.

Years later I will find that place useful for hiding, for avoiding the reality of a lover who has changed, her face mirroring the man who has stolen from her what I am also missing. The something else in her eyes will shift and smoke, becoming fear. I will watch her as she hovers over me, a dark triangle, watch my lover become the thing I am most afraid of, simply because she is afraid of me.

I will fantasize about killing him, her father. I will fantasize about it in great detail, until one day in my fantasy his face, the face I know only from photographs, becomes the face of the man with the red car.

At home, in the vestibular space of my bedroom, between my parents' world, the red car, dancing, and school, I write poems. In the poems I am water, and the man with the red car is a duck. I slide down his back in drops.

In my journal I write that I love him, that I want to marry him.

And so I stop eating, because I cannot find a way to reconcile the worlds I inhabit, and because starvation is the only speech I can afford.

Sometimes, like the goose girl in my favorite fairy tale, I speak to a familiar, hoping my familiar will answer. One day I am talking to the man with the red car. He is eating a sundae and I am watching. I ask him one of the questions they've taught us in beauty school: *if you were an animal, what would you be?*

He does not have to think it over. "A squirrel," he says, and I can tell he's proud. He slurps the last of his sundae through a straw. He does not ask what I would be.

I think to myself, *I would be a man.*

It is 1986.

When I move to New York City for college, I find it smeared in blood. There are bloody handprints everywhere, prints of names, names of politicians. I read the posters as I rush to the studio each morning—*Mayor Koch, Our Blood Is On Your Hands,* then a logo I don't understand, a pale pink triangle. *Act Up* it says, and *Silence Equals Death.* But death feels far away; silence, necessary.

In college I study English with a Great Man. I love his excitement at a strong line, a keen metaphor. I love his excitement, but when I whisper this to the girl next to me, he slams his hand on the podium angrily.

"I won't have you talking about me," he says, his voice husky with cigarettes. Later, I learn that he is sleeping with her. He praises her body to us on the many days that she is absent.

After class, girls whisper to each other: *don't let him shut the door to his office when he asks you in.* When the Great Man asks me in, I stand in the crevice the door makes, triangular, afraid of the bright light of his desk lamp and the blue light of his eyes. He hands me a copy of his latest book, then summons me closer so he can sign it. The book is complicated and clever; inside the word *lips* appears many times.

I take four classes with him so that I can learn to be a writer. We do not read a single woman author. Once someone asks why, waving his arm from the back row like an alarm that has suddenly decided to go off.

The Great Man answers without losing his place in *The Waste Land.* "There are no British or American women writers worth reading."

"Dickinson?"

"Too domestic."

"Plath?"

"Too angry."

"Woolf?"

"Derivative."

"Stein?"

He laughs. "I think Stein's problem is self-evident."

I am sitting two rows from the front, vibrating with a new understanding of how a poem is composed. The Great Man has given me Stevens; he has given me Pound. He has also taught me the difference between bad and good poetry. When he asks us to write for his class, I know that I must not write about the man with the red car. That would be an angry poem, or maybe a domestic poem, or, worse, an angry domestic poem. That would be, I now know, a bad poem.

Instead I write sonnets about clouds, six each semester. Twenty-four poems about terrible weather. Sometimes, while I am writing, my pen skids to a stop before *nimbus,* before *cumulus.* Sometimes I see no point in finishing that week's poem, however fluffy the cloud, however silver its lining, simply because I am a woman, and women, as I now know, write bad poetry.

I get an A.

One of the boys asks me what I did to make the grade.

At night, after class, I ride the subway to my apartment. One of the girls from class rides as far as my stop. Often we sit across from each other, acknowledging each other's presence only by proximity. I know she sees me; I know she knows that I see her.

It takes me a month to realize who she reminds me of.

By then I feel it, the something else I cannot name. There are jokes—gay people call it gaydar—about the thrill and terror of recognition, about its power. But there is no proper name for what I feel and, without a name, without witness, Jessica's bond with me vanishes, becomes wholly body, body and then energy, energy and then vibration, motion without signifier, unrecordable.

I do not see her.

The joke goes, "She could've saved you five years."

But I deny her. I turn from Jessica's new incarnation, this woman who sees through me, who inspires in me a charged knowledge that elaborates, magically, on something I do not yet claim. She sits across from me on the subway, dyke Christ to my Judas, vowing to haunt me. And I see Jessica after Jessica, year after year, until I finally give in and open my mouth in an ecstatic communion.

I come to hate studying. Thin, too thin, I have trouble concentrating. Words waver in front of my eyes. When I faint, the stairs to my brownstone redden and dissolve to dark.

For several days I cannot leave my apartment. Every time I begin a task, fears stall me, until unlocking the door is impossible. I pace, taking pieces of myself apart, until I am saved by a crack whore.

Her name is Corinne.

Her name is Corinne, and she lives down the hall. I know she is a whore because her clients ride the elevator with her, and because her pimp stalks her. Once, I step off the elevator to find him pounding on her door, first with a folding chair, then with his thick body.

"Corinne, goddammit, open the fucking door! Prazzie wants to see you, you shitty slut. Corinne!"

I know she's on crack because she buys in the park two blocks away, out in the open the way crack deals happen in my neighborhood, her palm glowing with light, with the tiny glass vials.

The week I cannot leave my apartment, Corinne breaks the spell, pounding on my door one sweaty midnight. Her desperation does something to my nervous obsessiveness and I open the door in a rush of glad freedom. All she wants is rubbing alcohol. In exchange, she lets me visit her apartment to see her murphy bed and seven cats.

I tell the man with the red car that there will be no more visits. His phone calls stalk me, plaintive and poignant, his grief at our breakup similar to the sound of the girls I dance with when they puke in the sink. Eventually the calls stop and the lies begin—lies to my parents, who still hope for a wedding.

I am distracted for the next several years. The man with the red car has distracted me. But I do not blame him. I look at my lips in the mirror—bow-shaped, like my grandmother's. She was a singer, but instead of a voice, she bequeathed me her lips.

Her name was Buena Vista—*good view.*

Her marriage to my grandfather saved the family farm.

I like my lips. I do not blame him, the man with the red car, for wanting to touch them. I look in the mirror every morning before I make up my face with all that red. Sometimes, thinking of Tara, I touch myself.

The smile I see isn't mine.

It will be years before I bleed again, before the color red means something else. It will be years before I drive myself, long hours on a deserted highway, to see a woman with red hair. It will be years before someone watches me eat, watches my lips with a stare that is neither calculated nor appraising, but wicked. It will be years before wickedness appeals to me, before I stop wearing pink, before a red car means little or nothing, before the face in the mirror opens its plain mouth to speak.

"Do you have anything darker?" my girlfriend asks the skeptical blonde behind the counter. We are shopping for lipstick because I want to kiss her and leave prints.

"I'll go check," the salesgirl says, and heads for the back of the store.

She does not return.

So we steal things—silver eyeliner, blue nail polish, men's cologne. For a week, on a dare, my lover and I wear blue nail polish until it scabs off and we find ourselves picking at it with our teeth. But for that week, her hands on my flesh look like bruises, as if someone has hit my thighs, arms, belly. Her hands on my flesh look ugly, and I beg her to remove the color, to make her nails clear again.

For our beauty school graduation dinner, we're instructed to bring something fattening—something *sinful*, Glory Sue says. I bake a pumpkin pie. When it is cool, I cover it in plastic, tucking in its edges.

Years later, I will enter my lover's kitchen, lured by a sweet cinnamon scent, buttery and warm. "Pie," she says. "Sweet potato." We stand in the kitchen, sipping coffee, waiting for it to cool. When it is done, she cuts two large slices and motions me to join her. She walks through the kitchen, living room, hallway. I follow her, and I follow the pie. She pushes open the door to our bedroom with her shoulder, flicks the light with her wrist. Then she sets both plates on the bedstand and sits on the quilt.

The slices are wrapped; for a moment I think she wants me to touch and taste through plastic. Instead she smiles, removing the barrier.

The beauty school classroom mirrors are veiled in gauzy streamers; at the center of the room is a table draped in silver cloth. We place our pies, cakes, cookies, and pastries in a seductive chorus line and then stand, soldiers at a peep show.

We wait for the word.

Eat.

We expect to hear it any minute. But we are well-trained; we do not flinch. We watch each other through the streamer-draped mirror and we do not know that we are watching hunger.

Glory Sue hands each of us a rolled-up certificate, stamped with a red seal. Her lips part. Again we expect it: *eat.* Instead she stands with her back against the table. "Girls," she says, and she does not mean *women,* "thank you for your participation."

Years later a student enters my office and drops a paper on my desk. Before I glance at it, she rolls up her sleeves. Outside, it is raining; the light in my office is pewter-blue. Through the gloom, I notice that her arms are covered with bracelets. As my vision adjusts, I realize they are scars.

Her name is sweet; her hands are graceful. In the faint light we look at each other and do not say a word. We do not need to; we speak the way women have always spoken to each other. My face tells her I will remember; her body tells me she trusts nobody.

When she leaves, her inked-up paper clutched so tight I know her scars must sting, I bend my head to my book again. I try to bring myself back, back to language, back to the words that will make her tale untrue. I try to read my way out of what I've seen, but the letters won't let me. Late late nights and early mornings I write, trying desperately to communicate without using my body, sick of knowing only that one language, the language of flesh and blood and pain. I want access to the words men use. I want in, into the club, where the light is strong and arms can carry someone. I want to enter. And I realize that I have known this from the beginning.

Glory Sue's lips part again.

"Touch yourselves."

We look down, at our red shoes.

"Touch yourselves." She puts her hands on her waist. "I want you to feel how fat food has made you. *This,*" and she pinches her flesh until her fingers are full, "is cake. *This* is pie. Feel it. Feel your fatness. Feel how much of yourself you would like to slice off."

At first we're shy. We aren't used to our own skin. Mine feels flaky, dry, crusted. Beside me, Tara gnaws on her thumb. But soon someone puts a hand on her upper arm.

"I hate this," she says. "How it jiggles. I wish I could cut it off."

We begin to move.

Jasmine puts one hand on her hips; someone else cups her breasts in both hands and bends forward. I touch my nose. Tara puts both hands on her legs; I see her in the mirror. I watch as she runs both hands up and down her thighs, over and over. Soon I follow, imitating her, running my hands up and down my thighs, over and over, along with her, dispossessing my flesh. We touch ourselves, cutting our limbs in half, winnowing and winnowing, and it feels, even now, describing it, like bloody handprints marking every inch wretched.

I see Tara in the mirror, undoing herself. She is watching her own hands, her own eyes. But in the midst of our feast, her gaze meets mine. We stare at each other in the glass, we stare, and the cutting, the severing, the slicing and winnowing become something else. I watch her watch me, my hands on my thighs, and I watch her hands reply, parting her lips.

It will be years before I can name the something else in her eyes, before a woman names the something else in mine. It will be years before I can name it, desire; years before a woman bleeds into my hands and I think *yes yes* this is what blood is for, salt and not cotton, *yes yes* this and not children, *yes yes* and *please.* It will be years before I learn to scream, before my name matches the mirror, before the words I speak spell something besides *rape* and the foods I eat become poetry; it will be years before I name the difference, name it *desire,* name it *anger,* name it after a color women feel but cannot see. ■

Riot

Joelle Fraser

Female Visitors
Items Not Allowed:

Tank tops
Halter tops
Shirts/tops which bare the midriff
Low cut, sleeveless, or cutout shirts
Shirts, blouses or dresses which expose undergarments, cleavage or back
Culottes, skirts, dresses shorter than one inch above the top of the kneecap
Wrap around type skirts, shirts or dresses with full length openings
Dresses or skirts too tight to allow pat search of inner leg
Clothing with holes
Spandex, lycra, or other rubberized or elasticized garments
Garments made of sheer or transparent fabric
Bib style attire
Swimsuits

I ask myself on the drive west out of Spokane, the empty road cutting through wasted snow, snow no longer smooth after weeks of dry cold. I ask myself because others ask me. Why not the high school, the nursing home? Why a prison? A men's prison, medium security. My students could be murderers or rapists, drug dealers, sent to this eastern Washington facility for the rest of their terms. But these men need help also, I remind those others. It's easy to talk of the cathartic benefits of writing classes—*it's an expressive outlet.* I can explain myself and be admired for my courage and altruism.

The truth is I don't expect to make much of a difference. I've volunteered because I'm getting something out of it. These men are the forgotten, the outsiders. I want to get close to their dark territory, to get close to the edge of whatever shadow it is. The thought unnerves me and I turn up the radio. In the distance the prison is lit up, a stadium for the fallen, and all around it is dark.

卐 卐 卐

The first night of class, I'm hidden in a black tunic of a sweater, the neck choking me. Wool tights confine my legs under a dark skirt. As advised, I wear flat shoes that I can run in. Over the weeks, I'll shed clothes the way some women shed inhibitions, carefully and one at a time. On the night of the fight, I'll be wearing a T-shirt and black, narrow pants.

I look up and Mike, who's here for drug running, is staring at me. "You're so intelligent," he says. He says it like he wants to say something else. Certain personal comments are ok: *Are you a writer? You are a good teacher.* But other comments are off limits: *You're in good shape—do you work out?* His hair is glossy, caught in a long ponytail. He is not handsome, but there is something.

The volunteer coordinator had warned us many times that the men are manipulative. Do not bring them stamps or newspapers. Tell them nothing personal. They will use it against you. Mike has a son with cerebral palsy he has not seen in three years, and one day he passes me a note: "Can you help me find my boy?"

卐 卐 卐

Offender Manipulation

1. *Be aware of the verbal and non-verbal messages you send, watch body language.*
2. *Know your personal and professional goals. Understand your value system.*
3. *Learn to be assertive and use the word "NO" appropriately.*
4. *Do not do anything you would be ashamed to share with your peers or supervisor.*

After class I drive the streets of Spokane, the sprawl of the city surrounded by dark prairie. I've been here two years and still feel like a stranger. No one's waiting for me; my husband is not at home. He's bought a business that is losing money faster than he can make it. He comes home rarely and when he does, he sometimes walks through the house and stares out the window or sits and looks at his hands. One day, he will watch as I leave.

When I do see him it is like having a stranger in the home, though this is really *his* home; I was brought into it like a mail-order bride, the place already fully furnished and stocked. In the middle of the night I go to the other bedroom, where the sheets are as cool as damp cloths against fevered skin. I stretch my arms and legs. Later, when he discovers I'm gone, he will sometimes stand over the bed, deciding whether to wake me, or perhaps just looking at me. I pretend I am asleep. When he does not come home, I stay in our bed and make it mine.

⌐ ⌐ ⌐

Miguel writes sometimes in Spanish. *Hace mucho tiempo que yo he sido con una mujer.* I think he writes both what he wants me to know and not to know. Years ago, in college, I spent a summer in Mexico with a boyfriend. We lived in a tent and got stoned every day and drank Coronas the temperature of piss. We surfed when we could and afterwards he'd pour a gallon of water over my head, but it was never enough, my skin always itchy and raw from the salt. One day at dawn, four *federales* searched our campsite and our car, and after taking the last six joints one of them scrawled a ticket for $214, which happened to be the exact amount we had left. One of the men, younger than I, traced his gun between my breasts, but he looked me in the eye.

Sometimes after reading Miguel's work I dream in Spanish: *jugar* means to play. *Calor* is hot, *frio* is cold. The word for broken is *roto*, but it can be applied only to an object, not to a person. You could not say, for example, *Ella es una persona rota.*

⌐ ⌐ ⌐

The men in my class aren't supposed to ask if I'm married. That's a "boundary issue." But I know they wonder. I don't wear my ring. I am full of secrets they sense but cannot name. This is supposed to be a one-way street, where they write their history and memory for me and I respond with encouragement: *powerful; great image; I like this opening.* But it's deeper than that for me, and perhaps they know I want something from them, some kind of knowledge or intimacy. Over time I begin to feel I should give something back. If I wanted, I could reveal the truths of my life one at a time, in subtle ways; for instance: *This passage really captures the isolation one can feel in a marriage.*

The house is carpeted thickly, even the bathrooms, orange stuff crawling up the base of the walls like thick fur. I can walk around and make no sound. No one would know I'm here. I disappear in my home which is not my home. The men at the prison. Do they miss carpet? I would tell them they're not missing anything.

⧉ ⧉ ⧉

I teach the class with Kelly, who is athletic and nice-looking in a wholesome way. She is nervous and concerned about her appearance. She puts on chapstick with strokes that flatten her pale lips and asks me if it's too glossy. I consider telling her the truth, that it doesn't matter, that the men will look at her mouth anyway, but I just tell her no, it's not too glossy. My husband told me I could teach in a garbage bag and it would make no difference. One day she says to me after a class: "Mike, the one in the ponytail. I don't like the way he looks at you."

We never asked about the backgrounds of our six students. It might prejudice us. "I don't want to know," she told me, which made sense to me. But we find out anyway, learn that Ron, who always comes early and is quick to laugh, had been raised in a Satanic cult, where he did "a lot of bad things." He's a Born Again now, and absently rubs the crucifix that dangles from his neck, as if for good luck. Mike is half Lakota, and if any of the men make me nervous, it is Mike. He seems to be the most aware of the fact that we are women. Jim always wears sunglasses, which he'll take off halfway through the class, and an old jean jacket. He is handsome in an easy, rugged sort of way, the kind of man who could pick up a girl in a country bar. He likes to write about his days in San Francisco in the sixties.

If any of them have raped or killed, we'll never know. Sometimes, during a class, I find myself thinking of the lies I'd told in my life, the hurt I'd caused because of weakness or apathy. I thought about the time in high school when I stuffed a shirt in my jacket and walked, robotlike with terror, to another store, where I wandered aimlessly until the woman who had seen me do it found me. A policeman gave me a ride home, and I was full of a shame so hot it seemed to sweat from my very skin.

⧉ ⧉ ⧉

It's always tense when we arrive. We know what will happen, because it happens every time. On the way to the educational building we have to cross the yard. It is winter and the sidewalk curves a path through dirty snow. Later in the spring, the snow will melt to reveal the bare ground. Thirty yards to our left is the gym. Men flock to the window and begin beating on it and shouting, their need both angry and desperate. The sound is muffled, a distant poundingpounding, the frenzy a blur in my peripheral vision. Kelly and I don't speak of it. What we have caused by our presence:

it is both a power and a powerlessness, and it is too big for us. We ignore it, which perhaps makes them more crazy.

After the first time, I follow Kelly's example and no longer look at them—that's what women are supposed to do. (But I want to look. A part of me even likes it. To see all that power, that self-control, *vanished.*) Instead I focus on details, the white cauliflower of a hearing aid in an inmate's ear; the tips of cigarette butts in the snow; a rabbit in the distance, bounding as if spooked. Later, I avert my eyes because it is enough to see them in my dreams, where sometimes they break through that window and hunt me down.

卐 卐 卐

In the Event of a Riot

1. *Stay clear of the altercation.*
2. *Remain where you are.*
3. *Find cover.*
4. *Keep a low profile. Avoid the appearance of observing crimes that rioters commit.*
5. *Look for a place to dive or roll if either authorities or offenders attempt to assault your area.*
6. *Do not attempt to negotiate. Your credibility as a negotiator is almost nonexistent.*

卐 卐 卐

Mike has written some good stuff about his escapades at the juvenile treatment center. The others laugh when he reads it aloud—how once he climbed a street sign to get close enough to read it and find his way home, he was that out of his mind. I didn't know it then but Mike would be one of the men in the riot, and his sentence would increase by eighteen months, and in an indirect way this would be partly my fault.

I have seen many fights in my life. I like to watch men fight, but I've learned this is not a good thing to admit. Fights in grade school, high school. Bars. Mostly they are over quickly after a rough push or a punch before others pin them down. But sometimes they don't stop, and if whoever I'm with will let me, I will watch to the end. Once, a boyfriend was jumped by two men, and later, bathing him, I blotted away the blood, my tongue catching whatever was left.

I watched while one man broke my mother's nose.

With another man, I would go to amateur boxing matches, bouts in the backs of gyms amid the smell of bodies and rubber and steel. I both loved and feared the thud and slap of fists on skin, the slide of their bodies when they embraced to rest, the spray of sweat like heavy mist. Later, in bed, the sex is rough and our bodies repeat those earlier sounds. And it is good.

That old saying, every bad person has a little good, every good person has a little bad. Why is it so easy for me to recognize their good, and so hard for them to see my bad? I've been using these men, and they look at me with such respect. I wade through their gratitude, their admiration—I could throw it against the wall.

I begin to meet with a counselor who has an office disguised as a living room. I sit on a loveseat and tell him my marriage is dying and that that might be all right with me. He wants to talk about my past but I resist. One day I bring him pictures of me as a young girl, black and white shots of a kid in overalls, with an expression so innocent and open I feel something very near grief when I look at them. I want to grab her and run with her and keep her safe. But I don't tell him that; I've never been able to expose myself fully to another. I realize that I trust the men in my class more than this professional man with his soft looking hands and delicate skin. I simply hand him the photos as if to say, here is my life, this is all I can tell you.

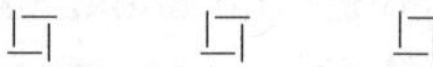

Our classroom is ordinary, except for the fact that we are locked in and a guard peers in every fifteen minutes. We begin by assigning pages of Tobias Wolff's *This Boy's Life*, thinking the boyhood memoir would be the perfect thing. But Wolff's boyish pranks provoke no more nostalgia than "Love Story" would for a porn actor. We quickly move on to the grittier *The Basketball Diaries*. Art especially likes this selection. The oldest and most hopeful of the group, he writes in allegorical language about the plague of drugs and about King Heroin, who rode down on a black horse and slew all in his path, including, almost, Art himself.

After the second class, we've put away our agenda because it feels cruel to impose structure on people who shower, eat, and defecate according to a schedule. And so when Mike talks about his father at length, we follow the men's example and just listen, even though in eight minutes this room will hold a Narcotics Anonymous meeting, and already half a dozen men wait outside. One man in a ski hat presses his face to the glass, his forehead like a potato. Art enjoys talking to me about journalism after our class, in the brief minutes I have before I'm supposed to leave. When I get out I'm going to be a cameraman, he tells me.

卐 卐 卐

Volunteer Agreement

1. *I agree to avoid undue familiarity. If an offender has a problem that is beyond the scope of my position, I will direct him to Staff.*
2. *I understand that persons under the supervision of the Department of Corrections have been convicted of criminal activity; that any offender I may have contact with may attempt to manipulate or take unfair advantage of me.*
3. *I understand that I am volunteering in a potentially hazardous environment and that I could be taken hostage or injured.*

While reading the men's life stories, I begin to write my own. I find it too hard to say anything—I don't know where to begin—so I write about my cousin who was killed six months ago by her boyfriend in front of their two small sons. He stabbed her forty-two times. But I write mostly about our childhood, about my memories of Karyn before she met that man. How she liked horses, how she taught me to do a backdive off the side of a pool.

I try to write about the men who are attracted to the women in our family, about the years of watching my mother pushed and pulled by so many of them, about my aunt who was almost beaten to death by her first husband. And I cannot ignore the irony of my own marriage—of my husband and his passivity. When I told him I was leaving, he was hurt, but I could only tell by the set of his face, the tension around the jaw. I wanted to grab him and say how can you let me go, how can you let me go without a fight. And sometimes I feel a passion, an anger so fierce I know it could drive me to commit the most dangerous acts.

卐 卐 卐

I think about the men in my class when I should think about other things: my Contemporary Rhetoric presentation, the search for a new apartment, the car's oil change. At the store, I wonder what the men would want for dinner. I wonder if they've ever had kalamata olives, or cabernet from the Carneros valley. I imagine us all at a river, the Snake River, with a cooler of beer and the Rolling Stones on the radio. The grass pricklysoft against my feet, the beer an icyscalding in my throat.

I wonder if they are allowed to have music in their cells—or anywhere. But I can't bring myself to ask. The question might offend them, as if my knowing that they were denied something so basic would be humiliating. I drive away in the evenings and turn up the radio. When I know the words, I sing.

There are ceremonies in prison. Gates and keys and bulletproof glass. It's controlled and locked and monitored, and yet it makes no difference. The danger is something I could pick up, like a weapon, and make it my own. It is something I could open myself to, like facing a hot wind. Some—and all women it seems—turn away from it. But I'm drawn to this shadow, there is something there I have to learn. Men on the outside don't like that I'm at the prison. It makes them uneasy. They look at me and shake their heads as if they know something I don't.

Something is different today, I know immediately as they walk in. Ron, who is the first one to class, is unusually subdued, but it is clear he doesn't want to talk about it. There are rumors of trouble, of lockdowns. The others come in one by one, and there is something in their exchange of glances that cannot be reached by me or Kelly, something in the way Joe sits back in his chair, arms folded over his chest, in the way Mike holds his pencil with his whole fist. I think about the boundaries in each of these men, where they lie.

After class Kelly and I are nearly at the copy room when the shouting begins. I feel no surprise, only relief at the inevitability of things, the way tension cannot last—the way skin will bleed when cut, and one will fall when pushed. Kelly runs to the door and looks back at me. *Come on.* I hear the instructions in my mind: in the event of a disturbance, lock yourself in. She whispers through teeth: *get in here.* The words are faint, as if they've traveled a great distance—through water, through the cement of a wall. I'm already gone. Then I've joined the crowd that has formed quick as cats to a struggling bird. Inmates huddle around the flurry, tense, hunched with hands on knees, gesturing and yelling as if they are a part of it, and soon they will be. More inmates from the gym stream down the hall and surround me. For a moment, it's hard to breathe, but then I find a rhythm, I move with them. I exist in a press of bodies, one woman now vanished. In the close hall the shouts of three dozen men ricochet and I am lost to all thought. I can see through triangles of elbows, through slits between legs. Two men scramble and punch and kick—the linoleum floor is smeared with blood now. A lip is split, a shirt torn. The bigger one tries to pin the other, is kneed in the groin and falls back clutching and cursing. It doesn't occur to me then that the guards, who run down the hall, their heavy boots hammering, can't see me. One of the fighters, darker and slighter, grips the other's hair in his hand so the man's head is arched back, mouth gaping, white throat exposed and bowed like the backbone of a small, pale animal.

Then the shoving begins all around and I duck, but not fast enough and I am slammed against the wall, where I sink to my knees and cover my face. Later I will think back and it will come down to a feeling, the feeling one has just before jumping off a cliff's edge to the river below, the giddiness that clings to any moment where there's an edge. One can exist in that surge of emotion for just so long.

Later, Kelly and the supervisor will look at me, their faces transparent with confusion and disappointment. And something else, something very much like repulsion. The kind that comes from seeing something contrary to nature. As if they'd seen a robin catch a mouse and gut it. Or witnessed a young girl expose herself in the most offensive way. I see myself in their reflection: I have committed a crime, I have run to something women are supposed to run from. But I cannot explain myself to my friend or my husband or the supervisor who orders me to leave. They would not understand that I am drawn to men who fight because it is one way I can get close to men: men exposed, no longer powerful and in control, but raw, open.

Halfway home, I pull over when it begins to rain. Class is over for me, and I think I begin to cry. I try to make out the blurred landscape. There is a woman in the farmhouse beyond, standing at the kitchen window. For a strange instant I think she could give me the answers, but the rain runs in rivulets down the glass, and I cannot see her face. There is only a shifting clarity.

How to Meditate

Brenda Miller

Day One

On arrival, huddle in the Volkswagen with your friends and eat all the chocolate in the car. Chocolate chips, old KitKats, the tag-end of a Hershey Bar—do not discriminate. Feel deprived, then light up your last Sherman, pass it around. Watch your fellow retreatants flow into the meditation hall. Note how elegant they look, even in sweatpants and black Wellingtons. Wonder where they get such nice sweatpants. Look down at your baggy jeans, your dim T-shirt and say, *I'm not dressed for this, let's go home.* Look beyond the meditation hall to the Navarro River, the cattails, the red-winged blackbirds. It will be raining, just a little.

Remember that you've forgotten dental floss. Take a deep drag off the cigarette and wonder what you're doing here. Take a close look at your companions in the car: your boyfriend Seth, who is so much older than you, and your friends John and Marybeth. Remember how the four of you, just days earlier, wound up tangled in a bed together, a soft bed with a down comforter, lazily stroking each other's limbs. Feel ashamed. Feel superior. Say, *Ready?*

A woman with bristled red hair leads you and Marybeth to the women's dorm. There will be a deck overlooking a marsh where the blackbirds clack and whistle in the reeds. Glance at the other women who are folding their extra pairs of sweatpants, their Guatemalan sweaters. Sit on the cot and pat it with one hand. It will be hard, unyielding, to help you obey the precept against lying in "high, luxurious beds."

Scope out the meditation hall. Set up your pillow, your blankets next to the wood-stove near the back door. Figure this will be a prime spot—easy in, easy out—and smugly wonder why no one else has nabbed it. Realize your mistake when, during the first sitting period, heat blazes from the stove, frying the hair on your shins. Slide away a little, quietly as you can, and bump the knees of the woman next to you. Irritation rises from her like a wave. Start to apologize but choke yourself off mid-whisper.

Sit cross-legged on your pillow, your hands palm down on your knees. Breathe. Your teacher, who is from Burma, perches on a raised platform, his belly round, his knees hidden under his white robe. He speaks in a voice so deep it vibrates beneath your skin. He repeats the word: *equanimous, equanimous*. Invent a strange animal, an *Equanimous*, half-horse, half-dolphin, gliding through the murky sea of your unconscious. Feel where the breath enters and leaves your body just below the nostrils, like a fingertip tapping on your upper lip. Concentrate on this sensation. Within seconds find yourself thinking about Marybeth's hand on your breast. Go back to your breath. Find yourself thinking about pancakes, eggs, bacon. Go back to your breath. Spend your first hour of meditation this way. They call it "monkey mind." Picture your brain swinging through the banana trees, its little hands clutching the vines.

Feel the pain begin in your knees, between your shoulder blades. Shift a little and feel the pain travel up your neck, down into your hips. Open your eyes halfway and surreptitiously glance at the meditators around you. They look perfectly still, their backs straight, their *zafus* round and plump. Look at your own flat pillow spilling from beneath your thighs.

You don't have the right equipment for this. You'd better leave now, before you're paralyzed.

DAY TWO

Read the rules again: No talking, no reading, no sex, no drugs, no eye contact. Vipassana, they say, is the art of looking deeply. Be unsure about how deeply you want to look. Read the schedule six times—4 A.M.: waking bell, 4:30–5:00: chanting in the hall, 5–6: sitting, 6–7: breakfast, 7–9: sitting, 11:00: lunch, more sitting, nap time, more sitting, tea at 4:00, no dinner, Dharma talk at 7, more sitting. Add up the hours of meditation and come up with the number 16. Figure this must be a mistake and perform the calculations obsessively in your head, your own private mantra. You're already so hungry it's difficult to concentrate. Think longingly about the chocolate in the car, and hate yourself for not saving just a little.

Go to breakfast. Hold a simple white bowl in your two hands. Stand in line with your fellow retreatants and note the radiant colors of their shawls, their scarves, the blankets they have draped over their shoulders. Shuffle your way to the breakfast table. There will be large urns full of porridge. Take some. Take too much. Take a banana. Realize that your boyfriend Seth is opposite you at the table. Watch his hand as it chooses a pear, puts it back, takes an apple, puts it back. Feel a surge of love and annoyance. Out of the corner of your eye see a glint of Marybeth's blond hair. See a flash of John's denim shirt. Feel grateful and angry at the same time.

Sit down at the long picnic table and begin to eat your food. Realize you need some honey and scan the table, spying it at the far end. How do you ask for it without speaking? You decide to get up and fetch it yourself, to avoid making an embarrassing faux pas. When you stand up your knees hit the table, knocking over your neighbor's teacup. Irritation rises from her like a wave.

Go back to your room and lie down. Fall asleep. Hear bells ringing in the distance. Know that you are supposed to be somewhere, then sit bolt upright and run to the meditation hall. Slow to a casual walk when you approach the doors. Stand and listen to the silence a minute. Listen to the breathing. Open the door, which creaks on its hinges. Tiptoe to your seat, aware of everyone aware of you, of your every move. Settle in. Breathe. Fingertip. Nostril. Etc. Feel an overwhelming desire to run screaming from the meditation hall. Think about pizza. A cigarette. A beer. Feel your breath for one, maybe two seconds. Feel your neck slowly seizing up. Fantasize about yourself paralyzed. Imagine Seth and John and Marybeth caring for you, running cool cloths across your forehead. Imagine the three of them kissing you all over your numb body, trying to restore feeling. Gasp when the bell rings. Hobble out of the meditation hall.

Go to lunch. Hold a simple white bowl in your two hands. Shuffle forward and ladle yourself miso soup, rice, some wilted bok choy. Take too much. Reach for the tamari. Notice Seth watching you from the opposite side of the table and dab it on sparingly. Sit down and eat slowly, slowly. Wonder if there's dessert.

DAY THREE

When you wake up, you might hear two women whispering in the bathroom. If so, take the opportunity to feel superior. Calculate how long it's been since you've last eaten. 16 hours. This seems impossible. Wonder why everything adds up to 16.

Drape a blanket over your head and walk outside, toward the meditation hall. Notice the red-winged blackbirds, the budding lilac, the silver cast to the sky. You'll think it's beautiful. You'll think you'll have to get up earlier at home from now on. Pause for a moment and notice your breath, like a fingertip tapping on your upper lip.

When you enter the hall the chanting has already started. Your teacher seems to chant the word *Betamite* over and over, with variations in pitch and speed. Wonder what Betamite is. Think of it as a breakfast spread, sweet and salty at the same time. Think about breakfast. Calculate the amount of porridge you will ladle into your bowl. Top it with honey and a pear. Breathe. Notice yourself breathing. Notice yourself noticing yourself breathing. Your neighbor tips over, asleep, and wakes up with a stifled cry. Feel sympathetic. Smile a sympathetic smile to yourself.

In the afternoon take a walk down by the river. You do not have Wellingtons, so your feet get wet and cold. Your hands are freezing. You miss your friends. You feel alone in a way that is foreign to you. Try to remember if you've ever been so completely alone in your life, and realize how surrounded you've always been, how supported. Remember how you laughed in bed with Seth and John and Marybeth. Remember the release of it, how it felt not so much like sex, but like love multiplied ten-fold.

Wonder if you'll ever be able to speak again. Try it. Open your mouth. Feel a tiny bit of panic tremble beneath your upper arm. Feel hunger in your belly like a wild animal.

Day Four

Just when you think you have it down, just when you've noticed yourself noticing your breathing for unbroken seconds at a time, your teacher tells you everything will change from now on. Now you must become aware of the sensations on the surface of your skin. Now you must scan your body, *sweep* your attention from head to toe, noticing the sensations arise and pass away. Arise and pass away. *Equanimous.*

Start with the top of your head. Feel your skull like a dumb shield, hard and unyielding. Feel nothing, then feel a slight tingling, a teardrop of sensation. Notice it. Move your attention like a scrim down the crown of your head, to the tips of your ears. Feel an overwhelming desire to run screaming from the meditation hall. Return to what you know. That fingertip. Settle in with the fingertip tapping on your upper lip. Feel competent. Feel sly.

Thirty minutes later open your eyes halfway and, without moving your head, try to see toward the men's side of the room. Move your gaze past young men with straight spines, men whose faces seem chiseled, calm, focused, unconcerned. Find among these men your boyfriend, Seth. See his furrowed brow, his downturned mouth, his clenched fists. See him trying so hard. Look past him for John. Try to find John anywhere in the room.

When you walk back to the dorm, see Marybeth flossing her teeth on the deck. Stop behind a tree and watch her floss and floss, the movements of her hand so practiced, her teeth so white. Feel at a loss when she turns around and heads back inside, the deck now so empty.

At lunch, take the right amount of salad, half a baked yam, stir-fried snow peas with tofu. Hold your bowl in both hands as you find your seat at the picnic table. Sit in the same seat every day, though you could sit anywhere you like. Try to eat with chopsticks, the way the people in radiant scarves do. Drop bits of food all over the table. Try to brush them away, casually, with the back of your hand.

You've memorized fragments of the people around you: a hand, a wrist, a thigh. You know their shoes: Birkenstocks, rubber boots, thongs. You recognize their smells: rose water, underarms, unwashed wool. Feel at home in this. Then feel surrounded by bits of people disintegrating.

At night, you'll have trouble sleeping, though you're so tired you think you might go insane. Breathe in and out. *Equanimous. Equanimous.* Your teacher's voice is the only one you hear all day, and so you listen carefully to every word he says. At night, when you cannot sleep, briefly worry about brainwashing. Think of your brains heaped in a sink, rinsed repeatedly in cool water.

DAY FIVE

At 5 A.M. you'll feel as though you're in a film. Drape your blanket over your head, clutch it closed at your throat, so you're cowled like a monk. Think of an appropriate soundtrack, something with gongs and birdsong. On your way to the meditation hall, you might see someone furtively smoking a cigarette. If so, feel superior. *Sweep* your attention from the top of your head to the bottoms of your toes. Make it to somewhere mid-torso before you begin craving kisses, wine, a cigarette.

After breakfast it's your turn for karma yoga, which means you have to wash the dishes. Stand at the sink with a man who, out of the corner of your eye, looks incredibly handsome, radiant. He moves efficiently through the kitchen, drying the dishes you hand him with a rough towel. Imagine the two of you communicating without words as you plunge simple white bowl after simple white bowl into the hot water. Imagine you are married to him, that you have a house in the country with two dogs and a meditation room. Imagine the children you will have together, their terrible beauty. Feel him close by your side. He hands back a bowl you haven't washed properly; a gob of gray porridge clings to the rim. Feel as though you want to die.

Walk to the meditation hall in the rain. Think, *equanimous, equanimous.* Feel the water evaporate from your skin as you *sweep* your attention from the top of your head to the bottoms of your toes. Think about Marybeth's hand on your breast, Seth's mouth on your lips, John's lips on your thigh. Try not to feel like a harlot. Try to remember how *natural* it all seemed at the time. Calculate how many different relationships must be nurtured in this foursome. Come up with the number 16.

At the Dharma talk that evening, discover that you will now have periods of "strong sitting." Now you must not move a muscle, no matter how painful the sitting becomes. Practice "strong sitting" for a half-hour before going to bed. As soon as you begin, feel an overwhelming urge to run screaming from the meditation hall. Feel a sharp pain radiate from your hip, your ankle. Resist the urge to move. Feel the tension in the room rise.

Then, inexplicably, feel your body relax. Feel the pain arise and pass away, arise and pass away, a continuous and fluid thing, impermanent. Begin to feel a glimmer of understanding. Begin to see your body in these terms, arising and passing away. Even the muscles. Even the hard bones. Even the core of you. Begin to wonder if the body that melted under the touch of Marybeth's hand is the same body that now arises and passes away. Feel a bewildered sorrow. Return to your breath. Wait for the bell to ring.

DAY SIX

In the night, when you're not sleeping, have a terrible dream. Feel your body dissolve, turn into nothing but air. Not even air. Jerk yourself back. Lie there gasping for breath. Resist the urge to wake up Marybeth, to lie down next to her, to feel her impermanent skin against your own.

DAY SEVEN

Decide to ask your teacher about this experience. You will go up to him during the question/answer session after the Dharma talk. Spend all day worrying about this, about what exactly you will say, what words to use. Worry that your voice might sound harsh and ugly, like someone diseased.

Wait your turn. Kneel next to the stage, and know that Seth can see you, and Marybeth. Try to look serene. John, you think, has stopped coming to the meditation hall, has decided to find enlightenment on his own. Bad boy. Envy him his initiative.

Move forward on your knees. Kneel before your teacher. His face is large, larger than your head. His eyes are kind but almost all pupil, and you feel yourself drawn into them, spiraling the way you did in your bed last night. So lean back a little, take a deep breath. His wife, next to him, smiles at you and you suddenly want to cry. Say, *I felt myself. . . .* Start again. Say, *I have so much fear. . . .*

He laughs. Fear is fear, he says, impermanent, passing away. He waves his hand in the air and for a moment it seems to vanish in a flash of white. Thank him. Return to your place near the wood-stove. Breathe. Feel the fingertip tapping on your upper lip.

In the last meditation period of the day, have another dream. Think of yourself pregnant, squatting behind a chair, giving birth to a baby girl. Feel yourself split open. Feel the beating of your heart, your blood.

DAY EIGHT

Breathe.

Arise.

Pass Away.

DAY NINE

Begin to dread the breaking of Noble Silence. Begin to appreciate how much of your life is taken up with small talk and inconsequential matters. Swear you will get up earlier when you get home, you will speak only when necessary, you will be an equanimous person, even if you never touch Marybeth or John or Seth again. Work hard at your meditation, so hard you break out in a sweat during "strong sitting." In the afternoon, realize that Marybeth has been sitting behind you all along. Wonder how you missed her there, all this time. Before going to your seat, watch the back of her head, the set of her small shoulders. See her as a body already dead. See the flesh passing away until only a skeleton remains. Wonder how you will live your life from now on.

Begin to lift your head and look at your fellow retreatants. Notice that everyone seems a little worn down, pale, sallow. Look forward to washing your sweatpants, sleeping in your own bed. Wonder if you will be alone in that bed. Memorize a speech you will give to Seth, John, and Marybeth. Swear you will love them no matter what happens.

Eat a pear for breakfast. Some rice and tofu for lunch. Steal some floss from Marybeth while she's in the shower. Stop in your tracks at the whistle of a blackbird. Whistle back, a small sound made of nothing but air.

DAY TEN

Break the Noble Silence. Feel the buzz in the room. Everyone's giddy. You've all just returned from a trip to a foreign land; you all have pictures to show, stories to tell. Even the strangers look familiar to you. Say *Don't I know you?* to everyone you meet. Notice the subtle glow around everyone's cheekbones. Sit with Seth and John and Marybeth at a round table on the deck. Hear the blackbirds yukking it up in the glade.

Well, Marybeth says, holding John's hand to her heart. *We've decided to have a baby!* A baby. The words seem so loud, so rough-hewn, you have trouble getting them from your ear to your brain. Marybeth's gaze slides across your face. John looks straight at you and grins. Seth puts a hand on your shoulder, and takes it away again.

Forget the speech you were going to give. Start to tell them about the night you dissolved in your bed, about your fear of becoming no one, but halfway through sputter to a stop. Try to feel your breath like a fingertip tapping on your upper lip. Feel an overwhelming urge to run screaming from the dining hall.

Walk a path through wet grass down to the Navarro River. Say good-bye to the blackbirds and their red shoulders. Think you will always remember this, and know that you won't. Feel yourself rising and passing away, there by the river. Look upstream and then down. Feel yourself like a boulder in the middle, worn by the rushing water. Hug yourself. Feel your hands strong against your upper arms, holding yourself in place. ▪

Baked Alaska

Karol Griffin

Gwen and I were breaking up, which is a strange thing to have to say, since Gwen and I were never lovers. At least I don't think we were. Not in the usual sense of the word. Our friendship was based on food; food we shared, food we talked about, food we loved. Sometimes it was soup, warm and comforting. Sometimes it was bread and cheese, nourishing and filling. Sometimes it was wine, giddy and intoxicating. In the end, it had been Baked Alaska all along, complicated and deceptive. Judging by the warm, soft meringue on the outside, you wouldn't guess that there was a hard, cold core in the middle. You wouldn't know that the surface and the interior were nothing alike until it was cut and served. And when it turned out all wrong, you wouldn't know until it was too late.

"I don't know quite how to say this," I said, "but we can't do this any more. I'm sorry."

Two bright circles of red warmed Gwen's cheeks, and tears welled up in her eyes. We were standing side by side at Leonardi's delicatessen, staring at cheeses.

"I don't understand," she said.

"Our friendship is . . . inappropriate." It wasn't the best word, but it was the only one I could think of to explain what had gone wrong.

"Did Paul put you up to this?"

"Not at all. It's just that you've been giving me . . . things, saying . . . I don't know . . . I need to get that from Paul. I ought to be getting that from my husband."

"So, what are you saying? You're going to make him your sole emotional support? You honestly think that's going to work?"

"I hope so." I studied a wedge of Cambezola and rearranged the pasta in my shopping basket. I wasn't explaining it right. It sounded frivolous and stupid.

"Well," Gwen snapped, "it would be nice. Wouldn't it. If it worked. It'd be absolutely fucking *sublime*."

I shook my head at her sarcasm and put the Cambezola back in the cooler. I tried to not to cry. I said I was sorry. Again.

"You," Gwen said, "*let* me treat you like a lover." She said it like a dirty word, like I was a dirty person. I left my pasta on the counter and went outside, hot with shame. Gwen followed. She grabbed my arm, spun me around, and hugged me like she was never going to let go.

"I'm sorry," I said again.

"Why are you doing this to yourself? I love you!"

I hugged her quickly and walked away.

"I'm so glad we never got involved," Gwen screamed after me. "You would have broken my heart." When I turned around and saw the look in her eyes, I got the feeling that what she meant to say was that I had broken her heart anyway.

Gwen was a bundle of insecurities held loosely together by raw nerves, but it wasn't the sort of debilitating character flaw you'd notice right off. She was one thing on the surface and something altogether different underneath. She was ethereal and well-traveled, an artist. I envied her certainty, her aesthetic, her aplomb. As time went on, I learned that underneath the glossy confection of impeccable styling and European sensibilities, she was hiding a melting core of pain and vulnerability, covered with a crusty shell. She was like a fancy layered dessert, a surprising combination of flavors and textures. Sometimes sweet, sometimes bitter.

Gwen and I fell into a friendship sparked by a click of compatibility that rarely happens when friends of friends meet. It was 1993, and I was new to San Francisco, naive and newly married. I had a hard time making friends. A woman I worked with invited me to go to the beach for Easter sunset with her friend, Diane, and Diane's friend, Gwen. We piled into Penny's car with sweaters, blankets, a fifth of tequila, two boxes of pink marshmallow Easter chicks, and a lemon.

We parked at the north end of Ocean Beach and walked down, away from the Golden Gate Bridge. The beach was nearly deserted, and a cold, salty wind blew off the water. The clouds were heavy and low, turning the city lights into a twilight that hung suspended in time. We stopped periodically and huddled together in the cold, blankets whipping in the wind. Gwen carved slices of lemon with her pocketknife and passed the tequila. We drank from the bottle and danced around, grimacing as the tequila burnt our throats and warmed our bellies. We stopped in the concrete shelter of the sewage release station and built a fire from soggy driftwood and roasted the marshmallow Easter chicks. Gwen held a melting chick skewered on a long stick across the fire for me to eat. I sucked the hot, gooey sugar off the stick and raised the chick on my stick to Gwen's mouth. Penny and Diane fed each other across the fire, too, an impromptu, ceremonial ritual of camaraderie. The caramel smell of burning sugar mixed with the salty, decaying smell of the ocean. In that moment, it seemed that the four of us would be friends forever.

Penny and Diane, the friends who introduced us, fell by the wayside as though their only purpose was to bring me and Gwen together. Gwen and I worked in the same part of town, it turned out, and we had a lot in common. When we met, we were easily accessible lunch companions for each other, but by summer, we were friends. We talked about clothing and art, lipstick and sex. We talked about food. Despite Gwen's smorgasbord of stories filled with bisexual innuendoes, I never asked her outright and she never said. We were friends.

I was working as a temporary secretary in a downtown building a few short blocks from Gwen's office, a gloomy room where she kept the books for a disreputable art dealer. We ate lunch together almost every day, picnicking Gwen-style, sumptuous, dramatic lunches of hors d'oeuvres, finger foods, or Gwen's leftovers from dinner the night before. We ate exotic pâtés and pungent, creamy cheeses sandwiched between pieces of crunchy, chewy baguettes that Gwen pulled like magic wands, still warm, from her leather satchel.

Gwen learned to eat in Paris; at least that's what she said when I asked her how a nice girl from San Jose acquired a taste for *pâté avec truffes et Cognac*. She could pack it away, too, even though she wasn't much over five feet tall and couldn't have weighed more than a hundred pounds. She tore chunks of bread with her teeth like a jackal at a zebra carcass, yet with a grace that seemed, well, Parisian.

Gwen wore vintage men's clothing that gave her tiny frame a continental look, with a fresh flower or two as a garnish behind her ear or in her lapel. Her tangerine hair was cropped close to her head, framing wideset, gooseberry eyes and delicate features. Her lips were like crimson taffy, stretching to amazing dimensions to accommodate her smile. Her speech was peppered with French words, a habit that was neither affected nor self-conscious; it complemented her conversation like a spicy vinaigrette. Gwen swore like a sailor and spoke, loudly, of bondage and sex toys, tops, bottoms, fisting and queens, in a foreign vocabulary of slang terms and sexual shorthand codes. Her stories were explicit and graphic and involved paramours with androgynous European names. Maybe it was just that she told these stories while she ate, but it seemed that her lovers and her meals were devoured with the same ferocity.

⌐ ⌐ ⌐

I expected to be the token straight chick at Gwen's lavish 30th birthday fete. Gwen's Russian Hill flat was filled with drag queens and club divas and artists, all honoring Gwen with presents and champagne in a party atmosphere of candlelight and clove cigarettes. Even though Gwen cleared away the furniture to make a dance space and filled the CD player with loud dance music, the living room was crowded wall-to-wall with boisterous partygoers and there was no room to move, much less dance. The kitchen table was piled high with fruits and cheeses, quiches, pastas, pâté. The food platters were bookended by a forest of champagne, wine and beer bottles on one end, and baguettes stacked like firewood at the other.

In addition to the usual crowd of Gwen's urban acquaintances, she had invited some high school chums who drove up from San Jose for the event. It was difficult to believe that Gwen had come from the same place as these women. Her former best friend, Colleen, was a hip-hick suburbanite with frosted, permed curls and long, coral fingernails. She tapped her nails incessantly on her wine glass and chain-smoked Virginia Slims. It came as no surprise when she announced that she was a cosmetologist.

Colleen's fingernails clicked more and more frantically as the evening wore on. A Marin County drag queen named Harry—wearing a stunning, floor-length, leek-green, sequined evening gown—carried a birthday cake on a platter into the living room. Before the Happy Birthday song had been completely sung, Gwen tore a fistful of cake and frosting from the cake and fed it to a stunning platinum-haired lesbian with her left hand while sliding her right hand up the woman's thigh. The police came to the door just as Harry was cutting the mangled remains of the cake with a butcher knife. There was frosting on his sequins, and his wig was askew. The policemen didn't look especially surprised by Harry's appearance. They hastily disarmed him of the cake-covered knife, asked him to turn down the stereo and left. Colleen looked as though this were not the sort of party to which she was accustomed, and clung to me like a heterosexual raft in a tempestuous storm on a gay sea. She cornered me near the buffet table and proceeded to tell me all about her life. She rummaged in her purse and produced a wallet filled with Olan Mills studio portraits of her family: a husband, an infant son, and a rabbit named (I swear this is true) "Fluffy." She chattered in baby-talk about her big strong boys and her adorable bunny, and, after a few more glasses of wine, the grueling details of her difficult labor and subsequent birth of her child.

Colleen paused for a moment and looked across the quiches at me. She leaned over as though we were sharing a moment, and gripped my arm with her coral talons.

"Tell me something," she said. "Is Gwen straight or gay or what?"

"Gwen," I said, "is a *people* person." I disentangled myself from Colleen's grip and left her to her own devices.

She was telling the story of her son's first words for the third time when Gwen decided that enough was enough. Gwen shoved the wallet of photographs back into Colleen's purse, thrust it into Colleen's solar plexus.

"This is a dyke's 30th birthday party," Gwen screamed. "NO MORE MOMMY TALK!" Colleen blanched and left in a hurry, and there was a smattering of applause.

When my downtown temp assignment ended, I was sent to a small law firm closer to home. Gwen and I didn't have lunch every day any more, but we spoke often, personal calls on company time. Sunday-morning coffee became our new routine, replacing our weekday lunches. We met at the Falling Dog, a deserted Mission District cafe with delicious espresso and a lion's head fountain that spit water into a basin of emaciated goldfish. One Sunday, everything changed.

"I don't know if you know this," Gwen said, "but I find you wildly attractive."

My eyes widened over the cappuccino cup frozen midway to my lips.

"Really," I said.

Gwen was sitting on her hands. She leaned forward and squeezed her shoulders together as though a sudden draft had swept through the room.

"Oh yes." She nodded emphatically. Her nose crinkled as she smiled. "You're a mango, a ripe mango. I just want to take a bite out of you." Her lips closed over animal teeth and she shook her head back and forth quickly.

If she took a bite out of me, it was bound to hurt, but I'd be lying if I said that I wasn't flattered. I thought of my wedding ring as an amulet, warding off the interest of everyone but my husband, a magical piece of metal that would render me instantly unappealing, or at least unapproachable, to everyone but the man I had married. I thought that the knowledge of Paul's presence in my bed was a sure sign of my sexual preference. I explained to Gwen that even if I weren't married, I was straight.

"I thought you knew that," I said. Gwen laughed the whole thing off as though it had been mostly a joke anyway, and we finished our coffee in an awkward silence.

That conversation bubbled beneath our friendship. From then on, Gwen flirted openly with me, acted like it was a joke, and then flirted some more. I pretended it was a joke, too, even when she left lengthy, breathless, mango messages on my answering machine. Eventually everything was back, more or less, to normal. Gwen cooked up a few flings, and we'd spend less time together while she was embroiled in steamy affairs that never seemed to last long. In between, she was just Gwen, serving up unusual food and laughing and telling rambling stories about why she liked men, why she liked women, why she liked me. Gwen quit telling me that I was a mango, but from time to time, she'd kiss my cheek and say "you're really *quelque chose*."

Maybe it was the challenge that Gwen liked. Maybe it was the certainty of failure. Whatever the reason, Gwen seemed to savor the idea of this unrequited love simmering on the back burner of her mind. She liked to stir things up. My husband, Paul, never liked her very much. He called her my "little lesbian friend." She flirted relentlessly with me in front of my husband, saying things she never would have said had we been alone. The three of us had dinner together. Once. Gwen cooked for us. She served succulent, gamy mushrooms in a tangy garlic-and-butter sauce over plump mounds of fresh pasta, accompanied by red wine and a hot sourdough baguette. During dinner, Gwen fondled everyone's legs under the table.

For dessert, Gwen made Baked Alaska. It seemed a lot of complicated effort for a bit of ice cream and cake. I thought that it was one of those desserts you'd find only on the pages of certain novels or on dessert trays in expensive, traditional restaurants. But there was Gwen, scooping rich raspberry ice cream into the shell of a homemade chocolate cake. She whipped up a stiff, sugary meringue in her state-of-the-art mixer. I watched in amazement as she shellacked the cake-and-ice-cream concoction with meringue, topping it with an interesting design of peaks and swirls, twirling meringue with a practiced hand. I was impressed, but then Gwen was always impressive. The oven was already set to broil. Gwen popped in the unbaked Alaska and opened another bottle of wine.

She was regaling us with stories of Paris when she remembered the dessert. She flew to the oven.

"It's ruined! It's fucking ruined." Gwen was distraught. The meringue peaks were a little on the dark side, and melted ice cream oozed out from underneath like cloudy raspberry blood. Maybe it didn't look like a Baked Alaska was supposed to look, but it looked like it would taste just fine.

It was midnight when Gwen finally walked us to the door, an arm around my waist, an arm around Paul's.

"You're a lucky, lucky man," she told Paul when she hugged him goodnight. "I keep trying to convert her, but she's just too damn straight and too much in love with you." She gave him a kiss that made me wonder whose jealousies she was trying to pique.

"She's an honorary lesbian, though," Gwen said, trailing her fingers down my arm and squeezing my hand.

After that, Paul liked her even less.

In the next two months, my relationship with Gwen became even more confusing, with too many ingredients and complicated undertones of contrary flavors. Women know what women want in a way that men never will. Gwen made tapes of Etta James and Aretha and Nina Simone for me. I often found gifts, large and small, in my mailbox, usually with no note. No explanation. She picked flowers to surprise me; she left bouquets on my desk at work. She made sensuous collages for me, magazine images spliced into her own paintings. She brought me perfect fruit. Gwen said all the things a woman wants to hear from a lover, and she said them at all the right times. I wished that Paul would look at me the way Gwen did. When he was too preoccupied to notice me much, I had extra helpings at Gwen's emotional buffet. I kept the compliments I wanted, and pretended not to notice when her words strayed outside the boundaries of friendship.

I gave Gwen presents, too, but the only thing she truly wanted was the one thing I couldn't give her. If I hadn't been married, I would have slept with her, not so much from libido or pity, but because she was my friend and I would have done almost anything to make her happy for a little while. But it wouldn't be enough. Gwen wouldn't be content unless she swallowed me whole.

⌐ ⌐ ⌐

I didn't hear from Gwen for a long time after I broke off our friendship. I couldn't look at a wedge of Cambezola without thinking about her, missing her. Six months later, Gwen wrote to me. From Texas. It was a friendly letter, hesitant but warm. I wrote back.

It seemed that the past was forgiven and forgotten, and for a while, Gwen and I wrote to each other regularly. Gwen's penmanship was like a child's cursive, an almost indecipherable salad of overlapping curls and jags. Her letters were like her conversations, drifting stories that were by turns *ôutré* and amusing, scrawled diagonally on vanilla-colored, perfumed stationery. The letters became less and less frequent, dwindling until we were left with one of those Christmas-card friendships. Almost every year, Gwen's card had a different return address. She'd promise to write and tell me all about the move, the new lover, the career, the last-minute plans she'd made, but the details in her annual missive were a meager appetizer for a meal that never came.

Yesterday, out of the blue, a box of exotic French cheeses and Italian salami appeared in my mailbox, postmarked Paris. There was no note, but I think it means that Gwen has finally found something she can sink her teeth into. ▀

Fast Food

Alex R. Jones

I applied at the Taco Bell in Ventura, California, because it was out of my hometown and not likely to be frequented by anybody who might know me. I was twenty years old then, a junior in college, and I needed a job for the summer. In small towns like the one in which I lived, jobs are had through friends and their fathers. Some kids worked for their dads driving delivery trucks around town for ten dollars an hour. Those were the good jobs. I'd never had one. I'd picked avocados the summer before for four dollars an hour, and I was glad to get it. But I was also aware that everybody I knew considered fast food work to be the lowest form of human enterprise, and Taco Bell to be the lowest form of fast food.

Low or not, I found myself interviewing with an assistant manager named Rick who wore a clean white shirt—blemished only by a single spot of red sauce on his breast pocket—and a Taco Bell–issue tie. Instinctively I felt sorry for him. He looked to be about 40, which is like Methuselah by fast food standards, and as he slid the paperwork across the table toward me, I had the feeling that the application process had, for him, lost meaning through repetition and futility.

After he gave me a math test, which I nearly failed, we progressed on to more vital issues, such as a code of conduct. He handed me a yellow sheet of paper with the Taco Bell version and told me to read it as he sadly stared out the window into the parking lot. I'd never had a code of conduct, and I scanned it with apprehension: One must always come to work on time. Being hung over was no excuse for absence. Employees showing up with wrinkled or dirty uniforms would be sent home. No tattoos could be displayed. No drunkenness would be allowed. Serving free food to friends would result in termination. Coming out more than a dollar short in your cash till was also grounds for termination. When I finished, I looked out the window and saw in the parking lot an employee sweeping up trash. That's going to be me, I thought. I left feeling nervous, but with an oddly comforting feeling that I was in the gentle but firm embrace of a higher institution: perhaps the Pepsico Company, which owned Taco Bell.

Crucial to an employee's integration into the Taco Bell experience, I found, was the uniform. Back then, it was an excrement brown, edged with an orange trim thought to offer a Southwestern flavor appropriate to a restaurant serving Mexican food. A marvel of science, it was 100 percent polyester, absolutely stain resistant, and, in the absence of heat or flame, virtually indestructible. The required brown shoes were not provided. However, assistant manager Rick strongly recommended a trip to Kmart in order to purchase plastic imitation topsiders with the requisite no-slip soles. The uniform was topped off with a baseball-type cap that was also brown and emblazoned with the Taco Bell logo. With his hat pulled low, usually out of shame, the average Taco Bell man half-heartedly clutching a broom looked like a weary Civil War veteran: too young to be fighting, but already jaded.

The mission of Taco Bell then, as now, was to sell the food of a brown minority to a white majority hungry for the exotic and, in doing so, make a huge sum of money. The design of Taco Bell stores was therefore an amalgamation of Disneyland comes to Old Mexico. Just as our uniforms were supposed to lend the crew members south-of-the-border spice, when half of them hadn't been as far as Los Angeles, the store that I worked at was, like all Taco Bells, an elaborate prop. It was a cement bunker rusticated with a facade of uneven brick and a red tile roof. Inside, the dining room floor was tiled in earth colors and lined with Formica tables and plastic plants. Because most Americans considered Mexico to be synonymous with filth, care was taken to ensure that the kitchen was visible from the dining room, to eliminate mystery.

Marketing Taco Bell to suburban whites must have been tough. When I was a child, my father used to refer to Taco Bell as "Crappo Bell" and refused to take us there, no matter how much we whined for tacos and nacho chips. He was from the Midwest and despised Mexican food, though he'd never had any. But my father was just the sort that Taco Bell had to win over. In those days, the late sixties and early seventies, in suburban white California, people didn't refer to tacos and burritos as Mexican food, but rather as

"Spanish food." I remember as a boy being taken out for "Spanish food" with my best friend in the back seat of his parents' Cadillac. It was a wonderful, ignorant time. It's different these days. Now, when people refer to Mexican food, as often as not they don't mean the food of Mexico, but rather the food of Taco Bell.

卐 卐 卐

My first day arrived. Assistant manager Rick escorted me to the back of the store. There, outside his tiny office, I was shown a training film from a small projector set up on several sacks of pinto beans. The film, complete with upbeat music and smiling employees wearing crisp uniforms, was designed to instill loyalty and a sense of heritage in the Taco Bell tradition. It told of the formation of the first Taco Bell by Glenn Bell, whose solitary vision had grown into an international fast food chain. I've always been susceptible to commercials and marketing in general, and before the film was over, I was all theirs. Up to that point, my life had been unmarked by conflict, war, or any real sense of purpose. I'd never realized how empty my life was without those things. I found I was a soldier waiting for a cadence call. I was ready to take my place in the long brown line. With my cap pulled low over my eyes, my name tag clipped securely in place, for the first time in my life I felt as though I belonged to something. I was ready, if untrained, for whatever lay ahead.

The crew members of my Taco Bell were actors in its theater. Mostly, they were white kids who came from families on the bottom fringe of the middle class. In Ventura, they lived on the edge of a continent, close to the 101 Freeway that surged north to San Francisco or south down to Los Angeles. The greatest ocean on the planet roared and seethed at the shore. Everything around them touched the edges of possibility, but the crew had learned to manage their expectations.

The guys had mustaches and crooked teeth, and swore with color and originality. They greeted each other with a simple raise of the chin. Like the men, the women on the crew preferred fast cars, usually old Camaros or Mustangs with torn seats and sporting high school tassels dangling from the rearview mirrors. Some of them got pregnant, and some of them loved the idea of having a child, and some of them hated it. Each crew member lived in a world of dusk lit by the neon of liquor store parking lots, not far from the streaking headlights and Doppler howls of the 101 Freeway, which could transport them to Los Angeles. Los Angeles, more concept than place, sat in the back of their minds as an unrealized dream. The other unrealized dream was college, which the crew members regarded with equal parts envy and contempt. Meanwhile, they were aware of every week, month, and year that they passed in the employ of Taco Bell. They smoked cigarettes with unaffected style, drank beer whenever offered, and they liked to party.

Without contest the hero of the crew was Paul, the fry cook. He had blond hair, a shaggy moustache, and a slow way of speaking. He rode a black and chrome Yamaha with a cracked headlight. Every morning he roared down Thompson Boulevard before doing an illegal U-turn across traffic, rumbling back the other way and parking in the employee dirt lot across the street. He wore a black leather jacket with no shirt underneath. Before he came on duty he sat bare-chested on the table in front of the store, lit a Marlboro, and squinted down the street for action. After he finished his smoke, he checked his watch—it was 9:59 A.M.—then tossed the butt into the ice plant. From a paper shopping bag, he removed a neatly folded uniform shirt. He stood up, lifted his arms and slid on his uniform top in one smooth movement. He spat once on the pavement and strode into the store.

Paul was popular because nobody knew much about him. We crew members respected only what we didn't know. Everybody else talked incessantly about their plans for escape, going on and on about the places they'd go, and the wonderful jobs they'd have. That talk didn't amount to anything. Like convicts grousing in the yard between lockdowns, none of us felt we deserved to be at Taco Bell, but there we were. But Paul had been at Taco Bell for two years, which was like ten years at any other job, and, either out of humility or self-knowledge, he never spoke about his dreams. Also, as the fry cook, he did a difficult and sometimes dangerous job that nobody else could do. Accordingly, he made $4.10 an hour, while most of us got $3.35.

Mornings began quietly. Paul worked alone at the fryer in the corner. With his apron and long rubber gloves, he dipped the rack of tortillas into the vat. The oil hissed and spattered. He yawned and checked his watch. The rest of us did prep work. We shredded lettuce, diced tomatoes, browned hamburger and loaded the sour cream guns, all the while talking about last night's parties. Two of the guys, Marco and Ted, talked about the girls they had seen, and their unfulfilled desire to have sex with them. Nancy reminded them of the unlikelihood of their ever having sex, with anybody, for the rest of their lives. From the fryer in the corner, Paul smiled but he said nothing.

I made friends with Dan Frances, a nineteen-year-old who was perpetually good natured. Dan's good nature was improved even further by having discovered a dead body earlier that summer, and whether he was pushing a broom or washing a pan he'd stop, smile, and talk about his dead body. All summer long we listened with great interest while Dan recounted his discovery of the body, its level of decomposition, and Dan's multiple theories regarding the cause of death. (Coke deal gone bad? Lovers' quarrel? Suicide?) We crew members were fascinated with dead bodies and death in general. We believed that a good knowledge of the ways and means of violent death made one savvy and prepared for life. In short, we knew the score. Life—that world one entered after high school—was not some movie, it was real, and one had better be ready for its pitfalls. By possessing a knowledge of death, we felt certain we'd never die.

Although I was in the crew, and in time came to be treated as a part of it, I wasn't like the others. I had grown up on the periphery of their world, but I was going to college. Like them, though, I had dreams—not to be a policeman or a fireman, or to get a sales job at Penney's—but to turn, as if by magical transformation, into a great writer. I impressed myself with the dichotomy of my life. By day I drove to Taco Bell and mopped tables, made refried beans, and filled soft drink cups; by night I drove to the public library and scrawled out my first stories onto college-ruled paper.

My time at Taco Bell did not threaten this dream, but enhanced its possibilities. While being exposed to the "real life" experiences of dicing tomatoes or scrubbing bean pots, I could contemplate my secret ambition without threat of competition. After all, I had plenty of time. I relished the wealth of my youth, the number of years I could waste and still be a great writer. In every book I read, I always turned to the dust jacket to find out when the author was first published. Hemingway achieved greatness at 25; at 20, I still had five years to squander! The time seemed to stretch on in front of me, full of promise. As preparation, I read books that I thought were sophisticated, so that their sophistication would rub off on me. That summer I started *Catch 22* and didn't like it, so I put it down. Then I checked out *Rabbit Run,* which I also didn't like, and I put that down too. Nobody could tell me anything. I was certain that stubbornness was a virtue.

All our work in the morning was preparation for the noon rush. This is where all my training came to bear, and where my future in fast food seemed most limited. The hardest task was learning to stuff on the front line during lunch hour. Everything was made fresh, and as the orders came in they appeared in abbreviated form on a video screen, like flights in air traffic control: BN BU WCH TC EXL PEP. The steamer frowned up at the screen, pulled a couple tortillas from the steam table, and tossed them on the rack. Then he smacked each of them with an installment of beans, and slid them down to me to stuff. There was a lot to learn. I had to know the ingredients of each food item (Burrito Supreme: beans, ground beef, red or green sauce, lettuce, cheese, onions, sour cream, olive) and the correct amounts of ingredients (cheese: one pinch; sour cream: one squirt of the gun; green onions: sprinkled sparingly for aesthetic appeal), to say nothing of customer-ordered variations (extra tortilla, extra cheese, no cheese, red sauce instead of green, both green and red, a.k.a. rainbow). Plus I had to wrap each item.

"Your burritos look awful," Rick complained. I was slow, too. The orders stacked up. At lunch time, the customers formed lines six deep. The air was full of the tang of cheese and the hot damp smell of beans and the greasy spice of beef. Pots clattered; managers hollered. The drive-through speaker blared out unintelligible orders. Our faces were pale and gleamed with sweat. The floor became slick with steam, grease, and the moist innards of destroyed south-of-the-border food items. The customers were insatiable: old men with false teeth, kids with skateboards, and fat ladies who needed, I thought, a long break from Taco Bell. All of them wanted burritos stuffed with extra sour cream and onions, or tostadas topped with lettuce and cheese, or nachos, the sauce gleaming a soft yellow, topped with a black olive sliver diced either by me or Dan or Kelly or Nancy or Marco or Ted or somebody else in the ever-changing menagerie that was the morning shift.

As quickly as it started, the rush ended. The dining room emptied, and the crew slowed down. The afternoon light slanted sideways into the dining room. Outside the window, the asphalt parking lot shone with the heat. Sometimes there were revelations. "Check this out," somebody called one day, and we all ran into the dining room and stared out the window. In the parking lot there was a black Corvette convertible that gleamed with an inner power. We could hear the rhythmic burble of its V8 above the Muzak. The guy that drove it was in his early thirties. He wore a polo shirt and a dark tan. Beside him, laughing, sat a girl with sun-bleached hair and white teeth. Between the plastic potted plants we stood and stared out the tinted windows at the car, the guy, and the girl, a trinity. We held our brooms and wash rags as we watched them. None of us said anything.

⧉ ⧉ ⧉

At the end of the shift we went out and sat at the table in the front of the store by the Taco Bell sign. We took our hats off and watched the traffic go by, drank Pepsis with ice, let the sweat dry on the backs of our necks. Another day was done. Paul stared down Thompson Boulevard and exhaled plumes of smoke through his nose. For my part, I had, after taxes, earned $14 and change and was ready revert back to literary mode. À la Hemingway, this consisted of bouts of frenzied writing interspersed with drunken poetic observations. Usually I got together with my non–Taco Bell friends and we drove out to the pier with six-packs of beer. It was a picturesque place to drink. The fog came in puffs, and the deck was wet and gleaming. We drank and talked about our lives. Anything was possible. Life was profound. At the end of the pier, men cast their lines with huge poles, while at their feet fish twitched. The waves beat against the pilings of the pier. On the beach, the lights of the city shone yellow in the air, and the wet sand reflected them. With a silent rush, the white foam rushed up and then receded out into the blackness.

The summer finally ended. On my last day I went into Rick's tiny office in the back of the store. He was counting cash. I handed over my uniform, washed and neatly folded, as per regulations. Rick inspected it for cleanliness, and then carefully hung it on the rack behind his chair, for the next recruit. He gave me my last paycheck and shook my hand.

"Maybe you'll come back next summer," he said.

"Maybe," I said.

卐 卐 卐

We had a party before I left. Dan Frances and I organized it. We chose a night when his parents were gone and moved his stereo out on the patio. The whole crew showed up. The beer flowed. Nancy asked me to dance, put her hands around my waist and then kissed me on the cheek. Later on Paul showed up and danced with three girls at once. I remember being happy that it was a summer evening, and that there was so much of my life ahead.

One night a few years later I got a call from Dan Frances. I had my first real job with a law firm and was living in a small apartment in Hollywood. He was drunk and wanted to know if I could come up to Ventura and party with him. He had left Taco Bell and was working as a security guard, because the police department had turned him down. I didn't tell him much about my life, but my writing was at a standstill. My own failure was becoming apparent. I didn't go and see him that night, and I never heard from him again. But I remember driving around in his Mustang the night of the party. We were out on Telegraph Road coming back with the beer.

"Watch this," he said, and the put the pedal down. The car squatted and roared, and I was thrown back in my seat. Through the windows, shadowed orange trees blurred. The reflectors on the side of the road were illuminated by the headlights and shot by like stars. Dan's Mustang ripped down the road with a contempt for everything bound stationary to the earth. I felt in the pit of my stomach the thrill of living, and I understood for the first time the attraction of speed. ■

Fields of Mercy

Ladette Randolph

I first heard the story of Armageddon from my best friend's stepfather. A Southerner with a Southerner's sense of drama and elaboration, he told us about the book of *Revelation* without equivocation. This *was* going to happen, every bit of it, just the way St. John had seen it in his vision on the Island of Patmos. The graves would open, the dead would rise. A hellish cast of characters would cause the world endless suffering: the dragon, the beast, the Antichrist.

At fourteen I was primarily concerned with the suffering described in the story and did not take much note of the promises for eternal peace and bliss that would follow the years of tribulation. Though deeply impressed, I wasn't certain at first if I believed the story. At home I asked my parents about it. They were obviously displeased, but they confirmed that what I had heard was all there in the book of *Revelation*. They too believed in a literal interpretation of the book, though they never talked about it, and seemed to feel it wasn't a fit subject for children's ears or for discussion with other church people.

With an adolescent's preoccupation with the grotesque, I became fascinated. I was drawn to the details of the prophesied end of time in much the way I was drawn to horror movies. The delicious sensation of being scared out of my wits fit in perfectly with the intensity of emotion I was experiencing in other areas of my life in those years. My church friends and I obsessed about the spectacular end we imagined. We recounted the gruesome details. It wasn't only us, however, for the early seventies marked an increased fascination with predictions of the apocalypse. David Wilkerson, famous for his book *The Cross and the Switchblade,* wrote a book detailing his own vision for the end times, aptly titled *The Vision.* He claimed he had seen a vision that indicated the end was very near at hand. There were other books written by conservative believers, one more graphic and wondrously detailed than the next. I bought them all, and I loved them. I was waiting for the inevitable end, hoping, as the *pre*-millenialists prophesied, that believers would be taken up—raptured—before the seven years of tribulation began. But just in case I had to suffer through the tribulation, I also read Richard Wormbrand's *Tortured for Christ,* a graphic testimony of his ordeal behind bars in a communist block country; Corrie Ten Boom's *The Hiding Place,* an account of her years in a Nazi concentration camp because of her family's role in hiding Jews (which they saw as their Christian duty); and a book by a female doctor (the title escapes me now), a missionary in the Congo, who was raped and driven from her camp by the "heathen natives." I was riveted by these accounts of faith and endurance in light of the quickly approaching end of time, and I was consumed with religious fervor, set to become a martyr for Christ.

Conversion stories fascinated me as well. They were the stories I gathered from the adults I knew, from testimonials at church camp and revival meetings. I collected these stories and retold them to friends. It was inevitable that I began to evangelize, bringing numerous friends into the church because of my influence. (To my amazement, all of those converts have stayed in the church twenty-five years later while I, the evangelist, have left.)

* * *

I was a precocious believer. By five I was singing solos in church, and at six I was baptized by immersion. Because the individual must choose to receive this form of baptism, which in my church (Christian Church) was believed essential for salvation, there were at first doubts that my six-year-old mind had grasped the enormity of that step. Mine was a farm family. We lived near the great Sandhills of Nebraska, a stark landscape. There were no neighbor children. No parks. No museums. It was an austere place where I grew up, and I was a child who wanted to sing and dance, to play the piano, to make up stories and plays, to draw elaborate pictures of mythical worlds. Where else in that environment but the church would I have found the beauty I craved? Only the church provided music and color and words. Such beautiful words. I still hear the words I first heard with chills at a Christmas pageant when I was very young, "And lo, this night in the city of David a son is born, Christ the Lord." And there were the Old Testament stories too: such passion and commitment. Such spectacular human folly and sin. Sin. I understood well the salvation I was receiving by going under the baptismal waters at age six. I was making a choice for a grander life.

In many ways I was not disappointed. I had a grand interior life. Perhaps I would have my faith yet today if I had been born into a church tradition that hadn't demanded such literalness of belief, if I had been exposed to the silent ritual of liturgical worship. (Instead, I was privy to the sermon, to the Sunday School lesson where no story was valued or recognized for its symbolic content.) Or a Pentecostal faith with its emphasis on the gifts of the spirit, allowing for a quirky individual vision, might have been enduring for me. Even as I seem to mourn my lost faith, I know it is irrational. Still, there are things I miss.

I miss my fundamentalist friends. The camaraderie of shared assumptions, the likes of which I'll never find again, is worth a moment of affectionate nostalgia now and then. There was a real community with those friends. Every weekend we met to cook meals together, to take long walks, watch movies. And we talked. We talked long into the night. If through the years my ideas became more and more abstract and mystical, even dangerously ecumenical, and if now and then I alarmed my friends with these ideas, I was still one of the gang, and my house a central meeting place. Those conversations I now recall spiraled and billowed. Ideas blossomed and stacked gloriously, airy and high. Such conversations reflected an intense search for the truth that I no longer pursue. The truth I found took me straight out of the very group that had provided such fertile ground for thought.

I remember one night shortly before I left the church telling one of these friends that I wanted to know myself so well that I would be perfectly distilled, like a drop of water, know exactly who I was in any circumstance, while at the same time be so big, so capable of understanding anything human that like an ocean I could find room for everyone and every idea. "You want to be God?" my friend said that night critically. I hadn't thought of it that way, that paradox a perfect description for what some might call God. "Why not?" I answered.

And then I read Blake, "Everything that lives is holy." And the Tao-Te Ching, and Jung. This was no crisis of faith, but rather an ever expanding acceptance of broader truths.

It was at about this time I had a dream. In the dream I came into an old-fashioned college classroom. I was late for class and everyone else had left. There had been a test that day, and the professor, an old white-haired man, who showed no impatience with my tardiness, pointed to where I should start. The test involved a number of booths at which some mathematical principle was enacted. My task was to name the principle or the theory behind the illustration. This was *not* a math class, and as I went from booth to booth, my test paper blank, I grew angrier and angrier. Finally, in complete frustration I at last put the unfinished test on the professor's desk and began to cry. The professor and I seemed to have a friendly, or familiar relationship, and he came from behind his desk to hug me in a fatherly way. He seemed genuinely concerned as he tried to comfort me. I said to him in anger then, "If I fail, you fail too." The meaning is apparent. I was telling the God that I had created—a kindly, delusional, and ultimately cruel God—goodbye. I sometimes miss him, too.

⌴ ⌴ ⌴

When I left the church, I also left my husband of twelve years, and I think in the minds of many of my fundamentalist friends, I went insane. My ex-husband certainly contributed to this idea. He told people that a demon had gotten hold of me, and he meant it. Friends I had lost track of since high school wrote to say they'd received letters from him telling them about my insanity and how I'd made off with the children, endangering their souls with my harebrained ideas. He said he was raising money for a custody fight, would they please help? There were a series of these letters. My own family members, all still in the church themselves, received the letters. "He's saying horrible things about you," one of my sisters-in-law told me. "How can you stand it?"

I shrugged, "I knew I would have to take the blame," I said. "It's worth it."

After weekend visits with their father, my children tell me about their activities: A pro-life march, a chastity conference, a revival meeting, a Christian rock concert, a missionary talk, an anti-abortion film, a movie about Armageddon. My friends outside the fundamentalist Christian community are horrified by these reports. "You have to tell them . . ." they say, suggesting any number of counter-activities, counterarguments, as though the minds of my children are like seesaws and need to be balanced with more weight on my end. But I don't see it that way, even though I, too, am deeply disturbed by the things they are being exposed to, all of it in a frantic attempt to save their souls from my influence. The balance I had provided while still living with their father is gone, for I would never have permitted all of this excess, and their father, now terrified by his loss, has become a caricature of fundamentalist belief—on his dining room wall hangs a huge bulletin board with missionary newsletters and appeals, Christian music plays on the stereo all day, and the activities mentioned above occupy the three weekends a month he has visitation with the children. When he doesn't see the children, he writes them letters filled with Scriptural admonitions. He warns them against the "spirit of the age," and reminds them to read their Bibles. He'll quiz them later to be sure they've read the assigned passages. So, just as I gained freedom from fundamentalism and their father, my children have become more imprisoned by both. No, I could not set up counterarguments or counter-activities. Instead of creating balance, I felt it would tear their psyches to bits. I felt that their father's energy, his fanaticism, could not be matched, that in fact it would not be healthy for me to try to match it.

For those who sometimes wonder why I've stayed in the same city, why I didn't move to avoid these problems, I have to say this is a progressive city where I have supportive friends, good work, a rich life beyond my past.

⚏ ⚏ ⚏

These days, I often feel suffocated by a world that seems to be filled with a saccharine, commercialized belief. Television programs like *Seventh Heaven* and *Touched by an Angel* are not only popular among viewers but sympathetically reviewed. Evangelistic Christian music and books now constitute a huge economy. Young people, including my three teenagers, flock to Christian rock concerts where the music is not only derivative, but the look is mainstream rock. Audio Adrenalin, DC Talk. Their music flirts with the edges, defining "cool" by how far they can go toward "worldliness" without crossing over. Each time I'm confronted by this commercialized Christianity I'm reminded of the story of Jesus' rage in the temple, clearing the money changers out (still the heart of the zealot in me). I find this industry far from benign. On the front door of the local Christian bookstore is the cartoonish depiction of an apocalyptic world. It's the advertisement for a new book by Tim LaHaye, a fictional account of the end of time. LaHaye is familiar from my own days of fevered reading in the early seventies. What is new now is the dominance of the industry and the evolution from prediction (a form of fiction) to an open fictionalization of events.

In the ten years since I left the church not only has this commercialized Christianity gained a strong foothold in the economy and in mainstream American thought, but it has gained tremendous influence politically. I was disturbed by the rumblings of the Christian Right as it began to emerge in the five years before I left the church, but I could never have predicted that in 1994 the U.S. Congress would support Newt Gingrich's Contract with America, and that that year's election would seat several freshman senators with openly fundamentalist agendas. I could not have predicted that within the public schools, talk of religion in the classroom would become such an impassioned subject that support for a Christian-based curriculum would have enough backing to support legislative initiatives. I could not have predicted that these political/academic shifts would lead my beloved brother-in-law, a conservative politician involved in the grassroots of the Christian Coalition, to tell me in 1994—when I said I couldn't live in this country if Newt Gingrich had his way—"And we'll want you to leave." The chilling first person plural suggested far more of a plan than my paranoia had even seen coming. I was beginning to have apocalyptic flashbacks. The glee with which the wars and skirmishes in Iraq were met by some in the Christian Fundamentalist community—convinced the long awaited prophesies for the end of time had been fulfilled—signaled a dangerous collective thinking, a wish fulfillment of destruction. Jerry Falwell's glib announcement that the Antichrist would be a Jewish male in his thirties, who was most likely walking the earth now, was not as singular a notion as many people wanted to think.

I feel less burdened now, having laid my faith aside, but I feel life is less magical, less intensely personal, too. While I still had faith, I felt I was the center of a meaningful drama, part of the fight for my soul. The universe had a specific beginning and a prescribed end. There was a definite plot—a battle between good and evil that would inevitably end in a violent and glorious battle, with the good guaranteed to win. No action film could compete with my own psychodrama. Trumpets would sound. Every knee would bow. All tears would be dried and there would be peace between all things. Beautiful words. "There will be no more crying, no more tears. . . ."

I had a dream once about the Rapture. I dreamt I was walking downtown in a large city. No city I recognized, though it vaguely resembled the mythical Gotham City. It was a gray day, very dreary, and I was on the sidewalk between stores when suddenly the wind came up and whipped around the crowds of shoppers. The weather was frightening enough, but suddenly the sky above us was filled with black helicopters. The sound was deafening. Without warning I was pulled hard, as if by magnetic force, to my knees. I saw that everyone else around me had been pulled to their knees as well. We covered our ears against the noise of the helicopters. I exchanged a glance with a woman beside me on the sidewalk, and I said, "I wonder if this is the Rapture." The woman nodded in agreement. I shudder now in recounting this menacing dream, but the feeling during the dream and for weeks afterward was one of both terror and euphoria, for I had known without a doubt as I shivered and cowered there on my knees that I would be allowed to board one of those black helicopters, like my sister-in-law's story of being airlifted out of Vietnam right before the fall of Saigon. I would be spared all sorts of horrors, literally saved by my faith.

Such drama is hard to leave. My faith was like a thick curtain, like a flat-earth theory of the world. I felt safe and knowing within its parameters. If I ventured close to the edge, or reached out to pull back the curtain, I always retreated to the safe known world. The sense of safety, of clear margins, allowed me freedom of range. I had a sense of knowing where I was in the world. Now, with all sorts of intellectual freedom, I often find my world is strangely prescribed. Paradoxically, though the world seems more vast I opt not to explore as much. There is now nothing at stake. While my faith had certain limits, those very limits became the site of great intellectual work, defining, defying. My fundamentalist friends were smart and interesting, educated, well-read. I would still find certain conversations with them stimulating, I believe, but I gave up my passport to that world. I had to. And even as I miss that sense of belonging, it is in much the same way that I miss childhood. There is no going back.

It was not easy to leave. I'd been warned most of my conscious life about "out there," "the darkness," "the ignorant," "Satan's sphere of influence." The books that might have introduced reason into my life when all of this fervor began in adolescence were somehow never available. They weren't on the bookshelves at home, and in my school's curriculum the archaic reading material somehow never cut through the bulwark of my already captive imagination.

I'd like to say I was looking for something in my adolescence and never found it but, truthfully, I had a resistant arrogance. It was I who was privy to information others needed; I knew the truth; I had the key to salvation. What could penetrate such suspicious, over-confident armor as that? The changes had to come slowly from within myself.

By the time I graduated from high school those changes had begun. I was no longer quite so certain. Church ritual annoyed me. My father's ministry was in turmoil, and the church people had revealed themselves to be more cruel than any adults I had previously known. The seeds were there, but nothing had quite taken root, and I made a bad decision to go to Bible College, to the dismay of some of my high school teachers. Though I turned a deaf ear to their protests, I was miserable both the summer before I left and the year I spent at Bible College. How could it have been called a college? One hundred and sixty students. Course offerings such as: Personal Evangelism, Life of Christ, Sunday School Education. The bald-faced indoctrination hastened my realization that organized religion was foolishness. Being forced to attend daily chapel services and nightly devotions only added to my rebellion in ways that might never have happened had I not been forced to take part.

My frustration did not signal a loss of faith. I was still an adamant believer. The problem was that the church was hypocritical. I couldn't stand the inconsistency between what was claimed and what was practiced. I wanted the integrity of Richard Wormbrand's experience, the refining test of faith. I'd lost respect for the pedestrian nature of the church. On some deep level I was a fanatic. My faith was still intact, but I wished to leave the church; however, some strange inertia held me back. I knew of nothing else, no other life, and my vague yearnings had no specific goal. I wanted the challenge of a beautiful life, but kept feeling myself restrained by a squalid reality. My contacts were so restricted that I knew no one I admired outside the church. I had been trained not to want things, trained by my reading material, my church doctrine, my own passivity, my loyalty to friends and family to want only the familiar, but there in the midst of the faithful, I was miserable and wanted out. And then I fell in love.

That should have perhaps been the end of the story, the beginning of my adult life, a life still of faith though perhaps a more reasonable faith. I visit that time now and again as we do all ruptures and wonder what if. . . . It is unavoidably a turning point in my life, for I married the young man I fell in love with. My life of faith, though, had not prepared me for his sudden death six weeks after we were married. And if I trace my loss of faith to the fissure that resulted from my grief over his death, it is also the site of my momentary return to the church, my blind, headlong, free fall back into organized religion, into a wrong-headed second marriage. I found again, desperate to define a life that had suddenly gone to sea, my old familiar fervency, my passionate zealous religiosity. I went mad in my own peculiar way.

Funny, how years later when after hard work and careful thought I finally regained my sanity, I would be considered mentally disturbed by my fundamentalist friends and acquaintances. In a way, I was absurdly amused. I was so happy to be back to some semblance of myself that it didn't matter what anyone said, how they criticized. It didn't matter that some of my friends not only abandoned but betrayed me. How could such little things matter?

There were all those years to be accounted for, though. They seemed wasted, wasteful. I remember two distinct images of my second marriage: one, the feeling that I was on the wrong path, that I was living the wrong life; and two, how time and again in the midst of the most mundane tasks, I would think in these words exactly, "these are my years in the wilderness." And like the Israelites, forced to wander, the promised land glimpsed but ultimately denied them because they had sinned, I felt I was paying a penance. I had made my bed, and now I had to lie in it. My harsh world view, the strict demands I made of myself were only what many others had suffered before me who believed in a strict, moralistic God. Such a God is in some ways easier to leave than the gentlemanly, slightly doddering God of those "fuzzy headed Methodists," the God I finally adopted before leaving my faith altogether.

What I retain of my lost faith is a respect still for the abstract tenets of Scripture: love, mercy, grace, forgiveness. In the end it was not scorn that enabled me to leave the church, but these tenets. Another story altogether. While I agonized in that awkward juncture before leaving, I unexpectedly felt no condemnation, only fields and fields of mercy, a sense that as humans we are destined to be both absurd and lovely. Eventually, I understood there was no God judging me. There was no religious faith that was not in some way of our own making. What I decided to make for myself, instead, was mercy. So I did.

Within This Landscape, I Find You

Anna Moss

When I first love you, it is summer. There must be a cricket song for every square in the mesh of the screen window. You make me feel sexy. I don't use my imagination and the feeling lingers longer than morning. The land is stretched flat and burned tired by the sun. Mississippi is a long way from my Michigan home and the distance relieves me. The change in the land leaves me exposed and feeling somehow new, as if the shift from cornfields and sloping pastures to cotton fields and naked flatness finds its way inside me.

* * *

I was sent to Tunica, Mississippi by a domestic Peace Corps program, Teach For America. I applied to the program knowing nearly nothing about it. What I did know was that it would relocate me far from home and the difficulties of my parents' divorce. At the same time, it would give me a social service job to be proud of. I feel like a cheater when you tell me that as soon as you heard about the program and its efforts to alleviate the desperate teacher shortages in resource-needy schools, you knew it was for you. Now that I am here, teaching in a room where before there was, perhaps, a janitor starting a video but certainly nothing more, I can see clearly the reasons I should have had for applying to this program. As Emergency Certified Special Education Teachers, we're filling in where otherwise there would be no teacher at all. When you ask me why I decided to join the program, I lie and speak with the insight I didn't have until I got here. I want you to like me.

I met Laura, the third Special Education teacher at Tunica Junior High, before I met you. I had an "interview" two weeks before school started, but it really turned out to be a chance for the principal to tell me what subjects I would teach. Laura waited outside the school office and then took me on a tour of Tunica. She said this was her third year in Tunica and she wanted to help me get my feet on the ground before the first day of school. She drove me through all the subs our students live in. We started at Sugar Ditch Alley, "got its name from the open sewage that ran through it up until the mid-'80s," and ended with White Oak, "This one's rough. We'll just drive along the edge of the neighborhood." Along the way she showed me the cracked asphalt court the boys play basketball on and the places her students live. She pointed out the different shacks with dangerously sloping roofs, rotting wood, gaps where wall corners should meet, and missing front doors. She called her students honey, sweety, sugar, my babies.

"You know, it's best if you don't drive through any of the subs alone until you've been here several weeks and people recognize you as a teacher. Even then," she continued, "it's always safer to take a student along." I immediately felt like Laura was a mother figure. Partly since she's years older and partly because she is so wise in the ways of Tunica. I asked her why she joined Teach For America.

"I was working in publishing in San Diego. Editing science journals. But then I read Jonathan Kozol's book, *Savage Inequalities.* I couldn't just do nothing. My mother thought I was crazy when I up and left. Still does. Maybe I am." On the way back to the school she points out the nice homes in town where all the white folks live.

"You can see why nobody from Teach For America even tries to live in Tunica. There's no neighborhood for people like us. The blacks don't trust us since we're white and the whites don't trust us since we teach in the black school. That's why most of the Teach For America people who teach here live in Helena, Arkansas. There, it's possible to live at the edge of where the black and white neighborhoods meet. It's only 30 minutes away, just over the Mississippi River. Living outside of Tunica allows you to be neutral, anonymous."

Laura was the first person to mention your name to me. "You and Kim and I need to meet up before school starts and get organized. We should be fairly consistent in our rules and consequences, since the Special Ed kids will spend their whole day among the three of us."

I hope you didn't notice, but I barely heard a word of our first meeting, unable to listen and concentrate on you at the same time. You had on your maroon tank top and jeans. Your shoulders jutted out of the armholes in perfect smooth lines and somehow seemed to be both strong and delicate. I couldn't see how you could wear long pants in the heat. You said you were going hiking in the woods with your dog after our meeting. I wanted you to ask me to go with you. I thought I caught you watching me too, but I was sure it was just a figment of my wishing.

After spending one afternoon together with friends, that night you finally asked me into your apartment. I was disappointed with your enthusiasm for teaching me chess. I was even more disappointed when you were ready to send me home after I quickly lost. I could have played chess better; I just wanted the game to be over and to get rid of the playing board between us. I didn't think before I crawled across the floor we had sat on to play, and as I reached you, I became shy. Instead of the kiss I had intended, you only got a slight brush of lips. You ended up not sending me home at all. The entire night was only innocent kisses and holding, more intimate than any sex.

Before I left Michigan, my greatest concern about moving to the South was the legendary heat of the region. I obsessed over methods and tricks to cope with the discomfort of intense heat. I thought avoiding turning on the oven would help and began to collect recipes for dishes that didn't need to be baked. I wrote them on index cards and the pile grew slowly; gazpacho, green salads, fruit salads, salads with fancy dressings, Jell-O, ice cream pie, and chocolate peanut butter bars, a dessert my mother, who learned the recipe from her mother, makes for special treats, especially at the holidays.

A year and a half ago, I was home from college for Christmas, just as I had been every other year. The tree was in the same corner of the living room as it always was, next to the fireplace, covered with tiny white lights, just visible to the cars that passed by in the edge of the large picture window. The mantle was decorated, as always, with boughs (real, not artificial) that were also covered with white lights. All the little white lights in that one corner of the room cast enough light to read by.

That year I was trying to make plans to visit a friend in New York the week between Christmas and New Year's. I found my father in the living room with the newspaper. He was on the opposite side of the room from the tree, next to a lamp.

I sat on the couch adjacent to my dad's chair, and waited for him to finish what he was reading. He was holding the front page open and I read the headlines that were facing me. And waited. The last page of the paper advertised appliances at basement bargain prices. Finally I asked if I could talk with him. He let out a distracted "Mm-hm." The paper didn't move. I explained that I wanted to use one of the family cars, asked if he would mind if I went away for a few days, and waited for him to answer. Only the upper corners of the paper lightly trembled. I stood up and paused, giving him one more chance before I left the room. The newspaper stayed between us.

I went directly to my parents' bedroom where my mother was in bed. She had a new thick book, something about the history of philosophy, that rested on her chest as she read. I sat on the bed next to her.

"I'm trying to talk with Dad about going to New York and he won't even put the newspaper down."

"I know," she said. "I have to leave him."

I watched her face, her eyes already wet though not quite crying, and realized she meant really leave. She meant move out. She meant pack her things and go. For a horrible moment, it seemed I had convinced her to leave, that my complaints of Dad were what made her realize she had to get out. I wondered what exactly it was about my words that had brought on this decision of hers. This wasn't what I had meant. I wanted her to take it back and not make me part of her conspiracy. I wanted her to be making a horrible joke.

Quickly though, my shock gave way to obvious clues I hadn't understood until this moment. My parents hadn't been on a vacation together in years. My mom had passed up a chance to change her work schedule so it would be more compatible with her husband's. My father didn't put down the newspaper when he was talking with her, either.

She cried a little, quietly, and looking down at the comforter she smoothed with her hands. I asked how long she had been unhappy.

"Five years. I would've left earlier, but Austin was just a baby." My brother was ten, still the baby. She continued to cry and even though I felt I should have been more consoling, I wondered instead how this would affect my life.

"How soon will you leave? Where will you go?"

"I don't know any of that yet. Not until after Christmas."

I asked my mother if there was someone else and regretted the question as soon as I saw her smile. I was scared by these intimate secrets but also curious about the type of man my mother would love, the type of man she would love more than my father—enough, in fact, to leave my father. Curiosity was stronger and I asked his name. She was smiling, a tiny smile only at the edges of her mouth. Even with the tears still on her cheeks, it was the happiest expression I'd seen on her in years.

"Jim." This was as far as either of us let the conversation go.

I didn't mention the trip to New York again. Christmas morning there were more gifts than there had been any other year. My mom always did the Christmas shopping and this year, knowing she would be leaving, she tried to compensate prematurely with gifts. My two brothers and dad were thrilled. Just like every year before it, they thought this was the best Christmas ever.

卐 卐 卐

And this is where I want to stop telling you this ugly story. Where I become embarrassed and ashamed and want to claim no relation. I don't want you to think this kind of love and marriage and mean divorce is my inheritance. I don't want you to think I own this. It is not mine.

卐 卐 卐

My mother told my father she was leaving him on the second day of the New Year. By telephone. From Idaho. My mother and I were there to attend my cousin's wedding. We were sharing a hotel room with my mother's sister, Cindy. She received the news at exactly the same time as my father. My mother held the phone tightly, stood in front of a picture window looking out onto Lake Coeur d'Alene and the surrounding mountains, and said, quite simply through tears, "I need a divorce." I was a bridesmaid in my cousin's wedding and wore a beautiful long dress of black velvet and a shiny deep purple material I don't know the name of.

My father couldn't seem to decide what he wanted. He wanted her to take everything that was hers and never come back. He wanted her to stay, begged her to let him love her, to at least try counseling. He became a man of spontaneous tears. When we returned home after the wedding, he had taken down all the pictures of her. She packed her things the day after our return and left. My brothers, Austin, ten, and Peter, eighteen, had no idea she was going to be gone when they came home from school that day.

I felt guilty that I was with my mom when she gave him the news and that my dad was alone. I wanted to remain the unbiased third party. I asked him to drive me back to school so we could spend some time together. The drive to Ann Arbor took an hour and a half, and I thought that maybe getting out, with a purpose, would be good for him. We stopped for coffee at a McDonald's where my father, a distinguished man, tall and thin with silver hair and a trimmed beard, collapsed onto the trash station. He stretched his arms across the space reserved for dirty trays and held his head against them while he wept. People politely ignored him. I rubbed his back. I traced the letters of THANKYOU that decorate the door to the trash-can. I stirred the cream into his coffee. When he was able to walk out to the car he got in the passenger seat and I drove the rest of the way to school.

I did not cry or feel sad because I wasn't supposed to. Without my mother, my father had no one to take care of him, and I was the natural person to fill in. I called him nearly every other day from school. I worried he would try to kill himself. He wouldn't speak of my mother except to say that he wouldn't say anything ill of her in front of their children. Just the way he said that made his ill thoughts of her clear. He didn't even know where she was, staying in a new apartment close to downtown where Jim would come and spend nights with her. She had become so immersed in her new and free life that I hardly spoke with her for months. When I was able to reach her, Jim was always there and she was too distracted, giggly.

I wish I could ignore the distasteful and keep things between us only beautiful. You make me want to discover an artistic talent in myself and use it to create beauty for you, something to match what I feel for you, and this story I'm giving you is far from beauty. I stay up late writing you letters and am always unsatisfied. I want expensive pens and slightly textured paper for these letters. I want my handwriting to be fascinating, my words to be closer to poetry, I want to slip dried flowers and their scent into the envelope. But I have only the same amount of artistic talent I've always had, which is to say not enough. My letters are written on yellow legal pads and my handwriting is still uneven and childlike. The envelopes are plain and smell, if at all, of the sealant. The most beautiful expression I have known is our touching and for that I need you here. Now.

You ask me if I'm like my mother. It would be appropriate to tell you about the time, when I was in seventh grade, that the whole family visited the Madison Children's Hands-On Museum. There was one exhibit with a double-sided two-way mirror. My mom and I sat on either side of the mirror and it created an image of our faces blended together. There was a dial on one side and turning it controlled the degree to which our features were blended. At one end of the dial, only my face filled the mirror, at the other end only my mother's. Once we adjusted our seats so we were sitting at the same level, it was difficult to define our features at any degree of blending. Even when the dial was turned all the way to either end, it was hard to believe the other person's features weren't seeping into the image as well.

You have asked the question after looking at yourself in the bathroom mirror, examining your facial features and finding evidence of a matrilineal influence. We aren't talking about inclination for divorce or approaches to love. We're talking about both you and your mother having the same shadows around your brown eyes, we're talking about the slight hump your mother has on her back just where her neck starts and your fear of developing it, but I'm thinking of the squares of clean paint my mother left behind on the walls when she took the pictures she wanted. I can tell by the following silence you are confused by my sharp "I am not like my mother," and I know I should apologize, but I don't.

卐 卐 卐

School starts and I try to hide how nervous I am about us working together. I realize that the 30-minute drive to work is not a hassle but instead a needed separation between work and home. When we drive out of Helena in the morning, the sun is beginning to come up and the river, when the alignment is just right, becomes solid and unmoving with bright orange or pink color. There aren't many people on the road at six in the morning so it's easy for me to imagine we're starting on a road trip rather than going to work. The sign over us when we cross the bridge says, "Welcome to Mississippi," the S's clinging to each other in their bottom-heavy curves. Underneath, in smaller letters, it reads, "The Hospitality State."

The Teach For America teachers aren't readily accepted by the veteran teachers in Tunica. It is the first time I experience being inherently disliked before I'm even known. I'm not liked because I'm white and quiet and small and do group activities with my classes. The other teachers loom powerfully above their students who sit in very straight rows.

Mrs. Haley is the worst. She underestimates how quickly I'll catch on to the foreign Delta dialect and tells the librarian that I'm just a "snotty yankee girl who thinks she know somethin' 'bout nothin" while I'm three feet away from her. Before the librarian can stop her, Mrs. Haley goes on to say, "She just a damn yankee thinkin' how we do things here not good 'nough for her." Mrs. Haley isn't terribly large, but she seems to shadow me with her loud voice and big boned body. She manages to be both bottom heavy and top heavy at the same time, balancing shelf-like breasts and a large behind all on top of tiny high heels.

I try to phrase it right when I tell you that I'm scared at school. I'm scared to be with you, to risk someone figuring us out. I want you to understand it's not that I don't want to be with you. It's that I don't want them to know I'm with you. Even beyond that, beyond Tunica, it's that I don't want to be afraid to be with you.

We cross the bridge every night on the way home and pass under the sign that reads, "Welcome to Arkansas," in simple red letters and underneath, "The Natural State." At the very bottom, in even smaller letters, it says, "Home of President Bill Clinton." There are soybean silos and a pesticide plant close to the bridge and the smell varies day to day, with what is being done at each place and which way the wind blows. We try to describe the smells to each other, but never quite get it right. Like moldy rice. Grain rotting.

卐 卐 卐

Here, summer turns to fall turns to winter with only a change from green to brown. I miss the bright autumn colors of Michigan trees. I try to describe them to you. Growing up in Seattle, where it is lush green all year long, you don't know how many colors the leaves can be. The absence of color is at least partially made up for by the cotton fields, which, by late September, turn to long rows of popcorn. We make peppermint tea and drink it on the old uneven couch we've moved to the porch.

卐 卐 卐

We are collecting leaves to take home and press in the telephone book. You choose them carefully, taking into consideration the variety of sizes and shapes and vein patterns, looking for the selection you need to teach a science lesson. You are holding a leaf in your hand, and looking at the low branches of another tree, when you ask me who there was before you. I'm not exactly sure what you mean and am even less sure of what you want to hear. Is it the flat facts, the reasons and the justifications, the assurance that I want to be with you? I think, perhaps, the story I should tell you, the story that somehow answers your question, is of Molly.

We lived in the same house on Thompson Street; she had the apartment below mine. When I returned to school, after the Christmas when my parents split, Molly was the first person I told and the only one I cried with. After the tears, we went to The Brown Jug, our favorite campus diner. Together we consumed two baskets of fries and three pitchers of beer in a little over three hours. A faithful friend, Molly wouldn't allow me to be drunk or miserable alone. It was 11:30 when we left the Jug. The air outside was shockingly cold and smokeless.

When we reached our house, I stopped at Molly's door while she unlocked it. She turned toward me before going inside and hugged me. She put her lips to my ear and I could feel them form the sounds as she whispered in a sober voice, "I'm sorry." We held each other longer. Long enough for our faces to turn warm against each other. The kiss would have seemed merely a portion of the embrace except that it, also, lasted too long. That night I dreamt Molly naked. Her long red-blond hair just reached her breasts and matched the color of her nipples exactly.

I spent the rest of the year drunk and sleeping with boys, trying so hard to be straight. But this was the moment I began to wonder. Though I wouldn't have admitted it at the time, this was when I first knew you were a distant possibility.

This may be what you want to know, but there is something that keeps me from telling you. You are still standing under the branches of the same tree; the sunlight is filtered and moving, the leaf is still in your hand and I can't, at this moment, define loving you in relation to what I've felt with others. I think to myself I will tell you all of this later, and instead say you are the first man or woman I've loved like this.

⌐ ⌐ ⌐

Fall arrives and is almost indistinguishable from summer. The Southern heat lessens, just barely. I begin to have dreams of the other teachers finding out, of Mrs. Haley appearing at the Wednesday staff development meeting in a gold lamé disco outfit pointing with a drunken finger and saying, "You two dykes." And the rest of the teachers chanting, "Dykes, dykes, dykes." This doesn't happen, but Mrs. Haley does announce before we arrive at a faculty meeting that she is quite sure we are "funny together." We ride to school together every day, you have short hair, and neither of us wears dresses very often.

Matt Wilhelm is nervous too. Even though he is also part of Teach For America, he hears what the other teachers say about us. He tries to warn me. We are outside together, on bus duty, monitoring students before the bell rings for homeroom to begin.

"Don't take this the wrong way, but you need to be more careful."

"What do you mean?" I assume he is referring to my approach to bus duty, which is to interfere only when things are out of hand, as in someone will surely get hurt, and to otherwise let the students run wild.

"I mean you and Kim. It's obvious when you're together that there is something between you. Mrs. Haley said something again yesterday." He looks down as he speaks. My first reaction is one of anger, as if we are young giggly girls in love and incapable of thinking of anything else. One of my students, Evelyn, comes running near us, barely balanced on the delicate dress shoes she's wearing. She grabs my arm,

"Ms. Good, Ms. Good, Ms. Good!" She shrieks my name the last time. "Teddy is after me and he's going to get me!" I'm still caught on Matt's words.

Matt fills in for my silence. "Come on, Evelyn, you want Teddy to catch you." Evelyn releases my arm and runs off, with Teddy in pursuit. I become more conscious of the groups of students near us. I lower my voice when I speak.

"We are careful. I hardly see her at all during the day and when we do we keep our distance." It comes out more defensive than I intend.

"Look, Anna." He is turning red and getting flustered. The bell rings and students are dispersing to their classrooms. I wait for Matt to finish. He pauses while groups of students rush by before he continues. "I'm just saying that, even though you are careful about physical distance, your feelings are still obvious. It's not safe here." Before we go inside he puts his hand on my shoulder and squeezes.

I know Matt is right. The most powerful insults our students have for each other are "faggot" and "gay." The state of Mississippi just passed legislation to make absolutely sure no gay couples will ever get married on its soil. The one openly gay man in Tunica isn't out by choice but because he fits the stereotype too exactly to not be out. He is beaten in the bars on a weekly basis. When two seventh grade girls are caught passing notes that are deemed too affectionate, they are sent to the school disciplinarian. I don't tell you about Matt's warning. Instead, I suggest we start avoiding each other at school. It's easier that way, I claim. It feels too dishonest to see you and treat you as only a co-worker.

⌐ ⌐ ⌐

Dad comes to visit for Labor Day weekend. We have Monday off, and even though school has been in session just over a month, I'm grateful for the rest. He stays at the Holt House Bed and Breakfast, less than two miles from my house. He drives down, claiming that he loves to drive, but I know he hates flying more. I turn into a tourist for the weekend, visiting Oxford and Faulkner's home, eating at soul food restaurants and visiting the local blues bars. I'm anxious for you to meet him. He shakes your hand and says he's glad I've found such a good friend. Sunday night the three of us go to dinner together. I feel like a liar during the meal, trying to talk with you as if you are just a friend. After Dad and I drop you off, he and I go on a walk along the Mississippi River. In the dim evening, the murky water seems clear and the sound of the river is its power. My father and I stand on a lookout as the sun goes down and I watch the carved graffiti pronouncing that Mark will love Katie forever fade into darkness. Dad talks about my brothers and work and how he is feeling better. I ask questions and answer the ones he asks. I wish he would guess, figure it out and ask me himself. I consider not telling him until I go home for Christmas. Then I imagine not telling him at all, ever. There is a silence. Perhaps Dad is waiting for me to answer a question I didn't hear or maybe it is simply a pause in the conversation.

"Dad?" I know what is about to come out of my mouth, but my stomach still aches as if I'm undecided. "I'm gay."

"Oh." He doesn't turn his head toward me and I try to decipher his profile. It reveals nothing.

"Are you okay?"

"Yes, yes. Did you think it wouldn't be okay? I'm just, just a little surprised, that's all." He continues to look only in front of him and tugs at his beard. "I don't know what to say."

We are standing next to each other, still looking at the water we can't see through the darkness.

"Who else knows?"

"Only you."

"Good. I mean, I just think it's best that way. You haven't told your brothers, have you?" I shake my head. "Good. Yeah. Jesus, don't tell them."

He gives me an awkward sideways hug with his arm around my shoulder. "Okay then. You happy?" I nod. "Good."

My dad and I walk back to where we parked at the beginning of the river road. It has gotten late. He's leaving early in the morning, by six, he says. He tells me I don't have to get up to see him off; there's no reason to since he's leaving so early. We say our good-byes. At home, you are waiting up for me. I don't know how to tell you I think he is ashamed of me. I say everything went fine. It seems that telling you would only hurt you too. You fall asleep quickly, facing the wall, and I hide tears beneath your deep breathing.

I call my mom a few days later. With the news out to my dad, I decide that if for no other reason than fairness I should tell her too. Now it is her turn. I tell her I'm gay, over the phone, from Mississippi. She is shocked and then realizes, I'm not sure for what reasons, that it is not that big of a surprise after all.

* * *

Winter now. We are living together and the house where I pay rent has become nothing more than a storage place. When the light dusting of snow falls the people here spin into a chaotic panic. School is let out early and we are told to go home and stay put. We stop at the Piggly Wiggly for dinner food. Other carts are overflowing with non-perishables. We buy Merlot and that evening make love with moist fingers and lips. By morning the snow is gone.

When we decide you'll come home with me for Christmas I'm amused by your excitement over the possibility of more than an inch of snow. Two weeks before the start of our vacation, I ask Dad if he has told Austin, my 12-year-old brother.

"Told him what?"

"About Kim and me."

"Why do we need to tell him? He doesn't need to know."

"He's smart, Dad, he'll figure it out."

"Not if you act normal, he won't. Just act normal, let him have his childhood."

"This is not going to ruin his childhood. And it's not something that will just go away. It's better to tell him now than have him figure it out on his own later. Do you want to tell him, or should I when we get there?" I've never simply refused my father before. I'm more nervous now than I was when I came out to him.

"Austin does not need to know." His voice is shaky with fury. There is a long angry silence while we each wait for the other to compromise. I give in and speak first.

"Maybe we need to just talk about this later."

"Bye." The word fades and it sounds like he starts to hang up as he says it. I listen to the empty line for a moment. I consider calling him back but I don't think it will make anything better.

I learned stubbornness from my father. A week passes and I don't hear from him. Then I get an envelope in the mail. It is a journal article on how traumatic it is for young adolescents to deal with issues of homosexuality. Attached is a post-it note reading, "Thought you should see this." I try calling him then. I leave a message on his machine, letting him know the dates we will be in town and ask him to call please. He doesn't call and I make arrangements for us to stay with Mom.

卐 卐 卐

Rodrigo has been the cornerstone of my behavior management all year. A big 17-year-old, he is especially large for the eighth grade. Both his size and his age make him a natural leader to the other students. You and Laura tell me that he is a constant disruption during lessons and the other students follow his lead. However, his crush on me has transformed him into an enforcer in my class. He won't even allow others to talk out of turn while I'm teaching. But something changes just after Thanksgiving break. Instead of watching me intently, he gazes at the top corner of the room and makes sure his look is one of intense boredom. He begins throwing spitballs at other students during class and I have to ask him to take the pick out of his hair. I assume I've lost my enchanting newness and am just another teacher now. Two days before Christmas break, on a day when the principal, Mr. Bulloch, is out of the building, Rodrigo raises his hand politely during fifth period. I've just handed out a writing assignment and anticipate that he wants to use the pencil sharpener.

"Are you and Ms. Myers, you know," he holds out his hand in front of him, palm down, and tilts it back and forth, "funny together?" I am careful to keep my eyes on his. The class is the quietest it has been in weeks.

"How dare you." I am careful to keep my voice low and controlled. It is just loud enough for everyone in the room to hear. "How dare you even suggest such an insulting thing." I won't look away from him and can only hope that as my face turns red they all think it is from anger and not embarrassment.

"Rodrigo, you know that is the most disrespectful thing you can say to a person and how dare you say it to me. You're lucky Mr. Bulloch isn't here today, or I would have you in his office by the scruff of your neck and I don't need to tell you what he would do to you."The skin pulled tight across my collar-bone is shaking with anxiety, but none of the students seem able to look at me now. They are suddenly intensely interested in their writing assignment.

⌐ ⌐ ⌐

The drive North reveals the winter you have been waiting for. By the time we reach Michigan there are several inches of snow and the last bit of driving is slick. My winter driving scares you, but you just aren't used to the ice. We use the directions they sent us to find Mom and Jim's house. It is important to me that when we arrive there it is the first time for both of us. I see some familiar Christmas decorations, but more new ones, in this farmhouse that is my mother's new home.

Christmas Eve we stay up late with Mom and Jim. We eat sugar cookies and drink hot tea. Mom frets about us living in the Bible Belt. She points out that it must be the most unfriendly part of the country for us to live in. Dangerous, is what she calls it.

I can't help thinking of the Christmas before, the first one without my mother. The absence she left made the house cold and suddenly too big. My father had done nothing to suggest the ensuing holiday. All he seemed to do was work. Once he arrived home he would drink wine and watch the news. I had two younger brothers who needed at least some suggestion of good cheer. I took my dad's credit card and made him generous. I wrapped all the gifts. I bought a tree from a K-Mart parking lot and got a rash on my forearms just dragging it to the car. I baked five different kinds of Christmas cookies and read *The Joy of Cooking* to learn how to prepare a turkey. I hated my mother for leaving me with this.

This year, when I use my key to let myself into the house while I know my dad is at work, I am grateful you're with me. I find my old bedroom empty. He has packed my things and stacked them in the deepest corner of the basement.

I wait for a chance to tell Austin. I find him alone in the kitchen one morning while you are in the shower and Mom and Jim are at the store. I don't know how to tell him and am awkward with my words. I wish I had planned exactly how to say this.

"Aus, how do you like Kim?"

"I like her." This isn't news to me; you are a willing video game partner and persuaded me to join an indoor football game with him.

"Austin, I like Kim a lot. More than the way you like a friend. I like her the way some women like their boyfriends."

"Okay." He is watching his finger rub back and forth on the kitchen counter and is smiling big as if he knows all of this already.

"You don't seem very surprised."

"I'm not."

"What do you mean?"

"I overheard Dad on the phone with Mrs. Fox. They were talking about you."

⊑ ⊑ ⊑

The rest of the school year drags. I wonder if we will make it until the end of May. There are rumors about us. Jeff Fennell, a student, sees us driving on Old 61 one weekend and mentions it slyly during third period on Monday. I consciously perform a casual reaction before going into the teachers' lounge and throwing up. From then on, we drive separately to school and only talk in official meetings. I'm grateful for the 30 miles that separate Helena from Tunica. When there are rumors that Mr. Wilhelm and I are having an affair, I sit next to him during the school assembly and call him by his first name in front of some students.

Spring. The Mississippi floods. We buy 12-foot cane fishing poles and make pasta salad to take as a picnic. We fish after work. It's a short walk to the river from our front door. There are at least ten other people fishing and they seem to have been there all day. Some have on tall rubber boots and wade in as far as they're able. Most have large plastic buckets they've turned upside down to sit on. The river is at its highest level in ten years. There must be a language to describe how much a river floods. All I know is that the river road, which follows the course of the water, has been overtaken. I know homes that are accustomed to the temperament of the river have been caught beyond the cement block stilts that hold them up. The adjacent land that is normally tangled with tall grass and weeds, where there is always an egret to be spotted, is covered. Tips of four-foot-tall grass are barely exposed. We fish for three hours and never catch a thing, though everyone else seems to.

Eight weeks later the river recedes to its normal boundaries. It leaves a great expanse of barren dust land, riddled with dried-up cracks. No more tall grass or water, simply orphaned land. Now we go down with a Frisbee and play where we once threw our fishing lines. The wind is a third player between us as we get farther and farther apart. When we get tired and start walking toward each other, it is difficult to believe our throws reached so far.

Notebook of an Arctic Explorer

Dan Gerber

I woke this morning to the clattering call of sandhill cranes and lay for a moment trying to make sense of the beamed ceiling of my bedroom. A week earlier I had awakened to this same unmusical song in a tent on a nameless lake scarcely 200 miles from the Magnetic North Pole. Why, I wondered, are these cranes here now in this abundance, on a hot summer morning just west of the Teton range in eastern Idaho, while those other cranes are standing on the thin tundra soil, a few inches above the permanent ice shelf, where, already now in late August, winter is earnestly presenting its card. The movements of animals and the reasons behind them are matters of conjecture, even for scientists. These cranes are here and those cranes were there.

Just before I left, somewhat reluctantly, for my ten day trip to the Arctic, I told my wife that I really envied her the time she would spend there at home without me. Though maybe what I was really up to in going was trying to take a vacation from me. We see the world by the light of our own moon, someone said. The shadow it casts is no one else's. Though the Arctic moon was too pale for shadows, above a land that, in August, never gets dark. And in the low sun along the horizon, my shadow was the longest I've ever seen, all legs with no head at all.

I was watching the shadow of our 737 as it dropped down to meet us on the runway at Kaluktutiak, more commonly known as Cambridge Bay. And suddenly our shadow, the runway, and then the entire Arctic coastline disappeared in a cloud of smoke, which turned out to be a cloud of dust. I'd never before landed on a gravel runway in a commercial jet, and it alerted me to the fact that, with the possible exception of the Kaisut Desert, I'd never been quite this far off the beaten path. Just below the gravel is the permafrost, so you could, I suppose, say we were landing on ice. I'd also never flown in a commercial jet with moveable bulkheads sectioning off most of the fuselage for cargo, ahead of the six or eight rows of seats provided for passengers. Cambridge Bay (Pop. 1,400, mostly Inuit) is the demographic center of an Arctic island the size of Texas.

I had hoped to see what Polaris might look like this close to the pole and to see The Great Bear directly overhead revolving around it, but between prevailing cloud cover and the absence this time of year of anything resembling what I think of as night, apart from the sun I saw no stars at all.

⌐ ⌐ ⌐

Ostensibly, I came here at the invitation of my son Frank to fly-fish for Arctic char. This expedition is my sixtieth birthday present, and since I will have my birthday above the Arctic Circle on a day on which night will never really fall, I'm wondering if, technically, I remain 59.

The Arctic char is most closely related to the Dolly Varden trout, though greater in size; due to the lower light conditions and the greater density of colder water, as Barry Lopez points out,[1] Arctic fish species tend to have larger eyes and to be stronger swimmers than their more southerly counterparts.

Except in desert country, fishing is always a good excuse for travel and a ligature around which to build an adventure. We have no concrete information about fly-fishing for char, no guides to tell us what sorts of arrangements of feathers and fur might appeal to a char, so our fishing will be largely experimental. But then everything about this trip, into country so unlike anything we've experienced, will be largely experimental. We've brought just about every imaginable kind of streamer and dry fly, but find, oddly, that flies designed to attract tropical bonefish are the most effective. And I discover that the closest analogy I can make to fishing for char is fishing for the bonefish. You present the fly in clear water over a frequently sandy bottom and strip it in slow retreat, as to a bonefish. And when the char takes it, he makes a long, streaking run like a bonefish, and then, again like a bonefish, turns and runs right back at you so that you are reeling in line almost as rapidly as the fish has taken it out in order not to give him the slack with which he can throw the barbless hook. We had enough success with our bonefishing techniques to make char the staple of our diet: boiled char, fried char, char sashimi and char salad sandwiches.

The float plane, which meets us at an inlet near Cambridge Bay, takes us to our base camp and from there to our outpost camps, all the way up to the Arctic Ocean. We seldom fly at an altitude of more than 100 feet, and in the course of our time there we fly over hundreds of miles of tundra, with lakes and rivers everywhere reflecting each brief appearance of the sun, like fragments of fallen sky. And it occurs to me that this isn't really a land at all, at least in these precious few weeks of summer, but rather a great water with some land running through it.

Hiking up the Nanook River to a place where I imagine *I* might be holding in the current if I were an Arctic char, I splash through rocky pools in my waders and trudge lightly along the sedgy meadows as if I were walking on a great sponge. And, in fact, I am walking on a sort of sponge. Since the ice moved out—the ice as in the last Ice Age—there are places in this region that have been rising, like a decompressing sponge, as much as thirty centimeters a year.

I'm struck by just how dramatically my mood changes with the slightest appearance of sunlight on and above this barren landscape—from glowering awe and a sense of implied threat to deep contentment. A brief breakthrough, glorying the river rocks and the stippled water itself, brings an instant of complete clarity to the entirety of my life and death below the tree line. I can't say more about it than that. It's a rare moment without metaphor. Or, finally, it's all metaphor.

There are cairns everywhere on the tundra. Is it simple loneliness, I wonder, the desire to create some artificial being, some point of human reference in this daunting and almost featureless landscape? Or maybe, because even the slightest protrusion can be seen from a great distance, they are personal aids to navigation, a way of finding one's way back. Maybe they are built to assuage boredom near a campsite, maybe a way to say "I was here," though no personal "I" is identified. Maybe they are built because the rocks themselves asked someone to arrange them that way, though we, or even the person who arranged them, didn't understand the request in terms of language. Maybe they are vertical petroglyphs built by another form of the Anasazi. Maybe someone like me built them simply to make another someone like me wonder.

The lack of discernible color variation in any large-scale view of the terrain and the preternaturally clear Arctic air conspire to make a joke of my judgments of scale and distance. What turns out to be the antlers of a caribou, I at first took to be a set of radio antennas towering over the horizon. After a very few steps, a distant mesa or butte turns into a ridge of small rocks I can easily step over.

Canada geese are whooping it up somewhere behind me, and a seagull, perfectly white, hovers to see if I might be edible. I spot an igloo-like structure with a tall antenna on a rise to the north, but when I arrive it has shrunk to become another cairn, not more than a foot high, and the antenna, a plain piece of lath. I wanted it to be a tomb on this almost imperceptible hill.

The Arctic is a place without wood, as we think of it, the largest plant being the ground-hugging willow with roots and branches of about the diameter of a finger. The willows sometimes reach a height of a foot and a half and are the tallest plant that can survive here. One might imagine a log cabin in this wilderness setting, but if there were one, the logs, along with all the other supplies that support life here, would have had to be imported from that abundant country below the tree line. What wood one sees here is almost entirely plywood. Cambridge Bay is a plywood settlement, and the few cabins at our base camp, ninety miles to the north, are made of plywood.

The Arctic's abrupt growing season isn't limited to plant life. Muskoxen grow very slowly because they gain weight only during the relative (though still meager) luxuriance of July and August and are in a "neutral balance" or even in a weight-losing mode for the remainder of the year.[2] I think of Janis Joplin's "Get It While You Can." At first I thought of muskoxen as a sort of shaggy northern cape buffalo, though, up close, I see that they are very much smaller, a big bull weighing only 700 pounds to the buffalo's ton.

Sparse though it seems to me, this landscape is in its flowering now. I try to imagine it in winter. I try to imagine the life of the muskox through three months of solid, unrelieved darkness and unvarying cold. Here is an animal who has mastered patience and acceptance, I think. But then it occurs to me that acceptance is a human idea. The muskox simply *is* acceptance given form in the field of time. There is nothing he longs for beyond the endless polar day and the endless polar night. I will endeavor to be alert enough to embrace him as my teacher whenever I'm tempted to feel inconvenienced or put upon.

I observe the superabundance of water here, now in late summer, and think of how barren it will be, and for how long, a few months from now. There's little snow in the Arctic winter because there's so little moisture to draw on. Just how muskoxen manage to survive year round in country this barren, this harsh, even in the rare feeding areas, is still a mystery to scientists. They browse on the low sedgy grass and gain concentrated energy from the tenuous willows.

There's a man at our base camp who has come up here to shoot a muskox—a challenge akin to shooting a cow in a pasture—primarily because he's never shot a muskox. Like some violent and acquisitive birder, he wants to fill out his life list.

I have such a blissful sense of personal insignificance here. I am, at most, a curiosity to the muskox and the caribou, and also, most probably, to Jimmy Haniliak, our Inuit guide. On our first day of fishing, having been dropped off by float plane at a lake, perhaps ten miles from our base camp, Jimmy and Frank and I traveled a good two hours by seven-horse outboard toward the mouth of a nameless river. I was taking photographs of the shoreline, and it occured to me how difficult it is to capture anything of the grandeur of this country on film, as it is its very absence of features, the vast nothingness itself, that makes it dramatic. It was cold and empty whenever the sun was shrouded and I motioned toward our lunch pack and asked if we'd brought along any water. Jimmy looked at me as if I'd asked him if my nose was still in the center of my face and then, with politely suppressed mirth, he pointed to the lake. He slowed and took a cup and, after clearing a bit of foam and feather from the surface, dipped the cup into the water and handed it to me. When I was thirteen, at summer camp in the Tetons in western Wyoming, we carried no canteens and drank with impunity from the rivers and streams. But, having been so much a creature of the industrialized world, the idea of drinking surface water hadn't occurred to me in almost half a century. In this regard, this water, which is water such a brief portion of the year, must be among the last pure water on earth.

As Frank and I were about to depart for one of the outpost camps, Jimmy asked me how big my finger was. I held out my hand. He took off his wedding ring, and it fit my ring finger perfectly. "I want to make you something for your birthday," he said, "now you are one of the old ones." He smiled at me, and when we returned three days later, he gave me a signet ring, beautifully carved from a muskox horn with only a knife and a file. I've never worn rings, but I'll treasure this one. I like being one of the old ones.

A mere week in this remoteness suggests to me how minute and tenuous a presence man is and how the earth might appear to some disembodied observer if man were suddenly absent from it. I realize that the preceding sentence has the specious logic of an Escher drawing, but then so does the very life of the Arctic. No one discrete element or being within it would make any sense at all without the entire supporting cast that makes its part possible. In this sense the Arctic is the quintessential metaphor, a demonstration laboratory for the interdependence of all life's beings. Life feeding on life.

Here, where the Hamilton River, through Hadley Bay, enters the Viscount Melville Sound, we are well above the northernmost point of Alaska at a north latitude of seventy-four degrees, in a line with Baffin Bay and northern Greenland. We are scarcely 200 miles from the present location of the Magnetic North Pole—which is said to have moved more than 400 miles north in the past 200 years—though still 1,000 miles south of the top of the world. I pull out my pocket compass to investigate our exact relationship to the MNP, and the compass laughs at me. Its needle wanders forty degrees east and west and never settles down. "Would you ask Boreas, god of the north wind, which way the north wind is blowing?" it chuckles. "Would you ask the source where it came from? You are here," it says dismissively. "You are here now."

Due to the prevailing southerly winds this summer the sea ice has moved out to the northern edge of the sound, leaving only scattered icebergs. Their submerged portions have taken on a deep cerulean blue in the light of this cloudy afternoon, and their exposed tops have been sculpted into Henry Moore–like shapes by the sun and wind. We had hoped for a glimpse of polar bears, which would have been a good possibility if the sea ice hadn't been displaced by this year's remarkably mild temperatures during late July and August. Melville Bay, just beyond the sound, is also known as "the breaking up yard," as it is a place along the Northwest Passage where ships have often been trapped and crushed by the sea ice.

Frank and I are wading, chest deep, in the Hamilton, several hundred yards apart at the edge of the dropoff. I'm stripping a rather large orange streamer across the current, hoping, with each retrieve, to feel my line come tight. Frank has given me this fly, with which he has taken and released several "torpedoes," one- to two-foot-long silver lake trout. But I seem to be fooling no fish into believing this streamer might be a fleeing fingerling char.

Jack, our pilot, who has been flying this country since 1959, is waiting with the float plane that we have beached just off a pool closer to the river mouth. I have mixed feelings about the northward migration of the sea ice. I was thrilled by the prospect of seeing polar bears, but also thrilled less pleasantly by my imaginings of what our adventure might be if we should experience engine trouble over the ice-packed bay and find ourselves down there with our fly rods and those chillingly white bears on their turfless turf. So I'm content to be holding against the flow of the river and the rapidly incoming tide, fooling nothing, not even myself, knowing finally that no expedition could be an adventure without the spice of imagined possibilities.

The wind is a raw forty miles per hour and looking downstream, I can see the tight, persistent loops of Frank's fly line against the dark sky. I was fly-fishing while Frank was learning to walk, and I'm both pleased and peeved that he has become a better caster than I am, though, due perhaps to youthful impatience, he breaks off more of the fish he's hooked. Since he first pinned me in an impromptu wrestling match when he was nineteen, I've watched myself being incrementally surpassed in almost every arena, though I console myself with the knowledge—or perhaps it's only a trope—that one garners more wisdom in defeat. If this is true, he is making me wise indeed.

Finally there's an enlivening sense of mystery in simply being in so remote a place, engulfed in all this emptiness. The primordial quietness and space can, at moments, blot *you* out completely; the experiencer is gone, and there is only the experience. I've had such moments of bliss here, as I've often had in a trout stream, absorbed in imagining the world view of the trout. As my friend Jim Harrison has pointed out, fly-fishing is the most hypnotic of sports and, apart from the pure pleasure of casting a fly-line, its value to me is, like this landscape, a white ground of attention against which memory and imagination can do their work, unimpeded by the normally abiding governor of *me.* I can actually feel poems beginning to grow like geometric shapes. The char is my ally, not in catching her, but in simply realizing there is that possibility.

* * *

In our northernmost camp, near Hadley Bay, I drift in and out of my dreams to the thundering flap of a large Canadian flag being flailed by a forty-knot wind. The whir of the flag becomes a constant, alternately a sea, a storm, a helicopter searching for me on the ice flow. Now, as I lie awake in my cold tent, it is exactly the ripping sound of a flag at the South Pole, a flag I heard once in a television drama, the Norwegian flag that Robert Falcon Scott found on his arrival after losing his race with Amundsen by only a few days. The sound of defeat. It may well have been the last sound Scott heard as he perished with his men on their journey back. And now it's the sound of this very flag on this very morning in this very place where I am but can't begin to conceive.

⊏ ⊏ ⊏

Barry Lopez posits the fascinating idea that, after an Arctic river has frozen, one could cut through the ice and walk around on the dry river bottom, since the river's headwaters are also frozen, and that this tunnel of the dried-up river is a favorite haunt of the polar bear.

My walk up the empty corridor of the frozen riverbed under a translucent ceiling of ice will have to be in early spring, when sunlight has returned to this end of the earth. I visualize a dim fluorescent glow along the dark, meandering hallway. I am sheltered from the wind and the extreme cold and at every dark bend in the riverbed I face the fatal possibility of disturbing a bivouacked polar bear. I listen for the sound of his breathing, magnified in this serpentine echo chamber, and know that each of my footfalls on the river floor are being carried to him, perhaps miles ahead, up this immense auditory canal. The bear will, of course, eat only my choice parts, finding me not nearly as tasty as a ringed seal, and will leave the lion's share of me strewn along the river bottom where, in the brief season of flow the following summer, my spleen will provide unusual fare for the returning sea run char. Or perhaps the bear isn't there at all, and I trudge on 'til I'm engulfed in the cascade of melting headwaters, lifted on their roiling crests until I'm thrust up through the now-thinning ice and returned to the Arctic summer.

⊏ ⊏ ⊏

What I discover, now that I've returned to the tree line, is that I've spent more hours in reflection on my time in the Arctic than I actually spent on the tundra. And I suspect I left something there, some confusion I'm richer without.

Now, in September, while the aspens are just beginning to yellow in Wyoming, I know that if the country I flew out of a scant month ago remained as watery and fecund as it was when I left it, it would hold little magic. It's the mystery of a summer place all boarded up, the lakes already freezing, devoid of human presence and human observation, unchanged for the next ten months, more or less, from the way it was before humans crossed the Bering land bridge at least 14,000 years ago.

There are rings of caribou antlers I saw. A blind built by ancient hunters? And I saw a circle of stones that once probably anchored the skirts of a sealskin tent. In the middle of the circle there reposed a human skull. Who knows for how long—100, 500, or 1,000 years—in this place almost too cold for decay? And there are those few plywood cabins at our outfitter's permanent camp that undoubtedly give the winter wind a more haunting pitch, which only the muskox will hear. Though in truth, I'm still there too, for my discovery is that the Arctic isn't so much a place as a state of mind. I brought some of that dramatic, unphotographable emptiness back with me. I keep it, as in a shaman's pouch, and parcel it out over my little daily life when I forget who it is that I am.

NOTES

1. *Arctic Dreams* by Barry Lopez (New York: Charles Scribner's Sons, 1986)
2. Ibid.

A Brief History of Thyme
Cosmology on the Corner Lot

Melissa Haertsch

Whole villages sprang up within the confines of some villa rustica *sites.*
—*William Woys Weaver,* Heirloom Vegetable Gardening

The truant officer came around yesterday, looking for the boy next door. The puzzled man stood on the new sidewalk and scratched his ear with a pen, then looked toward my door: the boy was absent—common enough—but the house was gone too.

This is my doing.

1. How to Make a Garden (Long Way)

Build a family home in a boomtown whose economy is based on the smash-and-grab removal of a non-renewable resource by unregulated companies. Have the house belong to respectable people for a hundred years, then allow the last father to grow old and poor in the de-veined city. Have him die, and have the children fax from Arizona to say that the lawyer should sell the house and send them the money.

An upper middle class professional will invest in it. He will lease to average people; he will grow accustomed to his lifestyle. Then some of his growth funds will fail and he will stop putting the rent back into maintenance. Relocate the good tenants to Arizona. The landlord will bring in some guys on disability who spend their days hanging over the second story porch rail smoking cigarettes and leering at school girls, and whose checks from the government go straight to a P.O. box in the suburbs. Have the landlord spend the checks and not return calls.

Get a dozen recent immigrants and force them to live in the house; have the van from the restaurant pick them up early every morning and drop them off late every night. One of the busboys—irrepressible human—will sing Chinese opera in the shower anyway, but this unexpected beauty will not be enough.

Disintegrate the house: put holes in the roof, let the furnace fail, send an unlicensed guy to repair the plumbing in disregard of code. Let the yard grow wild, and fertilize it with trash.

Then have the woman next door birth a child and suddenly develop a snake-eyed intolerance for threatening behaviors in her vicinity.

2. How a Wiener Dog Brought a Three-Story House to Ruin

When we bought our house seven years ago, we chose it because it was in a good neighborhood close to the university where my husband, Stephen, teaches. Although the yard was small, a disappointment to such avid gardeners as we are, the house was pretty, with room out back under the ash tree to build a playhouse for Stephen's twin sons. The place next door was ugly and a little run down, an exception on that tidy street, but it had a nice gay couple downstairs and a nice sort-of-married couple and their baby upstairs. The weeds were mowed regularly. The gay couple kept pots of flowers out front.

Then the sort-of-married couple skipped town and the second floor hosted a series of people whose lives were not working out. One of them dumped her crack-smoking boyfriend, who returned in the night to murder her young daughter in the back bedroom. The gay couple left. The weeds were no longer mowed, nor the walks shoveled, nor the roof made whole. The last family dropped their trash bags off the second story porch into the front yard, where they exploded and were visited nightly by grateful skunks.

Enter the wiener dog. He escaped from his pen a few houses away and made a low red streak to the sweep of trash. I went out with a broom to drive him off, and he lunged at my shins. At that moment, a trash bag of anger exploded in me. I looked at the house on the corner and said, "I'm gonna get you."

The house had a file. The housing inspectors served the landlord a packet of citations; he took out a loan and secured a building permit. The permit expired, the house worsened, and in early winter I danced the snowsuited baby up and down the sidewalk while the inspector stapled a festive red and white CONDEMNED sign to the front door. In less than a month, a bank owned the place. They set an optimistic price; after months of lunging at their shins and being whacked with a broom, I made my final offer, and Drew, a lawyer friend who had once prophesied our ownership of that lot, gave them a deadline. On the afternoon of the last day, they grumbled an affirmative and I signed the contract. Drew and I spent an hour giggling and plotting designs for the new space: a picket fence, an arbor, beds of vegetables and flowers, a border of mixed evergreens.

Six weeks later, thoroughly in debt, I wrote a check, went home, and tore the padlock out of the doorframe. My twelve-year-old stepsons and their best friend joined me. After a quick look at the ground floor, we decided to smash a hole through the living room wall instead of pulling out a second padlock; we passed into the hallway and went upstairs. The C-shaped second floor apartment ended at the crime scene, a creepy little room with a broken drop ceiling and one small window that looked out on beige aluminum siding. Somebody had painted the bloodstained walls swimming pool blue and pasted up a cheap nautical border. While the boys gleefully sledgehammered the sailboats, I fled to the rickety porch, launch pad of trash bags. A workman across the street was trying to pull a yew stump out of the ground with his Blazer. When he saw me, he called over to be careful. "My uncle used to own that house," he added more cheerily. "He gave great dinner parties." The yew, tree of hedges and English cemeteries, stayed in the ground.

The last week of July we returned the boys to Texas, where they live with their mother during the school year. During that anxious drive, I had two recurrent nightmares. In the first I am returning home, and the place on the corner is on fire. As I pull around in front of it, I can see that the flames have spread to our house, too. In the second dream, I am again driving up the hill, but the corner house is being demolished wildly, parts flying everywhere. I tried to tell myself that overwrought nerves, not the gift of divination, generated these little horror movies.

On the last day of the trip home we were so tired of picnic food that we ate very little and passed the time—thirteen hours from Indiana to Scranton—trying to keep the baby happy in the car. Then we drove up the hill, and—oh my prophetic soul—our demolition contractor was rolling around in heavy equipment atop a pile of rubble, formerly the front half of the condemned house. An audience of children and parents lined the far curbs; in the back row stood people with dogs, boys on bicycles. My husband parked, trembling, in front of our house, and we unfolded ourselves from the car. As we stood staring at the big yellow power shovel, the crowds along the curb began to applaud. I cried.

When we'd finally bought the house, Stephen did not want to go inside. He just wanted it to disappear from the lot, like Dorothy's house in *The Wizard of Oz*. I, however, wanted to see it, wanted to break its walls, bust its doors, scavenge its parts, and eat its heart in the marketplace. I wanted to smash it irreparably, disperse it among my friends who were restoring respectable old homes, cut up its boards and stack them neatly in my basement. I also wanted, just as badly, to see every splinter of the property go to the landfill immediately. In the end it was even better than that, because the backhoe operator, a gifted man, sorted out all the copper from all the aluminum from all the wood and plaster, and sent them to three or four different landfills and recycling centers. A house that is in four landfills is not coming back.

3. Digging the Square Ditch

But that night when we came home and the house was partly gone, that night when I had had nothing much to eat and was still emotional from having to give up the boys until Christmas, that night after the baby went to bed and Stephen drove off to play Irish music in Southside, I felt very sorry for my crushed adversary giving off small billows of plaster dust under the orange streetlight. I felt sorry that a big, solid house, through no fault of its own, should come to this, should be hated by me and my family and all the neighborhood, that such an innocent and beautifully constructed house should now lie in ruins, and that that should be the best thing that could have happened to it. This demise seemed so immensely sad that it required bowls of blood to be poured out and chants chanted and the whole crowd reassembled from their dinners and TV and beds to sing out our sorrow over the body of the dead ogre. These ceremonies could not, of course, be arranged. So instead I got a bottle of Jameson's Irish whiskey out of the basement, put on hiking boots under my tan travel skirt, and climbed me up the ruins of that house to the top of the pile, where the power shovel sat with its neck curved down and its head quietly in its wing for the evening. I climbed onto the treads of the shovel, sat on its blunt midriff and drank that whiskey. I sang every song that backhoe knew: classic rock, Fred Astaire songs, my Irish repertoire, *The Sound of Music,* elementary school spring plays. I sang for three or four hours. Between songs I conversed with the house, and with the child whose life had ended there, and with the trees I had bought and stashed in the shade. Late in the evening, a station wagon stopped beside the Dumpster, and out climbed my husband and our friend John, another lawyer. They stood on the ground, hands on hips, and admired the great heap of destruction before them.

John said, "It's the salvation of the neighborhood."

And I, somewhat inclining to John Wayne even when I'm not drunk, said, "Is that right, counselor?" The two men looked behind them, looked on our porch, looked at each other. "Up here," I said, and they squinted into the darkness. I waved the bottle at them.

"Um, honey?" my husband said, but they both climbed up beside me. Stephen found the remains of the chimney stack and began to ferry armloads of brick down to a hoard beside our basement wall. John drank with me and made a cairn of smashed brick pieces, which I tossed one by one at the few unbroken windows in the back of the second floor. I don't know why no one called the police.

Later on, John went home and I departed consciousness on the front porch in an inch of plaster dust. My husband dragged me through the house to the more seemly dark back porch, where I found myself some time later in a regrettable state of collage. Stephen took me upstairs and washed me like a big dog that has rolled in a dead deer and now wants back in the house. The next morning, as I examined the exploded blood vessels around my eyes, it occurred to me that I no longer, as the mother of a small child, had any business putting myself so close to aneurysm, even for the sake of obsequies.

4. Fanfare for the Common Man

After the contractors had dumped the fill dirt and a thick layer of topsoil, our neighbor Llew, a high school English teacher, began to drop by with his coffee every morning at five minutes to eight. He would work with Stephen and me for four hours, eat the lunch his wife, Linda, brought over for everyone, and then work some more. At supper we drank beer, talked about how much research Linda had accomplished that day, and stared at the landscape slowly forming beside us. Llew would go home then and be out there again at five to eight the next morning with a cup of coffee, his tall frame parked on the pile of foundation stones Stephen had hauled to the curb.

The morning we began to fence the lot, John stopped on his way to the firm. He watched the three of us sweating and cussing a fence post into the ground and cried, "Damn! This is better than law!" He zoomed away and was back in ten minutes in jeans and leather gloves. With two people now working each hole, obstacles seemed to drop away as if Jupiter had traced his finger along the edge of the sidewalk, and where he touched the ground pickets sprang up. We left the intersection corner open for the stone wall Stephen planned to build. As we stood in the gap, admiring the new enclosure and dripping sweat onto the dusty topsoil, a long car with dark windows purred to a stop beside the fence. The window powered down and a man's hand, tanned and gold-ringed, swept majestically across the expanse of yard. A cartoon Mafioso voice said, "My compliments." Then the glass whispered back up and the car hummed away.

5. Romulus and Remus Get a Power Shovel

Ted, the power shovel operator, noticed our rock collection and began to pick up large, nicely shaped foundation stones and set them softly in the grass along the curb. He was so steady, so uniform and careful that it began to seem almost normal to be working a few feet below the swinging thousand-pound bucket of a twisting, grating twenty-ton machine. One morning after a break for water, Stephen and I came to the gate between the old garden and the soon-to-be new garden. The shovel was right outside, removing the foundation of the former back porch. As we waited in the shade of the big spirea, looking affectionately at the scoop like the head of an elephant about its daily work, it picked up a stone two feet long, a foot wide and a foot high—about the biggest stone Stephen could carry freehanded—and set it six inches from the toes of Stephen's boots. The scoop swung away; Stephen grabbed the stone and hustled off with it. While I was still bent over laughing, the elephant returned with a smaller stone and set it before me. All I could do was hold my heart.

Stephen built his stone wall fifteen feet long and four feet high across the corner of the lot. He planted an ash tree outside it. The wall provided the first feeling of place in the empty garden-space, and stood ready as a carcatcher in case of careening autos headed for the baby. It was beautiful and lonesome, the last end of a hall where harp players pocketed the tears of kings, as though we had made our camp in the deserted grounds.

6. Remember Man That You Are Dust

One autumn day when I was covered with dirt and the baby's lunch, a spiffy young reporter in a black suit appeared on the porch. She seemed familiar, but without pondering it I hurried off to change my dress. I walked around the garden with her and the cameraman, showing them the new oaks and the tiny chestnut tree we had dug up from my parents' woods. By rote I narrated the history of the house. As I pointed out the tomatillos Llew had transplanted into our new vegetable bed, I placed the suave reporter: the first time I'd seen her, she was outside my front door asking my boys whether they knew the murdered child, whether they had ever played with her, whether they felt anything particular, whether they would like to be on TV. I had told her to get off my porch (Pilgrim).

After the interview, I sat on the same porch and watched her walking and rewalking a stretch of garden path, hypnotically chanting that flowers waved where a child was MURDERED, tonight at six. The spot aired the next day and lasted two minutes; we taped it. Then my mother phoned. "You shouldn't be seen on TV telling a reporter it's OK for Phyllida to fall down," she said. "What will people think of you?"

After the baby had tired of grabbing the big, foamy end of the microphone, I put her down to waddle along the grassy path beside the veggie bed. While the cameraman took dramatic close-ups of the tomatillo flowers, Phyllida walked a few steps and flopped over, nothing terrible. The carefully coiffed reporter made a dive for her; I laughed. Through the tomatillo branches, the camera focused on us just in time for this mini-drama to unfold at the end of the two-minute snippet. I had been admiring myself, of course, and did not notice Phyllida. "Mom," I said, "nobody saw it but you." When the phone rang next, it was my sister, who thought it was scandalous that I would laugh when Phyllida fell down on TV.

7. Four Years to the Day Since the Girl

One lovely summer morning when the boys and their cousins were still asleep on a camp-out in the attic, I saw a police car on the corner. An officer cordoned off the next-door porch, anchoring one end of the yellow tape to the lilac bush in my dooryard. "Good morning," I said. "How bad is it?"

"As bad as can be," he replied.

When the TV trucks arrived and the crowd of neighbors had grown pretty large, I went out and asked the lady two houses down if she'd heard anything. "Is it the second floor?"

"Yes."

"Did she kill him or did he kill her?"

"I think it's the little girl," she said. I went into the house and closed the door.

The police came later to question us. They wondered if we had heard anything the night before, if they could have permission to search our garden for the weapon. They also wondered whether the children had heard anything. I went up to the attic and sat down in the twist of sleeping bags. The kids said they had slept soundly, but since there were policemen crawling around under their playhouse, I had to explain. The boys and their cousins spent the day on the front porch, waiting for the body bag to come out. It took many hours; they sent emissaries to the attic for games and to the kitchen for sandwiches.

The younger brother of the victim, a child of five who had found the body, sat on the back seat of a police cruiser across the street and ate doughnuts until somebody from Child and Youth Services took him away. His mother, toward the end of the morning, was led from the building by her boyfriend of three days. She left with some detectives and never came back. When the police finally brought the vinyl-sacked corpse out on a gurney and rolled it into the ambulance, my children were all hanging over the porch rail ten feet away. They were on the front page of the paper, in full color, right behind the body and the police. This fame caused them as much excitement as the crime had.

By the time the police tape came down, the gay couple had moved out. The place sat empty and quiet for a month, disturbed only for one afternoon when the grandfather and uncles of the dead child came to gather the family's belongings. They took the brother's toys and clothes, the mother's television and pots. They hauled away a bed, a dresser, two or three pick-up loads of earthly goods. Then they set by the curb three plastic trashcans filled with every toy and book, every blanket and dress and barrette of the murdered girl. On top of the last can lay a dark-stained bear. I recognized it as an object of great power, something you could work big magic with, but I could not take it. That terrible force went to the landfill, where it was joined in four years by its former home.

8. How to Make a Garden (Short Way)

Choose a place where trees won't throw shade. Dig up the earth. Amend the soil with something organic; provide moisture. Sit on the ground nearby, talk to the inhabitants about why they are good and special, and take whatever they give you.

9. JUDGMENT

Phyllida and I were working in the garden when I saw that she had jettisoned her sunhat in the front hall. I dashed in to get it, glancing out the window to check on her. She was in the evergreen border picking and squashing holly berries, the compromise we had reached between her desire to eat them and my desire that she not be poisoned. A clip-boarded stranger walked slowly by, watching the baby. The woman made my hair creep, so I ran out to plop the sunhat of ownership onto Phyllida.

"She's so cute," the woman said. "You know she's picking those berries?"

"Yes. She likes to do that."

The woman, smiling, got into her car and left.

The next week, a sensitive young person at my front door identified herself as Laura, a social worker from Child and Youth Services. She wanted to discuss my chat the previous week with another social worker who had witnessed my baby playing outside unattended, eating potentially hazardous berries. I couldn't understand what she was talking about until I connected her with the strange loiterer. I assured my gentle, sober guest that Philly was never outside alone for more than a few seconds, was by herself longer than usual that day, in fact, because I had to stop to scrutinize the woman at the fence. After Laura had taken my name, Philly's name, my husband's name and place of business—had allowed that no complaints existed besides those of her colleague who happened to be walking back to her car from another case in the neighborhood—after she had counted my Scottish terriers (three) and I had resisted the temptation to tell her I had eight hundred cats upstairs—she left.

Suddenly, instead of being the citizen who calls about the kids on the corner playing outside in their underwear in January, *I* was the one with the unmarried recent B.S. in sociology on my doorstep. I wanted to hit the supervisor of caseworkers over the head with my demolition loan coupon book and speechify on what constitutes real child abuse. Instead I wrote her a letter complimenting the pleasant professionalism of her minion's unnecessary and insulting trip to my home. While I waited for her reply I decided to scrap my next neighborhood project, getting rid of a violent young couple on the side street who appeared to be selling drugs. Their children were pale as cave fungus, it was true, but they were clothed, they attended school, and they spoke to each other and their parents in a relatively civil tone of voice. For a week I felt like throwing up, and resolved to spend my free time shoveling manure onto my rose hedges instead of trying to save the city.

The supervisor of caseworkers wrote back thanking me for my nice letter. She assured me that the visit had been satisfactory from their perspective too, that I had no file with the department, and that she herself had three dogs.

10. A TIME GARDEN

Phyllida and I spend most of our days outside. As I crawl down the stone patio, digging out the cracks, enriching them and stuffing in little plants, my daughter toddles along behind me, removing the labels. We have five or six varieties of thyme, I think, but I am no longer sure what they are. Next summer, the stone patio will be covered with all manner of bees and hover flies, different sizes and colors, landing and taking off and harrying. We will get down on hands and knees to watch them gather their daily bread, and to look for the rare honeybee, almost vanished since the mite epidemic and the downing of a big, partially dead tree on the next block. Our few honeybees now come down from the museum in the park, where they live in a display hive with a pipe to the outdoors. It is a keen pleasure to see them in the garden now, but in their relative absence we have also developed a new appreciation for the wild pollinators—bumblebees, moths, butterflies—in their vast and beautiful array.

Just before school began again, before Stephen and Llew and Linda went back to classes, we took one more end-of-the-day garden tour. The grass was starting to grow; nothing had died yet. Suddenly, on the stone path from the patio to the gate, Llewellyn bent to the ground, a dramatic sweep through space for such a tall man. "Look at this," he said, straightening up. In his huge palm lay a tiny coin, a dime. The date said 1919. "How about that," he said. "I wonder where it's been all these years?"

Where indeed? Did the coin fall from someone's pocket in 1920—the year Stephen's mother was born in Texas—and lie on the ground until the front loader scooped it up in the topsoil quarry down by the river? Or did it wash out of someone's coin collection in Hurricane Agnes, the flood of '72, when I was five years old and forty miles away on a mountaintop? Where *had* it been?

Wing-hatted Liberty, silent on her private story, now soars through mine. Even when you think you have scraped history away from a piece of land, the past rushes in to fill the void with dimes and pony shoes, leaden Labradors and tin fish, baby bottles and bathroom tiles, the fewmets of civilization. We clear the land and history plants a garden there, an insect metropolis where a curly blond girl has for playmate a heaven-striving, sturdy-armed yew named Sheena; endlessness of sky in absence of slum; sacred soil of an old country whose music swans through a valley in the new; where a dirty silver dime tossed to a singing beggar lands in the grass and itself begins to sing. ▪

The Romance Writer

Lisa D. Chavez

I opened the file folder and began reading, my eyes skimming quickly over the words written in Katherine's loose and loopy scrawl:"

"What about dinner," queried Evan, the handsome blonde lawyer who was Amber's boss. He leaned over Amber's desk so far she could almost feel the heat radiating off his sculpted chest, beneath the thin cloth of his white shirt. His smile was hungry, predatory and brutal.

Amber tossed her waist-length raven tresses over her shoulder tempestuously. "I think we'd be better off keeping this relationship professional," she purred, trying to still the hard beating of her heart.

Evan traced one lean finger over her high cheekbone. "And why would we want to do that?" he asked with a cruel sensuous smile. "Are you afraid of me, Amber? You, the hot-blooded wildcat?"

She stood up abruptly, to put distance between them. "Not afraid. Just not interested." Straightening her mini-skirt, she tried to appear disinterested, but she had never been so moved by a man before. Her manicured hands trembled.

Evan looked at her, his icy blue eyes roaming down from her furiously blushing face to her full breasts to her tiny waist. "We'll see about that," he said, then turned and walked away.[1]

I sighed. Drained my beer. Flipped through the pages in the file folder—nearly 20 of them. Jesus, I thought, is this really worth ten bucks an hour? Does anyone read this crap? I riffled the yellow pages with my fingers, wondering if what I was reading was typical of the romance novel genre, or if I was simply transcribing the strange and boring dreams of a young woman I'd just met—the woman who was paying me by the hour to help fulfill her fantasy of writing a romance novel.

[1] This is a recreation; I did not keep any of the things I typed for Katherine.

That year, the year I left my first husband, I lived in a ramshackle log cabin on the backside of Chena Ridge, in Fairbanks, Alaska. It was summer, and while I had left him physically, I hadn't quite left him emotionally or financially, so though I looked for a job, it was mostly in a desultory fashion. I spent most days reading, writing poems and writing in my journal, and I took long slow walks with my dog. I had just finished an MFA program in creative writing, and the habits of being a student—long days of reading and writing—did not fall away easily. My husband was still hoping for a reconciliation, so he gave me money and didn't ask too much about what I was doing in Fairbanks, hoping that eventually I'd work the restlessness out of my system and come back to him.

This story is only partly about me, however. It is about me in the way that any story told is about the teller, even if the characters inhabiting the story are very different. It is about me in that it is a story out of my life, and a story filtered through my eyes, my mind, my memory. It is a story about me in that what I know about Katherine, the woman who this is ostensibly about, also says something about my life; I wouldn't have remembered her so many years later if her situation did not have something to say about my own at that time.

I met Katherine when I answered an ad in the *Fairbanks Daily News-Miner* for an editor/typist. The ad simply asked for someone with typing and editing skills, and I immediately sent off a letter outlining my qualifications, knowing they were excellent. I wondered about the ad—who could it be? A small press? I knew almost all the literary types in Fairbanks, and couldn't imagine who would place such an ad, but eventually I got a call from a woman named Katherine, who told me that she wrote stories and novels, but she had no computer and wanted her work on disk, plus neither her typing skills nor her command of grammar and spelling were strong, and she needed help. She said she'd been published; she even claimed she had an agent. I was dubious, for being a writer myself, I knew a bit about the publishing world, and I couldn't imagine how she could flourish with her self-proclaimed handicaps, but she said she'd pay $10 an hour plus expenses, so I agreed to meet her downtown for coffee and more details.

At three o'clock on a Tuesday, Pasta Bella's was nearly empty. As I walked in, my eyes flickered past a heavily made-up young woman wrestling with a toddler, past a couple lingering over glasses of wine, to a neatly dressed woman in a tweed jacket. She was reading a book at the table tucked back by the window. I stepped toward her, but her head never lifted in expectation, so I paused. Then I heard someone say "Lisa?" I turned to face the young mother, hand out to greet me.

I shook her hand, and we looked one another over. Katherine's name did not fit her, as if she had tried it on for size, but hadn't yet grown into it. She was small and busty, with long dark hair pinned up on her head, and round brown eyes ringed with make-up. Mauve lipstick on full lips. She was Latino, maybe, though much lighter-skinned than me, or maybe Italian or Greek. It was her clothes, though, that seemed most un-Katherine-like to me: leopard-print leggings, a bright blouse made of no material found in nature, and a black shimmery scarf wound round her neck. She wore flashy spiked heels, and her nails were long and scarlet—"fake" she told me cheerfully. "I have them redone twice a month. But you can see why I can't type." With that as an introduction, we sat down.

Already she was puzzling to me. Pretty, and younger than me—I later learned she was 26—she was obviously, like me, from a poor or working class background. Her cheap clothes and heavy make-up gave her away. The boy looked like her—dark-eyed and attractive, but he was querulous and ill-behaved. What did she write? I couldn't imagine.

But Katherine was friendly too, and as interested in me as I was in her. We sipped our cappuccinos and I gave her a quick run-down of my qualifications: the MFA, the editing work, the adjunct teaching. She was so impressed by the college teaching that I knew she wasn't well educated. Anyone who was would know that my experience was far from remarkable.

"How old are you," she blurted the moment I paused in my recitation. Try as I might to keep this odd meeting professional, she seemed equally concerned with making it personal, like a coffee date between friends.

"29," I said.

"But you've been to college!" she said. "I want to go. But his father," at this she pointed at the boy, "doesn't want me to." She shrugged.

I was immediately angered, thinking of my own past, and the struggles I'd faced to get an education. I wanted to encourage her to go anyway. But then I remembered that this was—sort of—a job interview.

"It's not everything," I said, lying diplomatically. "You can still write without it."

This led us back to a discussion of business. She'd give me her stories and her novel, and I'd type everything up, fixing spelling errors and punctuation, but not changing anything else. She gave me a manila envelope containing one short story—I should fix it up and give it back to her in a week; if she liked my work, we'd be in partnership, as she put it.

She talked blithely of her agent, gesturing with a beringed hand as she spoke. Her agent was eager for her work; it was only a matter of getting it typed. The novel was guaranteed to be published—the agent told her so—and it would be successful just like her earlier published pieces. I didn't know the names of any of the places she claimed to have published—they were not literary markets—except *Alaska* magazine. I was both skeptical of what she said and envious. While it was true her story seemed unlikely—though she did say she had worked with another writer like me in Oregon who typed for her and cleaned up her work—I was greedy enough for my own success to envy those words, true or not. Guaranteed publication. Nothing had ever been guaranteed for me.

We had come to an end of business, and the child was even more whiny and restless than before. Katherine paid for the coffee, then handed me a $20 bill.

"For what?" I asked in surprise.

Again she waved her hand, gold nuggets flashing. "Supplies. Paper. Printer ribbons. Whatever. Just give me a receipt, keep track of your time and what you spend so I can pay you."

I took the money, pleased but puzzled. What happened to my trial period? On the way home I bought a box of computer disks and a 6-pack of Alaskan Amber Ale.

❖ ❖ ❖

The story was dreadful. It was so awful, in so many ways, that I despaired of fixing it. The grammar was weaker than what I saw in my worst freshman composition students. Spelling and punctuation were quirky, tenses shifted back and forth, even point of view changed from third to first and back again. And those were only the grammar problems.

I immediately realized that even if I completely rewrote the chapter against Katherine's wishes—for that is what it was, though she had called it a short story—it still would be dreadful. Apparently it was an attempt at a romance novel, the type that some women take away from the library in shopping bags. It was a romance, but so bound in cliches that I couldn't imagine even the worst romance publisher wanting it.

The main character was buxom and raven-maned, named Amber or Tiffany, a name suggesting jewelry, and someone's idea of class. She was in love with her boss, Evan, who was, inevitably, square-jawed, brooding, handsome and brutal. (I couldn't resist suggesting another adjective for the last—did she really want the love interest to be brutal? She assured me later that she did.) He was a lawyer, and Amber or Tiffany—for now I can't remember the actual name—was his secretary. The story continued from that unpromising opening scene I tried to recreate, proceeding through the expected stolen kisses and swooning and heaving bosoms. Really, I couldn't imagine how any work got done in that law office. All I could think of was sexual harassment suits. Finally, I typed it all in, correcting mechanical problems as I went along, and occasionally making the most minor of suggestions. I let the big problems go.

When I labored over the manuscripts in my cabin, armed with a beer and a promise to myself that I could stop for awhile if I finished five pages, I was certain that this romance story was individual to her, that these details were something she had invented. Years later, when I decided to write about it, I did a little research. I skimmed over several romance novels and delved into a book that gave guidance to aspiring writers of romance. What I learned was that Katherine's novel was utterly ordinary. What seemed to me a recipe for a sexual harassment suit was standard fare, as was the description of heroes as brutal.

Obviously I had never been a romance reader myself. After looking over a few—some of which were fairly sexually explicit—I began to think of them as pornography's timid cousin—titillation dressed in the modest clothes of romance. Certainly the men in these books were no more unrealistic than the women in Playboy—they were all impossibly handsome, usually rich, sexually available and skilled. The heroines were fiery or spunky, yet always in need of rescue. The stories were as standarized as a pattern stamped out by machine.

It was that conventionality that bored me most. The characters were types, and not types that interested me. While I spent time that summer daydreaming myself, my fantasies were of a different sort. I'd grown up in Alaska, where even governors wear jeans and flannel shirts. Men in suits appalled me. I was looking for the archetypal Alaskan guy, jeans and hiking boots, beard and a pickup truck. And yes, I expected him to approach me. Evidence enough that I hadn't escaped a type of convention myself. But reading Katherine's stories, I was also aware of how different I was. I was coming out of a six year relationship, and I wasn't interested in any traditional ideas of romance. Just a few months later, a female friend said of a man I was sleeping with that he was not my "prince," and annoyed by her phrasing, I shrugged and said "I don't want a prince; I just want to get laid." She laughed, but it was true: when the same man told me he loved me, I brushed off his words irritably. Whatever I wanted, I knew it wasn't romance.

That evening, after my first meeting with Katherine, I took my dog for a long walk along Rosie Creek Road, thinking about what I knew about my employer. The story had only confirmed the impressions I garnered from our first meeting. She was a housewife, obviously; the child and our daytime meeting told me that. I figured her husband must have a good job, because the gold nugget jewelry she favored was expensive, and she wore a lot of it. I knew she was young, probably ill-educated, raised on TV and trashy novels, but with enough imagination to try her hand at writing her own version of the novels she no doubt consumed by the dozen. She was an awful writer, but something about her absolute confidence amused me rather than put me off. And she had got things published, hadn't she? That stopped me a little. I thought my own writing superior, but though I'd had a handful of poems published in literary magazines, I wasn't meeting with much success yet. I had just come out of an MFA program that had very nearly crushed all my confidence in my own skills. I envied her confidence, though I also found it sad, as all self-delusion is.

Our acquaintance that summer proceeded like this: Katherine and I met briefly, for coffee, usually, and she handed me what she had written, which I corrected. She made it clear she wanted nothing changed but spelling and punctuation problems: the square-jawed attorney remained brutal. I argued hard for letting me make the tense consistent, and finally she agreed, but she clung stubbornly to her shifting point of view, and since it was clear to me that she didn't really understand what I was talking about when I discussed first person and third and which does what, I finally shut up. It's your money, I thought. After I finished a new section, I mailed it back to her, telling her how much she owed me, if anything, for she often paid in advance, always in cash. As we met, details began to emerge about her, for she was talkative and I was interested, and both of us had plenty of time.

I knew she and her family had moved up from Anchorage recently, "for a change," she said, and it would be another day, later in the summer, when I would find out why that change was necessary. I knew that her husband—whose name I never knew—was a carpenter, and that like most construction workers in Alaska, he made good enough money, but he only worked seasonally. I knew they had bought a house, and I knew it was expensive. And they had the child, Brenden. And an enormous 4x4, new and modified with a lift kit and huge tires. And then there were Katherine's little extravagances: the gold nugget jewelry, the nails that needed to be redone weekly, and me. So I wondered about money.

What did her husband think of her casual handing out of $20 bills to me—did he indulge her whims, or did she go behind his back? My own husband was an engineer, and though he made enough money for us to live on comfortably when we still lived together, he had been a meticulous and fanatic manager of money—he knew to the penny how much we had at any one time. And though he said he didn't care what I spent as long as I told him how much so he could note it, he was really very concerned with every dollar I spent on books, or coffee, or clothes. Even when the money was my own. I saw this as part of his need to control me; it was one of the symptoms of the failure of our marriage. So I wondered. Did Katherine have a man that really didn't care?

The answer came by accident one afternoon as we sat at Hot Licks, the ice cream shop/coffee house near the university. Katherine drank coffee as usual, while Brenden quietly scraped at his bowl of ice cream.

"Brenden's father," she began, for this is how she always referred to her husband. "Brenden's father thinks I'm silly with all this writing stuff. He really does. It pisses him off that I spend the money, but hey, it's my money. I'll spend it on what I want."

She turned her nugget bracelet around and around. "He bought me all this stuff when we had money. We used to. But his job isn't good anymore, and I can't work, not really, not with the kid, so . . . but I do have some of my own spending money thank god, because he'd never give me any. Do you know Karen's Consignments?"

I nodded my head—it was a consignment store in a strip mall with the incongruent name of Teddy Bear Plaza, complete with a huge, hand-painted teddy bear in the parking lot. The shop was run by a Thai woman who also did manicures there—hence Katherine's elaborate nails.

"I work there," Katherine said. "Sort of. I just help out the owner sometimes. I can take the kid. She gives me a little if I sell things, plus she does my nails for free." She displayed her nails—this week they were painted an opaque brown, as if she had dipped them in melted chocolate.

"And I like it there," she added. "Someone to talk to. You should drop in sometime—you'd like Karen."

I knew this was an overture, casual but significant, and I wanted to accept it; I wanted to be friends. I didn't have a job, and all my friends that summer did. Plus, I'd been out of state for two years doing the MFA, and some of my best buddies had since moved on. I spent a lot of time alone, trying to decide what to do about my marriage—which was clearly over, and trying to seduce a male friend who wasn't interested but liked the attention. I needed more real friends. So, I tried, that summer, to become closer to Katherine in a desultory way, but even though I have overcome my childhood shyness, I am not good at making the leap between casual acquaintances and friends, unless I am taken in hand and managed by someone more confident than myself. So I tried, but somehow, my attempts and hers didn't connect. All her confidences aside, we somehow never quite became friends. Once I dropped in at the shop, but Katherine was not there, and I was a little intimidated by Karen, who tried to convince me to buy a white fluffy sweater I certainly didn't want. Once I suggested we go for a drink some evening, but Katherine said she didn't drink anymore, that her husband had a drinking problem. This seemed like a time to offer confidences of my own—to tell her about my marriage failing for the same reason—and I began to tell her, but she had to go, to pick up Brenden from the babysitter, and I was too reticent to bring up my own life again. And then in the fall, she was gone.

What I learned about her she told me, in Hot Licks again, later one summer afternoon. Brenden had been left with a babysitter, and perhaps she felt the time was right for confidences—we'd known each other two months. Perhaps I should have guessed some of her history myself, from the way her novel's narration slipped back and forth from third person to first and back, but I didn't, focused as I was on sheer tedium of typing it. I followed Amber/Tiffany's story with pain—her small-town-girl roots in Oregon, and her flight to Seattle, her romantic dreams and feisty independence, and her "tempestuous" affair with controlling Evan. At one point, in the story Evan slapped her, and I was disturbed by this plot twist for a number of reasons. I was angered by the way this violence against a woman was included casually, as if it didn't matter. And I was annoyed by how illogical and unrealistic it was given the story's context: lawyers did not slap their legal secretaries or call them "hot-blooded wildcats" in any law office I had heard of. It was clear Katherine really knew nothing about attorneys or secretaries, but had chosen this setting because for her, it was exotic, rich with some fantasy of an upper middle-class professional existence she was not privy to. The plot followed the romance novel outline, but as far as I had gotten so far, one element did not fit—Evan showed no signs of becoming the shining knight to save Amber from the drudgery of her job in his office, and the heroine seemed to be planning to flee from him too, on to an unnamed future. That was the story I typed out over the summer. Katherine's own story was much more interesting.

She was, of course, also from Oregon, from a small town I'd never heard of. And she, like her heroine, fled young, but she fled to Anchorage on a circuitous route.

It was August, and the late afternoon sun shone through the plate-glass window of Hot Licks, making me sleepy. My attention was less on her and her story than on thoughts of my own. I was making the final break with my husband, and I was dreaming, idly, of a man I hoped I'd meet: someone gentle, funny, smart and sexy. He would be neither square-jawed, nor tall, I thought, as I disliked those types of men, and he would certainly not be an attorney, but perhaps he would be dark and handsome. A bit wild. I didn't want love but I did want passion, and my only candidate was frustrating: the male friend who flirted outrageously but wouldn't be seduced. So as I did most of the time that summer, I drifted in my thoughts, barely listening to Katherine, which was why I misunderstood her statement at first.

"I was a dancer, you know?" she said, pausing to rummage through her purse for a cigarette, which she found. She rolled it between her thumb and forefinger meditatively but didn't light it—smoking wasn't allowed in Hot Licks.

If I had been paying attention, I would have understood her immediately—there is only one kind of dancer in Alaska. But I was drifting, and for a moment, looking at her everpresent leggings—today's shimmery black despite the heat—I thought she meant a ballet dancer. This puzzled me, because she was too short and plump to dance seriously. I recovered as she spoke.

"I danced at this club on Spenard," she said. Spenard is a section of Anchorage famous for its sleazy bars, and the joke it had inspired based on a well-known incident: what's a Spenard divorce? A gunshot to the husband's head.

"I met Brenden's father there. And I had Brenden. And then we got married."

I sipped my coffee, now attentive.

"It was ok, you know? The dancing. I mean, some other girls did other stuff on the side, went with the guys, but I didn't. I made enough to get by with tips and all from table dances."

I looked at her closer, trying to see if anything in her appearance gave her past away. Her make-up and clothes, while certainly giving her a cheap look, were still just that, a style, one many young women wore. I'd dressed like that myself—minus the make-up, in high school, a style encouraged by my mother, who had for years indulged in low-cut blouses and backless dresses from Frederick's of Hollywood catalogs, though I had never been confident enough—luckily—to dress as wildly as my mother suggested, and truthfully my typical outfit in those years had been tight jeans and concert t-shirts. In this small coffee house, with its tiny round tables pushed close together, I tried to imagine, for a moment, this woman naked, gyrating on a table—because at the time that is what I thought a table dance meant—while men watched, slipped bills into her g-string. I couldn't. She was just too normal to me, a plump pigeon of a woman, chirpy and sisterly. I could not imagine her in that other life, which I suppose shows my stereotypes, my own lack of imagination.

It was not a lack of experience that failed me. I'd been in those bars, had friends that worked at them, though they worked as cocktail waitresses, not dancers. Sometimes the dancers were beautiful; sometimes I wondered why anyone would pay to see them naked, and mostly they were just ordinary and young. I'd known women who had been prostitutes. There was never anything marking them, any thing that screamed out whore or nude dancer. And yet somehow I could not imagine Katherine doing it, perhaps because she seemed so innocent, lacking the hardness I'd seen in those other women. Perhaps because she did not fit traditional standards of beauty—she was not blonde, or tall, or thin, and though she was fairly full-breasted, she had the type of breasts that settle low, making her look more plump than anything else.

And her story continued. How her husband had been a "regular," and how he'd paid for table dances, but only from her, then talked to her on her breaks, then asked her out. Then a certain vagueness set in. There had been another man too, and she'd gotten pregnant, and who knows? But then the baby was born, and named, and the regular—Brenden's father—married her. And he wouldn't let her dance anymore.

"Not that I care," she said. "I mean it was good money, but not my idea of career, you know? I see myself more as a career woman." Ah. That explained Amber/Tiffany, though it was sad that being a secretary was Katherine's idea of a good career. My thoughts veered to the husband—what was he like? What kind of a man was he, paying to have a naked woman dance at his table while he drank? But Katherine didn't give me much time to think about it then. She turned her bright eyes on me, as if all the smoke and sordidness of her past could not dim her enthusiasm for life. "But I admire you," she said. "You got an education. A woman needs that. And you're a teacher. You have a career. So now I'm trying to do a little something. Write my novel. Maybe take some classes when I can." She patted the folder on the table between us containing her latest work, and I sighed inside for her.

"Why don't you got to college fulltime?"

Her face darkened, ever so slightly. "Well, there's the kid. And He doesn't want me to go." He was the regular, the unnamed carpenter I had begun to hate. She leaned forward. "Don't let this get around, but I may go back to Anchorage. Maybe. And if I do, I may take some classes. I've got the money." Then, as if aware of what that meant to our relationship, she added that we could keep working through the mail.

She sat back and looked at me reflectively for a moment. "Or you could come too. Why not? You've got nothing going on here."

It was true. At that point I had not even secured a job for the fall. Still, our lack of intimacy made the suggestion seem absurd. She seemed to realize this, for she laughed then quickly continued.

"Well, anyway. I might leave him. I don't know yet." She picked up her cigarette, and put it behind her ear, then withdrew some cash from the depths of her bag, which she pushed across the table towards me. "Anyway, I gotta run. Here's the stuff and some cash—see you soon!"

A moment later I watched her out the window do her absurd little leap into her truck—that monstrous 4x4, some poor boy's dream of the perfect machine. Katherine was maybe five feet tall. She leapt onto the running board, and pulled herself in with the handle on the cab. She left, as she always did, before I could ask her more.

⸻

The final time I saw her was the saddest too, though I didn't know at that time it would be the last. We met in Hot Licks again, but this time she didn't look so ebullient. She looked pale, which her even heavier-than-usual make up accentuated. She was puffy around the eyes, too, but she still seemed energetic.

"I'm starting over," she said, in lieu of a greeting. "I've got a real project for you now, something that will make it for me. Big bucks."

She handed me a clip from a magazine, and I felt a little queasy as I scanned it. I'd read it before in Poets and Writers. A contest for a novel, sponsored by Ted Turner. The novel was supposed to give a view of the future of America, some changes we could make in society, a re-vision. The prize was $100,000. I'd seen it myself, wished briefly that I wrote fiction, then more to the point, wished he'd give the money freely, to real artists not bound by his plan. I put it down on the table.

"I'm going to win that," she said, pointing to the paper. "And you're going to help me. I have a plan, even, for this new novel. But the big thing is time—we only have two months till the deadline. We'll have to really work to get it done."

She was caught up fast in her vision, and I didn't know how to stop it, but I knew I had to, or that at least I could no longer be part of her delusion, taking her money and keeping silent. I felt too guilty for that. In the past, I'd tried to suggest changes, gently, but she'd always told me to stick to straight typing. I continued to make small changes in parentheses, but she never asked me to revise based on those suggestions, even when the change was as basic as correcting a word incorrectly used. Like an anorexic who looks in the mirror and sees a fat person, she saw in her jumbled prose something real and valuable. I had encountered students like her before—those that truly believed that every word they wrote was wonderful, but this time she was paying me, and I couldn't coerce her into changing a thing. At least, I thought, she gets enjoyment out of writing it. I justified it to myself in that way.

But this was too much. She hadn't a chance and I knew it, even assuming she wasn't starting from nothing. And truthfully, I was tired of the work. The money was useful for odds and ends—a book I really wanted at the used book store, or a six pack of the expensive beer I liked, but mostly the work was just painful, a horrible sort of data entry, the English teacher in me tortured by the not being able to fix even the grossest errors. I suggested once that she write about her own life, which was light years more interesting than the drivel she gave me, but she seemed not to hear me at all, for she never acknowledged my suggestion. And now, at the table by the window again, she was weaving sheer fantasy—like her novel—and I was tired of it.

"So what shall we do for the plot?" she asked. "I have some ideas, but what do you think? What would they want?"

"Katherine," I said, taking a breath. I meant to tell her then, to tell her that she had no chance of winning that, that they would get hundreds, maybe thousands of entries, and that with her fractured prose she had no chance. But I couldn't. It seemed too cruel, and while I valued my honesty, I had never been able to be hurt people even when it was for the best. That was why I was still married. I knew it was over, but my husband was still hoping for a reconciliation, and whenever I saw the pain in his face, I was unable to say that no, never, there was no chance.

"Katherine," I stopped, began again. "Look, I'm not going to have a lot of time in the fall. I got a job. I'm going to teach three classes at the university. And honestly, I just don't think this project is a good idea." Please, I thought, just give it up. Don't make me say why it is a bad idea. I didn't want to have to destroy her dream, I just wanted out of it.

She looked quite surprised—I suppose her fantasy wasn't proceeding as planned. But as always, she made a quick recovery. "Well, ok. But if you could just help with the typing? You could still use the money I bet. I know I sure can." She tapped the ad with a long nail, painted metallic green as a beetle's carapace today, to match her leggings perhaps. "With this money, I can leave for good. Get my own place, get my life together. I'm tired of it all, so tired of being hurt . . ." Her hand unconsciously brushed her puffy eyes, and then I noticed only one eye was swollen, and the make up around it extra heavy. He beats her, I thought, and I wondered why I hadn't known before. And irrationally I hated Ted Turner, hated him and his money that gave such an absurd hope to this woman. I was so angry. No wonder she couldn't give up. She fled to these romantic fantasies like I fled to my cabin in the woods, though I had so much less to flee from.

I heard my voice soften. "Don't count on the money, Katherine. If you need to go, go. Do you need any help? A place to stay?" I offered this without thinking of my log cabin with its drafty plywood floors crisscrossed by voles and the occasional pine marten. No place for a guest, though if she'd accepted, we would have made do.

As she always had before, she pulled herself quickly together—shaking her head lightly as if she could shake off her worries and pain like a dog shakes water from its coat. "Oh no, it's not that bad. I mean it is, and yes I want to leave, but I'm biding my time, saving up a little here and there. Then I'll go. But let's at least start this, ok?" She pushed the contest announcement towards me. "As soon as I get something written, I'll give it to you. What do I owe you, anyway, for the last batch?"

"Nothing," I lied. "We're all caught up." It was easy to lie to her in this way—she never kept accounts. She owed me $30, but I figured she needed it worse than me. I didn't know her well enough to pry deeper into her life, but I hoped I'd made clear I would help her if I could. And I thought that not taking anymore money from her was one small thing I could do for her. I took her latest piece, and promised myself I'd find a way to terminate the work aspect of our relationship.

And so she left. As she hopped up into the cab of that absurd truck, she paused for a moment and leaned out the door. "Lisa, listen. If I win, I'll give you a cut too. Not just the hourly stuff I mean. We're in this together, ok? A partnership!" She closed the door, and drove off, a very small woman in a very large truck.

⊑ ⊑ ⊑

A month later, I got a letter from Katherine from Anchorage. She'd left the husband, she said; she decided she couldn't wait for her big winnings. She wondered if I would send her the last things I had of hers, and though she included a few country-western songs she wanted me to transcribe for her, and a request for a bill, I sent only the writing back, wishing her the best and telling her I wouldn't be typing for her any longer. It was easier to do in a letter. So she vanished from my life, except for the files of her novel on my computer, and I erased those eventually too.

And yet the woman herself lingers in my mind. When I told friends about her, they'd laugh and shrug. "Crazy," they'd say, as if I had told the story as a joke. But it wasn't funny, and she didn't seem crazy at all, only unable to evaluate possibilities. I remember a letter I transcribed for her, a long letter to 7–11, where she had once worked. It was a plan for how the corporation should be restructured to insure employee loyalty. She suggested higher wages—at least $8 an hour—because, as she pointed out, many employees were single mothers who needed to pay for childcare. She had a number of other suggestions to improve employee morale, to treat workers with respect.

All of her suggestions were sound, of course, but the touching part was that she actually believed the 7–11 corporation would be interested, would see the error of their ways. When she handed the piece to me, she said "this will really help working women" and she believed that. She was deluded, maybe, but with a poignance that was painful.

And then there are the parts of her life she never talked about, the parts I could only imagine, and try to reconcile with what I knew of her. Her life in a strip bar. What had she thought of, those nights, as she swayed and writhed on the smoky stage of a Spenard strip joint? Was it, as she said, just another job, the stripping off as uncomplicated as putting on the convenience store jacket? Even what had she wanted as a young girl—the house, husband and child—had not turned out like she'd planned. And with her own life so strange, so difficult, could she really believe those stories she wrote? I wondered if she'd read romance novels backstage while waiting to go on. I had a vision of her, in a thin robe, reading and smoking, being teased about her book by a hard-faced blonde in a g-string, but teased gently, because I imagined that backstage had the sort of camaraderie that develops among people who work together in shitty jobs. Perhaps her stage name had been Amber.

Perhaps she'd written stories as an escape, a vision of the way she'd wished the world could be. Our fantasies always contain a bit of truth about our lives, after all. Her dreams weren't too high even in the stories. The heroine who runs from a man who abuses her and fulfills her dreams of becoming a respected legal secretary. That's as far as I got in the story.

I hoped Katherine would be ok, that her husband wouldn't track her down, that she'd find a job, survive, even flourish in the end. When I thought of her, I couldn't quite imagine the fairy-tale ending she longed for, but I hoped for her happiness nonetheless. And maybe, somewhere between her flights of fancy and her practical nature, she'd find she could make a life for herself and her son.

And my life? A complicated year, a time when I found what I wanted in unexpected places. Two romances, one serious, one not. After a riotous winter, I shook myself, sobered up, and got on with my life. Like Katherine, I knew when to leave, how to protect myself. Eventually, I remarried, left Alaska for good. Got a decent job, published. My own happily-ever-after. And so I'd like to write this ending for her: Katherine laughing with her son and a new lover who is good-natured and kind. She's in a graduate's cap and gown, and the lacquer on her nails flashes like a promise in the pale spring sun. ■

Reflection Rag

Uncle Joe, Roberto Clemente, and I

Christine White

So much happened so quickly after Uncle Joe died. The tempo changed. This new rhythm blew aside the curtain and there it was, this other order of things that lies beneath or beyond: a hidden stage where we play out our lives and strange bedfellows mingle and the orchestra plays ragtime and spirits stand in the wings, feeding us our lines, leading us home.

Exit Uncle Joe

The year is 1999. The month is July. The day is 9. Uncle Joe dies after just a few days in the hospital. The obituary tells part of his story.

. . . born July 23, 1917, in Pittsburgh, Penn. . . . He lived nearly all his life in the Pittsburgh area before moving to Estes Park two years ago after Dorothy, his wife of fifty-three years, died. He received a degree in Petroleum Engineering. . . . Joe served as a Lt. Commander in the navy during World War II on Midway Island . . . Most of his career was spent as a white hat foreman for U.S. Steel. Joe enjoyed piloting his Cessna 150. . . . He was twice decorated and a recognized elite member of the Transcendental Explorers Club International. He is survived by his son Jimmy and his wife, with whom Joe lived in Estes Park, and four grandchildren.

At the top of the obituary is an old picture of Uncle Joe in his cowboy hat, white beard, and plaid shirt. Uncle Joe dressed that way a lot after his son Michael died. He looks like Gabby Hayes, like a real cowboy. He once was asked to be an extra in a Western movie. He looks like the real thing, Uncle Joe in that hat.

I know about Joe's years in the navy and his work with U.S. Steel, know how he loved to fly. But I don't know about the Transcendental Explorers Club International and the decorations. I thought I knew Joe pretty well but I don't know about that.

I think about Uncle Joe a lot after he dies. I wonder where he is. Just a few months before his death, Uncle Joe was with me in Illinois, and just two weeks before he died, he had driven his van back to Pittsburgh. Eighty-one years old and still driving from Colorado to Pittsburgh all by himself. Even Joe said it was probably the last time. When he couldn't drive back home any more, I guess Uncle Joe decided it was time to die.

Cousin Jimmy was sitting on the bed next to Uncle Joe when my daughter Gia walked into Joe's room at the hospice in Estes Park. Jimmy looked tired and scraggly. "Pappy has passed. Just a couple minutes ago," Jimmy told her.

Gia sat down in a chair at the foot of the bed. Jimmy left to give the undertaker information for Joe's obituary, so Gia remained alone in the room with her dead great uncle. She watched as an attendant removed an IV tube from Joe's limp arm. Then Gia called me.

"Mom," came her little voice, calling Illinois all the way from Colorado. "Uncle Joe died, right before I got here."

I didn't realize at first that she was still in the room with Uncle Joe's body. "Where is Uncle Joe now?" I asked.

"Right here. I'm with him now," she said.

I suggested she wait someplace else but Gia said being in the room with Joe was a good feeling, that the late-afternoon light coming in the window made the room seem warm and soft, and that Joe, lying alone on the bed with the white sheet drawn up to his white chin, his white hair and white beard and mustache in place, looked peaceful. "Like all the sadness has seeped away," she said. "It's not bad to be where Uncle Joe is."

"When is the funeral?" I asked. Ever since Jimmy had called me two days ago, saying that Joe was dying, I had planned to go to the funeral.

"There is no funeral," Gia said. "Jimmy's having a memorial barbecue and then he's going to scatter Joe's ashes."

The thought of a barbecue in lieu of a funeral didn't strike her as odd.

ENTER ROBERTO CLEMENTE

The year is 1999. The month is July. The day is 16. I am inside the Unity Church in Boulder, Colorado. Uncle Joe, or at least his ashes, will be scattered tomorrow in Estes Park. I am at a performance of the Rocky Mountain Ragtime Festival. Gia and a friend have brought me here. The friend's uncle is a ragtime pianist who will perform as part of the concert this evening. The uncle gave us free tickets.

A pianist named Scott Kirby walks onto the small church stage. Kirby is handsome, dark and bearded. He bows, elegant in a flowing white silk shirt and dark trousers.

"I am going to play 'Roberto Clemente.'" That's all he says as he settles himself on the piano bench. "I am going to play 'Roberto Clemente.'"

This juxtaposition of baseball icon and piano rag jars me. I hear Clemente's name and I am back in Pittsburgh all over again. Back where I spent the first twenty years of my life. Back where Uncle Joe came from until he left Pittsburgh two years ago to live with Jimmy. Moving didn't change anything for Uncle Joe. Until he died last week, but maybe even still, Uncle Joe is always from Pittsburgh.

Kirby plays "Roberto Clemente." The music comes in gently syncopated waves, lapping at my consciousness. Lovely, happy waves. Waves that cut to my heart and steal my breath. Haunting and laughing at the same time. Joyful, really. Joyful and never taking itself too seriously. "I am going to play 'Roberto Clemente,'" he said. Not flamboyant and racing like some ragtime, but thoughtful and elegant, this Roberto Clemente. The repeats bring new waves, each telling the same story, but reinvented. The melodies keep returning, first soft, then strutting, now brassy, now defiant, now poignant. And still joyful.

Editor's note: Shortly before we went to press, Christine White was killed in a tragic plane crash. We asked Lisa Knopp, Christine's writing teacher at Goucher College, to write the following memorial reflection on Christine's life and writing.

Once, Chris White literally fell on her face. "That fall was more than a headlong plunge down two flights of stairs," she wrote in "Big Dreams and Magic Places" (Sport Literate, *vol. 3, 2000). "It was an alarm reminding me of the fragility of life, warning me to not waste the days that now seemed a gift." Somehow the fall, which tore Chris's face, broke her teeth, and injured her back, transformed her into a daring adventurer: she hiked, rode horses, and snowshoed in western mountains; she mountain biked on slickrock in Utah and in the cornfields near her home in Illinois; she attended women's fitness retreats; and she entered the low-residency Master of Fine Arts Program in Creative Nonfiction at Goucher College.*

I had the pleasure of being Chris's faculty mentor during the fall of 1999, her final semester at Goucher, and during the spring of 2000 when she was one of my private writing students. When Chris entered the M.F.A. program, she was not new to writing. For many years she had written short, topical, often humorous pieces for

Oh, I wish you could hear it!

I am entranced, mesmerized by "Roberto Clemente." At intermission, I buy a CD with the piece on it. The next day, as I drive to Estes Park to scatter Uncle Joe, I play "Roberto Clemente." Over and over in my car, driving U.S. 36, climbing into the Rocky Mountains, I listen and, as if for the first time, I introduce myself to Clemente just as he had made his presence known to me, last night, at a ragtime festival in Colorado. The notes flow in my mind, run through my blood, the way the Fall River rushes downhill alongside my car.

Ever since that night in Boulder when I heard the piece called "Roberto Clemente," I've been governed by this music. Music I hear and music I sense. It's become a pulse inside me. I'm not sure why I feel this bond to Roberto Clemente but I know better than to ignore the pull of this music because I believe the universe works this way. Uncle Joe and Roberto Clemente and I, we were destined to interact with each other. It doesn't matter that Joe died last week and Clemente died over twenty-five years ago and I'm still around. That's how time works sometimes.

And, I am to find out, that's how writing is sometimes. I start out chasing one story and then another story starts to chase me. I want to write

---

the local newspaper and radio station. But during her four semesters at Goucher, she came into her own as a writer. During that time, I watched Chris search for the stories in her life experiences and undertake ambitious experiments with the form of the essay. She brought intensity and courage to her work as if she wanted to learn everything she could right now. *Perhaps it was because she had waited so long to write sustained, complex essays. Perhaps it was because she sensed that she hadn't time to waste.*

On June 11, 2001, Chris and her husband Michael died when their twin-engine, turboprop airplane crashed and burst into flames near Santa Fe, New Mexico. They left behind four children. And Chris left a manuscript, Grace Notes: Syncopated Musings on the Journey Home, *which she described as "a collection of essays about living deeply." In recent months, several of these essays either were published or were accepted for publication. "Reflection Rag: Uncle Joe, Roberto Clemente, and I" is part of this collection. I hope that through her essays, readers will witness the intensity, courage, wit, and grace that made Chris White such a remarkable person.*

—Lisa Knopp

about Uncle Joe but Roberto Clemente jumps in. And then other forces become involved. You see how it is. Sometimes a writer has no choice.

Uncle Joe's story is still warm; Roberto Clemente's trail is cold. As I write about them both, as I turn and chase them both, I re-enter the past and play games with time. I tell you, it's the best part of writing sometimes, to play hide and seek this way with the past, to live things again, and to write about ragtime.

Enter Scott Joplin

The year is 1896. The place is Sedalia, Missouri, a gathering spot for ragtime musicians, a town still part of the American frontier. It is night. The East Main Street that by day is a collection of feed and hardware stores and harness shops is now the "District."

Sundown fills the wooden sidewalks with gamblers, dance-hall girls, sports, pimps, and just regular men out on the town. Honky tonks like the Williams brothers' Maple Leaf Club are wide open in this tenderloin district. Bets are placed. Liaisons arranged. In the bordellos and clubs, black and white customers hang around the Victorian-style bars, pool and gaming tables. The hanging gas chandeliers do not give off light so much as haze but, even so, clearly visible through the smoke in a far corner is an upright piano and on its lushly-covered stool sits a black man. The piano player. He plays all night. His music both describes and accompanies the melee around him. He plays ragtime.

The man at the upright that night in Sedalia may even have been Scott Joplin himself. Joplin, who would become the Ragtime King, the greatest ragtime composer ever, had just arrived in Sedalia in 1896 and it wasn't long before he was at the center of Sedalia's ragtime community.

It's a mystery how the fabric called ragtime came to be. A rag was originally a simple black folk melody. Early ragtime composers, men like Joplin, collected these rags, these scraps of melody they heard in the air around them, and sewed them into extended musical compositions called piano rags. They built their rags around folk melodies and strong rhythmic variations called syncopation. Ragtime, while not exclusively black, blended the gaiety of freedom with the underlying sadness of slavery.

Yes, it's possible. Joplin's music might have been what the piano man played that night in the tenderloin of Sedalia: lilting, contagious, ironic, spirited but somehow melancholy, gentle music filled with repetition and melody and rhythm.

THE CROWD GATHERS

The year is 1999. The month is July. The day is 17. Jimmy's already grilling the memorial meat when I arrive at his collection of condos along the Fall River. Once Jimmy told me he would piss on Joe's grave but he apparently has reconsidered.

I walk into the convention center where Jimmy is hosting the barbecue and Uncle Joe is everywhere. A long table, draped with a bright red Indian blanket, is covered with photographs and personal articles that belonged to Joe. The decades I had shared with Uncle Joe spread out before me.

I take it all in, this majestically pitiful sweep of a life, decades compressed and expanded, recalled by this collection of Joe's things: The keys to his van. A road atlas held open by a magnifying glass. A travel journal. Two hand saws next to a dusty hand drill. Reading glasses and Civil War books. Joe's hockey skates. A bowler hat and a walking cane with a rattlesnake head. I study the photographs on the wall. There's Joe as a young sailor, Joe close up in his Navy uniform, Joe and Dorothy at the altar of St. David's Church, Joe with his first son Michael, Joe with Michael and Jimmy, Joe alone in his old house with his last dog, his blind Airedale Quincy. But Jimmy's memorial is about more than Joe. As I walk along the wall, past the ink sketches of the Homestead steel mill, I pass pictures of my dead parents, of other long-departed aunts and uncles.

Jimmy has been following me along the wall. "Everyone's here," he says, in his husky drawn-out way, his sly voice that could mean almost anything.

Everyone *was* here, gathered from only God knows where, come to Estes Park for the barbecue. In the photos, Dorothy ages along with Joe, but even as she ages, she dazzles. Dorothy and Michael, both smiling, sit side by side on the living room sofa, shortly before Michael died. We were all happy then. Dorothy's blonde hair is pulled back, her black dress low-cut and elegant. Michael wears what appears to be a cutaway jacket, white shirt open at the neck, his red hair thinning, his red beard impeccable.

A large greeting card sits in the middle of the table, next to Joe's ice skates. Dorothy had once sent this card to Joe. Joe had saved it and now the card belongs to Jimmy. The front of the card shows a rabbit and a donkey, apparently a married couple, sitting back to back, each one secretly fuming about the other. The donkey is thinking, "You dumb bunny." The rabbit is thinking, "You jackass." The sentiment inside the card captures Dorothy's wit and sarcasm and bitterness about her marriage: "It's so nice having these conversations with you." Yet, as if to show that one reality is never the whole story, in her flowing graceful script, my aunt had signed the card, "Love, Dot."

RAGTIME AGAIN

The year is still 1896. Ragtime music generates controversy when it first becomes popular in the 1890s. There is, first of all, the predictable moralizing about ragtime's low origins: prejudice, beer, and back rooms are undeniably linked to ragtime. Ragtime's syncopations, broken rhythms, and shifting accents also cause great uproar. "Who put the sin in syncopation?" critics want to know.

Syncopation, ragtime's most recognizable rhythmic characteristic, superimposes an irregular rhythm over a regular one and comes from the interrelationship of the right and left hands. The left hand on the piano plays the stride bass *or basso continuo,* keeping the pulse with the characteristic *oom pah* beat. The right hand plays the melodies and rhythmically works against the left hand, displacing the left hand's *oom pahs,* putting the beat on the offbeat.

Scott Joplin wants to make sure that ragtime players can take in all the rhythms, melodies, and counter melodies of a piano rag, and so his advice on tempo is categorical: "Play slowly until you catch the swing, and never play ragtime fast at any time." Play ragtime like a slow march, Joplin says. Joplin wants ragtime seen as a legitimate art form accepted by people of culture. Not that anyone calls ragtime illegitimate, but the implications are clear. It just isn't good enough for some folks.

COUSIN JIMMY PLAYS

The barbecue is underway and I hang on the fringes, watching Jimmy greet the arriving guests. He is gracious. A gracious host. I haven't seen Jimmy since last February when we had sat and talked, as we had many times before, over lunch at the Boulderado Hotel.

Jimmy, who in past years and for past lunches had sauntered into the Boulderado looking like Dirty Harry, rugged and sexy and slightly sinister in black leather jacket and orange sunglasses, this sunny day in February just looks weary. His thinning hair is no longer red, just dark blond and straggling, hanging to his shoulders, and his face has become his mother Dorothy's face: the same skin, the same dazzling teeth and crystal clear blue eyes.

I tell Jimmy he looks tired. He nods. Then I ask about Joe.

Jimmy tells me Joe is still drinking. Joe drinks in secret and thinks no one knows. Joe's knees are bad and he has a hard time walking but he still drives through Rocky Mountain National Park every day. Joe takes over Jimmy's kitchen each night, cooking food no one wants, ranting at Jimmy. Joe rants in the kitchen and Jimmy goes to Alcoholics Anonymous meetings. Sometimes Joe goes with him. Every day it's like this.

Jimmy grins his wide, almost demonic smile that is either very open or very closed, I'm never sure which, leans toward me across his plate, and says, "Christine, I don't need all this opportunity for personal growth."

We reminisce. "It's sad we're such a small family," I say. Cousin Jimmy smiles.

"We're small but we're getting bigger every day." He grins his grin.

"I have a daughter," he says.

"I know. Six-year-old Lila," I say.

"No, another daughter. Annie. She's twenty-one."

"Oh," I say.

Jimmy tells me about finding this daughter Annie. Since joining AA he's been trying to fix the broken places, smooth the ragged edges of his life. Jimmy's trying to make perfect time. Or make time perfect, I think. He answers my question before I ask.

"Annie's last name is Martinez," he tells me. His blue eyes are far away now. "That's why I couldn't marry her mother. I never could've taken a Mexican woman home to my dad. You know how it was back then, Christine. In Pittsburgh. Twenty years ago. You remember."

TIME TRAVELER

I used to think of time as something that flows like a river, a continuum that moved from the past, through the present, and into the future. "Roberto Clemente" has disrupted this linear view of time. How can I be floating down this time river, all nice and easy, and suddenly find myself upstream when I haven't walked along the bank to get there?

But it happened. Some tributary lost in time took me back to Pittsburgh that night I heard "Roberto Clemente" for the first time, back up the Ohio River, back to where the Ohio is formed from the waters of the Allegheny and the Monongehela Rivers, back to the place called The Point where the Ohio is born and where my grandparents lived with the other immigrants a century ago and where one day Roberto Clemente would play baseball at Three Rivers Stadium.

"Roberto Clemente" makes my mind play tricks with time, scrolling through events backwards and forwards in strange ways. I tell you the brain can be a time machine and sometimes, like when you hear ragtime, you can become a time traveler. Like this:

It is 1955. Pittsburgh is a smoky city, a dirty, tough steel mill town, still deeply entrenched in its ethnic enclaves of Germans, Italians, Irish, Latvians, and Poles, and Roberto Clemente, a black man from Puerto Rico, is a rookie for the Pittsburgh Pirates. The Pirates still play at Forbes Field. When Clemente comes to Pittsburgh, the Pirates are spectacular losers. Clemente chooses 21 for his uniform number, it is said, because his full name, "Roberto Clemente Walker," has exactly twenty-one letters.

Clemente struggles to gain acceptance in his new home. Pittsburgh has fixed racial barriers. Clemente describes himself as a "double nigger," both black and Latin, unable to speak much English, isolated and subjected to racial slurs, even from his own teammates and especially from the press. It's hard to look back and see how we were and have to say this is true. Sports writers, none of whom can speak Spanish, use phonetics to make Clemente look stupid, quoting Clemente as saying he "heet the peetch gut" and the weather was "veree hot." When his style seems flamboyant, Pittsburgh sports writers call him a "Puerto Rican hot dog." When he finishes eighth in the balloting for MVP in 1960, after the Pirates' dramatic World Series win over the Yankees, Clemente feels he was denied the award, or at least a higher ranking, because he is Latin American.

⌷ ⌷ ⌷

I tell some friends that an essay is hounding me that somehow has something to do with Roberto Clemente. They're skeptical. "You can't write about Clemente," one male friend, also a writer, says. "You don't know anything about baseball."

For a while, I agree with them but then I realize that I do know the most important thing about baseball: baseball is about running home. Here's what I mean.

No one but my grandfather ever took me to baseball games, and then only a few times, when I was in grade school, all the way out to Forbes Field near Schenley Park where we would sit on the bleachers in the hot afternoon sun and Grandpap would follow every play carefully and silently.

Grandpap loved the Pirates. He would sip from his silver flask and occasionally pass the program to me. He bought me Coke and hot dogs. I mostly remember how handsome Grandpap looked in his pearl gray suit trousers, his wide gray-and-white striped suspenders, and his starched white monogrammed shirt, his sleeves rolled up, his French cuffs disappearing for a few hours while we sat watching the Pirates play baseball.

I skim some biographies of Clemente. My interest picks back up. Clemente was wary of writers. He's a prickly, enigmatic character. Baseball transformed him. Some say he transformed baseball.

He also died on my birthday.

When I read that, or remember that, for I must have known it once, the headlines blared it so at the time, when I read again that Clemente died on my birthday, I know that, somewhere our paths have surely crossed. Roberto Clemente must be in this story about Uncle Joe's ashes.

Clemente Dies

The year is 1972. The month is December. The day is 31. Clemente boards a plane in San Juan, Puerto Rico, to personally accompany relief aid to earthquake victims in Nicaragua. Clemente believes that the military will not siphon off the donated food and clothing if he, El Magnifico, is there to supervise. He is tired. In his last game of what would prove to be his last season, he made hit number 3,000. He had felt the need to hurry and make this hit because, he tells reporters, he suspects he won't live to be old.

There are other premonitions that Clemente doesn't heed. His son sees the plane crashing. Clemente tells his wife "when your time comes, it comes." His father asks him not to go but Clemente boards the plane anyway. The plane crashes into the ocean about one mile off the coast of Puerto Rico, killing everyone aboard.

Thousands gather for days after the crash, standing at the ocean's edge at a place called Puente Maldonado outside of San Juan, watching the waves that stole Clemente's life. Clemente's body is never found. Clemente's sock, and later his briefcase, drift ashore. Everyone wants to know where Clemente is but the rescuers can find no trace of his body. When Pittsburgh catcher Manny Sanguillen hears about the crash, he runs to the beach and tries to jump into the water, but some of the waves that night are twelve feet tall. For the next five days, Sanguillen searches, making futile attempts to dive for Clemente's body. Thousands stand on the beach, just looking for some sign of Clemente.

MORE BASEBALL AND MORE RAGTIME

Ed Kaizer is the best pianist I know. We sit in his studio at Bradley University and talk about ragtime music and "Roberto Clemente." Ed understands both subjects. He is a classical pianist who also plays ragtime. He has played ragtime around the world. Ed also is from Pittsburgh and used to play semiprofessional baseball there in the late 1950s, but Ed never knew Clemente personally. Ed remembers once pitching a game in Forbes Field, though, when he was in high school. I guess you don't forget things like that.

Ed talks about piano rags and rhythm, reminding me how ragtime's distinctive syncopation comes when the left hand keeps the rhythm, the *oom pah* beat, while the right hand works out the melodies and plays the themes. Ed plays "Roberto Clemente" several times. When Ed's initial play-through doesn't sound like my CD, I realize how possessive I've become of the image I have in my head of Clemente. In Ed's hands, a different Clemente plays right field.

Ed hears what I hear in the piece. He goes with me back to Pittsburgh. "We can couch our memories in ragtime," he says. "It's nostalgic. It takes you wherever you want to go."

EL MAGNIFICO

Clemente was called "El Magnifico." The Magnificent One. A true Baseball Man. In the Caribbean there are a few who are called Baseball Men. For Baseball Men, baseball is a calling, a deep passion.

Dodger scout Al Campanis noticed the young Clemente when Clemente was seventeen and playing baseball in Puerto Rico. Campanis recognized his ferocious talent, called him "the greatest natural athlete I ever saw as a free agent," but did he know that Clemente would one day rise to the level of myth?

For eighteen seasons, 1955–72, Clemente was the mainstay of the Pittsburgh Pirate outfield. He won four National League batting crowns. His lifetime batting average was .317. In his career he scored 240 home runs and had 1,350 RBIs. He hit safely in all seven games of the 1960 and 1971 World Series and won the Most Valuable Player Award for the 1971 Series against Baltimore, where he batted .414 and hit two home runs. Clemente was a twelve-time All Star and twelve-time Gold Glove Award winner. He was the League's Most Valuable Player in 1966. He became only the eleventh player in major league history to record 3,000 hits. After his death in 1972, Clemente became the first Hispanic player elected to the National Baseball Hall of Fame. The Pirates then permanently retired Number 21.

ARRIBA! ARRIBA!

So skilled and alive and purposeful was Clemente when he played baseball that those who watched him have never forgotten. For Clemente, life was always about the right way to play the game, like when, in a game against the Astros, he ran flat-out into a wall, risking injury on a relatively meaningless play. "A catch for the ages," the *Houston Chronicle* called it, but some were dismayed.

Why did you *do* this? Why risk injury on a nothing play?

Genuinely puzzled because the answer was so obvious, Clemente answered simply. "I wanted to catch the ball."

Clemente put right field on the map. Throwing on the run from center field, Clemente let the ball loose at up to 110 miles per hour, it is said. He ran almost in desperation, as if chased by a beast, so furious was his speed. He slid with skill and at times hung suspended in air, parallel to the field, flat and fleeting as a shadow.

Clemente would swing at anything. He was a pitcher's nightmare. Someone once said he could hit .299 in an iron lung. And when Clemente hit, when his bat really connected with the ball, it would rise on a silent trajectory, kind of like time's arrow, flying away through space as if blasted from a shotgun. No wonder sports writer Roger Angell said Clemente played "a kind of baseball that none of us had ever seen before."

I'm surprised by how many people have a Clemente story. All this time there was a world of Clemente memories out there that I didn't know existed until now. Cousin Jimmy tells me this story about Roberto Clemente.

When he was in seventh grade, Jimmy and his friends liked to go to Forbes Field to watch the Pirates and they always sat in right field. He said they were drawn there. They tried to sit near Clemente. "He had a *baseball* look to him," Jimmy remembers. "Clemente was very proud and he would hold his head very high and move his neck." Jimmy calls this Clemente's "peacock thing."

In one game, Hank Aaron, who was playing for the Braves, hit a ball out of the infield and it rolled up toward second base. Jimmy says the ball lay on the ground about fifteen feet away from Clemente. Clemente never moved toward the ball. He dared Aaron to try for second. Aaron took off. Clemente ran so fast he scooped up the ball and threw Aaron out by a few inches. "It was the *Superman* move! Only Clemente could do that. We screamed '*Arriba! Arriba!*' We didn't know what that meant but we screamed '*Arriba!*' We couldn't believe it!"

As Jimmy is yelling "*Arriba!*" into the phone, jolting the lines between Illinois and Colorado, I notice that on my desk is a brochure for a new musical playing in Pittsburgh about Clemente that's called "*Arriba! Arriba!* The Roberto Clemente Story."

NO SIMPLE STORIES

I think it would be nice to write a simple story for once but there are no simple stories. Just simple ideas and little insights that take a long time in telling. All of this back and forth, the meshing of the pieces of this ragtime puzzle, is how I sort through the ideas that fill my head when I write.

So many lovely parts to this puzzle. I turn over all the little bits looking for the right fit: A rag, originally a black folk tune, grew to describe an instrumental syncopated march. To rag an existing melody is to shift the accents. "To rag" also means to tease, to incorporate surprises, to introduce an unexpected rhythm. The crowds cheer when a baseball player hits a home run. Ragtime or jazz musicians say the music is "coming home" when, in the last strain or next-to-last, the tempo changes and the rhythm increases.

There's more. Ragtime came to be a written music. That was important. And Joplin insisted that players play note-for-note from the written score. No one could change the parts he didn't like. "Play it as I wrote it," Joplin said. Joplin's first published work in 1899 is called "Original Rags" and the last, published after his death in 1917, is aptly titled "Reflection Rag—Syncopated Musings."

I told you before. We really don't choose our stories. When we're hot, our stories chase us until we catch them.

COMING HOME

Intense syncopation produces music that ragtime lovers call "hot." Clemente was hot. So hot in the 1971 World Series that the organist at Three Rivers Stadium played "Jesus Christ Superstar" every time Clemente came to bat.

Although the initial racial tensions faded and Pittsburgh loved him long before 1971, Clemente had always wanted national recognition of his baseball ability. Clemente wanted to be seen as the best ballplayer in the world. "I play as good as anybody. . . but I am not loved," Clemente said once. "I don't need to be loved. I wish it would happen. Do you know what I mean?"

Clemente was loved in Puerto Rico and he loved his homeland in return. Clemente's wife returned to Puerto Rico for the birth of each of their children, at her husband's request, and Clemente spent his off seasons in Puerto Rico. Clemente was always going home.

There's lots of ways to go home. It's instinctive, this returning, this circling the bases. Like birds and turtles and salmon, like Uncle Joe in his van making his loops between Colorado and Pittsburgh and like Roberto Clemente playing baseball, and maybe even like dying, we find ways to make that trip back upstream. Show me someone who has no desire for a return ticket and I will show you someone who has never heard ragtime.

Clemente: Dreamer and Poet

In the final analysis, I think, we matter for the qualities we embody in this life and for the depth of our dreams. Clemente's dream was to build *Ciudad Deportiva,* City of Sport, for the underprivileged children of Puerto Rico. Today Clemente's City of Sport sits on 240 acres, just a few miles from where El Magnifico died and where, since his death, over 100,000 children have learned about sports and about hope. My research turns up a poem that Clemente wrote one Father's Day during a game at Three Rivers Stadium. Here, I believe, I have tapped into Clemente's soul.

> Who am I?
> I am a small point in the light of the full moon.
> I only need one ray of the sun to warm my face.
> I only need one breeze from the Alisios to refresh my soul.
> What else can I ask if I know that my sons really love me?

I had never before thought of baseball players as wise men but Clemente is right. What do any of us need, after all, beyond the sun and the breeze and the love of our children?

Love Again Lost

The year is 1999. The month is March. The day is 5. Joe sits in my kitchen and tells me about Annie.

"I have a new granddaughter. She's a nice girl. Her name is Annie Martinez." At eighty-one, with time running out, Joe doesn't seem bothered any more by the sound of last names and the boundaries of old ethnic neighborhoods.

"She's getting married in September and Jim is giving her away. I gave her $10,000 for a wedding present." He chews thoughtfully on a piece of Italian bread. I almost choke on my spaghetti. Joe has always been tight with his money.

Ten thousand, I repeat.

Joe pauses and his fork with the spaghetti dangling stops in mid-air.

"Dorothy would have loved to have had a granddaughter. She would have loved to buy her pretty clothes. Annie would have made Dorothy so happy. I wish I had known." His voice trails off and I figure he's thinking about Dorothy's sad life and her despair at the end. The fork continues on toward his mouth. And then Joe starts to talk about his airplane.

Joe always was a traveler. Sometimes in his car and sometimes in his plane, he would just disappear. One day Joe told Dorothy he was going to the store to get groceries and he didn't come back for a week. When he returned, he said he had driven to the Outer Banks of North Carolina, just to look at it. Joe did things like that all the time. He drove to the place where the roads end just so he could drive back home again.

When we live our lives in metaphor like this, we risk that people won't understand.

Joe often went along to the AA Fellowship meetings with Jimmy. Sometimes Joe had a few drinks before he went to the meeting and sometimes he left early so he could have a few more before he went home. Because Joe's knees were filled with arthritis, he needed a comfortable chair and Jimmy had Joe's old brown living room chair moved into the AA hall. The brown chair still sits in the meeting room. I guess some other old man sits in it now.

Jimmy says he initially took care of Joe because it was the right thing to do, not because he loved him. Perhaps Jimmy loved his dad and doesn't know it yet. I asked Jimmy why he didn't have a traditional funeral for Joe. He thought for a minute and then said, "There was nothing to say."

Maybe saying nothing is better than saying the wrong thing. Silence is easier to take back or to amend. Scott Joplin had asked his wife to have the Maple Leaf Rag, his most famous work, played at his funeral. When the time came, she said no.

"How many, many times since then, I've wished to my heart that I'd said yes."

THE FELLOWSHIP

Most of the guests at the barbecue are Jimmy's friends from the AA Fellowship Hall. A man with tattoos on his arms and a bear claw around his neck arrives on a big black Harley. A pudgy man in brown trousers and flowered sport shirt says hello. Ladies carry plates of deviled eggs and fruit salads and bags of potato chips. While Jimmy cooks sausages, Annie sets out platters for the meat. Everyone is eating the sausages as fast as Jimmy can grill them.

Jimmy's friends take brief note of the pictures on the table. They never really knew the Joe who is in all these photographs. They just remember him as Jimmy's dad who used to go to some of the AA meetings with Jim and finally stood up one night and said, "My name is Joe and I am an alcoholic."

I only have Joe's version of what took place. Joe said he had been going with Jimmy to the AA meetings for months. He liked to hear the stories and needed some place to spend time, he said. He was lonely in Estes Park. He missed Pittsburgh.

Joe said everyone was happy when he finally stood up and said that yes, he, too, was an alcoholic and he said he told some pretty hair-raising stories of his own. But it wasn't because he had a drinking problem that he went to the meetings, he told me. It was because they had really good food afterwards and he liked having a place to go for dinner.

The last time Joe visited me, he signed our guest book, my family's way of keeping track of all the people who pass through our house. "AA Hall—Keep coming back!! Joe R., Estes Park Colorado, 3–5–99."

I remember Joe laughing as he wrote. "That's what they keep saying after those damn AA meetings, Chris. 'Keep coming back. Keep coming back.' Hell, I just like the food."

HYPERTIME

Time, modern physicists say, is really an extra dimension. Einstein understood this. He said that the distinction between past, present, and future is only an illusion, even if a stubborn one. Einstein also believed that the road on which we travel through time can curve and go backwards; it doesn't have to be the straight-as-an-arrow trajectory Newton envisioned.

I scan back and forth over my ideas and stories like a composer scans back and forth over a musical score. A musical score gives a solid shape to time, allowing the composer to hold past, present, and future in his hands all at once. Perhaps then composers live outside of time in what physicists call "hypertime."

David Thomas Roberts is the composer of "Roberto Clemente." He lives not in hypertime but in Moss Point, Mississippi. Roberts is also a writer, artist, and poet. He studies metaphysics. He is as deeply immersed in his musical compositions as he is in the landscape. The American landscape is his passion. "American Landscape" is also the title of his CD that I carry with me everywhere so I can listen to "Roberto Clemente."

Our conversation takes a seemingly odd tack in the beginning. Roberts tells me that a good friend of his had died the night before. I tell him I first heard "Roberto Clemente" the night before my uncle's memorial. Is it a coincidence, I then ask, that I sit talking to you about your composition the night after your friend's death?

"Synchronicity," he replies, "is built into our reality, and there may be no such thing as coincidence."

WHAT THE MUSIC MEANS

Roberts was moved to write "Roberto Clemente" after seeing a film about Clemente during the 1979 World Series, and he describes the piece as a "folk elegy" and a "country funeral." After viewing the film, Clemente became for Roberts "a myth to be recalled with affection." I wonder, but do not ask, if Clemente has become for Roberts a part of the American landscape he loves so much, just as Uncle Joe has become a myth to me, a myth *I* recall with affection, a key figure in my personal landscape.

As a musical composition, "Roberto Clemente" has four musical themes or melodies. These themes vary and repeat, vary and repeat, returning with nuances and interpretations determined by the composer and the performer,

To me this sounds a lot like life.

"Roberto Clemente" is not, Roberts says, a retelling of Clemente's life and career as a sound poem might be, but the music evokes "the man as I had viewed him via the documentary." Roberts tells his concert audiences that he heard elements of the first phrase of the second theme in his head as he watched the Clemente film and that he associates this theme most implicitly with Clemente the man. Even so, he cautions. "Don't say 'that's what the music means.' . . . The symbolism is more elusive. More fragile. You can't reduce the irreducible."

Roberts then tells me something he has never told anyone. The Clemente documentary used footage of waves washing up on the shore in Puerto Rico and footage of Clemente circling the bases. Roberts can't recall if the pictures were actually superimposed in the film or if he just remembered them in conjuncture. But it was these two images, the waves on the shore and Clemente circling the bases, running home, that he wanted to communicate in his composition.

Roberts has written about the "plaintiveness" and "gentle anguish" that is associated with ragtime, and I tell him I feel this gentle pain when I listen to "Roberto Clemente" and think about Clemente's life.

"I was touched by the mingling of tragedy and hope that is all around us," Roberts tells me. "And I was asking myself this question: *What is so meaningful in this tough school which is what I believe the earth is?"*

"Do you think Clemente's death was unfair?" I ask Roberts.

"I think we choose our births and deaths," he tells me. "We are unconsciously fulfilling what we've mapped or assented to have mapped. I don't believe in tragedy in the conventional sense any longer."

Grace Notes

A grace note is a musical term for a quick note frequently used in ragtime that is usually attached to another note and is out of time with the rest of the piece. Roberts describes the grace notes in "Roberto Clemente" as *lagniappe*, a Creole term for "a little something extra" or "a show of appreciation," and points out how the grace notes in "Roberto Clemente" add to the Latin feel of the piece. Ed Kaizer calls these extra notes "embellishments" but I prefer to say "grace notes."

To me, grace notes, in music or in life, are those unexpected blessings that pass by so quickly we take them for granted unless we listen very carefully to the music. Grace notes, like synchronicities, are really little miracles.

The Hoax Revealed

Jimmy says there really is no Transcendental Explorers Club International. He tells me he made it up when, after talking to the undertaker, he felt Joe's obituary was lacking in accomplishments.

I think Jimmy is mistaken about there not being a club for transcendental explorers. Why else would we wonder where we are and where we're going and what exactly we have to do to get home? Why else would life go round and round us like ragtime, defining itself by the off-beat, dangling the hope ahead of the tragedy and offering us the occasional grace note? Why else would Roberto Clemente speak to me in a song?

I think *Jimmy* is really the elite member of this club, twice decorated, as he said of Joe. Otherwise he would have set lower sights for Joe when he added the grace note to his father's obituary. After all, he could have said Joe was the Grand Pooh-bah of the Shriners.

DOROTHY'S ASHES

The month is July. The day is 17. The year is 1999. There's no formal announcement. Those of us who really knew Joe just sense that it's time and we gravitate to the river. Jimmy and his wife and son climb across some boulders that reach out into the Fall River. River is really too big a word today for the water that flows by Jimmy's resort, just a fast-moving mountain stream it is, dashing among rocks and leaving trails of white foam at every turn. Joe's ashes are going to be scattered in this stream, but because Jimmy's condo construction had caused a fish kill in this same river last spring and the Environmental Protection Agency had levied a substantial fine against him, Jimmy hasn't talked much about his plan. The ashes have been kept under wraps.

I walk down close to the river's edge, so I can say goodbye to Uncle Joe as his ashes pass. Jimmy opens the container that holds Joe's ashes and removes the plastic bag. As he hands the bag to his son, I see another small brown cardboard box out on the rock. Jimmy opens that box and removes another plastic bag that he holds close to his heart for a moment. Dorothy's ashes. Jimmy still has his mother's ashes.

The year was 1996. The month was February. The day was 21. Dorothy's funeral. Gentle anguish, Roberts would call it. As the priest talked about the pain that had lived in Dorothy's heart for too many years, I heard the ragtime piano player in the bawdy house back in Sedalia. His *basso continuo* pumped out the rhythm, the relentless *oom pah,* of her life. In the end, the priest had nothing more than words for comfort. After all, he's not a piano man.

But I hoped Joe was listening. Roberts understood the question: What is so meaningful in this tough school which is what I believe the earth is? Did

Joe hear the repeats and the themes returning? As he buried Dorothy, I wanted Joe to hear the grace notes.

After mass, Joe and I sat in the pew. Joe turned to me and in a loud annoyed voice complained about the sermon. He said his hearing aid wasn't working right.

"Will someone please tell me what that damn priest was talking about? All I could hear was every now and then he said 'Dorothy.' I couldn't make out any other damn thing he was saying."

COMING HOME AGAIN

That was three years ago, the last time I saw Dorothy's ashes. Today Jimmy holds his mother close to his heart and then, as he dumps her into the Fall River, his son pours Uncle Joe into the river alongside Dorothy. The current rushes past me. I listen to the water. The voices are clear as the ashes pass by.

"Dumb bunny," the donkey says.

"Jackass," the rabbit answers.

Swirling from eddy to eddy, they're after each other again. Alive and sad and angry and hopeful. Playful, the tumbling ashes are. Rolling over large stones, like the stride bass of a piano rag. In a hurry. Defying Joplin's advice about never playing ragtime fast. The music is coming home now.

I wanted to catch the ball, Clemente said. *I don't need to be loved but I wish it would happen. What more can we ask if we know our children love us?* The piano shakes as the rags roll out. The left hand plays *oom pah, oom pah* and won't quit. The right hand spins and re-spins the melody. *Ragtime takes us anywhere we want to go.*

Keep coming back, Uncle Joe wrote in my book. *Never say that's what the music means,* Roberts told me.

The time of our lives. Time torn in pieces. Time sewn back together. Little bits of melody plucked from the air. Jagged time. Ragged time. Ragtime.

"Dumb bunny."

"Jackass."

I close my eyes and remember all the ragged times and wonder if this damn ragtime will ever stop. I don't want a life played out like a piano rag anymore and I'm tired of the tragedy even if it carries along a little hope. Then I remember the grace note. I remember that Dorothy had signed her bittersweet card to Joe with "Love."

"Love, Dot."

The music softens and the notes dance around silence. The crowds are waiting, hoping for another home run. A Superman move. Clemente jerks his neck, unwinds his bat, and seeks another meaningful connection.

"*Arriba! Arriba!*" we yell as the ball disappears over the stadium wall. ■

Positive

Danielle Ofri

She was a tiny woman, but she had me cornered near the 16-West nurses' station, practically grabbing the lapels of my white coat. "Are you accusing my niece of having AIDS?" she hissed, her face only inches from mine. "My niece doesn't do drugs, she doesn't hang around nasty people, she's never had any bad diseases. She's a good girl!"

Her voice began to rise as she pressed closer into me and the singsong of her Jamaican accent became more dissonant. "You doctors think every Black or Hispanic kid who comes in here has AIDS. I've been at Bellevue for 25 years and I've seen how you doctors are." By now she was nearly screaming. The gray strands in her dark hair shimmered with rage. "Don't you ever talk to my niece like that again. And you're only an intern! I want her transferred to a real doctor."

I tried to edge backward, but she locked her glare on me. I could feel her angry breath hot on my face. She plunged one firm finger into my chest. "I don't trust you. Stay away from my niece!"

A few people stuck their heads out of offices to see what all the commotion was. I tried to use my most diplomatic voice. "Mrs. Stanton, I'm not saying that Yvette has HIV. It's just that the type of pneumonia she has can sometimes possibly be associated with HIV."

"Don't give me no a-sso-ci-a-tions." She sputtered each syllable at me. "I know my niece and she does not have AIDS."

"I'm not saying that she has AIDS." I tried to take a breath, but there wasn't much air. "Could we sit down in the lounge and talk about this?"

"There ain't nothing to talk about and we can do it right here." Mrs. Stanton crossed her arms in front of her chest and drew her cheeks in tightly.

I lowered my voice. "I'm not trying to say anything bad about Yvette. It's just that in the remote chance she has HIV we should know now so she can get the most effective and appropriate treatments."

"The 'appropriate treatment' is for you to stop harassing her about taking that AIDS test. My niece does not have AIDS. Period." She paused and shifted her posture so that her head was cocked even closer to me. I could see right down the part in the middle of her head. "Do you hear me? Period!"

⧉ ⧉ ⧉

It was only last week when I was scrutinizing Yvette's chest X-ray in the cramped radiology room in the ER. All the normal lung markings were scrunched up, like she hadn't taken a deep enough breath. Yvette was short of breath, true, but she didn't strike me as sick enough to explain these dense markings on the X-ray. Not in a 23-year-old. It was only midway into my internship year, but I'd already admitted enough patients to Bellevue Hospital to have acquired some amount of clinical intuition. I marched over to her stretcher. "This X-ray isn't good enough," I announced. "We're doing it again, but this time take a real breath!"

The second X-ray was essentially unchanged. The crowded lung markings could have been ordinary pneumonia or might have been consistent with PCP (pneumocystis) pneumonia. Yvette just didn't seem like AIDS to me. Something didn't fit.

I waded back through the noise and general chaos of the ER to Yvette to interview her. With her silky brown complexion, large rounded eyes, and generous supply of baby fat, she barely looked 16. But she was panting. I could see her gulping for air between sentences and there was a fine line of moisture on her forehead. The muscles of her neck and chest weren't straining, though, so I wasn't worried that she was going to "crap out" and need a breathing tube.

"It's only recently, doctor. Maybe a few weeks ago that I started having trouble breathing. I've never been sick . . . ever." Yvette paused, adjusting the oxygen tubing that opened into her nose. She inhaled heavily. "With the cold weather, and all . . . it's making me feel like an old person."

I asked her if she'd been a physically active person before these symptoms started. "Well, not exactly," Yvette said with a chuckle. "As you can see, I have a few pounds to lose. But I," she stopped for a breath, "I get around fine. My two little ones keep me moving.

"This breathing stuff just knocked me out. I mean, in the last few days, what with Christmas and New Year's. All the guests and everything . . . I could barely make it across the kitchen floor." Her voice rose for emphasis, but then she had to pause for a breath. "My aunt—we live with my aunt—

kept telling me to come to Bellevue, but I've never needed any doctors. I've always been healthy. You probably know my aunt . . . she works in medical records. She knows *everybody* at Bellevue." Yvette managed a sarcastic grin and rolled her eyes.

Yvette told me that she was interested in the paralegal profession. She had graduated high school and was contemplating college, but was raising her children full-time. She blushed when I questioned her about risk factors for HIV. She had never used drugs, never received any blood transfusions, and did not have multiple sexual partners.

When I asked about the man who was the father of her children, her tone hardened and dropped in pitch. "Him? He's long gone from my life. I don't want to know from nothing about him."

I paused, debating if I should pursue this. "Can you tell me a little about him?" I ventured. "Was he generally healthy?"

Yvette shrugged and looked over at the oxygen tank near her bed.

"Do you know if he ever did drugs, or had a blood transfusion?"

"Listen, I have nothing to do with him," she said flatly, her eyes remaining on the oxygen tank. "He's not part of my life."

"I know these questions are uncomfortable, but they are important."

Yvette continued staring at the oxygen tank with the pressure monitors and warning signs attached to it.

"Do you know if he had a lot of other partners?" I asked.

"He is out of my life. He doesn't exist." She turned her eyes back toward me. "Can we just get back to me already?"

I nodded—I'd gone too far. "You're right. I'm sorry. We'll stay with you."

I looked at the X-ray again with its bunched-up lung markings. Could this be PCP or was it just garden-variety pneumonia that could be easily treated with erythromycin? In my gut I did not think that Yvette had AIDS. Her history wasn't consistent with HIV and she didn't have "the look," as Bellevue interns would say. She was, if anything, overweight. Her skin glowed with youthful health. She didn't have any risk factors.

I reminded myself that HIV could obviously be transmitted heterosexually, but the actual rate of HIV transmission per heterosexual encounter was very low compared to homosexual transmission and IV drug use. I was still an intern, but I already had a fair amount of experience with HIV. This didn't smell of AIDS. To reinforce my feelings, and perhaps to convince those around me, I ordered the first dose of erythromycin to be given *stat*.

But just to be sure, I decided to repeat the X-ray one more time.

I hauled Yvette back to radiology. Ignoring the technician's complaints about three chest X-rays in one hour, I hounded Yvette like a football coach. "Okay," I said, "this is it! This time you are going to take a deeper breath. The deepest breath in the world. Stretch out those lungs! Get that air in! *Breathe!*"

I was back in the tiny radiology room again, squished between the old metal desk and the file cabinets, staring at the third X-ray. Two other interns were jostling me for the same light box to read their films. I tried to will Yvette's lung markings apart. I ordered them to disengage, to separate, to untwist, to disconnect. But they wouldn't budge. I flipped the X-ray backwards and forwards. I scrutinized it under the extra bright "hot light." I blocked the heart image with my palm to eliminate distracting shadows. I varied the ambient lighting. I squinted and covered my weaker eye. I removed my glasses and pressed the X-ray right up to my nose. But it was no use. The lung markings wouldn't part.

Harrison's *Principles of Internal Medicine* lists 40 diseases that can present with "increased interstitial lung markings," but in New York City in the 1990s there was only one. I couldn't deny it any longer.

I slunk back to the ER and reluctantly switched Yvette's antibiotic from erythromycin to Bactrim, the most effective drug for PCP. I lowered my eyes as I wrote the order, avoiding the "I told you so" stare from the ER nurse.

"I can't be sure exactly which type of pneumonia you have," I explained to Yvette, "until we do a bronchoscopy to get a lung biopsy. But I am concerned that you might have PCP. PCP pneumonia occurs in illnesses that suppress the immune system."

"What kind of illnesses do that?" Yvette asked, looking straight at me.

"Well," I said, trying to sound nonchalant, "if you are on chemotherapy or steroids. Some rheumatologic diseases like lupus could do it. Cancer could do it." I swallowed. "And HIV could do it too."

Yvette continued to stare directly at me, but didn't say anything.

I lowered my voice to a whisper. "I think you should do an HIV test." Yvette pursed her lips and shook her head firmly.

Yvette improved surprisingly fast after she was started on Bactrim. She continued to refuse the bronchoscopy and the HIV test, but within a few days she was breathing normally and able to walk around without oxygen.

Aside from our daily disagreement on morning rounds over testing, we got along well. I never got to meet Yvette's kids because they were too young to come up to the wards, but she told me how Stephan babbled nonstop on the phone. Apparently his great-aunt was reading extra stories to him at night so he really didn't miss his mother all that much. Sarah was just learning how to talk and was a little intimidated by the phone, but she was having fun with the snow.

Yvette had an easy affability about her and a catchy smile. When she grinned, two big dimples illuminated her face and you couldn't help but smile back. The three older women who shared her room became stand-in grandmothers, boasting about Yvette's progress to all the other patients on the ward. Yvette's nightstand was piled high with the cookies and candies they hoarded for her.

⌷ ⌷ ⌷

Mrs. Stanton was exhaling hot breaths at me as I tried to explain how Yvette's symptoms went along with PCP. "The way she got short of breath over just a few days sounds like PCP. And the chest X-rays are really suggestive of PCP."

"Don't talk to me about no X-rays," she pushed in. "I've been working here at Bellevue for 25 years. I know how things run around here! You residents don't know nothing about reading X-rays. I want to show them to Dr. Johannsen."

Dr. Johannsen was one of the best radiology attendings at Bellevue. Aside from her expertise in chest radiology, she was especially known for her friendly personality and her love of teaching. She was always happy to answer questions and was on a first-name basis with many of the housestaff.

We went down to the radiology suite on the third floor, with Mrs. Stanton marching resolutely in front of me. I carefully laid out the X-rays in front of Dr. Johannsen. I could tell from the way her eyes reflexively widened that she knew right away it was PCP, but she took her time. She carefully examined the three identical chest X-rays, holding each one up to the hot light. She treated the X-rays of Yvette with the same respect she would have given Yvette. Mrs. Stanton nodded proudly, and then shot a glare at me.

Dr. Johannsen thought for a good while and then turned to Mrs. Stanton. "Isabel," she said softly, "it may very well be PCP. I can't tell you absolutely, but it certainly looks like it. I think you need to do the bronchoscopy to get a biopsy of her lung tissue. It's the only way to be sure." She reached for the other woman's shoulder. "I know this must be terrifying for you, but Yvette will get the best treatment once we have the exact diagnosis."

Part of me wanted to exalt in the joy of being right, of making the correct diagnosis, of saying "I told you so," but I could not—Mrs. Stanton's face had crumpled inwards. The eyes that had locked me in their glare had now clouded over and hovered rootlessly without focus. The jaw that had been set so firmly against me now trembled with a helpless cadence. The fingers that had pointed at me with such anger now hung at her side, reflexively drawing together in a half-remembered gesture, then faltering and falling limp. "Okay," she whispered, the words barely making it out over her lips. "I'll talk to Yvette."

The bronchoscopy was done the next day. I reviewed the slides with the pathologist. In the microscope I could see hundreds of foamy bubbles. They looked like the snowdrifts that were piling up outside of Bellevue, coating the nineteenth-century brick columns with wedding veils of white. "They're all PCP," she said. "Every last one."

Yvette still refused the HIV test. While an HIV test required consent, a T cell test did not (at least at that time). T cells are the white blood cells most affected by HIV. Normally, humans possess well over a thousand T cells in a milliliter of blood. Fewer than 500 is typically when HIV treatment is begun, even though patients are still asymptomatic. Below 200 is when most opportunistic infections begin. Without Yvette's consent, we sent her blood sample for a T cell count. On the day of her discharge it came back at 8.

I wanted to share this result immediately with Yvette, but her discharge day did not feel appropriate. Too many conflicting emotions. She already had an appointment scheduled in my clinic for the following week. It could wait a few days, I told myself.

That evening I bundled up and walked down to the Little India neighborhood on East Sixth Street. The block was lined with Indian and Pakistani restaurants, crammed one against the next. Sitar music and curry fragrances wafted along the entire stretch. Colored lights festooned the windows all year round, but at this time of year, tourists could be forgiven for assuming that these were in honor of Christmas. Young men shivered outside, pressing flyers into the hands of passing pedestrians, offering free appetizers or 50 percent off the second entrée, anything to convince the undecided customer to choose this particular restaurant over that one. There was little else to distinguish the establishments. The restaurants proffered identical menus, the same assortments of biryani, tandoori, and vindaloo. Saag panir and fluffy poori bread were identical from one to the next. There were those who were convinced that there in fact existed only one kitchen that stretched along the whole of East Sixth Street, dispensing cheap, greasy, but serviceable Indian grub for the entire block.

I stomped the snow off my boots and popped into a random restaurant with the intention of sitting down for a meal. But my mind felt restless and resisted the confinement. I ordered two samosas to go and continued down the block. How was I going to tell Yvette? What actual words could I use?

The heat of the vegetable patties radiated through my gloves to my waiting palms. I bit into the crisp outer layer, releasing a vaporous warmth of garam masala spices. I couldn't recall a single lecture in my four years of medical school that had addressed this issue. There wasn't any chapter in Harrison's entitled "How to tell patients they have a terminal illness." I sank into the potato and pea filling, inhaling the pungent flavors of coriander and cumin. There was a bite, though, from the chili peppers.

I could keep hinting until she figured it out. *Yvette, remember what I said about that certain kind of pneumonia? The kind that can happen when the immune system isn't working so well? It's like what happens when you get chemotherapy, but in your case you're not getting chemotherapy.* A mustard seed caught in my throat. That was too horribly vague and ambiguous. I would hate for a doctor to talk to me like that. She deserved the respect of clarity, no?

I swung around the corner to St. Mark's Place. Brightly lit souvenir emporiums jutted onto the sidewalks hawking T-shirts, leather vests, silver chains and fake Rolexes. There was a café offering tattoo-and-cappuccino specials just next to one that provided high-speed Internet access along with cappuccino. The condom shop on the west end of the block had been replaced with a body-piercing parlor. Even on a cold winter night the street was teeming with teenagers from Long Island jostling with incense vendors in dreadlocks. Tourists struggling with their ungainly subway maps gawked at leather-clad girls with nose rings and tongue studs and overly-hennaed hair. As I trudged along the block I passed in and out of several clouds of marijuana.

I could be blunt and lay it on the table. *Yvette you have AIDS.* That would certainly eliminate any ambiguity. I started on my second samosa, which was already cold by this time. *You have AIDS.* There was a leaden thud to those words. In theory it seemed easy, just speak the truth. But the truth was so awful. It was a declaration of war on Yvette's life. How could I look into those liquidy brown eyes and say that? How could I possibly launch those bellicose words? The outer layer of the samosa, now that it was no longer hot, had turned to greasy mush. The potato filling was bland without the heat to energize its spices, and it piled up its stickiness on my tongue. A knish by any other name was just a knish.

I stopped in front of one of the jewelry displays. Tiny diamond studs sat side by side with heavy silver chains sporting pendants of skulls and daggers. There was a selection of thick gold-coiled chains that could be wrapped around the neck several times. Brass knuckle rings and handcuffs dangled from the edge of the display case.

Should I ease her in slowly? Should I be direct? Should I couch it in clinical terminology? Should I have a psychiatrist in the room with me? Should I ask my attending to do it?

I picked up a pair of earrings with small circles of pewter. It reminded me of the jewelry I used to buy in the Arab markets of Jerusalem, with the pressed copper that the vendors swore were actual ancient coins. I still had a few in my possession that I had purchased—bargained for—when I was 14. I held the pair in my hands, tracing the fine floral patterns that were etched into the metal. They glinted in the yellowish light of the streetlamp. I closed my palm around the earrings, feeling the chill of the metal eat into my flesh.

No matter which method I chose, there would be that one sentinel moment when the true meaning of my words would become evident. It almost wouldn't matter what my approach had been. Once it became apparent that I was telling Yvette that she had AIDS, all of my carefully selected words would tumble to the wayside. No matter what poets might say about the power of words, the most delicate and thoughtful prose is quashed by the leaden weight of a terminal illness.

I slipped the earrings back onto the table. My stomach was lurching from the grease of the samosas and my ears were beginning to sting from the cold. I plodded back up Second Avenue, my feet scratching against the salt that had been sprinkled on the sidewalks.

The night before Yvette's appointment I stayed up late memorizing different versions of my speech. I was determined to be straightforward with her. It was the least I could do, I thought. In the tempest of unknowns and fears that I imagined would ensnare anyone given a diagnosis of AIDS, I wanted to be a ballast of comfort. I wanted to have the *equinimatas* that Sir William Osler spoke of, to provide emotional support to my patient by being clear and steady. But I didn't want to compound her hurt.

I sat on my bed with a pencil, scribbling on the back of an envelope. I erased and rewrote my lines, then erased again. I telephoned all of my friends who were psychologists and social workers. Everybody had a different opinion, but they were unanimous in their relief that *they* didn't have to do it. I jotted a new speech down. I would be honest and forthright, but not harsh. I snatched my Roget's from the shelf, tearing through the pages to find the right words. They had to exist in there somewhere. "You will find words and phrases to express all the shades and modifications of that idea," the back jacket of my 1975 edition promised. Compassion, honesty, reliability—I looked them all up. Ambiguity—I checked the antonyms. I dug through the elaborately delineated categories that Peter Mark Roget, himself a physician, had teased out of the English language a hundred years ago. I scribbled more words on my envelope. I can do this, I told myself. Just be respectful but straightforward. *Yvette, I'm sorry to have to tell you this, but you have AIDS.* I tried out my lines aloud in front of the mirror. *Yvette, I know this will be hard to hear, but you have HIV.* I circled around my bedroom. *Yvette, this may be difficult to accept, but the virus, you know, the one that causes AIDS . . .* I fell asleep at three A.M., still mouthing variations on my theme.

When I arrived at clinic the next day, Yvette and her aunt were already waiting for me. My eyes felt too heavy to keep open and I'd been too nauseous to eat anything. "Well . . . you see," I started, trying to control the sour gurgitations in my stomach. Suddenly I couldn't remember any of the carefully planned speech that I had memorized. "Certain types of pneumonia . . . well different types of pneumonia . . . occur with different types of immune systems." My tongue seemed disengaged from my speech; its movements consistently one step out of sync with my words. "If T cells . . . one of the important parts of the immune system . . . aren't, you know, working so well, or aren't around in enough numbers . . ." I could feel myself drifting into babble. What happened to clarity and unambiguity?

I tried to take a deep breath but the air couldn't get very far. "Certain kinds of opportunistic infections, um . . . infections that normally don't, or usually don't, happen with the T cells around . . ." Where was I going? "Certain risk factors, see, can be associated with immunosuppression, and in those cases you can get different kinds of pneumonias . . ." What happened to Roget's perfect words that I'd written and rewritten last night? I tried to lasso in my rambling mouth, but contorted explanations spilled helplessly into the tiny exam room.

Yvette began to weep softly as my tongue garbled convoluted clauses about "lymphocyte ratios" and "seroconversion." Mrs. Stanton's breathing started to grow heavy, then became raspy and asthmatic as I felt myself choking over antibody reactions and Western blots. Mrs. Stanton heaved into loud sobs and my throat ground down, twisting to a halt around "lymphadenopathy" and "interstitial pneumonia." I stood there frozen, my fists plunged deep inside the pockets of my white coat. My eyes twitched around the small room, from the blood pressure cuff to the exam table to the stack of yellow X-ray request forms. Nothing would move; nothing would step forward to rescue me. I tried again to speak, but nothing would emerge—just a hoarse stutter that wilted against my teeth.

Tears began their ascent. Inside the pocket my hand clutched the bell of the stethoscope. I coddled it between my fingers, absorbing the cool smoothness of the stainless steel. They climbed steadily, the tears, steadfastly ignoring my plea to stay down. The clammy pulse of my palm evaporated the metal coolness of the stethoscope. The tears continued to push forward and the metal bell grew sticky from my heat. The tears bulged past the knot of muscles in my throat, overrunning the vise of gritted teeth. They rose in a pitch, rumbling forward, barreling upward, insistent in their path, until they hit their peak and spilled over.

And then there was the strange harmony of three people crying, each caught in a private dissonance. The room strained and the walls grew heavy around my head. But there was a relief in the absence of words. A relief to escape the tongue-twisting jargon, those lumbering, multisyllabic words intoned from textbooks, thesauruses, and professors; polyphonous clinical terms that were supposed to capture the essence of the disease. Words that I'd rehearsed and memorized, words that I'd thought would clarify and explain, but in fact served only to stymie. It was a relief to escape their tyranny and to lapse, for a moment, into the sanctuary of the nonverbal world—a world that required only the physical lexicon of the body. We cried together, sharing a language that paid no heed to linguistic proprieties, socioeconomic differences, or ethnic barriers.

Gradually the loud cries softened to sniffles and hiccupped sobs. "Could it possibly be anything else?" Mrs. Stanton asked, when she could finally speak again.

I wiped my eyes with the back of my sleeve and shook my head. "I'd still, um, though, like to do the HIV test. Just for documentation."

"It won't change anything, will it?" asked Yvette. I paused, then shook my head again. She declined.

I cleared my throat. "We should talk, though, about your, uh, situation." Back to the unwieldy world of words. "We need talk about your T cells and what medicines you need." T cells, medicines . . . words . . . how ungainly. "We checked your T cell count while you were in the hospital." Yvette looked up at me, uncomprehendingly. "Your T cell count . . ." I faltered, ". . . is, well, eight."

She continued to gaze at me without any change in expression. "What's normal?" she asked.

I swallowed hard, my tongue parched and immobile. "Well, it's, uh . . ." The words choked as they hacked their way out. "It's, uh, usually over a thousand."

There was a long silence. All three of us looked down at the gray linoleum in parallel gazes.

I didn't want to overload Yvette with information in this first visit but there was so much to do. It was imperative to get all her vaccinations updated, to set up appointments for regular blood tests, to apply to the Department of AIDS Services for additional healthcare coverage and to see a gynecologist and an ophthalmologist promptly. The short list of medications she had to start taking included Bactrim, one tablet once a day; AZT, two pills three times a day; rifabutin, two tablets once a day; Mycelex, one tablet five times a day; and a multivitamin once a day.

Then I gingerly brought up the subject of her children and the need to get them tested. "No," said Yvette, her tears drying up. "I will not interrupt their lives. I will not allow them to be tested." When I mentioned that we should also contact her ex-boyfriend, she became furious. "I probably *got it* from him. I hope he dies a slow and painful death!"

⌐ ⌐ ⌐

Yvette came regularly to all of her clinic appointments. She was by far my most reliable patient. She was scrupulous about her complex regimen of medications. She called me for refills well before her current prescriptions ran out. She remembered to do her blood tests every six weeks to the day, even when I forgot. And she always had a warm, dimpled smile for me, sometimes accompanied by homemade brownies or a bag of red seedless grapes that she knew were my favorite.

We never did do the HIV test. In fact we never even used the words HIV or AIDS. Yvette couldn't bring herself to say them, and nor, I found, could I. At the beginning of each visit when I'd ask her how she was doing she would reply, "I feel fine. If you didn't tell me that I was sick, I wouldn't know that I was sick." And with the smooth glow in her cheeks and that perfect-teeth smile, it was hard to argue with her.

She continued to refuse an HIV test for her children. I asked her to please let me at least speak with her pediatrician, but she said no.

"About your ex-boyfriend," I said, "it's important that he know so he can go to his doctor."

"I don't give a damn what happens to him," Yvette replied.

"You don't have to get involved at all. I can call him myself. Or, the Department of Health can do it anonymously. All they'll say is that he should consider getting himself tested. No names mentioned."

"Screw him. He's already screwed me. Why should I do anything for him?"

There was no chapter on this in Harrison's either. I conferred with several attendings about this issue and opinion was mixed. I finally consulted our legal affairs advisor. Regarding her children, it seemed, disclosure was not only possible but could even be required.

I confronted Yvette at our next visit. "I know this is a difficult thing to have to think about, especially now when there is so much on your mind, but there are a lot of people who potentially can be affected by this."

Yvette looked over to the "Children of Bellevue" poster on the wall.

"Listen, I can't force your children to be tested, but I do have the legal authority to call the pediatrician and tell him or her about *your* health status."

Yvette continued to stare at the poster. It was a calendar from three years ago that had brightly colored children's drawings decorating the 12 months of the year.

"I'm prepared to do that," I paused for a breath, "but I'd much prefer if I had your permission." I felt like I was cornering Yvette, and I didn't like having to do that.

I saw Yvette's eyes wander from January down to June, past the blue and green snowmen over to the bright orange flowers. Then down to her lap. "Okay," she mumbled, barely audibly. "You win."

⌐ ⌐ ⌐

Spring pressed along. The spindly trees on First Avenue were starting to bloom. The men who lived in the Bellevue Homeless Shelter congregated outdoors on the sidewalk, sitting on old milk cartons, enjoying the gentle sun. July would be coming soon, marking the end of internship. Once I'd taken care of the initial needs for Yvette—getting all of her medicines in order, setting up a regular schedule for blood tests, filling out all the Medicaid forms, talking to the pediatrician—there was suddenly a lull. We didn't have a whole lot to talk about during our visits. Especially since she felt perfectly fine. I had more time to ponder and a fear began to grow in me. Yvette seemed so healthy now, but she could get sicker and possibly die during the course of my residency. In the two years left to my residency I might actually witness the painful slow decline that would culminate in her death.

It was true that I had already seen a number of hospitalized patients die during my internship thus far, but they were different—they had already been visibly sick when I'd first met them. With their droopy gaunt faces and sallow skin, they'd already had their "terminal illness" label pinned upon them. Their arms were black and blue, and they had long since given up complaining about the needle sticks. They lived in their hospital beds, permanently attired in saggy blue gowns and regulation green Styrofoam slippers. They were perpetual patients—*only* patients—and nothing else. I had never seen them as healthy, functioning people and, frankly, I couldn't even envision them out in the world wearing real clothes, riding the subway, paying taxes.

Most of my clinic patients, on the other hand, were relatively healthy. They had hypertension, arthritis, or back pain. During our clinic appointments they'd tell me about a daughter graduating high school, or how long the wait at the pharmacy was, or what a lousy job the mayor was doing. We never had to discuss chemotherapy or DNRs. Maybe I'd fiddle with their blood pressure pills or remind them to get a mammogram, but I'd never had to think about blood transfusions or breathing machines. I'd tend to their winter colds and annoying heartburn, but most of them would never see the inside of the hospital. The vast majority would amble along without any major medical catastrophes during my next two years. And when I finished residency, I would pass them along to a new intern in basically the same condition that I'd inherited them.

But Yvette straddled both worlds. Now that she had fully recovered from her PCP, she seemed as healthy as my other clinic patients, if not healthier because of her youth. But over the upcoming two years there was a high probability of her getting cryptococcal meningitis or tuberculosis or lymphoma or AIDS dementia or any of the other brutal illnesses that follow HIV's coattails. These two years of my residency could be an unending series of medical disasters, each one wrenching her condition down another notch. Each one sapping her hold on life. Each one driving home the point that everyone with AIDS dies no matter how young or how healthy they start out. During the course of my tenure at Bellevue I might have to watch Yvette wither away from this robust woman sitting in my office to one of those skeletons that limped around on the AIDS ward upstairs on 17-West.

During Yvette's hospital stay back in January, one of my senior residents had made an offhand comment during rounds. "A T cell count under 50 and one opportunistic infection? Her life expectancy is less than a year." Whether that resident had been quoting data from a published study—this was in the days before protease inhibitors and combination antiviral drugs—or was just talking off the top of her head, I never knew, but those words stayed with me. I obsessed over those words. I obsessed over that prediction. Less than a year. I was going to watch Yvette shrivel and die and I was not ready for this.

Internship ended in July and I continued to see Yvette in my clinic. We went over her medications, refilled prescriptions, but there wasn't a lot to do because she felt so well and her blood counts were relatively stable. Several times I offered to transfer her to the HIV clinic where she could benefit from seeing the AIDS experts. She could also enroll in clinical trials for the newest experimental medications. Yvette would have nothing of it. She wanted to stay right here in the regular medicine clinic, with the healthy people.

I wasn't going to escape.

Occasionally, I ran into Mrs. Stanton in the hallway or down in the medical records department. We now had a strong working relationship, united in a common goal. She often brought me forms from Yvette that required my signature, and I frequently gave her prescriptions to save Yvette a trip to the clinic.

Yvette didn't acquire any other opportunistic infections. She never even caught a cold. I felt rather ridiculous writing "23-year-old Black female with HIV, T cells = 8" at the top of each of my clinic notes, when this woman with sparkling eyes and dimples in her baby-soft cheeks was sitting in front of me. Less than a year? She didn't look anything like the emaciated AIDS patients on 17-West. In fact, she was concerned about being overweight and wanted to know if I could prescribe her diet pills.

Maybe Yvette was the exception to the rule. Maybe her HIV wouldn't kill her. Maybe she didn't actually have AIDS. After all, we never *did* do the HIV test. I savored that thought in my head for several weeks. I even went so far as to ask one of the immunology professors if maybe a person with eight T cells and PCP pneumonia could have something other than AIDS. She rolled her eyes at me and I hung my head.

卐 卐 卐

Midway through my second year of residency I was doing a month rotation of full-time work in the emergency room. The hours were long, the surroundings dirty and chaotic. The stream of patients was endless and there was no place—physical or psychological—to rest. We switched backed and forth between 12-hour day shifts and night shifts every few days. My body was thrown in and out of time zones on an erratic basis. Working nights, sleeping days, working days, sleeping nights—I never knew if I was coming or going and the concept of "morning coffee" became a relative one. Like most other internal medicine residents, I spent my time counting down the 30 days until the end of this awful rotation.

Since there was never any end to the patients on line, there was no natural lull in the 12-hour shift in which to relax. Much energy was expended in finding creative ways to look busy while actually doing nothing so that the ER attending wouldn't plop another chart in your hand. My favorite method was to sit at the computer and aimlessly scroll through the lab results of my clinic patients. I could always say I was checking on labs for one of the patients in the ER. This technique spared me more than one drudgerous four A.M. patient evaluation.

One night, while shirking my duties in this manner, I came across Yvette's lab results from three weeks ago. She had done her regular six-week blood test, and I would normally get to them at our next visit in a few weeks. Suddenly I noticed that her RPR, the test for syphilis, was now positive, whereas in the past it had always been negative. My stomach froze and I sat bolt upright. How could this have happened? Normally a positive RPR was treated with three quick shots of penicillin. In patients with AIDS, however, syphilis could run a vicious course, with a predilection for the central nervous system. A positive RPR in the setting of HIV mandated an immediate spinal tap and could require a hospital admission for ten days of IV antibiotics.

I was most horrified by the fact that these results were three weeks old. Abnormal lab results always got placed in my mailbox for review. Even if I were absent from clinic the results would go to my attending. How could this have been missed? The irony of it was that the computer automatically flagged *any* value out of its preordained range. The majority of these "abnormalities" were so slightly out of the normal range that they were clinically insignificant, but they nevertheless piled up in my mailbox because of the asterisk. Here was a very significant abnormality and it had been missed. Just my random search, out of boredom, had uncovered it.

Yvette needed a spinal tap right away. I didn't want to hospitalize her just for a 20-minute procedure, but I wasn't going to be back in the clinic until after this ER rotation. I called her at home and explained the situation. Somehow saying "You have syphilis" felt so jarring to me, so archaic and judgmental. I mumbled something about an antibody suggesting possible exposure to syphilis. Clarity and unambiguity.

Yvette seemed calmer than I was, and simply asked what needed to be done. I decided to take advantage of my forced servitude in the ER. Yvette came to the emergency room and I whisked her to a back room before the nurses could even register or triage her. I tiptoed around gathering up all the supplies—the iodine, the local anesthetic, the test tubes. If anyone found out what I was doing I could get into a lot of trouble. For one thing, there was the legal issue of doing a procedure on a patient who wasn't officially registered and the possible malpractice ramifications if anything went wrong. But it was only a spinal tap—what could go wrong? For another, I'm sure the ER attending would be angry if he knew I was using the ER as a private office for my clinic patients. And any time I spent with Yvette was time I wasn't spending working through the crowded waiting room of ER patients.

I scooped up sterile drapes, a couple of syringes, and a 21-gauge spinal needle. My hands relaxed around the familiarity of these objects. These tools were old friends by now. The click of the stylet, as it snapped neatly within the hollow bore of the spinal needle that I was preparing, eased my nerves. I wasn't goofing off, I was just taking care of my patient. That's what I'd tell the ER attending if I got caught. Still, the idea of doing something even vaguely against the rules sent a jitter through my stomach. Just keep your mouth shut and act normally, I told myself, and the attending would probably think I was doing a regular ER evaluation.

I pulled the curtain around the stretcher. Yvette lay on her side with her knees pulled up to her chin as I had instructed. I examined her back, running my finger down her spine to find the right spot. I had to get the needle into the spinal space without, obviously, hitting the spinal cord. The spinal cord ended between the first and second lumbar vertebrae (L_1-L_2) so I wanted to sink my needle between L_4 and L_5. I drew an imaginary line between her hip bones, as I had been taught to do, and marked the point where it crossed her spinal column. That was the spot. Massaging with my finger, I tried to feel the space between the vertebrae, the space that would allow me direct access into the spinal canal. When I was sure I had it, I pushed the needle firmly in. I had done so many spinal taps by this time that

I didn't flinch. Yvette did, however, despite the local anesthetic I'd already injected.

"Sorry about that," I said. "That'll be the worst of it." I maneuvered the needle deeper, but it wouldn't budge. Bone. I'd hit bone, damn it. I pulled the needle back, angling it just a bit more southerly, and pushed in again.

"Ouch,"Yvette called out. Bone.

"Sorry. It's almost there." I aimed more north. Bone again. Finally, I pulled the needle out entirely and reoriented myself to my landmarks. Hip bones, spinal column, L_4- L_5. I dug my finger deeper into the flesh of her back. "Just a little pressure right now. I'm finding my spot. You okay back there?"

"Yeah. I guess," came the plaintive reply. "It's going to be fast, right?"

"Absolutely. I've done a million of these." Spinal taps were usually two-minute procedures in AIDS patients because they were so emaciated. The landmarks stuck out like Mt. Everest and there was barely any muscle for the needle to go through. But Yvette was not the typical AIDS patient. She had so much bulk that when she lay on her side, the symmetry of her back was confused. Her spinal column was obscured by the soft folds of muscle and fat. I was annoyed at the trouble I was having with the tap, but secretly it made me hopeful. Yvette was not the typical AIDS patient. Maybe she'd never die.

Finally I sat her up. I had her rest her elbows on the bedside table and hang her head down. In this position, everything "hung" evenly and her spinal column sat right in the middle. The needle slid in on the first try. I felt the gratifying "pop" as the needle entered the subarachnoid space. I removed the stylet and a bubble of fluid appeared at the mouth of the hollow needle. I took a big sigh and could feel the tension in my shoulders ease. I was in.

The crystal clear cerebrospinal fluid dripped into my waiting test tubes. Cell count, culture, protein, glucose, AFB, RPR—I counted the tubes as they filled, drop by drop. I remembered a resident telling me that cerebrospinal fluid had the highest concentration of HIV viruses compared to any other body fluid. Yvette's fluid looked so clean and clear. How could it contain such a deadly poison? It just didn't seem possible.

After the tap I snuck Yvette back out of the ER. I ignored the nurse who kept calling after me, waving a registration paper in her hand. In the doorway, Yvette and I smiled like successful conspirators. "I'll call you," I said, "as soon as the results are available. I promise."

The next morning I called the lab. "Vee don't do cerebrospinal RPRs on Tuesdays," the technician informed me in her heavy Eastern European accent.

I called on Wednesday. "Vee only do them on Mondays and Thursdays."

I called on Thursday at 8 A.M.—right after I'd gotten home from my night shift in the ER. "Vee start the assay at 9:00 if vee have enough samples."

I slept for a few hours, then called at noon when I'd awoken. "Zee assay is running now. It takes time."

I couldn't fall back to sleep and I was too agitated to do anything else. I decided to go to a matinee movie—one of the few perks to be gained from working the night shift. I called one more time before I left my house. "Zee assay is still running."

The theatre was on 19th and Broadway. The sun was shining brightly and the streets were filled with business people on lunch break. They scurried about in their dark suits, carrying briefcases, looking exceedingly focused. I slumped along, dragging my sleep-deprived feet. What could be on their mind, I wondered, to make them look so determined? Was it lunch with an important client? A conference call with a partner in California? A deal worth millions about to be sealed with a couple of martinis? My back ached and the sun was too strong for my eyes. I hadn't had a normal night of sleep in weeks. I doubted if any of these expense-account executives were worried about an RPR test on the cerebrospinal fluid of a 24-year-old woman with HIV.

I arrived at the movie theater and bought my ticket. "Hurry up," the cashier said, "the show's already starting." I was straggling through the carpeted hallway over to the darkened theater when I noticed a pay phone. One more time, I thought. I fished in my pockets for change and called the lab.

"Zee assay has just finished. Vee have results now."

"Stanton," I barked, "Yvette Stanton."

"Just one minute. Stanton . . . Stanton . . . Let's see." I could hear papers rustling in the background. "Vee have them . . . Stanton . . . Ah yes, Yvette Stanton. Zee cerebrospinal RPR is negative."

"Negative? It's negative?" I almost didn't believe it.

"Ja, ja, it's negative."

My feet—the ones that had been so leaden just a few minutes ago—could hardly keep from dancing while I dug madly in my pocket for more change to call Yvette.

"It's negative," I sang into the phone when she picked up. In the theatre next to me I could hear that the previews had ended and the feature film had begun. "It's negative. You don't have to stay in the hospital for ten days of IV antibiotics. Nope, we can just treat it with three shots of penicillin in the clinic." I felt like I'd just won a lottery. I settled into the plush theatre seats with a huge vat of popcorn and promptly slept for two solid hours.

冂 冂 冂

Yvette got her three shots of penicillin and felt fine. But then again, she always felt fine. I was thrilled that she didn't have neurosyphilis, but the fact that she had any syphilis at all meant that she'd gotten her second opportunistic infection. This could be the beginning of the end, I worried. Now Yvette might decline like all the other AIDS patients. I never pursued how it was that she might have suddenly gotten syphilis and she never offered. In her chart I simply indicated that she had a "positive RPR."

But miraculously, Yvette continued to be healthy. She never felt weak or sick during my entire second year of residency. Or my third year. Her cheeks never lost their rosy luster. Our frequent clinic visits seemed almost absurd for someone who looked so well. We religiously reviewed her blood test results, prescribed new medications as they became available, kept track of her Medicaid benefits, and updated her files as necessary. Yet we never uttered the words HIV or AIDS. I found myself guiltily joining her in euphemistic gymnastics. I sometimes even "forgot" to do a physical exam during her clinic visits. Yvette wasn't going to die.

The end of my three-year residency was drawing near and I gingerly brought up the issue of setting Yvette up with a new doctor. I once again offered her a referral to the HIV clinic, but she wouldn't hear of it. She preferred to stay in the regular medical clinic. She did, after my endless badgering, agree to enroll in the NYU/Bellevue AIDS clinical trials. I was happy because it would keep her in contact with the HIV experts, even if they weren't her primary doctors.

After one of our visits I went out to the waiting room to give her some prescriptions that she had forgotten. She was there with Sarah and Stephan, now aged 3 and 5. They were healthy, bouncy children, and they did not have HIV.

Yvette introduced them to me and they seemed to intuit that I was someone important in their mother's life. Sarah climbed into my lap and Stephan leaned in close to me. We spent 15 minutes talking and drawing pictures while Yvette filled her prescriptions.

I'm not the type of person who oohs and aahs over little kids, but I was so drawn to these two. They were adorable children, with large brown eyes and irresistible smiles. Sarah introduced me to Dino, her teddy bear, and told me confidently that she did not like broccoli. Stephan drew a picture of Bellevue, complete with the East River and the 59th Street Bridge. Then he added a woman with a black bag and said, "That's Dr. Ofri with her doctor bag." I felt honored to be accepted into their little worlds so readily, as though I had always been a member. I held them in my arms, breathing their sweetness, but overcome with guilt. They probably had no idea that the seminal event of their grade-school years would be watching their mother grow sicker and sicker and eventually die.

I felt partially responsible for their incipient loss of a mother. I had somehow initiated the process, but I wasn't going to be there for the end; Yvette's strong constitution had spared me the worst. I was going to abandon ship before things got messy. Part of me was secretly glad that I wasn't going to witness the ugly death that HIV brings. If my final memory of Yvette was as a robust, healthy woman I could maintain my end of the denial game.

Maybe I needed my denial to survive—I couldn't bear to watch Yvette shrivel and die. I'd always scorned the conventional wisdom that doctors shouldn't get emotionally involved with their patients. That view seemed so archaic and paternalistic. But wasn't I doing something even worse—taking care of my patient when things were easy, but then skipping out when the hard stuff came?

There was a gravelly sensation in my stomach, opaque and acid. The logic that my departure was strictly due to the termination of residency lurched about with my guilty relief about leaving before things got messy. I was deserting Yvette—if not physically or practically, then psychologically. Was this the type of doctor I wanted to become?

And I was mortified that any relief about escaping before the hard part could possibly slither into my head as I sat with Yvette's precious children in my arms, but it did. How could I be permitted to inhale their talcum fragrances or stroke their milky-soft skin when I knew I was abandoning ship? A fantasy flickered that I could adopt Stephan and Sarah after Yvette died, but they had their great-aunt who would raise them with a fierce devotion I could never possess.

I dreaded my last appointment with Yvette. For the whole month I had been saying emotional goodbyes to my clinic patients and I was already drained. I felt that I was abandoning them all. Yvette and I spent much of our final visit reviewing paperwork for the transition. I didn't bother with a physical exam. We studiously avoided eye contact until the very end.

"Please call me," Yvette said, "if you ever come back to Bellevue."

I was touched. We gave each other a big, satisfying bear hug before she left. Tears were in both of our eyes as we retreated to our respective sides of the clinic door. I took a few deep breaths and splashed some cold water on my face. The next patient was already in the room waiting to see me. ▪

Fire Season

Lee Martin

Maybe it was cholera, ague, typhoid, influenza. Or it could have been dropsy, nephritis, apoplexy, consumption. It might have been grief over the death of her daughter, Nancy. All I know is that for some reason lost now, my great-great grandmother, Elizabeth Gaunce Martin, died in the autumn of 1866, and her husband those 33 years—John Martin, who had taken her to Ohio and on to Indiana and finally to Illinois—was suddenly without her.

At the Brian Cemetery, on the day of Elizabeth's burial, the hickory trees would have been yellow; the nuts, their black husks splitting, would have lain in the brown grass. I imagine John's boots, freshly blacked, shuffling through that grass, his steps weary and halting, as he makes his way down the hill from the graveyard. His children are with him: William and Sarah, grown now, and the ones still at home—Henry, back from the war; George; Jackson; Robert; Louisa.

Louisa pauses at the graveyard's gate and looks back toward the hickories. "Aren't the trees pretty?" she says, and John hears the grief hidden beneath her bright voice.

Although he's not ordinarily an affectionate man around his children, he puts his arm around Louisa's shoulder—too roughly, he fears, because he knocks her straw hat, the one Sarah pinned to her hair, askew. Louisa stands there, the hat, tilted to the side, a silly look on her face, and she says, "Oh, Pa."

He straightens the hat for her, knowing that she's the one he feels most sorry for, the one who will miss her mother most. Prudence Louisa, named after Lizzie's sister, a name that now seems a mistake since Louisa is anything but prudent. She's irrational, indecisive. A mooncalf, Henry sometimes says. A twitterbug, chattering and giggling and buzzing about like a honeybee crazy for clover. She's always relied on Lizzie to steady her even after she became a grown woman. "Mommy, what dress will I wear?" "Mommy, I can't tie my sash." "Oh, Mommy."

John knows, this day as they leave the graveyard, that Louisa will never marry. He's sure that his other children will find their way in the world—have started to already—but Louisa, oh, his sweet, silly Louisa, she will always be his baby girl, too simple, too useless to be someone's wife.

"Yes, the trees are pretty, Lou," he says. "Now let's go on. Let's go home."

"Home?" she says, a crestfallen look on her face, and he knows she'll be completely lost without Lizzie.

"Yes, home," he says.

He herds her down the steps cut into the hill, feeling in a way he never has, his duty toward his daughter.

At bedtime, she comes to him in her sleeping gown, her hair undone, a wild bramble, a brush held in her hand. "Mommy always brushed my hair." She reaches out the brush to him. "Every night," she says.

He's sitting in a rocker by the window, letting the night air rush in, warm enough here at Indian summer to please him. It carries the scent of wood smoke and leaf must and the sounds of cornstalks, their dry blades scraping together. If it were a normal night—if Lizzie were still alive—she would join him here, and they would sit awhile, thankful for the harvest—corn and tobacco and pumpkins—and for Henry come home to them from the war, for Sarah and her good husband, Alfred Ridgley, and William, a grown man now, earning his own wage as James French's live-in hired man. John and Elizabeth would give thanks for all they had survived: the cholera that had almost taken him before they could marry, the birthings that she had managed, the journey they had made from Kentucky to Ohio and the drought that had driven them west, thirsting for rain. They had lost Nancy, but still, compared to other families who had buried child after child, they had been blessed.

"Can't you manage your hair tonight?" John says. He knows that if he touches Louisa's hair, he'll remember what it felt like a long time ago when Lizzie's pigtails brushed across his arm.

Louisa makes a few clumsy swipes of the brush. "It's all tangled up," she says. "Mommy always said the cats must have been sucking on it."

"Come here, then," he says.

And Louisa kneels at the window, her back to him. He drags the brush gently through her hair, glossy in the moonlight. He thinks of Lizzie with the angels in Heaven.

"A hundred strokes," Louisa says. Her head tips back slightly at the brush's tug. "That's what Mommy always did."

John feels something awakening in him, a tenderness the years and years of farm work have stolen from him. How odd, he thinks, here at the time of Lizzie's death, that he should find himself returned to love.

"All right," he says. "A hundred." He counts the strokes softly with the slightest whisper of breath, imagines Lizzie counting with him, the two of them, brushing their daughter's hair.

卐 卐 卐

It's hard for me to write of death these days. One of my oldest and dearest friends is fighting for his life. He lies in a burn unit at Loyola University Medical Center near Chicago while far away, in Texas, I wait for news. One week ago, at 1:45 in the morning, my friend's house exploded. Brad was alone in the house, sleeping in his bedroom on the second floor, which at the moment of the blast ceased to exist, the house reduced to rubble, engulfed in flames.

It's only occasionally, in the privacy of my mind, that I can work up the courage to imagine the details. I won't evoke them here. Let me say the words: gas leak, explosion, fire. You can imagine the rest.

And I think it's important to practice this empathy, to imagine the sequence of events, to feel as much as is possible the horror Brad woke to, to imagine me in his place. It's the step we don't take when tragedy's victim is a stranger to us. But when the face on the news, the name in the paper, belongs to someone we love, how can we help ourselves, for what we learn at these times is how deeply and richly we're connected. So I make the journey out of love, out of some hope that Brad's spirit, whether it rests now in some calm dream or twists in frenzy and chaos, will know that there are people who would have it come back to them.

卐 卐 卐

John, after Lizzie's death, keeps waiting for his life to feel familiar to him. He wants to wake in the morning and not have the terrible ache in his chest, the realization that he faces another day without his dear Lizzie.

Indian summer fades, and the cold winds of November sweep across the prairie. They strip the last of the leaves from their branches, and when John goes to the graveyard, the hickories are bare.

He and the boys make ready for winter. They butcher hogs and salt down the meat. They store fruits and vegetables in the root cellar: apples and turnips, potatoes and squashes, cabbages and dried beans. They build an ash hopper out by the cistern and cobble a roof over it to keep the ashes dry until soap-making time come spring.

John shows Louisa how to scrape ashes from the home fires and carry them out to the hopper. "You remember how Mommy did it?"

"Yes, I remember Mommy."

"Well, you're the mommy now."

Louisa giggles. "Oh, Pa."

"You are, Lou. You're the woman of the house. You're the one who has to keep things going."

He knows that he's blowing hot air, that his words, even as he speaks them, are flaming up and falling away to ash. Louisa can't ramrod this house. Through winter, John and Jackson and George and Robert will all do their share. And Sarah will come by, when she can spare the time away from her own home, to lend a hand. But come spring, when it's time to plow and plant the fields, John and the boys will be on the run from daylight to dark, and he wonders how they'll manage then.

One Sunday, when Sarah and Alfred are there, John asks her to write a letter to his sister, Malinda, back in Indiana.

Sarah's hand is sure; the nib of her pen scratches across the paper. "Dearest sister," she writes. "It's news of no count I send you."

She sits at the long table in the kitchen. John paces back and forth behind her, telling her what to say. He says that Lizzie is dead, that Louisa is lost without her, that they are all managing tolerable here in winter, but he dreads the spring and summer when he and the boys will be working all day in the fields and Louisa will be alone in the house. How will she have their meals ready for them? How will she clean and mend their clothes? "Sarah is a blessing," he says, "but so busy with a family of her own." He asks after Malinda and Joseph's children, the eight of them. The oldest girls are 30 and 26, and like Louisa they still live at home, but they are able and full of their father's smarts and their mother's common sense. "You're so lucky to have Ursula and Matilda," he says. "I'm sure they ease your way."

Sarah lays down her pen and blots the ink dry. "Louisa can't help it she's simple," she says in a quiet voice that injures John. He hasn't meant to be hurtful, only to state the facts.

"Of course she can't," he says. "I didn't mean her any harm."

But he was sharp with her that morning in church when she began to giggle during the sermon and he clamped down on her wrist. "Louisa," he whispered. "You hush." He squeezed until she whimpered and then went mute.

He feels guilty now, and guilty still the next morning when he carries a harness over to Ed Phillips' place to be mended. A hame has snapped in two, and one of the traces has torn and won't last another season.

Ed is out in his barn lot stacking barrel staves, layering them in crisscrosses so the air can move freely over each one—so sun, rain, wind, and frost can cure the wood before he cuts the staves and hollows them with his adz, joints them, and sets them into hoops which he stamps and punches and calls good.

John knows, because Ed has told him, that from the time he fells an oak tree to the time he uses the staves for barrels two winters will go by, the wood losing water little by little until it's cured enough to hold tight. But what neither John nor Ed know this day—what they can't know—is that Ed will die before this batch of staves is ready for his hand

"I'll put your harness right as rain," he tells John. "Soon as I fire up my forge. You go on up to the house. Get in out of this mess. Eliza's still got the coffee hot."

Eliza is the third child of James and Elizabeth French—a tall, willowy girl, the same age as Louisa, but here she is—Eliza—already kneading dough for noontime biscuits. The breakfast dishes have been scrubbed and stacked. The floors have been swept. A pile of mending waits for her darning needles. And just as Ed has promised, a pot of coffee warms on the hearth.

"Oh, I can feel the cold on you," she says, as she helps John off with his great coat. "Has it started to snow, Uncle Johnnie?"

"Starting to spit," he says. "Ed told me to come on up and get warm."

She's called him Uncle as long as he can remember—since the days when she played with his young'uns and from time to time he gave them all a penny stick of candy.

"Sit down here by the fire," she says. "Let me pour you a cup."

The boy, Hosea, toddles over and places his hands on John's knees. The newborn, Laura, is sleeping in her cradle by the fire. It nearly breaks John's heart, the sweetness of these children on this bitter cold day. How long it's been since his own were babes. The youngest, Robert, is now 13, growing into a man. John remembers one evening in Ohio, when he was at his grindstone, honing an ax blade, and Sarah and William came running to him to show off their cornhusk dolls. He set the ax aside and scooped them both up into his arms. He carried them into the house to Lizzie. "Aren't these the most handsome children you've ever seen?" John said, and when Lizzie answered her voice was shaking. "Oh, they are, John. They truly are."

And now she's gone, and his life is his, and the gravity of that thought—the notion that he is without a helpmeet, solitary now in the world, saddens him, and when he takes the cup from Eliza, he sees that his hands are trembling.

"You must be near froze," she says. He lets her cover his hands with her own and hold them steady. He feels the heat of the cup, the warmth of her skin. He tries to take a breath, but it catches in his throat, and when he tries to let it out, there's the noise of a choked sob, a cry that he's been carrying inside him since Lizzie died. It comes out now, and Eliza says, "You don't have to say a word. It's not for us to know the pain a body carries." He loves the soothing whisper of her voice. He knows she's speaking to him the way she does to her children when she wants to calm them. "Your heartache is yours. I'd take it from you if I could. You just sit here now. Sit here as long as you want. I've always thought it peaceful by a fire. Just look at little Laura."

"I'm an old man," John says.

"No, you're not old," she tells him. "You're just put upon right now."

卐 卐 卐

The ancients trusted in fire. The Druids used it to divine the future. They studied the vertical shapes of smoke, its wisps and spirals, its puffs and trails. I'll admit to a similar fascination. I've always watched with wonder flames licking up from logs in the fireplace, or from candles, or from patio chimeneas. What primal instinct is it that draws me so? I remember, as a child, begging my mother to let me light our fuel oil stoves. She rolled a cone from newspaper for me, and as I held its narrow end, she struck a match and touched it to the flared cone. I stood still a moment, admiring my torch. "Light it quick," my mother said, and she guided my hand through the open hatch into the burner's drum. Together we swirled the cone around the drum's circumference. Fire blazed up with a whoosh. We pushed the newspaper inside and I watched it blacken and curl and turn to ash, mesmerized by this vanishing act.

Now, since Brad's tragedy, I've fought to keep myself from thinking about the way skin burns, the way it disfigures. That first evening, after my wife and I had received the mind-numbing news of the explosion, we both were careful not to mention the extent of Brad's injuries. We spoke with friends in Kentucky and Pennsylvania, friends who had managed to stay in touch since college days, who had made trips together over the years, stayed in one another's homes, remembered birthdays and anniversaries, were as close as family. Now one of us was in trouble; it was the first time this family of friends had been threatened with such a permanent and aching loss.

Finally, our friends in Kentucky were able to get through to the hospital and speak to Brad's fiancée. The news wasn't good. Brad was burned over 80 percent of his body. The next 72 hours would be crucial. My wife and I held each other; we cried. Sorry, I can't beat back cliché here. We did what you do in real life when someone whom you love dearly might die.

That evening, we watched the news report on WGN Chicago and saw amateur video of flames rising from the rubble of Brad's house high into the night sky. We sorted through details that we had gathered from this report and from newspaper articles we had retrieved from the Web. The fire chief said there had apparently been a gas leak inside the house, but that he didn't yet know the ignition source. He said that Brad was "fairly severely burned" and that he had injuries to his arms—injuries that Brad's fiancée had described earlier as "deep lacerations." The man who lived in the duplex next to Brad's house said he had smelled gas a few months back after the gas company had installed a new meter. The gas company had to return to repair a loose pipe. The neighbor said he smelled gas a short time later, but when the gas company returned they said they didn't find any problem. Another neighbor reported that he had walked past Brad's house at seven P.M. and had smelled "a whiff" of gas. The neighbor's wife claimed that she had been smelling sewer gas the past few days and that at nine P.M. on the evening before the early morning explosion it had been "really strong." Finally, the *Chicago Tribune* reported that Brad had been conscious when firefighters pulled him from the rubble and he had told them that he had smelled gas in his home that night and hadn't reported it.

Why in the world, my wife and I asked each other, hadn't anyone picked up the phone and called the gas company and stopped this horrible, horrible thing from happening? If I could practice pryromancy, I would divine the answer in fire.

⊑ ⊑ ⊑

Come spring, John covers his tobacco seedbeds with brush and sets it to burn. In this way, he kills weed seeds and insects and hastens the warming of the soil. The dry brush crackles as it catches fire, and soon the heat is so fierce John and the boys have to back away into the shade of the deeper woods where the May apples are growing up from the rot of last fall's dead leaves.

John watches the shimmery waves of heat wrinkling around the fire. It's been a winter now since Lizzie's death. It amazes him that he has made it through this season of days, through the gray skies and the short light, and come out here on this fine spring morning with so much left in the world that pleases him: the babble of creek water in the dark woods, the ringing of a woodpecker, the bright green of the May apples' broad leaves, the way Jackson and Robert and George squat down, their weight on the balls of their feet as if at any instant they might spring up like deer. John squats down, too, feeling the strain in his knees, a stretching of tendon that tells him he's still flesh and bone and not wasted away by grief as he imagined the day he sat in Eliza Phillips' house and felt as small as a tobacco seed, as puny. The wind, he thinks, could have lifted him and carried him away. That's how gone-to-nothing he was. But here he is now, another birthday gone. Fifty-seven he is and amazed, but also saddened, that without Lizzie, he can still feel joy.

He imagines the charred ground after the brush has burned to ash. He and the boys will hoe the plot and rake the dirt and ash to a fine tilth before sowing the tobacco seed. They'll tamp the ground with the flat sides of their hoes, and by May, after morel mushrooms have popped up among the May apples, and the May apples themselves have bloomed and set fruit, the tobacco starts will be ready to transplant. Another crop begun. Another season of growing.

"Where's Henry this morning?" Jackson asks.

"He's helping out over to the Ridgleys'," George says.

John listens with pleasure to their strong, clear voices ringing out in the quiet woods.

"Sweetening up Mary Ann is more like it," says Jackson.

"She's a honeybee," says Robert. "Henry better look out or he'll get stung."

Robert makes a buzzing sound and corkscrews his fingertip into Jackson's ribs. He does the same to George. Soon the boys are shoving at one another and wrestling around in the May apples.

As much as John enjoys the show, he can't bear the thought of those May apples crushed or, worse yet, wallowed up by their roots. He claps his hands together twice, and the sound is sharp enough to catch the boys' attention and bring their horseplay to a halt. Again, John can hear the creek running, and the woodpecker, and the crackle of the fire.

"You leave Henry's business to Henry," he says. "Don't you know it's a sin to begrudge a man love?"

"Henry's in love." Robert, who hasn't completely shed his boyishness, giggles and squeals.

"Robert," John says with heat. "You hush."

John thinks he could sit here forever in the lush woods with his boys. But then he sees Louisa through the flames of the brush fire, her hair unpinned, her chest heaving. "Pa, Pa." She waves her arms. For a moment, he's afraid she'll try to walk through the fire. "Oh, Pa," she shouts. "Come quick."

卐 卐 卐

We're in fire season now in North Texas. It's mid-August, and we haven't had rain since the end of June. The prairie grass turns to tinder; the longhorn cattle chew the leaves from mesquite trees, the only thing still green in the pasture. Grass fires break out. All it takes is a spark—a burning cigarette tossed from a passing car, a loose muffler dragging over the pavement, a rancher's mowing blade striking a rock in a pasture—and something catches the brittle grass, and it starts to blaze.

From my neighborhood on the northwest edge of the city, I sometimes see the black smoke rising up along the horizon. Sometimes the fire's intense heat induces a smoke tornado, a vortex that sucks up smoke and flame. I've seen photographs in the newspaper of these white tornadoes, glowing orange close to the ground, these spirals of smoke churning through the air, their cloudy funnels obscuring whatever lies beyond them. Suddenly, it's impossible to see what's on the other side. What a wonder it is. What a horror.

On winter days, when I was a child, my father would drive along our township's roads—perhaps we were on our way to the Berryville store, or to visit my grandmother, or to the Lukin school for the annual Christmas pageant—and out across the snowy fields we would see the chimney smoke rising from homes, some of them hidden down long lanes. That smoke would be the sign that the people who lived in those houses were safe and sound. If ever we didn't see smoke, we knew there was trouble: illness or poverty or worse.

In the summer of 1978, Brad and I shared an apartment. This was the summer when the woman who would later become his wife, and then his ex-wife, called things off with him. Every time he saw her out with another date, it hurt him, but I'm not sure someone would have known that unless that someone happened to be living with him and saw how late at night, when the two of us were alone in the apartment, he sometimes went quiet—a rarity for Brad since he has always been one of the most effervescent people I've known—and stared off into space, having traveled to some secret, inner place.

I had a similar place inside me. My wife was an hour and a half away acting with a repertory theatre company in Vincennes, Indiana, and though I drove down and saw her on the weekends, I secretly worried that at the end of summer, caught up in the glitz of theatre life, she would refuse to come back to me.

Although Brad and I occasionally spoke in earnest about our pains and fears, we also understood the importance of keeping each other from falling too far into our respective caverns of gloom, those dark chambers of the heart where we could get lost and never return. We brought each other back with humor and hijinks, some of them adolescent enough to be embarrassing to recall now: ringing telephones answered with boyhood one-liners ("Joe's Bar and Grill"); midnight commando raids on another friend's house, letting ourselves in through an unlocked back door, creeping upstairs, sneaking through the dark house until we pounced on our friend in his bed and shouted like maniacs.

And why? For the pure joy of it, for the idiotic laughter that came bubbling up from the gut, filled the chest and throat, that laugh-until-you-cry glee we remembered from when we were boys.

I was an only child. I had lived with my parents and then my wife. I had never lived in a college dormitory, never gone away to camp, never been a member of a fraternity. That summer with Brad was as close as I had ever been to having a brother. And what an excellent brother he was: companion, confidant, comedian. His booming laugh could fill a room, could catch me by surprise no matter how many times I had heard it. My god, how could anyone love life so much? He had a knack of making people feel better about themselves, a skill that served him well in his career as a school psychologist working with troubled children. I can't imagine anyone who could help but feel they were damn lucky to know him.

The summer of 1978 ended happily for both of us. My wife came home. Brad and his girlfriend got back together. The next summer, they married. A few years later, they had a child, a daughter, and our circle of friends, four couples, went on seeing each other at Christmas, at shared vacations arranged in various cities across the country. Then, in the early 1990s, Brad's wife filed for divorce, and as sad as that was for those of us who loved them and their daughter, even this coming apart seemed amicable. Brad and his wife arranged joint custody, agreeing that they would do everything they could to make the situation as easy as possible for their daughter.

The years went on. Brad became engaged to a woman who is as full of zest as he is. On the night of the explosion, she was staying with her mother who was ill. Since it was a weekend, Brad's daughter normally would have been home with him, but she was with her mother and stepfather, sailing on Lake Superior.

In the most recent photo I have of Brad—a photo he sent with last year's Christmas card, he and his daughter are sitting on the floor in front of their fireplace, their black lab between them. Brad's daughter is 12, and even though she's wearing braces on her teeth, she's smiling with abandon, unashamed, a smile so much like Brad's own. The two of them have a shiny garland of red and green Christmas tinsel wrapped around their necks, a glittery strand linking them. It would be clear to anyone, even a stranger, that this father and daughter adore each other. The old sparkle is in Brad's eyes, the glint that says anything is possible.

Eight days after the explosion, I found a report in the online version of the *Chicago Tribune,* a report from the Illinois State Police Crime Lab that jarred me. My wife wandered into the room.

"There's news," I said. "Someone deliberately cut the gas line to Brad's kitchen stove."

"Murder?" she said. "Who would want to murder him?"

"Not murder," I said. "They found blood throughout the house. The lacerations on Brad's arms happened before the explosion. They're on the insides of his arms, from his wrists to his elbows. The police are using the term, 'progressive suicide.'"

⌧ ⌧ ⌧

How surprised John is when he gets to the house and sees Ursula and Matilda Fite. Ursula has on an apron. She's a tall woman with a long neck. Tendons stand out along its length when she strains to lift a pan of dishwater. Matilda is shorter but just as lean. She's sitting at the kitchen table paring potatoes, her small hands working with speed and grace; the peelings come off in long spirals and fall into the pan on her lap.

"Mama sent us," she says to John. "She said you needed help."

"All the way from Indiana?" he says. He's stunned for a moment to know that there are people in the world who would go to such lengths—uproot themselves from home—all on his account.

"Yes," says Ursula. "All that way."

Louisa is at the fireplace raking out the ashes the way John has taught her. An ember pops and lies glowing on the hearth. John sees Louisa reach down with her fingers. He starts to shout, "No, don't. It's hot." But before he can speak, Ursula has reached out and snared Louisa's hand. She speaks to her in a kind, motherly tone. "Oh, honey. You don't want to touch that coal. It's hot as sin. You don't want to burn yourself, honey. You come on over here and help me dry these dishes."

John lets all the breath that's gathered in him come out with a sigh. A few years later, he'll remember this moment, and he'll think this was the instant when so much began to change. Ursula took Louisa's hand and saved her from fire, and so many things became possible because for the first time since Lizzie's death there were women in the house. John knew—had known most of his grown life—it was women, good and decent and earnest, who had always taught men what it meant to have a family and a home. Without women, men were lost. They were the cold water slapped on the face come morning, the ticking of a clock when no one was in the room to hear it, the gray ash of a fire long burned cold.

On this day, when the Fite sisters have come, they make soap. They pour lye water into a kettle in the yard and build a fire beneath it. They let the lye come to a boil and then they test it for strength. They set a fresh egg on the surface and it floats; they dip a downy feather into the boiling lye, and the feather's down and shaft dissolve. Soon there will be cakes of soap—brown, soft soap that makes John's skin tingle when he uses it, that leaves its lye smell on his clothes when Matilda or Ursula washes them. It is soap that cleans in a snap, that eats away dirt, that makes you feel as bright as a new penny.

The trees are full of bud-swell. Soon the leaves will unfold like babies' wrinkled hands reaching up from cradles, and by the time the trees are full and the tobacco starts are growing in the fields, Henry will marry his sweetheart, Mary Ann, and buy a 20-acre plot of his own. One by one, John's boys will set out on their own. Jackson will marry Matilda Fite. Robert will marry Ursula.

Shortly after the last wedding, when it's once again John and Louisa alone, he goes to the Brian Cemetery and there he sees Eliza Phillips come to put chrysanthemums on her husband's grave. It's autumn, just past midday, and the sun is high and warm. The wind moves through the golden leaves on the hickories. A squirrel chatters in the high branches, disturbed by the presence of these two humans.

Eliza is kneeling by Ed's grave. John offers his hand to help her to her feet. She takes it without hesitation, and they stand a moment, her palm across his. He's 64 years old; she's 28.

"It's Indian Summer," he says to her.

"Yes," she says, "but winter's coming."

He hears the misery in her voice. He thinks back to that day by her kitchen fire when his breath came out in a sob, and she was so tender with him. He covers her hand, holds it between his two, and she doesn't move to withdraw it.

How lucky they are, he thinks, to be here on this sunny day, two people who, despite all they've lost, still believe in love.

"Winter comes," he says. "It goes. It doesn't kill us."

"Sometimes I get so lonely," she says. "Don't you?"

And he tells her, yes. "Yes," he says, "I do."

They marry in April, a season of daffodils growing up from the warming earth. Surely people talk about the 36 years difference between them. Surely there are family members who shake their heads. But who are these naysayers—who are any of us—to say what sparks and blazes in another person's heart, in the secret chambers where longing flames.

Brad, dear friend, I don't know what happened in your life to make you want to leave it, but I'll wager it had something to do with love, though few will believe it.

I've heard that the police have a letter that you wrote to your daughter, a letter that they found lying on a neighbor's lawn after the explosion. I imagine that letter's graceful flight—blown high above the flames that night, a patch of white fluttering like a moth, tumbling down and down, past all the chaos to lie, finally, still and safe, on the green grass.

Sort through the rubble, sift the ashes, turn the bones, and that's what we'll find. It's what we always find—the words that survive, the yearning, the knowledge that sometimes, in a dry season, you can want your life so badly, all you can do is set it on fire and let it go. ∎

Family Geometry

Diane Comer

The table is our first geometry: square, circle, rectangle, or the pecan oval of my childhood where I am a fixed point beside my sister, across from my brother, with our parents at the head and foot. I did not always sit there. In a photo taken on my second birthday, I am sitting in a highchair, beating my hands on the metal tray smeared with cake, wearing a chocolate frosting grin. I am tangential to the family table and the picture shows me straining to get out of my highchair to attain a place at the bigger, better table. In a later photo I am consoled with the dregs of someone's wine glass. At two, I already understand something: the party is at the other table, the table I am not seated at, the table a short distance from my highchair or across the room in the restaurant or across the room of memory.

When I was in first grade in Belgium my best friend was Julie—small, dark-haired, dark-eyed. Julie possessed everything I wanted: long hair, a mother with long hair, a pair of miniature stuffed mice wearing tiny taffeta crinolines that poofed out from their soft white bodies. I coveted the mice whenever I held them, stroking their whiskers, their skirts, their white fur. Finally Julie invited me to spend the night. Her family lived in an old two-story farmhouse surrounded by fields of sugar beet. I was enchanted by the gleaming marvel of the walnut stairway and mezzanine, the final swoop of the banister where we leapt off before crashing into the carved newel post. I stood on the threshold of her parents' room with its four-poster bed, the bentwood rocker with an afghan thrown over the arm, the cool light spilling through the northern windows, awed. My envy was complete when I saw Julie's room with its canopy bed sugared with lace, the immense mahogany wardrobe with the silver key, and finally, the mouse house, a miniature world of antique furniture, peaceful and still as the house where she lived.

We ate dinner that evening in the warm light of September at a battered harvest table in the kitchen. Julie's mother dandled the baby on her lap while she heaped food on our plates, wild rice, flank steak, green beans. It was the first meal I remember enjoying. No father at the head of the table to worry us. Laughter. I touched the bare wood on the underside of the table, trying to understand its charm: solid, rectangular, the wood marred and worn by generations, the kitchen snug around us. I hungered for the ease with which Julie's family ate their meal and I knew I would want a table like this, a kitchen like this, a life like this.

Twenty years later I was in Salerno, Italy, at an eight-foot walnut Shaker table laden with antipasti: the best prosciutto, four different cheeses including fresh, butter-soft mozzarella made from water buffalo milk, black and green olives, sparkling wine, red wine, mineral water, fruit, bread. Our host, Gaetano, concocted a divine pasta sauce while his wife, Maria, assisted.

"Do you like this wine?" Gaetano asked.

"I love the wine, the food, everything," I said as I tore a paper-thin piece of prosciutto in half and ate it.

From my seat at the table I watched the meal unfold. As he juggled dishes, Gaetano explained the virtues of garlic, the character of the olive oil from Maria's family orchard, and the secret of the can of tomatoes in his hand, "These are the best tomatoes. The ash from Vesuvius, you know Vesuvius? makes a special kind of soil, and only on this plain below Vesuvius, outside of Napoli is this soil." Cooking had never been this communal, instructive, and entertaining in my mother's kitchen. Here was a method I could use.

At the oval table of my childhood dining was serious. My mother closeted herself in the kitchen, stewed over *Gourmet,* and drank martinis, emerging hours later, victorious or otherwise. We ate at eight o'clock, two hours later than anyone I knew. The dogs were not allowed into the dining room, whose champagne beige carpeting was plagued by the color's inherent desire for dirt. Before eating we prayed the same prayer, "Bless us O Lord and these thy gifts which we are about to receive through thy bounty through Christ our Lord, Amen," mumbled in a continuous rush by us three kids and intoned clearly by our father. I do not remember my mother praying or even bowing her head. She remained defiant of God and my father's Catholicism. Food was her religion: the grace finished, now we would worship.

Linen napkins were unfurled. We each had our own napkin ring. My father's was solid silver with his initials and graduation date from West Point, while the rest of us had ugly orange melamine rings painted with different flowers to distinguish them. Our first plates were white Ironstone octagons sold in a garage sale. Later a discontinued Wedgwood pattern called Blue

Pacific summoned a world I could only long for outside this plate rimmed with ocean blue. The silver remained the same, plated, floral, with the family *H* on the handle, the forks so large and unwieldy in my child's hand they were more weapon than utensil. I suffered through many meals. Moussaka with its hidden sickening ambush of eggplant. Cauliflower and Brussels sprouts bitter and hateful in my mouth. Meat I chewed and chewed, then hid in my napkin to sneak to our pair of poodles. My mother set her jaw, "It's not poison. Eat it. It won't kill you."

My father supported her culinary terrorism, "You will eat everything on your plate young lady or—" The threat varied, but to be sent away from the table was the final shame. I do not know what was worse, to be forced to eat food I loathed, choking on tears, or to be banished from the table. That I do not have an eating disorder as a result of the regimen and discipline of these family dinners amazes me, but I suppose in a way I do—some days I forget to eat or cook.

My mother was a brilliant cook. Some dishes were too intensely flavored for me, while others were legendary favorites: Flemish beef stew on riced potatoes (the secret ingredient was beer); Hungarian goulash on buttered noodles with poppy seeds, redolent with sauerkraut, caraway, pork, tomato, sour cream, and dill, a dish my sister hated and I loved. I would eat anything Italian: lasagne, manicotti, minestrone, spaghetti sauce steeping fragrant all day long in the dented aluminum pot. As an adult, the food I enjoy cooking must be simple, unlabored, and delicious. If it can be made quickly and in one pot, I like it even more.

Last fall I stood in a discount store staring at a hunter green Dutch oven made by Le Creuset, a company famous for cookware that fuses enamel to cast iron. Every pot comes with a 100-year warranty. The Dutch oven was 80 dollars. I lifted the pot. It must have weighed ten pounds. I saw a winter of soups and stews, whole chickens roasted with rosemary, and I heard a voice behind me say, "You'll have it for the rest of your life." I turned around and saw my friend Jana smiling at me. That clinched it, that and a soup made for me in the orange twin of this pot 13 years ago in Ireland. I was in Dublin to study classics and theology at Trinity College, but really I was drinking Guinness, rolling and smoking cigarettes, and lying in bed until noon. I was learning about clothes and food; studying Hebrew was far down on the list. Natalie was my unofficial guardian, a generation older, a bank manager, unmarried, she had a snapping dry wit, with splendid taste in everything: her home, her clothing, her cooking. When I was 12 and she was 32, we had shared a room in a private clinic in Austria. We had both broken our legs skiing. She had a spiral fracture that required surgery and pins. I had three clean breaks and boasted a pair of thigh-high plaster casts with slits down the center to accommodate the swelling. During that week, despite or because of our age difference, we became friends.

For my 21st birthday Natalie took the day off to make a celebratory dinner. What a gift, everything made with care from the *Cordon Bleu* cookbooks: cream of onion soup, a lovely fish, spinach with cream and nutmeg, profiteroles swimming in dark chocolate sauce. Good food, dear friends, all gathered around Natalie's pale oak circle of hospitality. I was of age now and knew what I wanted: a round table. A round table creates communion, everyone's glass within easy reach for toasting, everyone's elbows to themselves, no one sitting at the head or the foot, a democracy of dining.

I did not buy the round table first. I had an aborted affair with a mahogany veneer gate-leg table that was branded with the number seven. I thought, good, the rectangular surface is already marred. Later I discovered the table got a mark if you looked at it too long. Water, heat, the brush of the day-to-day destroyed that table. What had started out as a handsome Duncan Phyfe knock-off with a single flaw turned into an obsession with 0000-grade steel wool and touch-up stain. A piece of African fabric found at Goodwill hid the cursed surface until I made tablecloths from drapery fabric.

I knew I wanted a round table, but the color and style escaped me for over a decade until a New Year's Eve dinner in Iowa City—dead plain round oak with two or more leaves, no claw feet, a mismatch of oak chairs around it. Between courses, I nodded to my husband, Jeff, and tapped the table, "This is it." The following Christmas Jeff sent me out to buy fresh tortillas for dinner. When I returned a round oak table festooned with bows sat in the middle of the dining room. "Do you like it?" Jeff asked. "Is this what you wanted?" I smoothed my hands across the warm tawny surface: a pedestal table, dead plain, no claw feet, circa 1930. I nodded, wordless.

Two years later in an antique store I saw a pine harvest table covered with vintage cheese graters, potato ricers, jelly molds. I asked the owner, "John, that table you're using to display old housewares, is it for sale?"

John wheezed tobacco into my face, scratched his head, and said, "Yes."

"Is it old?"

"The legs are."

I laughed. "How much if I take it off your hands now and write you a check?" He named his price. I hauled it home in the back of my boss's Subaru station wagon, the old legs jutting out as I drove along Highway 24.

The round table was a gift from husband to wife, but the harvest table was a gift to myself. Few things have made me as happy as the harvest table with its scarred surface ready for battle with cutlery, crockery, spills, crayons, the human condition. The name says it all, to harvest, to bring in. The moment greetings are exchanged, friends and strangers gather at the table, as though invited. And they are invited, a table in the kitchen says, come on, sit down, have something to eat and drink, stay for awhile. I do not like the round table any less, but it serves a different purpose, something more formal and less essential. The harvest table defines our house. The kitchen will need to be big enough for all six feet of it. Everyone ends up in the kitchen at a party for a reason, not because the stove is the modern equivalent of the campfire, but something else, something unconscious, beyond the warmth of an imagined hearth: the inborn need to gather together when the darkness surrounds us and tell stories. Give everyone a large table, preferably battered, where they can sit, eat, drink, linger, and tell stories in the one room where they want to be. Our pine harvest table does this for us.

Jeff's cousin and his wife and two kids came to visit while Jeff was away on business. The first evening they brought more chairs from the dining room and arranged them around the harvest table. Without thinking they knew here is the center, here is where we want to be, not in front of the TV, but around the table. I began to make marinara sauce while we were chatting. Fourteen-year-old Nathan got up and joined me at the stove, "What are you doing? It's not from a jar." I laughed and shook my head and gave him garlic to peel and Parmesan to grate. Later when I looked at us all eating around the table, I understood why the table hungered for more than just Jeff and me. Two people at a large table seem to be missing an invisible family. A month later we hosted Thanksgiving for the first time. We ate in the dining room, but more hours were spent around the harvest table, peeling potatoes, eating hors d'oeuvres, talking over tea, over wine, over nothing.

When I was a child our dining room table brooded silent and handsome during the day. Sunday morning, I am five or six, and we are not going to Mass. The house is sleeping. I crawl beneath the dining room table with my stuffed animals and look out through the filmy lace tablecloth. I feel safe. This is our house, our ark, here under the table where no one can see us. Whenever I see children playing under a table by themselves, drawing their world in, I wonder what the weather is like above their heads that drives them below to pretend, yes, here is a safe place. What Julie's kitchen table revealed to me nearly 30 years ago was that a family could gather at the table to eat, talk, work, and play, and the table could be a welcoming place, a haven for all. Table as haven, not battleground, was unthinkable to me then. We never talked around our family table. We ate and we argued, but we never talked. Once I could clear my plate and hold my own in an argument, I was a force at the dining room table. Out of habit, I still tend to argue too much in company around a table.

After years of formal dining rooms where the pecan oval table reigned in concert with the buffet and china closet filled with Italian linen, Bavarian bone china, Waterford crystal, sterling flatware, my parents took to eating in the kitchen at a rock maple dinette set. Not exactly the kitchen, but the transitional space between the kitchen and the family room. Eating in the kitchen was slumming to my mother. She had grown up in cramped apartments, eating bad food, often alone, in the kitchen. She vowed never to eat in the kitchen again. And she didn't. Not for years. The shift was gradual, first the occasional meal on a TV tray, then the maple dinette appeared in sight but not in front of the TV. Just as my mother quit buying lovely things to wear, she quit eating in the dining room. I would come home from college and chide her about not using the linen, the silver. Then I would iron a tablecloth and polish the silver and she would make a dinner I was finally old enough to appreciate.

My mother complained the dining room was dark. It was. By then everything in her life was blurring from years of drinking, and the eat-in kitchen—something she had always despised—was easier to manage. She did not have to concentrate or perform there in a way the dining room demanded. In the evening she could fumble through cooking, pick at the food on her plate, and then watch TV or read. Maybe the dining room table reproached her. All those years of glorious food. The stellar dinner parties. Everything she loved, everything she let go—she who cared about every detail of the table, the place settings, the progression of the courses, who sat where. All I wanted was to be her dinner guest, to have her full attention the way only others seemed to have. Now I see it was I who was not paying attention.

In April the phone rang during lunch, in a distant room, and we did not hear it. Later I picked up the remote phone and heard the stutter tone of a message waiting. "Diane, it's Dad. Listen, I found Mom unconscious on the kitchen floor this morning. She was still dressed. She never came to bed last night. I sleep like a log and never heard anything. I tried to rouse her. I kept saying 'Jo, Jo,' but there was no response. Then she vomited a lot of blood, a pool the size of a card table. I dialed 911. The fire station's only a few blocks away and the paramedics got here in minutes. She's in neurosurgery now, down at Presbyterian. Diane," his voice breaks, "I think we're going to lose her." Click. End of message. I stood by the harvest table and began to wail. A friend sitting at the table stood up and put his arms around me. Sobbing and gulping for air, I could hardly relay the message.

The pool of blood the size of a card table—I know that size, the nights my parents hosted bridge, two card tables of four, the cards with their gilded edges and Florentine backs, the little dishes of savories and sweets on each table, the coffee urn on the buffet with the battery of china cups and saucers, and the marvelous dessert I must not touch. I imagine my mother's body on the kitchen floor, beside the rock maple dinette, a wood so hard a nail cannot be driven into it. The previous dinette set had been made of equally hard material: wrought iron.

All those years she sat at the dinette in the kitchen. I remember her mounting stamps for the collection while sitting at the wrought iron table, a tall glass of Coke beside her, a Pall Mall straight burning in the beanbag ashtray before she quit smoking. She would hold the mint issue stamps with tweezers as she placed them in their protective sleeves. As her small shadow, I loved the stamps with flowers and animals. "They're pretty, but they're worthless. British Honduras," she would snort. When I was three the wrought iron table sat on the screened-in veranda of our house in Santo Domingo and we ate outside, I in my highchair, my family in the four available chairs. Large pale moths attached themselves to the screens and the Dominican Revolution exploded in the distance. A time of fear: the family poodle that bit me, jagged glass atop the wall surrounding our house, nearly drowning in the O-club pool, tarantulas our live-in maid killed with the mop in one blow.

I did not believe death could be so sudden, not hers. I thought my mother would live to see my children get married and have children. I thought our lives would run parallel, not touching, but parallel. We were going to Italy together next fall. "Not Florence, not Rome, Rome is dirty. It's not the same," she said on the phone four days before. "Maybe Tuscany or Umbria. The hill towns. Do you remember Assisi?" I remember Assisi. I was eight. The rest of the family stayed behind at the *pension* while we went together to the church where the exhumed body of St. Clare lay on a bier behind glass in a shadowy chapel guarded by nuns. The saint's wizened face was black, ancient, and frightening. To cleanse of us this horror my mother took us to San Damiano, the original convent of the Poor Clares, and we walked in the cloistered garden amid bees and flowers eight centuries after St. Francis wrote his "Canticle of the Sun" here. Above us in the hill town of Assisi the church bells tolled the hour, but we were quiet together. Now I cannot break the silence.

In Albuquerque my mother's absence filled the house. The dining room table was covered with her last cataloging of the stamp collection. Magazines, cookbooks, conjugations of French verbs, piles of recipes and grocery lists were strewn across the rock maple table, as though she had just risen from the chair where she always sat, her back to the kitchen, her world. I could not bear to sit at the dinette and what little I ate in my father's house I ate outside at the battered redwood picnic table on the patio, my back to the kitchen. Her world had vanished, despite all the details of her existence covering every surface. End tables, coffee tables, night tables, countertops, the desk, each bore the mark of her daily life: half-finished knitting, novels with her place marked by grocery coupons, letters to answer, earrings, tissues, makeup, her glasses. I held her glasses to my chest. Everything she would never see appeared before me—our house, our garden, our children, our ordinary lives moving forward into the invisible distance.

My father comes to visit. Without my mother beside him he is smaller, almost frail. As I embrace him I feel his mortal bones as he feels mine. We both have lost weight we cannot afford to lose. I strive to make food he will enjoy, recipes of my mother's, knowing he hardly cooks. He sits between me and Jeff. I watch as he eats, pasta with tomatoes and cream, lime tarragon chicken, second helpings, extra bread, pouring wine only for himself. All those years at the head of the table he said the prayer, barked the orders, and thrived. Now he tastes nothing, only eats. How strange to have him here without my mother sitting silent over her morning tea with the newspaper at the harvest table or sated with a dinner I labored over, snapping down cards with sweet determination as she set my dad in bridge, a glass of cognac beside her on the round dining room table.

That last winter after 12 years of playing bridge with my parents, Jeff and my mother against me and my father, we finally switched partners. My mother and I won. She was pleased I understood the game well enough to bid correctly, to follow her lead, to know when to slough and when to trump, how to work the crossruff, the finesse, the bad split, all those lovely subtleties in bridge, and yes, to beat my dad.

Now I play bridge against the computer. While the computer does not chastise me when I lead the wrong suit as my father did, it does not smile a secret smile when I take it to game, as my mother would. Jeff, who partnered my mother for years, never fully understood the intricacies of bidding. Each bid is a code, and he often mistranslated, ending up in the wrong suit and overextended. His standing joke with my mother was, "Five hearts, and you're playing them." My mother would no sooner enter our house than he'd be chanting, "Five hearts, five hearts," while she waved her hands at him to stop, as though trying to still a playful dog. I think about the five honors in hearts he placed in her coffin and I feel like we are what is left of the deck, impaired, unplayable, useless.

The people I love have always been at the table where I am seated. The table's shape or location alone do not give it meaning. My sister's oak trestle table covered with bowls of fruit, toys, scars, stains, and the wearing love of three children. My in-laws' teak rectangle, bare during the day and battened down with padding and tablecloth (vinyl for grandkids) during meals. My sister-in-law's cherry Mission reproduction piled with no fewer than six Indian dishes made by her husband, for which I minced ginger and garlic at the melamine table in his kitchen. My other sister-in-law's solid oak round table built for her by a friend who said, "Hell, Liz, if I'd known you were going to have four kids I'd have made you a larger table." My friend Jana's expanding Scandinavian rectangle covered with heavy tapestry and her generous heart. Our friend John has not one but two tables in his enormous kitchen and another picnic table on his porch. John has no wife or family but he understands something fundamental: the table and the people at the table are the focus in any room, in any country.

My mother favored the oval and all of her tables have been variations on the ellipse. How like her the oval is, not the first shape that comes to mind, not an everyday shape, but used everyday. Neither rectangular nor round, the oval is the shape of compromise. "I'm a Libra," she would say. "I can't make up my mind and I hate arguing." Although when pushed my mother could have the final word and silence. Like her oval table, my mother was graceful and defined, exacting and pleasing, with just enough curve to draw you close and just enough edge to make you keep your distance. I doubt my father could have been a tyrant at a round table, and as it was he was reduced and moderated by my mother and her oval table. The real power, I believe, sat at the foot, not the head, of the table. She was our go-between, our diplomat, the voice of reason in his ear. "Tell him," I would rage, "tell him this." And she would, tempering my message.

During one of her last visits I was struggling to cook a meal beyond my scope (taking it to game, as it were). I was peeling garlic with a knife, fresh garlic whose papery skin clung to the cloves. My mother asked, "Why don't you smash it with the handle of a knife and then peel it?"

"I know that!" I shouted. "I want the cloves to be whole to mince."

She fled the kitchen. I finished peeling the garlic and walked into the living room. She sat in our overstuffed chair, crying.

"I'm sorry I snapped at you, Mom."

She nodded and said, "You've never spoken to me that way."

I put my arms around her and kissed her cheek, "Come on," I said, "help me finish dinner."

At our harvest table I sit across from Jeff, my back to the stove. At the round dining room table I sit beside him, my back to the kitchen. Like my mother, I do not want to see the world where I work—it's like sitting next to the waitress station in a restaurant, all clatter and distraction ruining the meal. Most cooks will sit with their back to the kitchen or the stove, regardless of their sex, and yet close enough to spring up for the next dish or the salt shaker. But my mother never got up from the table.

This is what I imagine happened. The local news finished and my father went to bed. My mother sat in her customary place at the rock maple table, sorting through recipes or reading or making her grocery list, while the blood that had been wearing a weak place in the artery for 63 years finally broke through. Cranial aneurysm, quick, merciful they say, except for those who loved her. Seized, she falls to the floor. The long night. If I think about the long night she lay on the kitchen floor I will not stop crying or blaming my father for not finding her sooner.

If I think about her dying in the kitchen there is some comfort in that because she loved the kitchen and preferred to be alone in it. She had complained of a headache earlier in the evening. This is the last supper but they do not know it. He does not pray at the table unless all the family is assembled and this is rare. What we pray for now is not possible. Come back. Let us all sit down together. Everything and everyone in their place, like dishes in the cupboard, the simple order of the everyday, what we expect will continue, but does not. I sit at the harvest table in her absence and wonder what to cook, even as she did in her kitchen. The basket of acorn squash, the last of the basil, the tomatoes coming on, fall. ■

On the Mowing

Leslie Lawrence

JULY '98

It's a good year for blueberries and I love blueberries, but I'm worried about where such abundance might lead in the long run.

The demise of the mowing?

The mowing is what brought me here, and the mowing—not the cramped, moldy cabin with its annual infestations—is what has kept me coming back for more than a dozen years.

I learned of the place from an ad in the paper: *Quiet cabin with view of Monadnock.*

"Quiet" was good—I was hoping to complete a novel—and "view" was essential—how else could one bear all those inside hours. But writing is lonely, and I didn't know a soul in New Hampshire. Born in New York City, now settled in Cambridge, Massachusetts, my hunger for country had generally taken me down roads with less dire license plates. Week after week, I noticed—and skipped over—that ad, but after rejecting a slew of too-suburban places in Massachusetts, I finally dialed 603, the *Live Free or Die* state.

The next day I followed the landlord's directions—along the familiar numbered routes, to the unfamiliar ones, to the ones that had no numbers or names. *Right at the fire station; right again at the little red house; then follow the dirt road.* I followed and followed, through a forest so thick it offered barely a glimpse of rooftop or daylight. I hoped this guy was on the level, and I was beginning to lose faith when I spotted the promised "Y" with its tree laddered by two-by-fours sporting a variety of stalwart names.

Pulling into the next driveway, I saw a skinny, fifty-something man with thick glasses, looking up from his woodpile. Was that a smile? Confronted by such tentativeness, my own voice boomed. "Are you Harvey Tolman?"

"Yup."

I offered my hand. He dropped his axe. We shook.

"We could take my truck," he said, "or walk up to the cabin through the mowing."

"Let's walk," I said—almost always the better choice, I've discovered, and "the mowing," whatever *that* was, reminded me of "the gloaming" from that song in *Brigadoon* that had once flared all my adolescent longings.

So off we went behind the woodpile, Harvey and I, weaving our way through a thick stand of trees until suddenly we were blinded by an astounding light.

There, sprawling in front of us, was what I, raised in Queens, probably would have called a field. And a field, let's face it—even a small, flat, shorn one—is a good thing any old place or time but especially after a long, dark drive. And this one—five acres, ten? I don't have the acreage sense, but it was big. A whole world. Irregularly shaped, climbing and dipping and climbing again, you couldn't take it all in at one glance or guess how far it went. All you knew was the glory of so much tall grass doing what it does best—swaying in the bluesy spring wind. The cabin was nowhere in sight. But just a step or two into that honey-colored expanse and I knew this was the place for me.

My first June "on the mowing," as I quickly learned to think of it, was cold, buggy, and lonely. Now and again, I saw station wagons parked on the western edge near paths that led who-knew-where, but I never met their drivers. The cabin I'd pass near the bottom of the mowing was clearly uninhabited. As for the one about 20 wooded yards from mine, it lay eerily empty except on weekends when a jeep full of rowdy teenaged boys arrived, sometimes with parents, always with rifles they liked to fire at unpredictable hours and at targets I didn't want to imagine. Mostly I stayed at my desk, from where I could look down the dirt driveway onto my slice of heaven. Often in parka and woolen hat, I sat there from morning until evening, save for a jog or garbage run—both of which took me down the mowing and up it again. At night I'd try to get out, just so I wouldn't get too weird. I'd go to one of the free chamber music concerts held in far-off churches, or to the weekly contra dance in the Nelson Town Hall where, neither welcomed nor shunned, I stumbled through reel after reel and spoke only a few words. More often than not, "mowing" was one of those words. I pictured it with an apostrophe instead of a "g" and though I couldn't have told you its precise definition, just hearing the word fall from my lips made me feel more at home and in-the-know; the snob in me judged the in-the-knowness of strangers by how bliplessly the word registered with them.

Whether the excursion had been a balm for my loneliness or salt on the wound, I loved returning to the mowing at night. To its absence, really—its blackness glittering with fireflies. I'd stand at the end of the driveway, the sky above, Montana-big, the jaunty fiddles and eerie bagpipes still in my ears, the simple *allemandes* and daunting *hay-for-fours* making my body hum. Still sweaty from dancing, I'd stand there, unable to name the feelings that kept me there long after the chill set in. If this was loneliness it was delicious. If it was serenity, it was fringed with terror.

That was in '86 and '87. Since then, I've lived on the mowing every summer except one. Our friend Miriam Goodman now rents the cabin I first rented; I've moved to where the gun-happy family used to be. All agree, its jutting porch on stilts offers the best view of the mowing. I've had a nine-by-twelve writing studio built for me a few yards from there. I've also gained a life partner, another woman, and given birth to our son, Sam.

Mowing is of course the present participle of the verb *to mow,* but it is also three nouns: the act of mowing, the yield of that act, and the place where that act occurs. Furthermore, in the OED it is an adjective, as in, "My little mare had provided for herself by leaping out of a bare pasture into a lot of mowing ground . . ."

No fool, that little mare.

On our mowing, the life of our nontraditional family resembles a Norman Rockwell painting, and however hard I try, I can't summon the cynicism to knock it. The mowing is where we have celebrated seven of Sam's ten birthdays—with puppet shows and piñatas, scavenger hunts and pajama relays. The mowing is where we play the kinds of ball games his age demands; where we engage in high-spirited marathons of hide-and-seek tag or try to fly one recalcitrant kite after another. Both clock and calendar, the mowing is where we camp out to watch the meteor showers. Where we spy deer and wild turkeys; where we eat our breakfast when the cabin is too cold; drink our gin and tonics when the sun hasn't yet set.

Where the grasshoppers in August announce the coming of fall.

Where even low-slung city dogs become gazelles.

Where we scattered the ashes of one of those graceful hounds.

Where, weeks later, Sam put blueberries, still dusted with those ashes, into his one-year-old mouth.

It is where, I always assumed, someone would scatter *my* ashes; for it would be no sacrifice for the living to journey here.

It was Nina, Harvey's ex-wife, who first put the fear of too many blueberries in me. It must have been shortly after their divorce. She was still living in the same house at the base of the mowing where I first met Harvey; and he with his new wife, Frankie, had moved to the neighboring farmhouse where he grew up. Walking with me on the mowing, Nina observed that Harvey had been neglecting the mowing, and if he didn't get on it soon—"Here, look!" she tapped her boot on a rock, "You can already see the signs—spongy moss!" She toed a sapling. "Maple trees!" She swept her head around and said matter-of-factly, "All these blueberries!"

"Signs of what?" I asked, already worried.

"Well, if you don't mow a mowing, pretty soon it becomes a forest."

Not such an original idea, I realize, but one that had never occurred to me. I had no more thought to question the longevity of the mowing than I had that of Mount Monadnock. Certainly I know nothing lasts forever, but I assumed that, barring forest fires and greedy developers, large-scale features of the landscape remained the same for generations. Didn't we return to such places year after year precisely because we liked to measure our own fickle selves against their steadfastness?

A few seasons back, I had been startled when a shiny car appeared on the mowing. Out came an older man in city clothes, his clean shirt tucked neatly into crisp khaki slacks. And when I nervously approached (we don't get many intruders here), he explained that some 30 or more years ago he'd summered on the mowing and just wanted to say hello to the place because—he shook his head in amazement—"it changes less than any I know!"

"Now Harvey's father," Nina continued, as we stood there contemplating the mowing's future. "To him maintaining the mowing was like a religion. If he had to be out there 24 hours a day, that's where he would be!"

Before that conversation with Nina, I often noticed how the mowing would change from minute to minute as the sun and clouds engaged in their operatic battles, and occasionally from day to day, if Harvey or his son Colin happened to be out on the tractor mowing a stretch—an event which always brought mixed feelings since it made walking easier, but gazing a little less blissful. Naturally, I also noticed the gradual changes from early summer to autumn. But now, I began to notice changes from year to year.

At first glance each June, everything looked the same—the same graceful descents to the south and east, the same roughly zigzagging swaths of browns and yellows and greens. But on closer inspection, the darker greens seemed to be gaining on the lighter ones, the terrain was becoming bumpier, the bordering trees growing taller and creeping inward, the view of Monadnock shrinking just a bit. "Eh, you're imagining it," others said. But one summer a visiting friend twisted an ankle in a hidden hole. And whereas once I could blithely pick dozens of wildflowers, now I had to wonder if a handful for me would deprive my neighbors.

And the blueberries! We used to enjoy searching for them during those couple of weeks in late July, enjoy the batch or two of pancakes, the blueberry something we'd bake for Sam's birthday party. (Poor guy, he prefers chocolate, but I always feel compelled to make use of the berries.) Now with them covering most of the mowing, arriving in early July and staying through mid-August at least, we're wearily searching our cookbooks for ever more exotic concoctions.

Before Nina's comment, I generally regarded the mowing as a beautiful expanse of emptiness, a welcome absence of trees and irritating human and vehicular life. A place for stretching the legs, any old time but especially in the morning and evenings when the light is best and the bugs, alas, are the worst. A quiet, meditative place to rest my eyes when they drift from the monitor.

Afterwards, propelled by fear—and embarrassment over the utter lack of curiosity I had shown for everything but the name of my beloved—the mowing held new interest. It became not just a place for, but the object of, contemplation. And instead of spending the bulk of my time reading and writing fiction, I combed the local library's history and geography sections. Instead of walking the mowing for sheer pleasure—or to get to the lake or the eggs Frankie sold—I began to tromp around, Peterson guide in hand.

I saw, of course, tall grass, but now I knew that there are over 5,000 species of grass. And I knew the answer to that crucial question I had never thought to ask: Why is it that you can mow down grass and it just keeps growing back? The answer, I learned, is something felicitously called the "*meri*stems," the tissues that produce new growth. In most plants, they reside near the tips, but in grasses, the meristems are safely hidden away near the base.

And along with grass, which I had thought of as the mowing's more or less sole component, I saw moss, lichen, twigs, stumps, oak and maple saplings, pygmy bushes, acorns, mushrooms, ragweed, milkweed, tall meadow rue, red clover, and yarrow—not to mention the countless varieties of insects, spiders, and other critters going about their business. Now I understood why one naturalist spoke about the "drama in every bush"; another about "a riot" in his nearby meadow. I wondered if I would ever again be able to think of the mowing as a quiet, contemplative place. And I fretted over what all this multifariousness might bode for the mowing's future.

Enter Tom Wessels's marvelous book *Reading the Forested Landscape*. No doubt, "reading the landscape" is not a new idea. It's what hunters and gatherers have done for thousands of years. But the practice, as Wessels rigorously applies it, was new to me—and enthralling.

His point of departure is always a specific landscape. Then the observations and questions begin. Why is that apple tree so gnarled? This juniper so stunted? What can we surmise from this curious mixture of old and new growth? Each question leads to a hypothesis that is usually discredited by some bit of previously overlooked evidence that raises new questions, demanding we look farther afield, and further back in time so that soon Wessels is talking about the Pleistocene era, about Verrazano and John Winthrop and Chief Greylock. Reading Wessels, I began to understand the travesty of teaching about nature piecemeal—by simply identifying and categorizing this or that without wondering how one species impacts on another; and how human inventions, philosophies, and politics leave their marks on fields and forests and streams. I learned, for example, that Napoleon's defeat of Portugal transformed the landscape of New Hampshire. But I'm getting ahead of myself here.

The indigenous people of New Hampshire were largely nomadic, so that when the "first" settlers arrived in the 1600s they found almost no clearings—just trees, trees, and more trees. To the Europeans' way of thinking, since the natives didn't clear, enclose, or cordon off land, they didn't own it; and by extension of this bizarre logic, the Europeans concluded that they themselves, who almost immediately starting cutting trees and making fences, did own it.

They chartered the town of Nelson in the mid 1700s—and a rugged bunch they (and of course their predecessors) must have been. One only has to live in our drafty, wood-heated cabin in early June or late August to start wondering how people survive the winters here now, let alone centuries or millennia ago when there were no shelters, no wells, no roads, no stores, no nothing. According to one history of Nelson, many of the "first" residents "would chop down his acre of heavy timber in a day, and drink a quart of rum, and chew a 'hand' of tobacco while doing it." Clearly these people were made of different cloth than we are today, and there seemed to be no shortage of them. When the British defeated the French and Indian Alliance in 1760, even more people came, and by 1790 Nelson had 7,621 people!

Which brings me back to Napoleon and his defeat of Portugal in 1809. This defeat ended the embargo on exporting Portugal's valuable merino sheep and began the period called "sheep fever," in which half or more—some say 80 percent—of the mostly wooded land was cleared.

In those days, people worried about the vanishing forests; now the process is in reverse. Farmland and pastures and mowings are rapidly being reclaimed by forests. No doubt there are social and historical forces that accelerate this process—the demise of small farms, the overgrazing of pastures, the advent of Polartec, and the diminishment of some mowers' commitment to mowing—but apparently this is also simply the way with clearings: sooner or later, they are overcome. "Succession" it is called—ironically, to my mind—it feels so much like failure.

Sooner? Or later? Will this mowing be here in five years? In fifteen? Will Sam someday be that man who returns to the one place that hardly changes at all? Or will he search in vain for the landscape that obliterates the years between his *now* and *then*? For questions about the pace of change here, I always go to Ben Smith, owner of one of those station wagons parked near hidden cabins I didn't venture near until my second or third summer. Ben has lived in that cabin nearly every summer of his nearly 80 years. When I ask him how the mowing has changed, he says, "Hardly at all." But then he adds, "They used to put manure on it and that made for better hay. Even so, the hay was never that great. Too many rocks.

"And there was an ice house behind the barn. And Rodger's mother, Mildred, used to make donuts. We would get our milk from there—unpasteurized. The mailman brought chickens and eggs.

"Before they had the dam at the lake, you could walk to the island, and that's where we had our sleep-outs."

To Ben, apparently, the "mowing" encompasses all a man might remember about his boyhood summers. I try to rein him in.

"We set up a badminton net," he recalls, "and tether ball. And once I got it in my head I wanted to be a pole vaulter, so I brought out a bamboo pole and it broke.

"In my mother's paintings, you can see clear down to Harrisville, whereas now that's all trees."

"Was the mowing ever used for grazing?" I ask, wondering how many years we might have before it, too, becomes "all trees."

"Not since I've been here," he says, "but yes—sure—way back. It must have been used for sheep when Ebenezer first came. His house used to be where the French cabin is. Rumor has it some local schoolchildren were doing an archeological dig and located Ebenezer's well there."

The "French" cabin (so named because for years a Parisian family summered there) is the one that sits near the bottom of the mowing, a hundred yards or more above Harvey and Frankie's place, which borders the dirt road. Ebenezer was Harvey's great-great-great-great-grandfather, I learn. Born in 1748, he fought in the battle at Bunker Hill and settled in Nelson in about 1787. One history of Nelson quotes Ebenezer's praise for the town's "enchanting hills," but whether he was referring to wooded hills in the distance or clearings in his own backyard, I cannot say. I do know that by the early 1900s the land was probably cleared because that's when Wilmer, Harvey's grandfather, built the five "camps," as they call rustic cabins around here.

August '98

Our neighbor Miriam says the blueberries are nothing to worry about. If they're more plentiful this year, and she's not sure they are, it's merely because we had such a rainy spring.

I feel reassured, until she adds, almost as an afterthought, "Now the blackberries. If you're looking for bad signs, look at them. They're tougher and thornier, and they used to grow just on the borders, but now the whole area near Ben's cabin is covered with them."

It's true, I see one evening as we walk to Ben's for dinner.

Of all life's pleasures, walking to someone's place for dinner is one of my favorites. In Cambridge, we indulge only during snowstorms, but here in Nelson we do it often. And when we do, with a hard day of work or play behind us—and ahead of us, a feast—the walk offers pause enough to wax pensive. Tonight I'm filled with wonder and gratitude. How far I once strayed—the drugs, the sex, the Grateful Dead concerts, the near arrests in D.C., the hitching from Germany to Greece—and here I am, clean and fresh in the perfect light, one hand clasping a child's, the other, a straw basket cradling a still-warm pie.

Yes, wonder and gratitude, but also a touch of alarm, for Miriam is right: the land near Ben's is rife with blackberries.

We are setting the table on the porch and here come Harvey and Frankie, first just their heads, their torsos, then their whole lengths as they climb the mowing.

Once we're all settled at the table and well into the meal, we make our proposal—something we've thought about for years, so why not now since we plan to summer here for as long as we can still walk: an expansion of our cabin—a dormer upstairs so Sandy can have a proper study with a view of the mowing!

Harvey and Frankie eye each other. Sandy and I prepare ourselves for refusal.

"That might not be worth your while," Frankie says gently. "Sometime in the next few years we plan to tear down the cabin and build our retirement home here."

For this we are not prepared. I take a gulp of wine. My eyes sting. As the Native Americans know all too well, knowledge, time, and love don't determine a claim's legitimacy, but even if they did, I cannot pretend that my 13-year affair with this spot rivals a Tolman's multigenerational intimacy. No, there's no comforting myself with outrage here. I must settle for anger's more difficult sister: pure, inescapable grief.

July '99

Another summer, another dinner with Harvey and Frankie. This time they arrive by car, probably because Frankie has brought her portfolio—bulging with a thick batch of her newest watercolors.

Trying to come to terms with our impending loss, I am practicing a disinterested curiosity. "So, what about all these blueberries?" I ask, nodding to the mowing just beyond the front porch. We have another bumper crop this year, despite a much dryer spring.

It's true, Harvey says, countering Miriam, the blueberries are a sign that the mowing has not been properly maintained. He admits he ought to mow more—fertilize, too. "The fertilizer encourages the grass," he explains, "which discourages all these coarser plants we're seeing now."

I'm surprised he doesn't seem much bothered by this. Could it be they've changed their plans about retiring here; that we, after all, will be the ones to witness the mowing's gradual succession?

After dinner, Frankie brings out her paintings. They are stark stylized landscapes with thrillingly fearless colors, and, having recently done a little painting myself, I feel silly for working so hard to try to capture the exact shade of minty green to indicate the lichen on the two huge trees that grace our porch.

I brave the question. "Is this our last year here?"

"Depends on whether we can round up the cash," Frankie says. "But whenever we do, we hope to find you a place somewhere around here. Would you consider the French cabin?"

"Yes," we say, without enthusiasm. It's already occurred to us, but we'd so miss the view.

I offer up some more pasta, pass around the Parmesan. "Have you designed the new house yet?" I ask. It is an active, deliberate process—this letting go.

Frankie describes their plans. A long, one-level C-shaped house with kitchen, living/dining room, and studio all facing the mowing.

Until I catch myself, it is *I* that I imagine in that kitchen, in that living/dining room, in that studio, in front of my easel, no longer worried about finding that perfect green.

"M-o-w-i-n-g-g-g": my first email password.

"The best thing I've ever done," I've more than once thought and said, meaning finding this place.

The first few years I was up here, I looked around for something to buy. I saw houses that were more substantial, cottages right on ponds; places that cost far more than I could afford, but even they didn't interest me—probably because, as I now read in my *feng shui* book, the ideally located home is the one we have here—protected on three sides by hills or forest and fronted by downward-sloping land. Maybe now's the time to wrap my mind around a totally different sort of summer. Never mind that mine are supposed to be for writing, we should rent a villa in Umbria, drive cross-country and do the parks.

Daily, on my walks down the mowing, I wander around the French cabin. If it's empty, I venture in. I look out the windows from every side, imagine an addition, a porch, and I stand where I would be if I were inside that porch, and I look up the mowing—or the small patch of it visible from there. The view's not great, but I remind myself it's the same one I had when I first stepped into the mowing—and that was enough to sell me. Also, I like seeing the barn and apple orchard, absent from our spot on high. I recall that it was good enough for Ebenezer, and that our friend Caitlin who rented the French cabin last season thought it the sweetest.

This summer, bored with my improvised blueberry-peach pie in its ginger snap crust, and even with Miriam's sublime blueberry-lemon teacake, we have attempted a sweet yeasty blueberry *fougasse*. And I'm determined to try a *clafouti,* if only for the name. That still leaves mousse, pudding, bombe, buckle, Charlotte, fool, and grunt.

(Happy Birthday, Sam!)

If, as I recently read, all landscapes tell a story and all stories are about time, it follows that this story is the same old one—of life relished and squandered, the farmer growing tired, the child growing up, the parents growing old, the dogs dying, the hard truths faced and flung aside. And if this is the end for us (whether sooner by landlords or later by berries and biodiversity) we may as well enjoy it. That's what I tell myself as I sit on the porch watching Sam set off his rockets made from tubing and plastic soda bottles; as I throw sticks for the dog; as we part the tall grass on our way to Ben's for dinner. ■

Physics and Grief

Patricia Monaghan

> In nature nothing remains constant. Everything is in a perpetual state of transformation, motion, and change. However, we discover that nothing simply surges up out of nothing without having antecedents that existed before. Likewise, nothing ever disappears without a trace, in the sense that it gives rise to absolutely nothing existing in later times.
>
> —David Bohm

"Actually," Dan said, "I've been reading a lot of physics." He looked down at his empty paper plate and shrugged one shoulder, then the other. "I don't suppose that makes any sense."

Dan had not spoken to me in almost a year. We'd seen each other occasionally; we had too many common friends for that not to happen. But when it did, Dan made certain to stay on the other side of the room, to find himself in need of a drink when I came near, to turn suddenly away when I tried to catch his eye.

That was the year when I was a new widow, and Dan was about to become one, his partner, Steve, descending into a hell of lesions and pneumonia and fungal invasions of the brain. Even in the blur of my loss, I felt no anger toward Dan—though anger is so predictable a part of grief—for avoiding me. I knew the cause: I already was what he most feared to become.

Six months after I was widowed, Dan joined me in that state. Steve gave up his obdurate struggle to remain alive, asking to be kept home when the next crisis hit. It was only a week. Friends told me that Steve's death was gentle and that Dan bore up as well as could be expected. Dan dropped from sight for a time, disappearing into memories and pain.

Now it was summer, and we were sitting under blue canvas at an outdoor festival. Dan had approached me with an apology for his actions. I had embraced him with understanding. We were sitting companionably together, catching up on each other's lives, when I asked him what most helped him deal with his grief.

Physics.

Dan met my eyes, and his brows came together, then raised. "Relativity. Quantum mechanics. Bell's Theorem. You know?" I think he expected me to be surprised. But I was not. It had been the same for me.

To explain how physics came to be important on my journey of grief, I have first to describe the problem with my keys. There were five of them, bound together with a wide steel ring: a big silver skeleton key, for the embossed brass Victorian lock on the front door; a round-headed key that opens the more modern deadbolt; a little golden key to the garage; an institutional "do not duplicate" key to my office; and a black-headed key to the Ford station wagon.

I remember the day—the hour—that the keys disappeared. It was late spring, less than three months after Bob died. Walking out the door to go shopping, I had reached into my jacket pocket, where I always kept my keys.

They weren't there.

At the instant, it seemed inconsequential. I'd mislaid keys before; hasn't everyone? I was inside the house, so I had used the keys to enter. They were, therefore, somewhere in the house with me. I merely had to look carefully and I would find them.

I was unperturbed. I did what I did whenever I had mislaid something. I looked in all the logical places: in my coat's other pocket; on the shelf near the front door; next to the telephone; in the kitchen near the sink. Nothing.

I was still not overly concerned. I must have been distracted when I entered, I reasoned with myself; I must have put the keys in some unlikely spot. So I began methodically searching the house. Entry hall. Living room. Pulling out furniture, looking under pillows. Nothing. Dining room. Kitchen. Opening cabinets, reaching to the back of shelves. Nothing.

Okay, then, I must have carried them upstairs. Guest room. Bathroom. Moving around each room slowly, looking especially in places where keys were unlikely to be. Behind pictures. In rarely-opened drawers. Study. Nothing. Linen closet. Nothing.

In my bedroom, I suddenly grew frustrated. I needed my keys! The only key to my car was on that ring; I could not go to work without it. What would I do without my keys?

I started to cry.

I had been crying for months, ever since Bob had finally died, fighting cancer to the last. The six months before his death were exhausting. For three months I was his sole caregiver; then, during his final hospitalization, I visited him two, three, even four times each day. Economics forced me to continue working, so I had neither physical strength nor emotional resources left when he died.

In the days before Bob's death, I had been with him constantly, telling him stories of the future we should have had, praising his work and his son to him, reminiscing for him about happy times when he could no longer speak. I did not sleep for perhaps forty-eight hours as I held vigil by his bedside, leaving only for necessary moments, for he had been shatteringly fearful of being alone at the moment of death. And so I was with him when that moment came, holding his hand as his breathing slowed, singing old songs to him, stroking his face through its paralysis.

It was the hardest thing I have ever done, witnessing as he "departed from this strange world a little ahead of me," as Einstein said when his oldest friend, Michele Besso, died. When I left that hospital room, bearing with me the amaryllis that had bloomed only the day before, I felt that I was leaving all happiness behind, that my world had changed unutterably, and only for the worse.

I lived the months afterward in a trance of grief. There was a memorial service that I planned, I remember that. I remember a brick meeting hall with red tulips, a jazz pianist, readings from Bob's novels, visitors from many states. For the rest, I barely recall anything. I apparently kept working, and doing laundry, and feeding the dogs, and planting the garden. My body kept moving through the Midwestern spring. But my soul was in the desert, in winter.

That day in May, the loss of my keys reduced me to tears, though of course I was weeping for my greater loss, which every other loss would now reflect. Possibly I wept for hours; I did such things at that time. Finally the storm passed. I got up and set determinedly about to find the keys. To survive, I had to work. I needed to drive to my office. I could not manage without my keys. I would find them. I had to.

And so I repeated my search. I must have missed the keys the first time, I told myself. I started again at the front door and scoured the downstairs. Living room: no. Kitchen: no.

And so it went. After an hour or so, I found myself again in the bedroom, still keyless.

I began to weep again. This time, my desolation seemed endless. I could not stop crying. I lay on the bed, sobbing and flailing my arms. I soaked several handkerchiefs. I buried my head in pillows and drenched them with tears.

Then I became enraged. I got up from the bed and began to scream at Bob, furious at him for dying and leaving me so helplessly besieged by grief. I screamed that he was cruel and heartless, that I'd been there in his hour of need, and where was he when I needed him? I raged and wept, wept and raged.

I had not, before Bob's death, spent much time thinking about the question of whether or not there is an afterlife. I had been brought up with a conventional picture of heaven and hell. And I had studied enough other religions to realize that many wiser than I believed in some kind of survival after death. I had read believable-enough accounts of those who claimed to have been contacted by the dead. But the possibility of an afterlife was not something I dwelt upon. I did not wish to make moral decisions by weighing the possibilities of future reward or punishment for myself. Nor did the survival of my own small person seem especially important in comparison with the universe's vast majesty. So, for myself, what happened or did not happen after death was not a very important question.

Bob, by contrast, had been quite clear about his beliefs. A natural mystic, he had practiced Zen for twenty years. But he was also an unrelentingly hard-headed empiricist who believed the universe to be a mechanistic place in which consciousness was only a byproduct of the body's functions. Thus, when the body died, consciousness ceased as well. Bob believed, as Fred Alan Wolf put it in describing the Newtonian worldview, that mind—or soul, or spirit, whatever you call it—was just "a convenient by-product of the physiology of . . . the mechanisms of the brain, down to the remarkable electrical and mechanical movements of the nerve firings and blood flows."

He never changed his belief once he entered the hospital that final time, even though I, desperate for some reassurance that our love could continue after he faded from this life, talked to him about reincarnation and other possible survivals. But Bob would be no foxhole convert; he marched gamely toward that abyss which he saw as the likely end of his being. Death was painful to him; he had much to live for; but he would not grasp at hope of continued life just to ease his pain. Unless he had time to ponder, unless he could become completely convinced, he would believe as he always had. Happy lies held no appeal for him.

One thing I loved about Bob was this: he had more integrity than any person I'd ever met. That integrity remained to the end. He met his death with his long-held beliefs intact. He was frightened, but he was very, very brave.

Because I had no personal convictions on the subject, I held true to Bob's beliefs after he was gone. It was a way of remaining close to him. I, too, would refuse to grasp at imaginary straws just to ease my pain. If Bob believed that all traces of his consciousness would evaporate at his death, that only his physical works would remain, then I would loyally uphold that belief.

And so I lived in the desert. Life has never seemed so dry and meaningless to me as it did then. I would watch lovers kiss in a coffee shop and a whirlpool of pain would open beneath me, as I thought of one of them holding the other as they parted forever. I would stare at parents playing with their children near the lake and imagine sudden illnesses and accidents, wondering how life could create such joy only to obliterate it. I wept constantly: when I heard beautiful music, when I saw painful news, when I saw new flowers, when I went to bed, when I woke up.

But I adamantly refused to settle for those happy visions that religion held out, of dreamy heavens full of harps, of other lives to come, of eventual reunion in some cosmic void. I even rejected nonreligious spiritualism. When friends said they had dreamed of Bob, or felt him near, I received the information in silent disbelief. It was their need of solace, I told myself, that caused these apparitions. They had just imagined them. I, loyal to Bob's beliefs, would not settle for such self-deluding comfort. I would tough it out, looking reality right in its cruel face.

But the day I lost my keys, I could not be brave like Bob, not any longer. Seeing those loving eyes go dim had been the single most painful moment of my life. The idea that the universe could so wantonly create beauty, could bestow upon our lives the kind of love that seems like ultimate meaning, only to destroy it in a breath, had finally become too much for me.

I wanted so desperately to believe that Bob, and Bob's love for me, still existed somewhere in the universe, that in my furious pain I flung down a challenge. Standing in the middle of the bedroom, I demanded that he come back. Find my keys, I insisted. Find my damned keys! If there's anyone there, if there's any love left in this universe for me, find my keys!

After the fury had passed, I felt mortified. I had been screaming at a dead man. Standing in my room alone, screaming at a dead man.

Worse, it was all so trivial. If I were going to throw down the gauntlet to the universe about whether there is life after death, couldn't I have chosen something more important as proof? World peace? Personal economic security? A beatific vision?

But I'd spoken. I'd insisted that Bob prove his continuing existence by finding my keys.

Even writing about that day, I feel embarrassment cover me. It was such an excess of emotion about such a small matter, about such a minor inconvenience. Why had I broken down over such a silly thing? Why had I challenged the universe over something as unimportant as a key-ring?

But break down I had, and challenge the universe I had. And I could not bear the answer to be silence, negation, the absence of Bob forever, anywhere. Now I truly had to find the keys. So I resolutely began, yet again, to search. I started once more in the front hallway. But this time, I took a new tack. I might as well do spring-cleaning, I decided. I'd clean the entire house, front door to attic, and in doing so I would certainly find the keys.

There was more than a bit of desperation about all this. If I did not find the keys, all was indeed lost. If I did not find the keys, there was no vestige of Bob in the world. If I did not find the keys, I was alone in the cruelest universe imaginable.

Three days later, I was back in the bedroom. Except for that one room, the house was now clean, ammonia-and-paste-wax clean. I had taken down curtains and washed them, cleaned out closets, pulled up rugs. I had upended sofas and searched their bowels. I had repotted plants. I had pulled books from shelves and dusted both.

The house sparkled, indeed.

But I had not found the keys.

The bedroom was the final outpost of possibility. From the first corner around to the last, then spiraling in to the center, I cleaned and searched. I opened drawers and rearranged them, shaking out their contents on the floor. I moved pictures and dusted their frames. I worked slowly, with mounting despair, for the keys had still not appeared. I moved the bed and polished the floor under it. I shook out the bedclothes and aired out the mattress.

Finally, I was finished.

There were no keys.

I collapsed. This time my grief truly knew no bounds. I had asked for an answer from the universe, and I had—I believed—received one. Bob had been right. Consciousness was a byproduct of our body's functioning, and now that the ashes of Bob's body sat on the bookshelf in a white box, there was nothing, anywhere, left of the curiosity and passion and brilliance and love that had been him.

The depression that began that day incapacitated me. I was unable to work for nearly a week. Finally, however, I called the car dealership and got new car keys. I found the spare house keys. I began to reconstruct the openings to my life. I knew now that I was indeed alone, that I could not call upon Bob for help, that he was no longer present anywhere, in any form. It was a bleak and cruel universe, but at least I knew the truth of it.

What I experienced during that next year was more than simple grief and certainly more than emotional depression, although I suffered from both as well. It was stark existential despair. Life had no meaning, much less any savor. I tried to find what comfort I could in friendship, in earthly beauty, in art, in learning. But at my center was an abyss of meaninglessness. I could as easily have gambled all my resources away as built a garden; as easily have crashed my car as driven it safely across the Midwest; as easily have drunk slow poison as cocoa for breakfast. That I did one thing rather than another seemed only an arbitrary choice.

At last, however, I began to awaken from my coma of sorrow. I began to argue with Bob in my mind. As I gardened, I noticed again the resilient connection of matter and energy, how nature never destroys but only transforms. As I walked in the woods with my dog, I saw spring flowers emerging from the withered leaves of autumn. What hubris, I began to think, to imagine that human consciousness is the only thing this universe cares to obliterate. Surely we are not that important.

But these were fleeting thoughts, unconvincing, evanescent, ideas which did not in any case reach to the root of my grief. It was easy to accept that Bob's body would eventually nourish other beings, through the cycle of decomposition and recomposition. But it was Bob's self that I'd loved—not only his body, though certainly that. And although I knew and accepted, with piercing pain, what had happened to his body, that told me nothing about where the unique energy went that had invigorated it.

Every once in a while, I would think of the lost keys and sigh. I had, after all, asked for a sign, and I had been given one.

That was when I began reading books on physics. I had been reading a lot of spiritual literature, looking for answers to the appalling questions life presented. But I only grew more isolated, angry at the serenity that seemed forever beyond my grasp, despairing at my continuing inability to find any sense in death's senselessness. It was not that the answers which spiritual literature offered seemed implausible or incorrect; it was simply that I could not believe them, could not make the leap into not-doubting. The more rigidly codified the religious insight, the more it seemed to exclude—even to mock—my anguished confusion.

I can't remember exactly which book, which author, brought me to physics. Most likely one that pushed the boundaries of science to include spirituality. Fritz Capra, perhaps, or Gary Zukov. One of those wild minds who saw bridges where others saw barricades. But it wasn't the spirituality that gripped my attention. It was the science.

Where religion had failed me, being so certain of itself, physics offered paradoxes and complexities so bizarre that my hatred and fear of the universe began to be replaced with what can only be called awe. I'd known Newtonian physics before, from my days as a science reporter, but I had never ventured into quantum mechanics. There I found the most astonishing ideas, ones which smashed the clockwork universe just as Bob's death had torn apart mine. Ideas that read like Bob's beloved Zen koans, statements that strained the limits of my linear thinking. "Our universe seems to be composed of facts and their opposites at the same time," I read in Louis de Broglie's work, and "everything happens as though it did not exist at all."

Such statements seemed eminently sensible, reasonable, even straightforward. Yes, I responded passionately. Yes, the universe was that strange, that indescribable. Death is not an equal and opposite reaction to life; consciousness is not some strange form of inertia. I needed a new physics to describe the wild movements of my grieving soul. And a new physics I found.

Like my friend Dan, I found quantum theory immeasurably consoling. With an uncertainty-loves-company kind of logic, I lost myself in Heisenberg and the reassurances of the Uncertainty Principle. If we cannot conceivably know everything about the physical universe, then the abyss of doubt whereon I stood was as good a standpoint as any from which to view life. If we cannot know something as simple as two aspects of a subatomic particle's motion simultaneously, how can we know for certain that there is no life after death—or that there is? If our measurements may alter the reality that we measure, could not consciousness be a form of measurement, subtly altering the universe?

My deepest consolation, however, was not in speculating about whether a consciousness suffused, as mine was, with grief altered the world in a different way than one flooded with happiness. Rather, I drew solace from the dumbfounding absoluteness of Heisenberg's theory. We could not know everything, not ever, because in the moment of such knowing we may change what we know. I could not know—I could never know—if or where Bob existed, for each time I sought for him—each time I measured this universe in terms of Bob's existence or nonexistence—I was perhaps changing the conditions of the very universe through which I sought. It was as though Heisenberg, by enshrining uncertainty at the center of perception and knowledge, made anything and everything both possible and impossible at once.

Suddenly the world seemed to make sense again, although in a deeply paradoxical way. Where religion's certainties had left me bitterly bereft of comfort, quantum uncertainty allowed for unimaginable possibilities. Whatever measurement I took of the universe, I understood now, could be only partial. There would always be something that eluded my grasp. This was an enormous comfort.

It was not only uncertainty that captured me. Because this new physics was all about time and space, Einstein spoke to me like a voice from a burning bush. I, who lived in a time and space from which my love had disappeared, found respite in considering the ways that time and space were linked. "Any two points in space and time are both separate and not separate," David Bohm said. What salvation that seemed! As incomprehensible as this new spacetime was, it was more lively with possibilities than linear and planar realities. My separateness from Bob was real, but in some way, we were also still together.

In some way—this was most important to me. For this was not a metaphoric togetherness, a trick of language. This was science, after all. And not just science but the queen of sciences, physics. Physics which did not ask me to believe, did not ask me to have faith. Physics which observed and experimented. Physics which offered a description of the world, admittedly bizarre but as accurate as blundering language could make it.

I did not have to believe. I only had to wonder.

The fact that, as Max Born pointed out, the quantum world is utterly unvisualizable presented no problem to me. Visions of the subatomic world were metaphors, whose richness and limitations I amply understood. But unlike religion, which seemed hypnotized by its own articulations of the ineffable, physics acknowledged that any picture we hold of the subatomic world is by definition inaccurate, limited, inexact. No one has ever seen a quark, much less a Higgs boson. But they act; we see their traces. Such quantum strangeness spoke to my condition. I had witnessed something deeply incomprehensible when Bob died. Studying what Bohm called the "unanalyzable ways of the universe" mirrored that experience.

My grief did not disappear, for grief is a chronic disease which exists in the body. My body would still regularly writhe with sudden memories: when I automatically reached for Bob's favorite juice at the Jewel, when I passed the lake where we had taken our last walk, when someone uttered a phrase he had relished. The tape-loop of his last hours ran constantly in my mind, so that I would see the doctor, my friends Natalie and Barbara arriving, Bob's son Michael leaving, the amaryllis, Bob's paralyzed face, the doctor, Natalie, the amaryllis, the doctor. . . .

Because of the power of these death-watch memories, relativity especially absorbed me. The paradoxes of time preoccupied me for days on end. Einstein had seen the connection between the study of time and awareness of death's approach, arguing that death really means nothing because "the distinction between past, present and future is only a stubbornly persistent illusion." I envisioned those points in the universe where radio waves of Bob's voice, from a long-ago interview, were still new and bright. I invented scenarios in which I stretched time out like taffy, making Bob's last days as eternal as they had subjectively seemed. I relished that consoling insight that Einstein's equations were time-reversible, that perhaps time does not move in one direction but can flow backward as well as forward. I imagined moving backward through time, intersecting with a healthy Bob and recreating our life, always hopping back on the time machine before the diagnosis, living those happy times over and over and over. I knew these were fantasies, but I also knew that I no longer knew what time really was. There, once again, were limitless possibilities.

If my grief did not disappear, that crazed existential doubt did. Life no longer was so utterly senseless. It made sense again, but in a more marvelous way than I'd ever imagined. I found myself staring at graphs of the Schroedinger wave collapse, imagining a cat alive, dead, alive, dead, all at the same time—imagining Bob's continued existence as such a wave. I pondered the complementarity between particles and waves, especially the way an observer seems implicated in the emergence into reality of each. Particles dancing and leaping in a virtual world, flickering in and out of measurable existence. Or perhaps they were not even particles at all, but what Henry Sapp called "sets of relationships that reach outward to other things." To David Bohm, too, particles exist not so much as nuggets of virtual and actual matter, but as "on-going movements that are mutually dependent because ultimately they merge and interpenetrate."

Matter disappeared, at this scale, into flashing energy, particles into momentarily observable comets of being. Bob had been composed of these miraculous particles, these miraculous relationships reaching outward toward me, these mutually dependent and interpenetrating movements. And perhaps he still was, in some way, in some unmeasurable place. Our lives together had been lived in a space and a time, within a universe through which the mighty and unfathomable river of spacetime flows. Were we still connected, as Bell's Theorem hints, in some intricate and inexpressible way? Was I somehow still affected by the changes that he experienced—in whatever state those blinking-into-existence particles that had been Bob were now? And did my changes affect him still as well?

Far from compelling me toward certainty about where and how Bob still existed, quantum theory removed from me any urge toward stapling down reality within one interpretation. In the quantum world, Nick Herbert has pointed out, there are at least eight possible pictures of reality, any of which is more consoling than the Newtonian vision of the universe. Maybe there is an "ordinary reality," as de Broglie and Einstein believed; in that case the hard stuff that made up Bob is somewhere still in existence, and even now I am breathing atoms that had been part of him during his life. But the Copenhagen hypothesis of Bohr and Heisenberg questions whether there is any such "reality" at all. In their view, Bob and I had lived something like a dream together, and that dream had as much reality without him as it had with him. An alternative reading of the Copenhagen hypothesis is that we create our own realities, that reality exists only as we observe it doing so; in that case, I could create the reality of his continued existence by believing strongly enough.

These were only some of the possibilities. There was David Bohm's theory of the implicate order, which argues that there is an undivided wholeness that could wrap both Bob and me, in our varying current states, in what he called "indivisible quantum processes that link different systems in an unanalyzable way."There was the fantastic many-world hypothesis, which permitted me to envision that Bob and I still lived happily in another space-time, after he had survived cancer; in that reality, we are writing an essay together, perhaps this very one.

Or possibly, the quantum world is based upon no logic that we would recognize. In that case, life's either/or does not exist, and Bob's apparent lack of existence is no more true than his apparent existence had been. Or perhaps I created him, or he me; perhaps neither of us existed before we met, we came into being complete with memories when we created each other, and thus he continues in me, his creation. Perhaps, as Fred Alan Wolf has argued, the mind does not "exist in the physical universe at all. It may be beyond the boundaries of space, time and matter. It may use the physical body in the same sense that an automobile driver uses a car."

Or maybe all of this is simultaneously true. Maybe this world is so full of mystery that we cannot ever grasp its actual probabilities and probable actualities.

I pondered these extraordinary possibilities as I moved through my ordinary life. Slowly, the pain of my loss began, not to diminish, but to find its place in my life. If I did not feel joy, at least my pain had become a familiar companion. I continued reading physics, but with less crazed compulsion. I even began to accept the cruel existence of thermodynamics, with its arrow of time that threatened my happy time-travel imaginings, once I realized how connected to the richness of chaos it was.

Every once and again, I thought of the lost keys. In fall, as I was raking the front yard, I imagined that perhaps I had gone to the car for something, that spring day, and had dropped my key-ring into the crowded bed of hosta by the door. But no. In winter, when I decided to move the piano, I thought that perhaps I had missed the hidden keys during my frenzied cleaning by not moving that massive upright. But no. That next spring, after preparing for a dinner party, I sat in Bob's recliner and noticed a side pocket I had missed. There? But no: the keys were not there either. The seasons passed, and the keys remained lost.

Each time this happened, I thought to myself that finding the keys no longer mattered. That I had moved beyond the challenge I had flung out to Bob, to the universe, on that wild sad day. That unless the keys found their way back to me in some utterly strange way, I could not regard it as an answer to my desperate plea. I said to myself that finding the keys would be—just finding the keys. That if I found them in some ordinary way, it would prove nothing, one way or the other: I lost the keys, I found them, there was no connection.

And then I found the keys.

Friends were coming to dinner, and I was sitting in my study feeling sad, as I often did, and thinking of Bob, which I always did. I wistfully imagined him being with us, thought how much he would have enjoyed it. I felt my loss again, but poignantly this time, as a sad melody rather than as painful cacophony.

Then, for no special reason, I looked at the door of my study. It was open after having been closed all day. I kept it closed to keep my dog out and to keep visitors from wandering into my private space. That door had been opened and closed scores of times in the preceding year. When I entered, nothing unusual had caught my eye.

My study door is decorated. There is a Celtic knocker in the shape of a squirrel, a St. Bridget cross made of Irish rushes, and a poster. The poster, mounted on heavy blue cardboard, is a memento from the publication of my first book. Issued by my publisher for promotional parties, it shows the book's cover, my name, and the huge black words "it's here!"

The door is one of those old wooden doors with six deep panels. The poster is tacked tightly to the middle of the door, covering the two center panels and resting on the lower. The edges of the poster are flush against the door, especially at top and bottom, with the exception of two areas on each side, halfway down the cardboard, where small gaps exist.

From one of these gaps, I noticed a key coyly poking out. I walked to the door and pulled sharply. Immediately, out tumbled the entire missing set.

I held the keys loosely in my hand and stared at them. I looked up at the poster, with its emphatic proclamation. And then I smiled and said aloud, "You always did have a great sense of humor, Bob Shea."

It would make a good story to say that everything suddenly fell into place, that all my questions dissolved, that I was somehow transported to a place of certainty and confidence in life's meaning. That I no longer felt that the universe was a place of uncertainty and chaos. That I recognized and accepted the proof of Bob's continuing existence.

But that would not be true. What I felt was bafflement and curiosity, together with a startled amusement. This could not be the answer to my crazed prayer. No. There had to be some other, more commonsense answer. The keys were behind the poster: effect. Someone must have put them there: cause. I had been alone when the keys disappeared. Ergo, I had put the keys behind the poster. I did not remember doing so; it must have happened accidentally. Somehow, it was clear, I must have dropped the keys behind that poster, that day a year previously when I'd lost them.

I set out to prove my thesis. I tried to drop the keys behind the poster. I stood at the door, held the keys up in my right hand, and dropped them on the door. They caught at first on the cardboard's edge, then bounced off the door mounding and slid down to the floor.

I tried throwing the keys at the poster from a few feet away. The same thing happened: they slid down and did not hold. I tried walking past the door with the keys dangling from my hand, to see if they would catch in the poster and hold. They did not catch and hold.

There was only one way to get the keys into the position I had found them. I had to pull the poster forward, push the keys along a little groove in the door, and shove the poster back in place. Anything else would result in the keys either not lodging behind the poster at all, or dropping out as soon as the door was moved.

I spent a half-hour trying to make the keys stay behind that poster. Natalie, when I told her the mystery of the found keys, did the same. We stood in the green-carpeted upstairs hallway, two grown women flinging keys at a door, over and over. Thinking of more and more peculiar ways that the keys might have wound up resting on that hidden shelf. Unwilling at first to accept that only careful, conscious effort could bring the keys to rest as they had been, but unable to find any other way to make the keys stay in that place.

A year previously, the answer that I had wanted was a simple one: that Bob still existed and, hearing my call for help, would return my keys to me. But once this particular and peculiar miracle had occurred, I resisted accepting it as an answer to that crazy challenge. I attempted to catalog all possibilities. I had gone into a fugue state, placed the keys behind the poster, and forgotten all about them. A visitor had found the keys and whimsically placed them behind the poster. A worker—the plumber, say—had found the keys and hid them rather than giving them to me.

These scenarios are possible, though fairly unlikely. Were this a court of law, I would argue that there was no motive for anyone else to hide the keys, and no evidence that I have either before or since gone into a state of mindless fugue. That my beloved Bob had somehow answered my request seems as likely as any of these interpretations. Also: Bob had a unique sense of humor, and he tended to procrastinate. So it would be in character for him to have taken a year to get around to giving me the keys back, and then it would be in a suitably clever fashion.

I have, many times since the keys reappeared, asked myself how I would have responded had I found the keys, in exactly the same place, during my original frenzy of grief. I would, I think, have accepted it as a dramatic proof of Bob's continued existence. Look, I would have said to myself, he returned to me in my hour of need. He loved me still; I could still call upon him and rely upon him; there was life after death. In retrospect, I am glad that I did not find the keys then. Although my pain might have been greatly lessened at the start, I would have been left with only an odd anecdote which, over time, would have grown less and less vital, would have held less and less consolation.

Instead, the loss of the keys had propelled me into discovering a way to live with the unresolvability of our most basic questions. During my period of grief, I became familiar—even comfortable—with relativity and uncertainty. Indeed, those theories polished the world so that it shone with a strange and compelling luster. The world could never again be ordinary once I had plummeted through the rabbit-hole of quantum mechanics. If there was uncertainty at the basis of the universe, there was also a ravishing mystery.

After the keys reappeared, as I considered the various possibilities for how they got where they did, I did not feel compelled to prove any one or another. I did not call every visitor and worker who had entered the house in the previous year; I did not have myself examined for unsuspected fugue states. Neither did I convince myself that I had proof of life after death. I was, and I am, willing to live with all the possibilities. I will never know exactly how those keys got on my door, but it does not matter. The loss of the keys did not pose a question to me; it set me on a journey. Finding the keys was not an answer to my question; it was just another station on the way.

I once asked a techno-junkie friend where my email is stored. I think I pictured a huge computer somewhere, where I had the electronic equivalent of a little mailbox. I think I pictured that mailbox sometimes full with mail, sometimes empty. But where on earth was the mailbox?

My friend guffawed. "There's no big computer," she said, "it's all in the fiber-optic network."

This answer was utterly mysterious to me. In the fiber-optic network? Where is that? How can messages be in a network, rather than in a place? My mind boggled.

But quantum theory teaches us that this is not, ultimately, a universe of hard mechanistic reality where mail has to rest in mailboxes. It is a universe of connections and relations, of particle-waves in spacetime where order explicates itself in form and enfolds itself in pattern. The universe is not a great machine, Jeans said, but a great thought. A great thought that expresses itself in matter and energy, ceaselessly changing places.

Whatever part of that great thought once appeared as Bob Shea still exists, I now believe, somewhere in the network of this universe. He has only "departed from this strange world a little ahead of me." Perhaps, as Einstein said, "That means nothing. People like us, who believe in physics, know that the distinction between past, present and future is only a stubbornly persistent illusion." If I cannot access the codes to find Bob in the universal network, it does not mean that he has ceased to be. But "being" in that other world must surely be something beyond our imagining in this one, something as different as messages surging through networks are from little metal envelope-filled boxes.

I am comforted by having my keys again. We live in story, and the story of the keys now has a pleasing symmetry. But I do not know what that story means. Or, rather: I know that it can mean many things, some contradictory, but perhaps all true at the same time nonetheless. And I am most deeply comforted by knowing that I cannot ever truly know, that the universe is so far beyond our understanding that miracles, even peculiar and rather silly ones like this one, are very likely to keep occurring. ■

We're Here Now

Floyd Skloot

I spent my adult life getting as far away as possible from my mother. For nearly forty years, I moved steadily west from her home on Long Island's south shore, living in Pennsylvania, Illinois, Washington, and, finally, Oregon. My brother followed the same pattern. He went to New Jersey, then California, where he lived for nearly a quarter-century till his death at fifty-seven. He would not even answer his phone, assigning that responsibility to his wife, since the caller might be our mother.

She was a flamboyantly disappointed, tyrannical, violent woman. Would-be aristocrat, thwarted star of stage and screen, silenced chanteuse, potential rival of Mary Cassatt, my mother married a butcher and believed herself under sentence in their tiny Brooklyn apartment. Her illusions of noble privilege and patrician style were desecrated; nothing was as it should have been. Not even when we moved to Long Island in 1957, where the sandy beach and briny air only provoked her to rage. For years, I thought mothers normally bit deep gouges into their own wrists when children spilled a glass of milk, then grabbed them by an ear, marched them into the bedroom, made them empty their toy chests, stuffed them inside, and locked the lid for two hours. I assumed "flu" was the medical term for a black eye, and the real reason other kids were absent from school too. I imagined all boys and girls listened while their mothers dialed the phone, asked to talk to the director of the county hospital's "insane unit," and asked if there were a room available for a little boy who disobeyed his mother. The only one available was next to The Mad Bomber? That'll be fine. Tomorrow, if he doesn't start behaving.

Having come to think of my childhood as The Big Bang, I saw my adulthood as a gradual slowing down of the family dispersal that childhood initiated. In time, I settled into distant orbit; my mother remained on Long Island, her heat, her pull, still felt. We spoke by long-distance. Occasionally my wife, Beverly, and I flew back for brief visits, but it never felt safe or even possible for me to linger. Then last year, when it was clear my mother could no longer live on her own, Beverly and I brought her to Oregon. She lives an hour away from us in the memory impairment unit of a Portland-area nursing home. We are realigned.

I know this is not a unique situation, but our particulars have a singular strangeness. I am fifty-five, and for the last fourteen years have been disabled by brain damage suffered in a viral attack. My mother is ninety-one and deep in the grip of age-related dementia. It is as though chance and fate have reasserted our inherent connectedness, dealing our brains complementary blows.

Neither of us is as we were anymore. Our memories have, to varying degrees, been shattered. As a result, the past we shared looks very different now: hers has vanished; mine is in random tatters with the most vivid, most intense memories enduring whole, probably because such memories are stored in a separate part of the brain, one that escaped the primary damage. Our brains have both undergone vast organic alteration and our minds no longer work as they did. So maybe, out of this weird wreckage, we can find something in the time we have left together that is better than what we found in the past.

This turn of events offers an opportunity for us to draw together at last. Offers? It insists. Because not only has our remembered past been radically rearranged, but so has our future. A month ago, she was diagnosed with breast cancer.

⌐ ⌐ ⌐

When Beverly and I arrive at the nursing home, my mother is playing bingo. She sits at a long table among two dozen residents, hunched over her card, face inches from its surface, shaking her head. Adamantly. Macular degeneration may have ravaged her vision and dementia destroyed her memory, but she still sees well enough and focuses closely enough to know her card is not filling up the way it should.

"Stupid caller," she mutters. "Can't even announce the numbers properly." She looks around, then places a marker over B-32, though the number called was B-23. "There!"

I pull a chair next to her. She no longer smells of cigarette smoke and heavy makeup. Her eyelashes are no longer darkened shanks. She is annoyed at the way this game is developing, at how difficult it is to see and keep track of her card. She hates when other residents win the game's twenty-five-cent prize. She grumbles at the aide who strolls between tables offering help and at the resident in a wheelchair to her right who keeps repeating the caller's announcements. I know she does not remember we were coming, and within moments of our departure will forget we were there. She will then demand that a nurse phone me at home, well before I have gotten there, to find out when we are finally coming to visit. If we are not available to take her call, she will be annoyed all over again.

But she will be delighted when I make my presence known. Since it is the one moment of her delight that I can count on during a visit, I savor the anticipation. This is a new phenomenon in my life. There will be an instant when she is not sure who I am, then another when she is not sure I am real. But I will say, *Hello, Mother* and then she will gasp: *Oh!* Her eyes will widen. She will touch my arm, just to be sure, then announce, *It's you! Oh, this is the happiest day of my life.*

Before arriving at this nursing home last year, my mother was never a bingo player. Bingo, she would have said, was a game for the hoi polloi. For people who drove their own cars, or wore uninsured jewels and domestic rather than imported fashions. People who ate stews. After all, did the nobility play such nonsense? Besides, bingo had a nasty mixture of narrowed fate—the card you were handed—and too much left to chance. It was simply a lottery and lotteries were, she felt, for the lower classes. In Brooklyn, when my father was alive, they hosted card parties at which she consented to play canasta with the women while he played poker with the men. Mahjong was possible, and in later life, with her second husband, Scrabble. Games of great skill, she felt. But bingo? About as likely as competition tiddlywinks.

As her dementia accelerated, my mother found herself compromising. She had increasing trouble managing her customary two-hour costuming routine in the morning and sustaining balance in her tight high-heeled shoes. Her last boyfriend, in the retirement hotel back in New York, was an eighty-five-year-old former mechanic who knew nothing of the fine arts and wore comfortable polyester pants. A man who winked, who took walks; a man who played bingo. As cognitively impaired as she was, he turned out to be fine, undemanding company, and they spent most of their time sitting in the lobby where other residents could see them and, my mother hoped, be jealous. She never called him by his first name, Irv, conveying her disdain by referring to him only as Dorfman. But now she herself not only plays bingo, she dresses in a T-shirt and cardigan, sweatpants and sandals. Her hair is its natural gray. She adorns herself with two beaded necklaces she made in the arts and crafts room. And though she is ticked off about the way this game is going, my mother is more civil and temperate than I ever remember her being.

"N-17," the caller says.

My mother studies her card and finds the correct square. She snatches another marker and is ready when B-4 is called.

"Before what?" she mutters. Now, with her card beginning to look a bit better, she smiles.

"I think you're going to win," I tell her.

She waves my words away, still smiling. She gets two more squares.

"You're on a roll, Mother."

At that, she turns toward me and says, "Mother?" She leans closer, peering. "Who's that?"

"Hello, Mother."

"Floyd!" she gasps, touching my arm. "It's you!" She spreads her fingers over her chest and rolls her eyes. "Oh, this is the happiest day of my life."

We hug. Beverly moves into my mother's visual range and triggers another gasp. "Oh! And, oh, and it's . . ." my mother says.

"Beverly," my wife says, joining the embrace. "How are you today?"

"Beverly!" My mother makes a sound that is part way between a laugh and a sob. Then she lets us go and says, "Let me look at you."

We are all smiling. This is a scene that would have been impossible to envision at any other time in my life. I savor it: my mother this openly happy, nothing complicating the moment, everyone embracing, love all around. What next, Lassie barking as she nuzzles my mother's hand?

"Oh!" my mother says again. "She's so beautiful, Floyd. You two should get married already."

"We are married," I tell her, "nine years next week."

"Nine years?" The expression on her face begins to change. We can watch the happiness melting away. She frowns and says, "When will you come again?"

"We just got here."

"I know, but when will you come again? Do I have to wait another nine years?"

⸻

My mother loves excursions now. It doesn't matter where we go or what we do, she's pleased just to be in motion. This is apparently true inside the nursing home as well, where we are told my mother never sits in her room, lies down for a nap, entertains herself. She cannot bear to be still or alone. *What do I do now?* she continually asks the staff. They tell her, and off she goes, smiling.

After checking her room to see if there is anything she needs, Beverly and I lead my mother out to the car. She takes a few steps within the scaffolding of her walker, then stops to speak.

"You're taking me out?"

"For coffee and cookies."

"Oh!" She takes a few more steps and stops. "This is the happiest day of my life!"

After another small progression toward the driveway, she stops to say, "Where are we going?"

"To Starbucks for coffee and cookies."

"Oh! You're taking me out?" I nod. She takes a few steps and stops. "You know, I would like to go out for coffee and cookies. Can we do that?"

"Good idea."

When we reach the street, she stops and looks up. "It rains every time you come here."

Because this is just the kind of thing my mother would have said in her prime, and because her husky voice sounds like it always did, I am suddenly angry. I needed to drive an hour into Portland for this? Hey, it always rains in Portland. It's not my fault!

She moves again, pushing the walker ahead, smiling a little. She stops and blinks when rain hits her face, then says, "You're here." She approaches the car and says "I can't believe my eyes." I take the walker, and my mother, leaning against Beverly to negotiate her way into the front seat, says, "She's beautiful." Beverly helps her settle, buckles her in. "You two should get married already." I walk around the car, seeing through the windshield that my mother is still talking, though Beverly and I cannot hear her now. As we settle into the car, my mother says, " . . . day of my life." I turn on the windshield wipers. "It rains every time you come here."

All I can do is laugh. There is, of course, no point in being angry. I must find a way to avoid this instinctive response to her voice and tone, because she means nothing by it. The words have little real significance and she no longer has the vital capacity to intend cruelty, to manipulate. At worst, her response and its tone are simply vestigial.

There are, naturally, two Starbucks coffee shops within a mile of the nursing home. The one to the west requires a tricky left turn across three lanes of oncoming traffic; the one to the east requires only a simple right turn.

"When will you come see me again?"

"We just got here!"

"I'm so glad to see you."

"It's good to see you, too."

"So when will you come to see me again?"

I decide to turn right.

"In three or four weeks."

"Three or four weeks? That's wonderful!"

"We always come every three or four weeks."

Her voice deepens and darkens. "Every three or four weeks?" She shakes her head. "No good. If I had a mother, I would see her every day."

She has a point. An hour's drive seems long to me because I dread our time together and how exhausted I feel for the next few days. We used to visit every week, when she first got to Oregon. Then every two weeks. Now every three or four weeks. I believe I am balancing concern for myself with concern for my mother, but I know she would not see it that way.

Once we are at Starbucks sipping drinks and nibbling cookies at a table, I notice how tense I have been. My leg and shoulder muscles ache, as does my head. I have been perched on the edge of the seat, focused intently on everything going on, responding to everything my mother says, cleaning up crumbs, reminding her to eat her cookies, drink her coffee. *This is ridiculous,* I tell myself, and realize I have just used my mother's voice to make that observation.

When I am home, even when I am heading to Portland for these visits, I understand they do not have to be ordeals. Her volatile personality has lost much of its edge; she is calmer and more capable of those instants of simple happiness. If the past tinges our time together now, it is because of me and what I import into that time. I am free to leave the past behind and to allow each encounter with my mother to be as fresh as it seems to be for her. A new start for us, each moment arriving without historical baggage. A chance to have an uncomplicated interlude together, for as long as she has left. It may lack the content of a genuine mother-son intimacy, but it can resemble that connection in ways that might be moving, perhaps healing. I know and believe all that.

Then I hear her voice, or a gesture triggers memories, or I catch a resonance in what she says (*it rains every time you come here*) that may not be there, and opportunity starts its transformation into ordeal. Usually, Beverly's smile will be enough to bring me out of it. I take a long breath, my mother moves on to the next stop along her narrow loop of topics, and I see things for what they are. But I know I am making these visits more difficult than they need to be. I must remember what it is possible to expect from my mother. Then I must recognize it for what it is and accept that her happiness in seeing us is genuine, her anxiety about the frequency of our visits is understandable, and her momentary delight is the only delight she can offer.

"Do you like your cookie, Mother?"

"What kind is it?"

"Chocolate chip."

She reaches for a piece, holds it up, and says, "This is the best cookie I've ever tasted." She puts the piece down and picks up another. "Next time, maybe I could have chocolate chip instead."

⊡ ⊡ ⊡

We have left Starbucks and entered a Fred Meyer One Stop Shopping store. My mother loves these places, reacting to the lights and merchandise with childlike glee. But today she is having trouble getting beyond the questions in her mind. She hardly notices where we are.

"When will you come see me again?"

"Soon, Mother. We come every few weeks."

"I'm so glad." She takes a few steps and stops. "How many years is it since you visited me last?"

"We're here now." I mean, of course, that we are visiting at this moment, so why not enjoy it now. But I also gesture toward a rack of lipsticks. Beverly, who moved ahead of us, selects an assortment to show my mother.

"Where?" my mother says. The ambiguity of my statement has made her even more confused than usual. "Where are we?"

"In the store, buying you lipstick."

"And look!" she says. "Your girlfriend's here. Isn't that a surprise. When are you two going to get married?"

"We are married, Mother."

"You are? How long?

"Nine years."

"Nine years. But you'll come again in a few weeks?"

"Absolutely." I point to the lipsticks in Beverly's hand and say, "We'll even buy you more lipstick."

She nods, looks down, and says, "But why do you have that stick in your hand?"

"It's a cane, Mother. I've been using a cane for fourteen years now."

"You have? Why?"

Even before her dementia worsened, my mother could not or would not remember my illness. It embarrassed her; it made no sense. *A virus? You caught a virus on a plane trip and it damaged your brain? Are you sure your doctor knows what he's doing?* No matter how many times I told her that I was disabled, that I could not work, that I was sick, she never accepted my illness. *You have memory problems? Cognitive problems? So what, I have them too. You're just getting a little older. Besides, nobody I know has brain damage.* Brain damage, like bingo, was not an acceptable turn of events.

"I'm sick," I answer. "I need the cane to keep my balance."

"You're sick?" She looks intently at my face. For an instant I wonder if she is going to check my brow for fever. "What's wrong with you?"

I put my hand around her shoulder and give her a hug. "I caught a virus that targeted my brain." She's still looking at me, trying to see, trying to comprehend something. I realize that one aspect of my anxiety over our visits is connected with fear. I can see in my mother's ravaged mind one possible future for my own. We are all, if we live long enough, at risk for age-related dementia. But I am at special risk, and in fact already dwell in the neighborhood of dementia, with my IQ diminished and memory systems compromised, my abstract reasoning powers dwindled and concentration often in ruins. And I'm her son, with half my genes inherited from this woman. I can only hope I have her longevity, and that the virus responsible for my brain damage has not hastened me along her path toward senility.

I also realize that I must have deeper compassion for her. This means I must think about her, and allow for tenderness, when five decades have accustomed me to blocking all thoughts of her. I must also, and finally, accept her as she is, not as she was and not as I wish her to be. Which is, after all, what I always wanted her to do for me.

I smile at her, the explanation of my condition now finished. My mother blinks and turns toward Beverly.

"It's you!" She beams. "Oh, dear, imagine finding you here." She accepts the lipstick from Beverly and says, "I wonder where Floyd is? Do you know what he looks like?"

卐 卐 卐

Although my mother no longer has access to her long-term memories and cannot form new ones, she does not seem to be lost in time. Instead, I imagine she is frozen in the Now. When I mention that she lived in New York for ninety years, she denies it. No, she never sang on WBNX as "The Melody Girl of the Air." No, she never was married to a butcher, did not spend years making greeting cards from castoff buttons or play Agnes Gooch in a community theater version of *Auntie Mame.* Her parents, two husbands, and brother; her older son who died and the beloved cousins from New Haven; New Haven itself, which she considered the most elite city in the East because her cousins lived there: all gone from her mind. Sometimes Beverly and I will find her sitting alone in the solarium, eyes closed. After the greeting, she cannot remember where she was when we arrived. *How did we get here? I like this room.* She says she was not thinking of anything, and I have come to believe her. She was not sitting there plotting, churning over imagined wrongs. She is convinced, simultaneously, that we have not visited her in years and that we are still engaged in our previous visit. Time has scant meaning for her, though she worries about its passage between visits.

There is, in the worst sense, nothing for her to keep track of beyond the immediate moment. Nothing else ever seems to have happened or be about to happen. Yet, because each moment has a host of potential associations—*this is my son; this is his beautiful girlfriend what's-her-name, whom he should marry; I am somewhere*—she can keep track of nothing.

Though this seems like torture, my mother is often quite equable now, according to reports we get from the nursing home staff. The thing that seems to agitate her the most is me. My presence suggests a past and a future she cannot grasp, cannot bring into focus. I think her efforts to figure out when we last visited, and when we will visit again, are her way of making sense of an elusive feeling of continuity that I trigger for her. Or, perhaps, of horrible discontinuity. She misses me most when I am actually there, because that is the time when she remembers that I was not.

In the early stages of my own illness, I had similar difficulties. Short-term memory was unreliable and long-term memory erratic. Days whizzed by, though time seemed to have stopped. But gradually time took shape again for me. I patched together a coherent sense of my past, working around the gaps and ragged edges, and grasped possibilities for my future. I also came away with a greater appreciation for the present moment. My mother is not graced with this good fortune. Time only spirals more wildly for her. I have had glimpses of that myself, and feel terrified for her.

After a few months at the nursing home, we were told, the passage of time was becoming unmanageable for my mother, and consequently for the staff working with her. When there were no organized activities, she had begun lashing out at the nurses, aides, and other guests, calmness gone, the old behaviors reasserting themselves. We had a meeting with the staff; they were considering the need for a psychiatric consultation and, perhaps, medication to help control her anxiety and explosive anger. But first, they thought, we should all pay a visit to the home's day-care center. Maybe a few days a week in day care, every moment filled with something for my mother to do, would be worth the investment for everyone concerned. And keep her off psychotropic drugs. Yes, they said, why not have a look at the facility; go see Arnie.

We found my mother in her room, standing at the bathroom mirror, smiling. Such bathroom sessions, we had been told during the meeting, were among the few things my mother does by herself. She sometimes remains in front of the mirror for fifteen minutes. It is, for her, an Activity.

"Floyd! It's you!" She turned back to the mirror and adjusted a pair of beaded necklaces that she had made the week before. Then she turned back and said, "Floyd! It's you! Oh, this is the happiest day of my life."

We led her into the hall. She stopped her walker in the doorway of her room, pointed to her photograph beside the door, and said, "This is my room." Then she took a few steps, stopped, and said, "You never come to visit me."

The walk from the memory impairment unit to the day-care center took about fifteen minutes. Yes, Beverly and I are married. Nine years now. Yes, she is beautiful. We were here a couple of weeks ago and we will return soon.

"Welcome!" Arnie said as soon as we entered the day-care center. He beamed. Small, tanned, white-haired, and full of warmth, Arnie radiated hospitality. He was so glad to meet my mother, had heard so much about her. He patted me on the back, shook Beverly's hand, smiled at my mother.

"I hear you're quite a singer," he told her.

"I am?" my mother said.

"We sing every day here." His hand swept outward, directing our attention across the room. "We sing, we tell stories, we share, we have programs, we play games. You'll love it."

At the far end, by the windows with their view of young Douglas fir, a net sagged in the afternoon light. Four wheelchairs were ranged on either side of the net, their occupants batting a balloon back and forth. Senior volleyball. Everyone seemed engaged in the game.

Arnie took both of my mother's hands in his. "I also hear you're a very fine artist. Would you enjoy painting here?"

My mother smiled. She actually batted her eyes at Arnie. "Of course, dear. If you're here."

I remembered taking my daughter to a day-care program just like this, run by Annie instead of Arnie. I never would have imagined my mother playing volleyball, but it seemed possible that she would enjoy being there, and that the break for the staff on the memory impairment unit would make it easier for them to work with her on the off-days.

As we headed back toward her room, I told my mother that she would be going to the day-care program three times a week.

"Three times a week?"

"Tuesday, Wednesday, and Thursday."

"Oh, Floyd!" She stopped and looked at me. "You'll visit me three times a week? That's wonderful."

⌖ ⌖ ⌖

My mother has three significant lumps in her left breast and one massive lump in her right. Late-life breast cancer works its sabotage slowly, and no one involved in my mother's care believes it makes sense to put her through intrusive testing, a double mastectomy, and chemotherapy. She forgets the doctor's visits as soon as he leaves her room, is symptom-free, and remains unaware of her illness. The doctor said this cancer may not even be what ends her life, given its languid progression in a woman her age. But if I had not been convinced before that the end of her life was nearing, I cannot ignore the facts any longer.

I keep dreaming of the cemetery in New York, of the family plot. It belongs to the Skloot family; my grandparents are there, with four uncles and two aunts. At the far left is my father, who has been there for forty-one years, and crammed beyond his grave, at the extreme edge, is my mother's second husband. She overrode his children's desire to have him buried beside his first wife—their mother—and was able to convince the Skloot family to squeeze him in where no outsider was intended to go. The result is that my mother's husbands now lie on either side of her waiting gravesite, their headstones listing toward each other as though sharing a dark secret. Her portion of the plot is narrower than originally planned, and slightly sunken. The last time Beverly and I took my mother there, she sat on the marble bench, looked in the general direction of her husbands, and grew still. She was quiet a minute or two, and I wondered what was going through her mind. Now, in my dreams, I hear her thoughts. *When were you here last? When will you visit me again?*

All my life I have tended to deal with my mother by focusing on the immediate encounter. She was too unpredictable for any other approach. As a child, this meant watching her intently, gauging her mood, dodging her latest explosion. Later, it meant handling the current phone call, deflecting the moment's problem. I knew there was no chance I could actually do something to make her content, or change the way she acted. All that made sense was to manage each episode individually. Either that, or do what my brother did and cut off all contact. It has, I see, been easy and safe just to keep my distance from her. But now we are here together and she is only an hour's drive away.

She cannot hurt me. She is genuine in her pleasure at seeing me, her need to see me, despite the fact that she forgets immediately and does not believe I ever come. And she is dying. For both our sakes, I must begin to manage closeness with her.

We stand in her room at the end of the visit. She asks us to wait while she goes to the bathroom, till she understands when we will be back next, till she is sure we are married. As we leave the room, she fights back tears. It is no longer the happiest day of her life.

"You'll be back soon?"

"Before you know it." ■

Chicago Torch Songs

Amy E. Stewart

I.

There is an essay that begins this way:

> *Everyone has a place, a city or town that they remember only in a romantic way. Everyone has a place, a city or town that they remember only ever fondly, that they remember only ever having been happy in, beautiful in, well-liked and bewitching in.*

But this is not that essay. This essay can't begin that way, because I want to write about the year I lived in Chicago six years ago. To start any piece with Chicago and only romance would be inaccurate, a lie, a tourist's story, not an inhabitant's. I love the city, that's true, but I still remember vividly the tricks it pulled on me, the way it forced some bit of bad luck on me nearly every month I lived there, so that, after a while, no matter how much affection I had for Chicago, it still felt like the city was always asking me to leave.

So my essay about my favorite place, city or town, would start more like this:

I moved to Chicago in September, and Chicago welcomed me by refusing to hook up my phone for the entire month and then for most of October too. Chicago introduced me to three men in October and November, all of whom were charming, all of whom I would have loved to know better, but all of whom were moving to New York City in a week or two. In December, Chicago stole the luggage rack, the spare tire, the passenger-side rear-view mirror off my car—and though Chicago was nice enough to at least leave my radio antenna behind, it would have been a better gesture if Chicago hadn't unscrewed it and raked it down the whole length of the car before throwing it where I might find it later in a snowdrift at the curb.

For the month of January, Chicago left me more or less alone, but then in the middle of February it mugged me on my way to the El, taking my wallet and pushing me to the ground so hard that when I caught myself, my teeth knocked against each other, chipping the pointed ends off both my canines. And the very next day, Chicago told me that my apartment was being converted to condos and served me an eviction notice.

March and May were fairly uneventful, but Chicago more than made up for that oversight by leaving a man for me to discover, bloodied and dying two blocks from my apartment. And though I feel more than a little uneasy claiming that as my bad luck when it was so much more his, had Chicago let him be found by someone better equipped to handle such an emergency, the outcome might have been different and that guilt, or rather *this* guilt, would belong to that person, not me.

Stop here and hold on this scene:

A young woman is sitting on a sidewalk north of the Loop, holding the hand of a man whom she doesn't know at all, holding the hand of a man who is slipping irrevocably away from being a man at all. He doesn't speak—maybe he is incapable of drawing in the breath needed to push out again into the weight of words. Blood is seeping from his chest, and she doesn't know whether he was stabbed or shot, though it hardly seems to matter. She does know that she shouldn't move him but can't help sliding her lower calf beneath his head anyway so he's at least able to rest against something softer and warmer than the concrete of the sidewalk. And when she speaks, all she can say is, *Hold on. Please hold on,* because she heard those lines in movies and in TV shows, and if she can think of this moment as scripted, then she won't be here, responsible in this way, someone else's blood soaking red and warm into her jeans.

Later that night, she will shower repeatedly in water so hot that her skin will tingle for days, oversensitive to the slightest contact with anything. And then she will lie in her bed, hoping to sleep, listening to the trains coming and going from the station on Addison. She will be able to hear a distant music of street performers, a trombone and trumpet clearly, everything else muted and untranslatable, but they won't be jazz. They won't be the blues. She will hear only reprise, only a repeat of the sirens heading her way, coming closer but too late as they wind their way north to the scene, to her, to the no-longer-a-man-at-all that she's nonetheless still begging to hold on, to please hold on.

And that is a story I have not told anyone, not once. Because I love Chicago, but it feels like every time I claim that, it should be phrased as *And yet, I love Chicago* or *Nevertheless, I still love that place.* But such turns of phrase would require me to explain the *and yet* or the *nevertheless,* and I have not wanted to explain.

Let those who hear I love Chicago think Art Institute, Adler Planetarium, Sears Tower, Chinatown. Let them think Chicago River, pale green and tied up with the concrete and steel ribbons of the Michigan Avenue bridge, the Wabash, the State, the Clark Street bridge. Let them think the changing face of Lake Michigan, placid and shining one day, driving itself in four-foot waves at the city the next, pluming up and over Lake Shore Drive to startle motorists and send them scattering to off-ramps and exits. Let them think blue sparks falling from train tracks overhead. Let them think Cubs or Sox or Bears. Let them think polish sausage.

That's easier than explaining how the unexpected, the surprises the city holds to throw at you just when you've stopped paying attention, are what make Chicago loveable. Not the food, not the music, not the towering buildings butting up against the lake—although certainly all of those things are nice, too. But in April, years ago, I held a man's dying hand. I would like to have not had to. But if Chicago was intent on his going, I am glad that Chicago was also intent on his not going alone, untended, without a hand to hold.

A month earlier, in March, the clerk at the neighborhood grocery stopped me before I could get out the door with my quart of milk and pack of cigarettes. One mitten was tucked into the sleeve of my coat, the other was not, and that disturbed him. *It's cold out there. You need to tuck that mitten in to save body heat.* And so he did, grabbing my hand and pushing the mitten into place. He sent me off then with a smile and a *Be careful out there,* and it was startling, that 6' 4" bear of a man being miscast for a moment as mother. I felt lucky for the rest of the night.

In January, while riding the El, I saw a woman take off her rain slicker and sling it over a seat that was filled with soda—poured there by a young man two stops back. The woman was standing next to a pregnant woman who had difficulty staying on her feet through the quick sway and shudder of the El's braking around the turns in the track. Taking notice, the rain slicker spread across the puddle, and the woman led the other to the now dry seat. A moment worth watching, partly to see such kindness between strangers, but also to see the expression that tripped across the still-standing woman's face, something like surprise at her own actions. Catching her maybe thinking, *What have I just done?* and *Why did I do it?*

And months before that, in October, I felt lucky again, when a man whom I had a terrible crush on (and I mean *crush* literally in the way that it was difficult to breathe when I was near him, and in the way that when I looked directly at him, I could see nothing else but him until it felt like I must be lightheaded, that I must be experiencing tunnel vision) walked me downstairs from a party. I couldn't have been more surprised when he took hold of me and pushed me roughly against the wall of mailboxes by the front door—one hand digging into my hair just behind my right ear, the other gripping my waist. Surprised that he should be interested in me in a sexual way, but more surprised by roughness from a man who had seemed so mild, so polite, so gentle. And I have not been excited again in that way, never so overwhelmingly again as I was in that moment, before he leaned in, before we kissed, before the rest of his body followed, pinning me there, in that moment when his hands first took hold of me and then the sounds of mailbox doors rattling and ringing in the hall.

And I think the same thing, the same kind of energy or whatever you want to call it, that sent the dying man to me in April—or more accurately, I think now, sent me to him—is also responsible for the maternal tendencies grocery clerks seem to have there in the city. And maybe it's the same thing that makes people behave counter to what seems to be their nature. A shy sheep of a man could want to suddenly grind the whip-quick length of his bones against yours, fiercely and with pleasure. A woman who is surprised to find that she has such niceness and caring in her might spread her slicker open to make a dry seat for a woman she doesn't know. And I would not want to have missed being touched by those things. I would not want to have missed seeing those things, those kindnesses and delicate moments in a city that rarely seems to care.

Stop here and hold on this scene:

A young woman is holding the hand of a man she doesn't know. She's sitting, doubled over, balancing his head on her calf, while she leans in close with her ear turned to his mouth. She's hoping to feel his breath ruffle the fine hairs there. She's hoping that when she puts her hand on his cheek, he will open his eyes or cough or cover her hand with his own. She's hoping that the pain in her own chest will snap in two because, of all of the things she can't believe she's doing or not doing right now, the one that confuses her most is that she's not crying.

But there is no breath left. He has died, despite her hoping, just as the ambulances pull up beside them, painting them in red and blue and white swirling patches of color. Suddenly, where it was all stillness moments before, everything is now alive with motion—the revolving lights, the hustle of the police and paramedics, the shrill whine of the sirens pulsing out and away through the neighborhood.

The young woman has said a prayer for the man—she who has not been to a church or thought of God in any way other than derisively, as the punch line of a joke, for going on five years. But she says a quick Lord's Prayer just in case, and then when she's done—as a police officer pulls her away and as the paramedics start their work—she doesn't know what made her say it at all.

What have I just done? and *Why did I do it?*

II.

There were nights when I thought I could feel the movement of the moon, detect its passage along its arc across the sky without ever having to look up. And maybe that's a good thing when there are very few other celestial bodies visible in the night sky over Chicago's buzz and glare. There's the moon, always the moon, but in that city, most nights, it looked alone and unfixed without stars to hold it in place.

But in March, a new comet (if I understood my mother correctly) had been discovered. It shone brightly above the moon and had done so for over a week. Had my mother not told me of its discovery—her voice thin and distant over the pay phone in the laundromat—I would have mistaken it for a planet, maybe Mars or Venus. Staring up at it from the El tracks, the moon the barest of slivers, I felt a sense of vertigo, as if the platform below me were swaying and might soon fall from beneath my feet. An almost nervous expectancy pooled in the pit of my stomach, dragging down to my thighs—feeling something like both fear and desire.

This on a night when, leaving the art supply store where I worked, I had ransacked all of the *have a penny, leave a penny* cups for stray nickels and dimes to be able to afford the train fare home. None of my fantasies about moving to the city had included such moments of desperation. I think I was probably crying. I cried a lot that year.

But then there was that white fire, the faintest trace of a tail visible, arcing toward the moon above Michigan Avenue, and I began to understand the importance of little things, of how the smallest details could save the day.

III.

I can't imagine having been the girl that moved to Chicago and lived there for a year just out of college. I can't imagine that I am she, that she wore the same skin that I do, that she is not some character I am inventing. But I remember clearly telling my parents about the move over dinner in Cincinnati and how worried they were—at first because I was taking such a big step, because I was moving so far from home, but mostly because I was moving to such a *big* city so far from home. I was almost able to read my mother's thoughts as she put on her brave smile of approval that she uses in situations when I am doing something she doesn't like but that she knows she can't talk me out of.

She was imagining me living in a cockroach-infested third-floor walkup in a building whose landlord would be willing to, on occasion, accept *favors* in place of rent on the months when I came up short. Or worse, she was inventing a menacing figure—dressed all in dark clothing to better blend in with the shadows under the El tracks, the shadows in the alley next to the building where I worked, the shadows in my apartment at night—who was undoubtedly awaiting both my arrival to Chicago and the opportunity to do me bodily harm. And knowing that my mother was having such thoughts, I know I talked too much about my plans, never allowing a moment of silence for her to jump in with her morbid *what-ifs*.

Once I was living in Chicago, though, I found out that my mother was right. I was mugged and had my wallet stolen early one morning not fifty feet from the door to my apartment. I wasn't badly harmed physically—two chipped teeth, slight abrasions of the knee and palm that stopped my fall when I was pushed from behind—but I was badly shaken up. During my next phone call to my parents, I thought about telling them I had been mugged, but the words wouldn't come. If I had told them, they might have tried to force me to move back home. And I didn't want to do that, because if I did—because of the mugging and the possibility of future muggings—I would have to give up the roar of the El train rumbling past my building, the ability to step out of my front door and walk six blocks to the shores of Lake Michigan, the smell of popcorn and the echo of the organ that drifted into my bedroom window from Wrigley Field on the nights when the Cubs were playing at home.

After living in Chicago for three months, I would not have been able to describe myself as happy. I didn't have many friends yet, and I felt terribly alone. I missed my family so much that sometimes I dreamt that they had moved into the apartment across the hall and that they stopped by each day to borrow a cup of sugar, to ask about the weather, to button my coat all the way to the top before I stepped outside into the cool night air. But I had already fallen in love with the city—whether I knew it or not.

I spent every day I had off from work exploring Chicago, haunting its streets, its alleys, its coffeehouses, its used bookstores, until I felt certain that

I knew the whole expanse of it as intimately as the creases that had grown deep into my palms. A minus ten degrees, not including wind chill, wouldn't have kept me away from the Michigan Avenue bridge where the Chicago River bisects downtown, a broad ribbon of pale green holding apart gray walls, gray streets, gray buildings. A minus fifteen degrees would still not have kept me from walking along the shore of Lake Michigan, or playing with the stray dogs that lived in the park there, or imagining that I could crawl down to the frozen surface of the lake and walk wholly into a new suit of skin, one of my own choosing that didn't understand loneliness, that wouldn't be able to feel the cold wind slicing across its eyes and nose.

IV.

Let those who hear I love Chicago think Navy Pier, Grant Park, Buckingham Fountain. Let them think Swedish bakeries, Irish pubs, Mexican taquerias, French bistros. Let them think impossibly young sailors dotting downtown white and navy blue. Let them think horse carriages all in a steaming row wrapped around the old Water Tower. Let them think lake-effect snow collecting along streets and sidewalks, in banks against storefronts and newsstands, camouflaging the gray and dirt of it all, proving that from time to time even a city as big as this one is capable of change, even of something beautiful.

Because Chicago wants to surprise. Chicago wants to perform magic tricks and sleights of hand. Chicago wants to put on a good show, and all it asks in return is that you keep your eyes open and watch. In April, that month when I held a lot of different hands—the dying man's, my friend's as she read her acceptance letter from the program in Missoula, the little neighbor girl's as I helped her cross the street to school, a near-stranger of a man's hand in a café on Ontario just before he looked away and sunk his teeth playfully into the tip of my thumb, his canine almost breaking skin—I also saw Chicago wholly disappear.

Driving to work, trapped in traffic on the Ohio exit off I-94, I was facing the whole downtown skyline from the Hancock building to well south of the Sears Tower. I had been sitting for ten minutes already, listening to the radio and staring at the city stretched out in front of me. The sky behind me was hazy and bright, but everything was gray and darkening out over the lake, revving up for bad weather I hadn't known was coming. And then suddenly, a thick white tendril of fog wrapped itself around the middle of the Sears Tower.

The fog looked like a giant white octopus arm embracing the building, like bad special effects from some B-movie—moving too knowingly, too solidly, and too fast. I sat there in my car watching it happen, wishing I weren't alone, wishing I could nudge someone and say, *Hey get a load of that.* But there was no one to nudge as two more arms wrapped around the tower from the opposite side, as the same fog bank tumbled over the tops of shorter neighboring buildings, as I noticed that the whole north half of the Loop had disappeared behind an opaque white screen while I had been watching elsewhere, as the whole city vanished, including I-94, the Ohio Street exit, and then even the cars before and after mine that held me trapped, idling on the overpass into the city.

When I finally made it to the intersection where I could turn left, north to Chicago Avenue, once the light was no longer red, a window washer appeared in front of my windshield as if literally from a puff of smoke—first not there and then magically there. I rolled my window down, holding a dollar out to him just as he was leaning across the car to make his first swipe, and said with a laugh, *I don't think that's going to help me much right now.*

He straightened up, took my dollar, and said, *Well, Miss, I guess I see your point.*

He looked at the fog billowing around us, the fog that made everything invisible, the fog that obscured even the beaming traffic lights out ahead of us. He shook his head, laughed, and disappeared as suddenly as he had appeared. Another chuckle and and *I guess I see your point* drifting out behind him.

And these are the tricks that Chicago plays. One sunny April day, it could decide to cast itself as Brigadoon, vanishing right off the map and not choosing to reappear until it's good and ready. The fog lasted through the day and on into evening. There was traffic again during rush hour, but the news shows couldn't say much about it. Not a single helicopter could make it into the air that night.

Oh, there was traffic, but there was nothing to report.

Let those who hear I love Chicago think fog banks that might be amused by notions like *little cat feet.* Let them think winds that blow so hard that I have seen them push people right off their feet, even at midday when those people are stocked full of too-heavy lunches. Let them think both deadly cold winters and sweltering hot summers falling on the exact same streets—both equally lovely and equally dangerous. Let them think ice-blue frozen lake, fog-bearing lake, pale green sailboat-dotted lake. And let them think of all of that as Chicago's tricks, as magic, as a kind of delightful sleight of hand.

V.

One of those mornings, years ago in Chicago, I rose up singing.

It could have been the October morning I woke up next to the man of the mailboxes. He was stretched out there on his stomach next to me, the sheets tangled around his waist. I was struck by how seamless his back was, how smooth and pale and unmarked by even so much as one freckle. We had not been gentle with one another the evening before—my teeth ached from having knocked against his so many times, my fingers were sore from his clenching them in his own against the windowsill above my head, whispering, *There's only so much a guy can take,* sounding like he really meant it—but there were no traces left on him of our roughness. His face was turned toward me, softened in sleep, and before my heart could skip or try to lay claim to him—because I knew he was leaving for New York in a week, because I knew what I was getting into before I got into it—I leaned over and sang softly in his ear, *Won't you come home, Bill Bailey? Won't you come home?* And before he even opened his eyes, he whispered back, *My name is Bob.*

Or it could have been the morning I woke up in my second apartment, in the Ukrainian Village, on Paulina, in late May. All of the picture windows that looked west over the neighborhood were open, letting a cool breeze sweep through the kitchen and living room. And maybe the parts of me that were still six or seven or eight years old—and admittedly there were far more of those parts left then, when I was only twenty-one and only really, after all, playing at being an adult—could smell in the air that a carnival was being set up only blocks away. Maybe I still had some sort of sixth sense that could feel the change in the air when the circus comes to town, that could feel the carnies setting up their carousel and their cotton candy machines and their tilt-a-whirl. All I do know is that I was happy the moment I woke up, so happy that my housemate caught me humming show tunes while making breakfast. And later, when I saw the Ferris wheel lazily turning in the alley between the dry cleaner's and the butcher shop on Chicago Avenue a few blocks east of Ashland, I was both surprised and not surprised all at once.

But I think it's more likely that the morning I am thinking of was in June, just a week or two before I would be leaving Chicago for grad school, for a small town in Ohio, for good. The truth of the matter is that it had not occurred to me to love Chicago while I was living there, or at least not until it was too late. I spent most of that year whining about the weather and my job and trying always to forget that I was lonely, that I was poor, and even that I had watched a man die blocks from my home. Forgetting the latter was easy enough because I still had to live there, still had to walk home at night alone from the train, still had to pass the spot where I had found him, and also because there are simply some things you have to let yourself not think about. But I wallowed in the poverty and loneliness.

The first time I visited the Art Institute, I went only to see Edward Hopper's *Nighthawks.* I had no interest in the Chagall Windows or the Albrights or the O'Keefes. I went only to see those lonely men and women in the corner diner, because I thought I would finally understand the painting, really understand how detached and sad Hopper's characters were. But the painting was on loan, touring on the road in a Hopper exhibition. So I went to the gift shop to buy a framed print of the painting to take home with me, but I couldn't afford it. Neither could I afford any of the glossy coffee-table books that included reprints of *Nighthawks.*

Eventually, I had to settle for Mark Strand's *Hopper,* but I hated it—a paperback that reprinted Hopper's paintings on a disappointingly small scale, in black and white. And Strand argued that Hopper's paintings weren't about sadness or loneliness, but instead about geometry and form. I felt betrayed. Couldn't Strand see that I was the pathetic solitary girl in *Automat?* Wasn't it obvious that Hopper's *Hotel Room* could just as easily have been my bedroom? Might I not also sit in a diner and be the woman that no one makes eye contact with or talks to—not the soda jerk, not the handsome man in the fedora sitting so close by that I could reach out and touch him?

For much of my time in Chicago, I was horribly self-pitying and pathetic. Except not on that morning, a week before I would leave—one of those perfect Chicago June mornings, when it's hot but not unbearably hot yet, the air is still clear, the sky impossibly blue, and cool winds are still blowing in off the lake—I knew, really knew that I loved the city. It had burrowed into me—the trains, the noise, the rush of things, all those honking taxicabs, and buildings so tall that they scrape sky—and I suddenly wasn't sure why I was moving in a week. *What was I doing?* and *Why was I doing it?*

I spent the whole day walking and riding trains. I walked from my apartment clear to the Brown Line Chicago stop. I hopped the train north, got off at Belmont to buy a samosa from Moti Mahal's, got back on and rode to the end of the line and back again down through the Loop. The city was parsed out to me, the way that the train lets you see only bits of things—a slice of the river, a square of sky between buildings, the backs of houses, and the endless scrawls of graffiti that sweep past too quickly to read. I think I was trying to memorize it all in that one day, because I finally knew that I would miss it.

And the memory of that day was the one thing that kept me from crying, a week later, when I crossed over Milwaukee Avenue toward the southbound exit of I-94 for the last time, leaving behind the butcher shop at the corner of Chicago and Paulina with *Vivo Pollo* painted in the front window, all of the singing ice-cream vendors and their quilted silver carts, the pale teal of the river trapped and tied in by bridge spans in the center of the city, jazz clubs and blues clubs, the Elbo Room, the Blue Note and Al Capone's smoke-filled Green Mill, the names of the El stops that I recited each day riding into work like the refrain of some old blues song about riding the rails: Addison, Belmont, Sheffield, Franklin. . . .

Let those who hear I love Chicago think whatever they will. It likely doesn't matter one way or the other. Because for whatever reason, I did love Chicago. I did. I always did. ■